JACK HORN

MANAGER'S FACTOMATIC

SECOND EDITION

PRENTICE HALL

Library of Congress Cataloging-in-Publication Data

Horn, Jack.
    Manager's factomatic / by Jack Horn.—Rev. and expanded ed.
       p.   cm.
    Includes index.
    ISBN 0-13-562927-6
    1. Supervision of employees.   2. Personnel management.   I. Title.
HF5549.H5297   1992   92-13095
658.3—dc20   CIP

Printed in the United States of America

10

Dedicated to Leo Silver—who was successful at encouraging people to do their best.

ISBN 0-13-562927-6

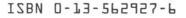

9 780135 629277   90000

ATTENTION: CORPORATIONS AND SCHOOLS

Prentice Hall books are available at quantity discounts with bulk purchase for educational, business, or sales promotional use. For information, please write to: Prentice Hall Special Sales, 240 Frisch Court, Paramus, New Jersey 07652. Please supply: title of book, ISBN number, quantity, how the book will be used, date needed.

PRENTICE HALL
Paramus, NJ 07652

On the World Wide Web at http://www.phdirect.com

INTRODUCTION TO REVISED AND EXPANDED EDITION

After doing the original version of this book, there are times when I thought I should have been a politician. Why? Because I would know how to handle constituents! Not because of reader complaints (and there were a few), but because of the volume and nature of suggestions. Most of the comments would start out with, "This is a good (or useful) book, but why not also include XYZ?" Well, one of the first things that one learns in management is that the customer (or the reader in this case) is always right.

In this revised and expanded edition there are many more of the daily manager problems covered. There are more alternative solutions to more of the pain-in-the neck situations. That is an important "plus" because undesirable situations are set in varying work-environment circumstances which require different solutions.

As most of the problems are caused by other people, more of the solutions are about how to handle other people.

ADDITIONAL PROBLEM-SOLVING HELP

In addition, the number of quick action checklists in the back of the book have been increased. Each of the over two dozen checklists have been expanded to be more inclusive. They can be used for quick answers to the more common problems.

EXPANDED PROBLEM AND SOLUTION LOOK-UP TOOL

In the back of the book is a Master Subject Finder. It is useful in looking up a management problem and then finding a desirable solution. It is a fast-working tool.

MANDATE TO MANAGERS: GET THE WORK OUT

Let's face it! Middle managers are caught between the executives (the brass), who want something done "yesterday," and their immediate subordinates, who are frequently content to "get around to it tomorrow." Most managers are experienced in trying to handle that paradox.

To help handle these daily problems, created by both the superiors and the subordinates, this new edition has over 1,000 good management ideas.

PERSONALITY AND LEADERSHIP

One of the skills that have to be sharpened and honed is the ability to deal with people. Some call it "political savvy;" others call it "interpersonality ability." Whatever its name, "people-handling" is a factor in almost every situation faced by any manager today.

Technical skill is still very important. But basically, a manager manages people. That is why we have cranked in more "people-handling" techniques for varying situation into this revised edition.

The people-handling techniques are not backed up by theory, but rather by battle-tested methods that are used by others. If the techniques work for them, they can *work for you.*

All of the techniques are presented in easy 1-2-3 step fashion for easy implementation. In minutes, you can have the solution to a problem that many have vexed you every working day.

A word about theory. Flip through the book. There are no pie charts, statistical tables, graphs and complex formulas. It is strictly practical, hands-on experience of how to handle most of the problems facing managers today.

UNION CREATED PROBLEMS AND SOLUTIONS

If your plant, office, or operation has more than it can handle with unions, Part 6 is must reading. It is good information for handling excessive grievances, seniority abuses, strike threats, unrealistic incentives, protecting management rights, and so forth. Also, there are the Japanese management secrets for countering unions.

YOUR PERSONAL MANAGEMENT DEVELOPMENT

Part 7 has been added for those managers and supervisors who want to be better promotion material. Nothing overnight or unrealistic, but rather good, solid proven methods for self-improvement for a more successful career in management. No seminars, no additional schooling, nothing but, "Here's what you have to do."

DOING A BETTER JOB FOR NUMBER ONE

When you signed up for a career in management, there was no promise of days of wine and roses. However, in most instances there was the challenge to do a better job. Finding new ways to improve performance, increase productivity, boost services, and to be more cost effective were and continue to be the demands of the job.

It has been said that there is no best way, *only better ways.* Those managers and supervisors who keep trying the better ways are the ones who will one day most likely find themselves in the executive suite, the ivory tower, headquarters offices, or whatever its called in your place. With that kind of your own personal career-oriented outlook in mind, read on.

FOREWORD—ORIGINAL EDITION INTRODUCTION

"I never met a man I didn't like."

Will Rogers, the humorist, said that and it wasn't because he never met a disagreeable, grumpy, uncooperative, complaining, or just plain unlikable person. He probably met many at work or elsewhere. However, when one gets to know a person and to understand personality differences, it is easier to tolerate those differences and overlook shortcomings.

A manager does not have to "like" all of the reporting supervisors and subordinates. But, if there is an understanding of them and their long- or short-range objectives, the manager can be more effective. The goal of the manager is not necessarily to be liked (although that is always a plus), but to gain the respect of subordinates and the higher levels of management while meeting productivity or effectiveness requirements.

Today, Joe Nice Guy cannot, through "niceness" alone, be a successful leader in a managerial capacity—but neither can Mr. Scrooge.

The workforce has greater mobility than ever before in that subordinates can leave one organization and find work fairly easily in another one. A manager must encourage participation in meeting requirements. There must be a balance in attitude between Joe Nice Guy and Scrooge in order to get the work out. It takes an even-handed, technically competent manager to instill the idea of production participation and teamwork in subordinates.

An organization that has made successful use of the participation doctrine is the Marine Corps. Every man and woman in the organization is a Marine, from the lowest private to the highest-ranking general. The noncommissioned officers (sergeants and corporals) are equivalent to middle managers in the business world. They are selected on the basis of their technical capability and their ability to continually inspire participation on the part of their subordinates.

And, by the way, this participatory principle is used by the Marine Corps units of most nations. The private is made to feel that the organization cannot be let down no matter what the private's personal requirements might be. The private, or any other rank, must meet the performance standards of the Corps.

While army units, the world over, are trained to defend their country and so forth, marines are trained in organizational loyalty.

The analogy in business and industry is not that far fetched. Those employees, who feel that they are participating in meeting their company objectives are less likely to be problem employees and are more likely to meet their productivity requirements. The participation doctrine has to evolve from the middle management people.

The companies that develop participation programs or team concepts are having more success in meeting the challenges to their market or industry position. As an example, such companies are able to make changes more readily to meet changing market requirements. They are not married to the concept that Department B can only make widgets or that sales reports can only be cranked out by Section C.

There can be more flexible utilization of resources when the corporate objectives are known to the lowest levels of the organization. Even rank and file employees want to participate—they, at least, want to meet their own personal objectives with the overall corporate objectives.

The successful techniques illustrated in this work rely to a major extent on the principles of participation management. That is; middle managers use methods that encourage the subordinates themselves to help solve problems, increase productivity, and improve cost effectiveness.

The participation doctrine has one other benefit. It reduces people created problems. And, then the manager can become a guiding hand rather than a "boss."

Jack Horn

ACKNOWLEDGMENTS

Most managers and supervisors are successful at their jobs. The reasons for success include the fact that these front line management people have made the most of training and personal experience as well as that of others. That sharing of experience is a two-way street. First, someone learns something that is new or different. Second, by actually sharing of one's own experience, there is a reinforcement of what was gained by that experience.

Many contributors to this volume submitted problem solutions and recommendations from actual practice—tested and applied successfully. They are from various types of industries and organizations.

Among those who gave invaluable assistance, in one way or another, or who provided encouragement for this work, are Marc Rick, Pinky Green, Anne Snipper, Edwin Frisbie, Al Geller, Howard Yaffe, Walt Meyer, John Biviano, Joan Daddio, and—without limitation—Jean Horn.

OTHER MANAGEMENT BOOKS by Jack Horn include *Executive's Factomatic* and *Supervisor's Factomatic,* which are available from Prentice-Hall, Inc., Englewood Cliffs, NJ 07632.

CONTENTS

APPENDICES: THE QUICK ACTION CHECKLISTS
AND FAST WAYS TO EASE MANAGER WORKLOAD   547

HANDLING EMPLOYEE-CREATED PROBLEMS

REFORMING THE CHRONICALLY TARDY EMPLOYEE

"I've been on a calendar, but never on time."
MARILYN MONROE, 1926–1962

Several factors can contribute to an occasional lateness of even the most conscientious employee. This type of latecomer is not a serious problem and most managers and other supervisory people are understanding about excusing an occasional lateness.

However, the chronically late employee is a vexation to the boss, a cause for the uneven flow of the workload, and an excuse to other subordinates who might become tardy more frequently. In addition, a half hour's lateness in time soon turns into an hour and increasingly becomes worse.

For many reasons, it is unwise for a boss to try to "live" with the situation created by the chronically late subordinate.

TAKING IMMEDIATE ACTION RECOMMENDATION

The manager must get directly at the problem by discussing it with the errant employee:

> "Listen, Charley, you will have to get your affairs in order so that you are at work on time."
> "I had to take the kids to my sister's this morning."
> "You probably knew that last night. You should have gotten up earlier or made arrangement in advance."
> "But, Mr. Stone . . ."
> "Sorry, Charley, you will have to organize your personal life so that you will get to work on time."

EVALUATION

Mr. Stone has used a soft approach. It will work on most people—at least for a while. Definitely, it will NOT work on the hardcore and frequently tardy employee

RESCHEDULE WORK RECOMMENDATION

Create deadlines for completion of certain tasks by 9:30 in the morning. If Charley is conscientious about everything else but his lateness, his anxiety about reliability and performance may make him get to work on time.

FOLLOW-UP RECOMMENDATION

The above recommendation is only useful if Charley is reasonably conscientious. If he is not AND he is also late to work, it is time to look for a replacement.

OUT-OF-SIGHT, OUT-OF-MIND PLOY

> "Charley, while you were out this morning, I gave Bennett permission to use your desk in order to get out the weekly production report."
> "Charley, this morning we had a departmental meeting. Too bad that you weren't there because we need your opinion on the new products (or procedures)."

BASIC GAME. After the start of the day, when it looks like someone is going to be late AGAIN, commence an activity to indicate that the team does not need the culprit all that bad.

RECORDED WARNINGS

An intermediate disciplinary step that is useful, PROVIDED that the employee is concerned about a permanent written record of the problem, can be handled as follows:

> "Charley, if you are late any more this week, I am going to send a memo down to personnel for inclusion in your file. The memo will state that you have been warned about being constantly late and it will be a part of your permanent record."

The manager would do well to keep a record of his own of all verbal warnings of this type. The record should include times and dates of lateness and the warnings.

RAISE REVIEW TIME STRATEGY

While most managers have more than enough mandated paper work, keeping lateness and other warning records can be useful. When it is time to discuss raises, these recorded warnings can be flashed to the errant employee as an indication of a lack of commitment to the job. After such a review session, the errant employee might mend his ways. With many problem employees, it is worth the try.

TRY THE SWITCHING ROUTINE SOLUTION

In most situations, the manager can switch duties around. (It is a good cross training technique which increases the pool of available skills to do this from time to time anyway.) The manager can suggest that there will be a change in duties for an employee if the lateness abuse continues.

The new duties could be *less* than desirable to the problem employee. After all, somebody has to do the dog work. Sometimes, a change, even for a short period, is very persuasive in overcoming employee reluctance to reform. This ploy may not be applicable in union shops where job assignments are well defined.

In some operations, it is even possible to switch errant employees to another shift for a while until they shape up.

UNION SHOP REQUIREMENTS

Union contracts frequently limit a manager's prerogatives with regard to disciplinary measures. HOWEVER, most union contracts contain disciplinary provisions of one sort or another. Accordingly, there is nothing wrong with bringing these clauses to the attention of the employee AND the shop steward.

Bringing the shop steward into the picture early in the game is an extra needle into the errant employee to change his ways.

WHEN ALL ELSE FAILS

The chronically tardy employee who will not reform is reducing cost effectiveness in the department. The work flow is disrupted and the manager may be spending too much time that could be better used on someone else. There comes a point where further effort is a waste. It is a managerial requirement to recognize that point.

At that moment, the employee has to be released. If for no other reason, retention is unfair to others who have good on-time records and carry more than their fair share of the load.

REDUCING COFFEE BREAK ABUSES

"There never has been a thirty-hour week for men who had anything to do."
CHARLES F. KETTERING, General Motors

Studies by some theorists indicate that some sort of break in the work schedule can increase production or performance. Although this may prove to be true in the more tedious types of activity, little credit can be given to the coffee break for work improvement when most monotonous jobs are done by machines.

COMMON ABUSES

Theorists cannot contend with the fact that not only is there time lost for the break itself, but some employees prepare for the break well before time—causing lost effort. And some also take their own sweet time about getting back to the grindstone promptly upon completion of the break time.

INFORMAL SOLUTION

Some firms permit the employees to have their coffee and snacks at the work station or desks. Fine! No particular time is set for the break. The break tends to fit in with the normal flow of work. *Any congregation is discouraged.* Most employees will not interrupt the flow of work, either because they use the more slack moments for the coffee and snack or because they frequently do not care to have anything to eat.

The casual observation of the work stations by superior personnel tends to reduce coffee break abuses. However, if several managers and supervisors tend to meet in one office for their own coffee klatch, the benefits of the informal solution are quickly eroded.

"Why shouldn't I take a nice break, the boss does?"

7

Rigid solution

Admittedly, the informal solution can be accomplished only in certain types of operations. The rigid solution requires fixed start and stop times. Where coffee break abuse could become a way of life, the start and stop times of the break have to be well indicated (by a whistle or a buzzer) and rigidly enforced by front line management people.

Rely on supervisory action

All of the managerial personnel down to the straw boss level must discourage employees from leaving their work stations or slowing down in anticipation of the coffee break.

"Hey Charley, why did you stop recording input?"

Similarly, at the conclusion of the break, the resumption of work must be monitored by the on-the-scenes supervisory personnel as soon as possible.

Without monitoring, the ten-minute coffee break can extend by five minutes beforehand and then at least five minutes afterward.

The front line managers and supervisors should be in their geographical work areas immediately before and after the coffee break.

The front line management people can make direct observation of abuses and encourage more productive use of time. How? By handing out assignments, checking on production progress and performing other supervisory and managerial functions. When? Prior to and right after the break time.

Look out for the goldbrick

Charley doesn't call it goldbricking. He calls it, "catching up on the news."

Despite efforts, some employees will look upon the extended coffee break as an opportunity to socialize. (Every plant and operation has its fair share of social lions.)

Only the conscientious effort on the part of the front line management people observing and curtailing break abuses will cause the segregation of those who occasionally abuse from those who will consistently abuse the time allotted for the coffee break.

ADDITIONAL TIPS

The relocation of the coffee and snack machines closer to work areas is generally a good idea. Large canteen areas tend to cause larger congregations of employees and greater opportunity for socializing.

The diffusion of the machines about the plant or operation rather than clustering them in one central location would generally cause less abuse. Geographically close management people can observe the scene about the machines.

Another consideration is to consider a lack of seats or benches near the machines which could reduce congregating and coffee klatches.

HOW TO MINIMIZE THE EFFECT OF ABSENTEEISM

"How does a project get to be a year behind schedule?
One day at a time."
FRED BROOKS, Chief Designer, IBM

In many business operations, the policy is to cross-train almost everybody—with minimal exceptions. The effect is to have a variety of skilled personnel available and ready to assume other duties in order to keep the work moving.

This technique can be accomplished even in some union shops. There may be some pay expense disadvantage. However, it could be worth the added expense if the flow of work is not hampered by absenteeism. Here's the basic formula: Absenteeism Costs Exceed Increased Pay Scales.

FREE BY-PRODUCT BENEFITS

Wilbur, the cross-trained employee, becomes more aware of how his regular duties fit into the overall flow of work. He can know more of what coworkers and others require in the scheme of things in order to do their job. Wilbur can more readily anticipate Roscoe's work problems because Wilbur has experienced how the other shoe fits.

Another benefit is that by cross-training, Wilbur is given some relief from boredom—a major cause of absenteeism in many industries.

IMPLEMENTATION OF THE POLICY

Increasing the inventory of skills (the talent pool) provides the front line managers with additional flexibility. People can be moved around more readily in order to meet higher-than-usual volume requirements in various areas.

Even where temporaries are brought in to take up the slack in the workflow, they can be put into jobs that require less skills. As a side benefit, lower level skilled temps can be recruited.

It goes without saying to experienced managers, there will be resistance to cross-training. The overcoming of the resistance has to start at the recruiting interview. A job applicant should be told up front that he or she is expected to learn and perform tasks outside of the regular functions of the job when called upon to do so.

"We may want you to handle customer calls occasionally."

A good selling point for overcoming resistance is to try to give employees reason to believe that cross-training helps improve personal job security. And, it does!

The cross-trained employee, being able to handle several functions, is of more value to the company than otherwise.

SIDE BENEFIT TO EMPLOYEES

Wilbur, who can now wear several hats on the job, is more employable when seeking work elsewhere.

"Yeah, I can do that also."

PROTECTION AT INTERVIEW

At the employment interview, a job applicant can be told in effect:

"While we are hiring you to do assembly work (or billing, or whatever), you are expected to learn spray painting (or invoice input checking, or whatever) and occasionally lend a hand to the other department. Do you have any objection to that arrangement?"

Of course, one does not have to have been around the track many times to know that objections can, and do, arise later. However, it is best to have raised the issue at the interview so that an employee cannot possible truthfully insist, "But, I wasn't hired to spray paint."

ADDITIONAL INSURANCE AGAINST RELUCTANCE

An additional ploy is for the interviewer to write on the job application in the margin or remarks section, "Spray Painting— OK," while the applicant is watching. Then, have the applicant initial the remark to assure the applicant's understanding of the *employment condition* and to minimize any possible future reluctance.

HANDLING BLUE MONDAY

From time to time, a number of people performing the same or related functions will be absent on the same day. This seriously hampers productivity—not only for that day but for the ensuing days as well. Catch-up usually takes a few days.

Switching over a few assembly personnel to the spray painting department, which is undermanned because of absenteeism, would NOT necessarily bring about full production. It would only bring a flow of work (perhaps the more urgent orders) through the plant or operation.

However, the flexibility of making the personnel switches allows the line managers to fill the bad spots and—very important costwise—tends to reduce idle or stand-by time resulting from work bottlenecks created by undue or high absenteeism.

"Wilbur, there's not enough work for you over here, so go over and see Elmer about giving him a hand."

HIGHER LEVEL CROSS-TRAINING RECOMMENDATION

"Roscoe, go over and run the drill press section."

The benefits that inure to the organization from having the rank and file cross-trained are much greater when the policy also applies to supervisors. An absent supervisor can be as much, or more, of a bottleneck in the workflow as any other employee.

The same ploys used to install cross training among the rank and file can be used on supervisors. Cross-trained supervisors are more valuable to the organization (resulting in greater personal job security) and can become more occupationally mobile (advancement possibilities).

THE ALCOHOLIC EMPLOYEE OR SUPERVISOR

"We are all serving a life sentence in the dungeon of self."
CYRIL CONNOLLY

Experienced managerial people will advise that any promise by an alcoholic subordinate that he can control his alcoholic habit must be viewed with suspicion. He would not admit it to himself, **much less his boss**, that he has a drinking problem. This makes for a strong distinction between the alcoholic and the other types of problem employees who will frequently admit to their short-comings.

Must people drink, and even though some may be considered to be heavy drinkers, not all become alcoholics. The few that do can be helped more successfully if help is offered in the early stages.

BEING ALERT FOR THE FIRST SIGNS

Generally, the drinker who has become an alcoholic, will begin to incur a heavy absentee record—not necessarily typified by the Monday and Friday absence syndrome. (Frequently, he has dried out by Monday, and if Friday is payday, then he or she needs the money.)

Partial attendance can be expected. Either related illness or discomfort forces him to be late, or he leaves after the lunch break. Food can make him ill. Sometimes, he will leave work to indulge his weakness.

When questioned about absences or the partial absences, the alcoholic cannot be expected to admit the real cause but will offer ostensible excuses. Closer query of these excuses could bring about a reaction which could indicate that they are not the true reasons.

RECOGNIZE THAT IT IS A UNIVERSAL PROBLEM

Management people should not be surprised by the type of personnel who become problem drinkers. Every level of employee from the president on down has a potential for alcoholism.

Nor, is there any limitation imposed by age, race, national origin, sex or any other background. Other factors that are deemed to have little influence are working hours, wage levels, length of service, commuting, or relations with a work superior. In short, anyone at any time could become an alcoholic.

WARNING ABOUT DISCHARGE

It is almost impossible to discharge an employee on an "opinion" that he was in an alcoholic condition at work. Without absolute and positive proof, the employee in court can demand and obtain job reinstatement and money damages.

Where is the employer to get a competent, unbiased and *expert* witness against the alcoholic? Without blood samples, even the Company's doctor or nurse would have difficulty proving a case for the employer!

"He looked bleary eyed."

"Charley smelled like a brewery."

"He wobbled when he walked."

All are conjectures and opinions; in most courts, they are not even admissible as any kind of evidence.

OTHER FIRING CAUSES CREATED

The alcoholic employee could present other problems in addition to tardiness and absenteeism, including theft of Company property as well as that of other employee, disregard of safety rules, indifference to productivity requirements, high error rate, drinking on the premises, and the encouragement of others to violate the Company's rules.

All of these associated problems can be cause for discipline including discharge.

CORPORATE ETHICS

The Company has a moral duty to provide assistance to the alcoholic's rehabilitation. Besides, it's good business. The Company that stands behind the employee suffering from this type of illness is the type of organization that good people will respect inside and outside of the organization. And a rehabilitated alcoholic can become a valued asset to the Company.

STARTING RECOMMENDATION

Usually, the Company doctor can counsel the alcoholic employee to seek professional help. A session with the Company physician will provide the employee with information on the current and potential adverse long-term effects of drinking on his physical well being.

Admittedly, it is a scare tactic. Its purpose is NOT to get him to stop drinking, but, rather, for him to seek help with his problem.

Thousands of alcoholics have been rehabilitated to normal working lives with the assistance of Alcoholics Anonymous and other organizations, local and national. They have been successful in returning people to productive and useful lives.

ENCOURAGEMENT

Managerial and other personnel will do well to advise the alcoholic employee that drinking is a problem that he hasn't been able to handle on his own, and that they understand that he has a problem and will do what they can to help.

Make no mistake. Only, he, himself can stop his drinking, but his associates at work can applaud and support his effort to overcome the problem.

OTHER ASSISTANCE RECOMMENDATION

Sometimes, a chat with the employee's family or his social contacts outside of work will provide further encouragement for him to come to grips with his problem. Where there is a close association, members of the clergy, who are more regularly involved in fighting alcoholism problems in families, can be of assistance, not only for purposes of persuasion, but, also for recommending local rehabilitation or treatment centers.

AVOIDING ALCOHOLISM COVER-UP

"In giving advice, seek to help, not please, your friend."

SOLON

A frequent attribute of the problem of the alcoholic employee is that many coworkers and even a number of supervisors wish to conceal the problem. Their motive? They have a desire to help the employee by not permitting the higher levels of management to become aware that one of their employees is an alcoholic.

For some reason, the cover-up is not tried with other types of problems. It is peculiar to employee alcoholism.

MISGUIDED COVER-UP LOGIC BY MR. HELPFUL

Joe Helpful wants to protect coworker Charley by hiding the fact that Charley is sometimes intoxicated at work. CAUTION: Many friends may help Joe in his misguided endeavors. Some of Joe's reasons used for covering up for an alcoholic at work might include the following:

1. Charley is a good worker otherwise. (Not always true!)
2. He needs the job and getting caught would put him "deeper in the bottle."
3. He has a many problems at home.
4. He would help anybody that he could.
5. It is an illness that cannot be cured by letting the management know.
6. It will only take a short while to sober him up.
7. The job (or pressure) caused him to drink.

COUNTERING WITH BRUTAL FACTS

One method of overcoming the willingness to conceal the problems of the alcoholic employee is to *set the record straight* with regard to all alcoholics. The reasons for tackling the problem head on and *quickly* include the following:

1. If Charley, while intoxicated, drives to and from work, he may be a deadly menace to himself as well as to any passengers in the car that are with him. In addition, others on the road may be in serious danger.

2. On the job, Charley could be a threat to his own safety and that of other employees. If while intoxicated, an employee injures himself in a job-related accident, the errant employee is usually not entitled to workers' compensation coverage. (Check your workers' compensation insurance policy.)

Further, if, while intoxicated, an employee causes injury to other employees, the others are entitled to workers' compensation and may also win a personal lawsuit against the intoxicated employee.

The other injured employees, in addition to workers' compensation and money damages against the intoxicated employee, may have grounds for suit against the employer for permitting an intoxicated employee to work and cause their injuries.

Personal safety is of prime concern. However, the legal costs and the damage awards can be staggering, especially since insurance companies are generally prone not to insure for the actions of intoxicated employees.

Insurance companies are quick to cancel (or fail to renew) worker's compensation coverage and public liability insurance at premises where there have been a number of accidents involving intoxicated employees. (Regardless of whether such protection is actually provided.)

3. An alcoholic does not get cured (or even rehabilitated) by someone's efforts to cover up for him. He continues to be a problem at work and at home.

4. The Company's community relations suffer if other organized groups in the community see in the Company image a tolerance of alcoholism.

5. If an employee has customer contact while intoxicated, he will cause a loss of sales for the Company.

6. Many employees, as well as some of the parents of some of the younger employees, are offended by the presence of an intoxicated employee on the premises.

7. An alcoholic can only be rehabilitated with the assistance of experienced persons who are skilled in such matters.

POLICY STANDARD

Managers, supervisors, and other managerial people should be made aware that the cover-up of the existence of an alcoholic employee should not be tolerated. Usually, the Company has policies and rules with regard to the handling of employees who are intoxicated or who drink on the job. If a superior is interested in helping the alcoholic there are ways, not by covering up, but by encouraging the alcoholic employee to seek assistance and eventual rehabilitation.

THE CORPORATE APPROACH

The Company should clearly inform all of management personnel and the rank and file of its alcoholic assistance rehabilitation program. The cooperation of both management people and the rank and file is required to encourage the alcoholic to enter a program for the well being of himself, his family, and his fellow workers.

INSTANT REPLAY OF RECOMMENDATIONS

1. Counter the arguments in favor of cover-up with the facts.

2. Develop policies and procedures for dealing with alcoholic personnel that aims toward their rehabilitation.

3. Encourage all levels of personnel to support the rehabilitation program.

THE BOTTOM LINE FOR EVERYBODY

Mr. Joe Helpful is not only thwarting Company policies with regard to covering up for alcoholic employees but he may be doing a disservice to himself and coworkers. In addition, he is depriving Charley of participating in an alcoholic rehabilitation program which would be to Charley's benefit. And, providing real help and assistance to our friends, who are in need, is what our system is all about.

Helping to reform a problem employee is not a one-way street. A reformed employee can be a very valuable asset to the organization—as well as to his coworkers, boss, family, and the community.

OVERCOMING RESISTANCE TO CHANGE

> *"I've been in this business a long time. I was on*
> *television, when it was radio."*
>
> MILTON BERLE, comedian

A technique of meeting and overcoming a subordinate's resistance to change is to anticipate the approach that a particular subordinate is likely to use. That subordinate could be a supervisor or a rank-and-file employee. (There are people in all levels who resist change.)

Such anticipation of resistance can be based on past experience or signs of an obvious attitude toward new suggestions for improvement in general, and is not limited to possible changes in the work environment.

RECOMMENDATION—ANTICIPATE THESE REACTIONS

Bill Inarut is slow to make changes. Some of his ploys against making changes could include one or more of the following:

1. THE PREMATURE JUDGMENT. This resistance is made *before* all of the ideas are fully expounded or have been explored. "Before you go any further, it won't work . . . "

2. CURSORY EVALUATION. The subordinate has considered only the attributes that are more readily obvious and has chosen to ignore the details.

3. SELF-SERVING ASSUMPTIONS. The employee has jumped to conclusions that he himself desires, twisting them from the available facts.

4. SINGLE-VALUED JUDGMENTS. The employee had judged the benefits or the drawbacks of the proposed change on the basis of only ONE criterion of value.

5. "EITHER-OR" JUDGMENTS. Comprehensive and complex sets of conditions are over-simplified in the attempt to arrive at "good or bad" decisions.

6. INACCURATE VALUE SCALES. The attempt is to set into an order relationship the elements of a complex relationship but use is made of an inaccurate scale of values.

7. SWEEPING GENERALIZATIONS. The employee stereotypes or labels people, things and ideas according to his experience, without regard to errors that occur in making generalizations.

8. SEMANTIC DEFENSE. Certain words and phrases instill an emotional response that has resulted from unfortunate, inconclusive or inadequate exposure to the facts.

BASIC LONG-RANGE RECOMMENDATION

In an ocean of changes that are evident everyday in almost every facet of life, the subordinate, who, for one illogical reason or another, is resisting improvements is a fish out of water. Most experienced managers and supervisors can easily recognize such a subordinate.

The long-range aspect of tackling the problems of introducing changes is to encourage the attitude that the Company is constantly on the *alert for improvements*. Present techniques, and methods are subject to change because the Company must meet the challenge of the competition. Meeting that challenge is represented by *improved performance and more cost effectiveness*.

As has been said in thousands of pep talks to managements in companies everywhere, *There is no best way, only better ways*.

FASTER ACTION RECOMMENDATION

"Mr. Inarut, management has ordered us to put this change in immediately. Using your good experience, let me know what the ramifications are."

The manager has taken the upper hand in the situation. First, he has complimented the subordinate about his background and how well he respects it. (A little extra grease in the gears is not going to hurt.) Second, Mr. Inarut's opinion is being sought. Therefore, when the change is implemented, Inarut is more likely to participate in the successful transition.

Old Bill Inarut has quietly and with finesse been made a part of the process of change. And, just maybe for his ego, that is what he wanted all along.

THE PARTICIPATORY PROCESS

If the manager knows what the subordinate's approach to change might be—not necessarily the detailed ostensible reasons—the manager might put in a counterpunch before the objections are voiced. Every effort should be made to bring the slow-to-change subordinate along in the process. In that way, the subordinate may feel that he is part and parcel of making changes for the better.

"Wilbur, let's get on this problem together."

"Wilma I'd appreciate your advice on this new project."

BRINGING *EVERYBODY* ON BOARD FOR CHANGE

If there is a corporate environment which encourages change, the front line manager's job is much easier. Those who resist constructive change are painting themselves into a corner because their skills are becoming outdated. Not only will they be out of work where they are but they will have difficulty in finding work down the street.

This is similar for companies. Those, who are still making "buggy whips" or outdated widgets, or whatever, are going to have less and less work. Front line experienced managers can see the handwriting on the wall—sometimes ahead of the brass.

Come on, face it, if the Company is not gearing up for changes, then it is best to update that old resume.

Performance orientation in not just for people, but for companies as well. Faster equipment, improved methods, new marketing techniques, better materials, lower-cost financing, innovative products, and so forth, are what companies, who want to stay around for the long haul, need.

You do not have to be a brain surgeon to know that if a company is still making toasters that grandma liked (instead of those "newfangled" pop-up kind), checking in with a couple of hot-shot employment recruiters or agencies may be in order.

DEALING WITH SUBORDINATE PERSONALITY CONFLICTS

> *"Those who in quarrels interpose,*
> *must often wipe a bloody nose."*
> JOHN GAY, Poet

If two subordinates do not get along, the one who suffers most is their section or department manager.

Mary and John may be great workers. However, they may be harassing each other or failing to cooperate. (One cannot know which is worse.) Whatever the manifestations of their personality conflict, their conduct hinders productivity.

If the conflict is the result of a work-related cause, the front line manager ought to be able to remove the cause and resolve that type of disagreement. But frequently, the real root cause may be something related to the basic nature of the two personalities involved. That condition makes the situation a more difficult problem for their superior.

SUPERIOR'S RESPONSIBILITY—PRODUCTIVITY, NOT PERSONALITY

A superior cannot change a subordinate's personality.

No matter how experienced or clever a manager might be, there is little reason to believe that he can be a "Sigmund Freud" and make lasting emotional changes in his subordinates. The most that can be hoped for is the goal of getting the two subordinates to function together in the work environment. That is despite their even admitted personality differences.

Subordinate personality differences notwithstanding, the responsible manager has to get the work of the department done.

QUICK FIX SUGGESTION

The outward, readily obvious manifestations that interfere with getting the work out should be stopped as soon as they are discovered.

23

CONTROLLING THE EFFECTS RECOMMENDATION

While not eliminating the cause of conflicts between two sub-ordinates (unless they are job related), the manager can reduce the effect fairly quickly.

One typical method that can have success is to call both parties into a private office. Let them state what they think their problems are. Then, the manager, acting as an impartial mediator, can try to resolve the differences in the interest of department productivity.

If, after a bit of time, their differences are not being resolved, the mediator-manager can try the following:

"Okay, so we don't agree on everything."

"That's right. John has a few things to learn."

"Wait a minute. We have to get the work out. If you two can't work together, I'll transfer both of you out of the department"

"That's not fair!"

"So? Let's try to make up our minds that both of you are going to have differences—you don't agree on everything. Okay, but do NOT let that interfere with getting the work out. For the good of the department, both of you have to work together OR neither of you can work in this department. Is that understood?"

"Yes."

"Yes."

"Good. Now, I would like both of you to shake hands even though you don't like the idea. You can shake hands on the fact that you are going to cooperate to get the work out. Okay?"

FOLLOW UP

While there may be an uneasy truce for a while, at least the situation should improve. It is best that the truce agreement be reinforced from time to time even with little comments.

ANOTHER RECOMMENDATION

One ploy that can work is for the manager to conduct a peace conference off the premises. A hassle-free environment may be best.

The manager can arrange lunch at the Blue Bird Tavern, or wherever, for himself and the two personality problem contenders. After a cocktail and lunch (paid for by the Company) and over the coffee and dessert, the manager can state the case. The subordinates would air their particular problems with each other. The manager, being a *peace negotiator*, can try for a truce agreement in the interests of accomplishing the department's workload.

AVOID PERSONALITY CLASH BACKFIRES

One of the worst things that can happen to a manager, or anyone in authority, is the accusation of being unfair. In subordinate personality clashes, right or wrong is almost immaterial. Impartiality is a manger's strength in handling problems between his subordinates.

Most managers are fair. They avoid having "teacher's pets" and can recognize apple polishers pretty fast. The trick is to maintain an even-handed approach to conflicts between subordinates.

PROTECTING THE ORGANIZATION

In most well-managed organizations there is the pressure upon its members to perform or to improve performance. Even stakes of minor recognition causes some people to try to outmaneuver any opposition or competition. Some of such goings on are healthy for the organization. New valuable ideas can surface brought on by the competitive factor.

However, such competition has to be restricted. In excess, the conflicts can lead to business "civil war" and the reduction of productivity and cost effectiveness.

PROTECTING YOUR OWN CAREER

Even in a small department, serious personality clashes have to be viewed with some alarm. Frequently, they are disruptive to the flow of work. Few managers can seek advancement to higher levels of management if they can not control their subordinates' personality clashes that tend to reduce departmental performance.

One does not have to be in the business world too long to realize that people in the higher levels of management have to have improved "people-handling" ability. (Higher-ups have to deal with a greater variety of types of people.) Therefore, in the interest of possible advancement, it behooves a manager to keep increasing the skills of getting people to work together as a team—even when they do not exactly care for each other.

USING THE EMPLOYEE CLIQUES TO ADVANTAGE

*"Do not join encounter groups. If you enjoy being
made to feel inadequate, call your mother."*
LIZ SMITH

In every well-managed organization there are lines of authority. The more prominent ones are laid out by the leaders of the organization. However, in varying degrees, there are subtle other lines of quasi authority, some of which may have a significant "hold" on organization members.

Wilma is a good billing input manager with plenty of potential for higher managerial levels. However, some of her subordinates look to Maria for guidance. Actually, Maria is glad that they do and encourages her friends in the department to ask her questions about their work. This situation may have arisen because of a variety of reasons such as social relationships outside of work. A counter organization or clique has developed.

CREATION OF PROBLEMS

These types of relationships can create front line managerial problems. Those department members, who are not part of the clique, can become uncooperative with those employees who are and vice versa. In other words, instead of there being ONE team to get the work out, there are two. Wilma could have an increasingly difficult time in directing the department's work effort. Further, in any dispute with Maria, the leader of the clique, further dissention by the others in her clique is created.

HOW TO EASILY RECOGNIZE THE CLIQUE

Members of cliques have a herd instinct. Clique members will try to socialize during the day—usually causing a reduction in the work flow. At lunch, they will all go to the Blue Bird Tavern, or wherever, or share the same table in the Company cafeteria.

Anyone who frequently does not lunch with the other members of the clique has a good chance of being ostracized.

As with almost any social group, the clique has a leader. Usually, the leader is the one who has the power of veto over suggestions of others, or can make the informal recommendations that are accepted by others. A typical leader decision is where the group should have lunch.

HARMFUL EFFECTS

Frequently, the chief discussion topics of cliques includes gossip about other coworkers, supervisors and managers. Mutual enemies may be verbally torn apart. An atmosphere that borders on antimanagerial feelings can be engendered. Sometimes, there is fostered a discernible disinclination to cooperate with other coworkers.

In addition, clique members usually look to their leader for some job leadership, thus conflicting with the prescribed chain of command. "Legal" countering of valid superior instructions could be clique inspired. Individual clique members are kept in line by the peer pressure of others in the clique.

RECOMMENDATION FOR OFFSETTING CLIQUES

Any very obvious attempt to interfere or try to break up the clique is NOT recommended. Such a ploy may create a unifying issue for the continuing existence of the clique.

1. Throw the leader off balance. A clique leader, at best, has only a tenuous hold on leadership. The superior can become a "friend" to the leader while trying something like the following:

   "Maria, thanks for showing John what to do with the foreign billing."
   "I didn't do much."
   "But, you did, Maria. I certainly appreciate your help."

Recognition of the leader's assistance—whether valuable or not—may take the edge off any antagonism of the leader toward the superior.

2. Create dissension for the leader. With finesse, indicate to the clique members that the clique leader has been more than helpful in increasing productivity, or reducing errors, or obtaining more cooperation from other departments.

   "Oscar, can you get the commission report out in one day like Maria used to do?"

3. Crunch the socializing. On-premises socializing should be brought to an immediate halt. Break up the opportunities for off-premises socializing by staggering the lunch hour for the department. Spread the clique members over the staggered hours. Coffee breaks can be staggered as well.

A valid and justifiable reason (if one is needed) for staggering is the desire to have at least a skeleton staff covering the department at all times.

A side benefit of the staggering of the clique's lunch and coffee breaks is that there is less likelihood of time abuses. Clique members are more likely to start and resume work on time if the clique is doing a minimum of socializing.

4. Disengage members. Minimize having clique members work together on joint efforts or where group effort is required. The ostensible reason for making the switches in job assignments can be that management wishes more of the personnel to be cross trained. Or, any reason can be used.

USING CLIQUES TO ADVANTAGE

Once the clique is no longer considered as being hazardous to the health of the organization and lines of authority are firm, the clique members can be useful as a tool of the department manager.

1. No matter how weak the leader has become, any new ideas can be presented to the clique leader as a sounding board. For instance:

   "Maria, we have a lot of work to get out this week. Do you think the department would like to work on Saturday?"

2. Or use the leader as a straw boss, like this:

"Maria, Instruct Paul on how to get out the shipping report. Also, ask Joan if the sales tax return data is ready. Thanks."

3. On joint projects, where teamwork is essential, the weakened clique can be more useful than a heterogeneous group of employees who may not be as harmonious.

BENEFIT TO THE BOSS

With proper direction, increased productivity on group activities is possible. A basic reason would be that members of the clique would not be competing with one another but would be cooperating for a common goal.

REDUCING BUCK PASSING BY SUBORDINATES

> *"If one tells the truth, one is sure, sooner or later,*
> *to be found out."*
> OSCAR WILDE, 1894

"I caused the snafu."

"The mistake was made by me."

"I take full responsibility for the error."

One does not have to be a very experienced manager to imagine that many people would not take the blame for their own errors. The driving force is that in a more and more complex production, service and managerial environment, it is becoming increasingly important to trace down even minor snafus.

Buck-passing is a serious corporate malady. It is a symptom of management's failure to affix responsibility properly so that the chips will fall where they are supposed to.

A CASE IN POINT

At one plant, buck-passing by managerial personnel themselves was so prevalent that few operating decisions could be made without some kind of committee meeting. An investigating consultant found the causes for the problem included the following:

1. Procedures and policies defining responsibility were not set down in writing.

2. When a goof was uncovered, someone was reduced in rank or was fired.

Severe disciplinary action for mistakes encourages buck-passing. After all, who wants to risk being canned by some front office head chopper for a mistake when there is an alternative to owning up to a mistake?

WARNING: Severe disciplinary action also causes lying, cheating, and the deep-sixing of mistakes so that no one will find them.

DRAWBACKS OF SEVERE DISCIPLINE

The concealment of operating mistakes causes irreparable harm to the Company. Product and service failures can be costly in short- and long-term sales and profit dollars.

First, there is the cost of immediate replacement of the product and service which is very expensive. Second, the quality image of the Company is impaired so that ultimately (sometimes too quickly) future sales are reduced.

MANAGERIAL CONTROL

There are two fundamental areas for affixing responsibility. Among front line managers, supervisors, and staff people, the definition of duties should be set down in some written media—a policy and procedures manual, and accounting manual, a job description manual, and so on. The manual must be updated regularly.

The second area is largely for the rank and file. This can be accomplished in a very straightforward manner. In most situations, the manager or supervisor provides instructions to the immediate subordinates.

REQUIREMENT: COMPLETE INSTRUCTIONS

It is insufficient for a superior merely to tell a subordinate how to do the job. The boss must also delineate exactly what the subordinate's responsibilities are that are part and parcel of the job. This reciting of responsibilities is not limited to job training. It should be reinforced from time to time. A typical example could be as follows:

> "Roscoe, you are responsible for correctly matching the freight bills to the duplicate of the receiving report."
> "What if there are differences?"
> "It is part of your duty to note the differences on the voucher to Accounts Payable. any mistakes in matching

and noting any differences will be your fault. Any questions?"

Even if Roscoe is very suited to the job, he will make mistakes. However, chances are that Roscoe will make fewer and fewer mistakes. And, he will not be prone to put the blame elsewhere for his goofs, especially if two factors prevail. One, from time to time, he is reminded of his responsibility. And, two, if Roscoe is not severely disciplined for any errors that do sneak through.

Over-disciplining may cause:

"The Traffic Manager said that it was okay to approve Zip Trucking bills—so I thought that this was okay also."

"Don't blame me for that one. Herman said that it was okay to approve it."

MANAGERS CAN SET AN EXAMPLE

Once in a while, admit to a goof.

Of course, example is important. Managerial and supervisory people will discourage buck-passing by employees if, from time to time, in the presence of their subordinates, they admit to making mistakes themselves. (Anyway, a little confession is good for the soul and deflates the ego.)

Not every one of the boss's mistakes need be admitted to in front of subordinates. However, the admission of an occasional goof on the part of the boss could demonstrate to subordinates that acceptance of responsibilities for error is desirable.

HOW TO ESTABLISH A PROPER DRESS CODE

"With an evening coat and white tie, anybody, even a stockbroker, can gain a reputation for being civilized."
OSCAR WILDE, 1891

Not many people in management can have avoided noticing that over the years there has been a considerable change in dress styles for both men and women. At times, there have been challenges to management's right to have rules regarding the appearances of its employees as absurd or unusual dress becomes more evident.

While some styles have become more socially acceptable, management can view certain attire as a threat to the Company's image—both to the public and to the customer.

LEGALITY OF DRESS CODES

The weight of legal decisions indicates that Company managements have certain rights in the control of their employee's appearance. In a landmark case the issue of dress was stated as follows:

> "Question: Either an employer has the right to prevent willful destruction of his goodwill (his public image), built up over many years, by making and enforcing reasonable rules, or he hasn't."

(Paul Masson, Inc. Vs. Winery Workers Local #186.)

The arbitrator in the case decided that the employer *has* such a right. However, a key word in the statement of the issue is "reasonable."

CAN MANAGEMENT TASTE PREVAIL?

The manager or supervisor, who expects employees to conform to his or her personal taste, is going to have some hard convincing to do. A confining (very restrictive) taste in clothes by management is no more desirable than the taste selected by an employee who comes to work dressed as Uncle Sam.

It is pointless to put into the dress code rules that have very little likelihood of ready acceptance. It would only damage managements prestige in a showdown.

LIMITED EMPLOYEE RIGHTS

When a person enters into an employment relationship, he has surrendered some of his personal rights. He has agreed to accept rules imposed by his employer. Old English law provides that a servant's individual rights are modified by his act of accepting employment from his master. It is a part of the doctrine of employment at will.

A nonemployee has every right of self-expression. However, as an employee, a person must conform to the employer's *reasonable* rules with regard to attire.

PUBLIC PERCEPTION OF REASONABLE

A reasonable rule of thumb governing the employee's dress might include asking what impression the employee's appearance, going to and from work, would make on the general public. Would the public and employment-related contacts consider the attire of the employee a discredit to the employer?

RECOMMENDATION FOR MOST SITUATIONS

Interview forms, merit increase applications, promotion or transfer applications, and so on should provide for the interviewer to complete a question as to whether the applicant's attire is satisfactory. Employees must be made aware that such a question exists on the evaluation forms. This will provide some impetus for the continuing improvement in appearance by most of the employees—although not all.

Certainly, those employees who have the opportunity and who wish to move ahead will carefully consider the types of additions to their wardrobe.

Handling Absurd Taste Subordinates

Despite the herd (follow the crowd instinct) and the conformity syndromes, some employees can be expected to arrive at work dressed in what many would consider poor taste. The immediate superior should be alert to the first instance when that happens, as it may be a test on the part of the employee to gauge the boss's reaction.

Assert Management's Rights Promptly.

The immediate superior can approach the employee, in a friendly way, and ask why the employee is so attired. The interview can best be performed in private. The superior might suggest that in the future the employee conform to a taste that is closer to that of fellow workers.

As an alternative, depending on circumstances, if the boss wishes to draw the line on that very first day, the following can be tried:

> "Charley, I think that it is best that you drop what you are doing now and go home and change into something that we both can consider more appropriate."

Handling Reluctance

In the event that the employee resists the suggestion for a change of attire, the superior can insist as follows:

> "Charley, you are off the clock as of now. You can get your things and leave. You can return this afternoon if you are dressed more in line with what others are wearing."

> "Sally, you are on leave without pay as of now. You can come back on Monday and resume work if you are properly dressed for work."

If the employee does not return, then the employee is considered to have resigned without due notice.

Importance of Dress Codes

There is some correlation between having meaningful, observed dress codes and how most people regard their work situation. It would seem that those who are properly dressed for work tend to have a greater respect for themselves, their superiors and the Company that they work for. Those who are extensive nonconformist as to dress rules may have a lesser regard for the other rules as well. Admittedly, not always.

The benefit of the doubt as to proper attire is for the front line manager or supervisor to determine. Even where there is no written policy statement on appearance, managerial people should apply certain appearance standards to their subordinates. After all, sloppiness, laxness, absurdity, and so on, by a subordinate is a direct reflection on the boss.

HANDLING DRESS CODE VIOLATIONS

"He's a modest man with much to be modest about."
WINSTON CHURCHILL

There are **three** major aspects of the dress code in the business world. First, there are the requirements of employee safety. These include safety shoes, hard hats, hair nets for machine operators, and so forth. The second aspect includes full or partial uniforms that are a part of the nature of the job, such as the apparel worn by plant guards or airline crews.

Those two aspects are more or less covered by in-house rules and frequently present little problem in either interpretation or enforcement.

The third aspect has to do with acceptable appearance and its effect on the attitude toward the job.

LACK OF DEFINITION

The absence of directives, memos, or written policy statements must be recognized as a tacit admission by top management that it does not necessarily consider a definition of the dress code to be that important. That actual policy says to executives, managers, supervisors, and rank and file employees, "Use your own judgment." But, who's judgment is to be used?

There is some indication of a corollary between sloppy personnel appearance and a lower opinion of the job function and the work environment by rank and file. Even work station and office area housekeeping may suffer.

In addition, the absence of a minimal dress code may create other adverse attitudes including a lack of pride in one's work that becomes obvious both within and without the Company.

THE MINIMUM CODE

One looks at the colleges for evidence of the breakdown of attempts to control dress and general appearance. A closer look reveals that seniors and those interested in campus interviews for jobs begin to consider their dress and outward appearance more carefully. They are quick to learn that first impressions can be durable and that in the business world, books (and other products) are frequently sold based on attractive covers (or packaging).

Coworkers, supervisors, top management, and outsiders form very quick opinions based in part on appearance and dress. The opinions so formed are a reflection of an attitude which, willingly or otherwise, the employees and the Company are projecting.

RECOMMENDED POLICY GUIDELINES

Depending on the type of industry or organization, the following points might be made in a policy statement:

1. Your Company is in daily contact with customers and other outsiders of various kinds including observation by various leaders in our community.

2. The Company regards good public opinion of itself and its employees as very important to the Company's success.

3. All of the employees are always representative of our Company. Therefore, the outward appearance of the employees should cast good impressions.

4. In order to maintain a good Company image and in consideration of the opinion of fellow workers, all of the employees should dress in comparatively good taste.

5. Dressing in good taste requires that the selection of clothing be based on what other employees and your immediate superior would consider as appropriate in the circumstances.

6. Any unusual attire or sloppiness in appearance suggests a lack of consideration for others and a low opinion of the job and of your Company.

RECOGNIZING THE VIOLATOR

Shorts and sweatshirts are more obvious departures from what many would consider as being in good taste.

The borderline cases are exasperating but they can be handled the easiest. Frequently, a small comment by the immediate superior is usually all that is necessary to instill more care in dress.

Outside of the obvious costumes, the usual hallmark of inappropriate dress is the fact that it is often occasioned by comments of other employees and of other managers and supervisors.

How to handle the situation

For most marginal cases, a short talk in private is all that is necessary. If reinforcement is needed, the written policy guidelines should be made available to the employee. When there is improvement in appearance, favorable comment can be made by the immediate superior, to encourage continuing care in appearance.

The more difficult subordinate can be told that a part of the job's responsibility is appropriate dress—that good appearance indicated the extent of commitment to the position. Promotions and other future benefits cannot accrue to one who does not have the expected commitment to the job and the Company.

Handling the hard core violator

With some people, disciplinary action may be required. A warning of disciplinary action may be made. After the warning, but ignoring any borderline compliance, the next time that a subordinate employee appears for work in what would be clearly outrageous dress, the employee should be sent home immediately. If the culprit fails to return to work, it may be presumed that he has resigned without notice.

The fact that a subordinate may have other favorable work attributes does not mean the Company and the immediate superior should be put up with one whose appearance in obnoxious.

Justification

An unfavorable reaction by just one outside contact to one employee's appearance can undo otherwise totally favorable relations. In addition, disrespect of a superior's instructions, company policy and the accepted norm of behavior by even one subordinate can cause *a reduction of employee morale*.

A manager is charged by higher levels of management with certain responsibilities including the appearance of his subordinates and the department's morale. Failure to shoulder any part of those responsibilities is an adverse indication of the ability to be a manager.

HOW TO HANDLE MATERNITY LEAVES

"Congratulations. We all knew you had it in you."
DOROTHY PARKER
(In a telegram to a friend who became a new mother.)

Some employers, in this day and age, do not have a firm and written policy or guide in the handling of maternity leave.

Frequently, there is the attempt to use last minute quick solutions which at times become inappropriate. All of which makes the employer appear to be a bigger unfeeling Mr. Scrooge.

A comprehensive and well thought-out policy and procedure protects the job rights of the employee and permits the immediate superior to gauge the work force requirements.

THE LAW

Most states have laws regarding the employment rights of pregnant women and authorize state labor department inspectors to follow up on any employee complaint. The company counsel should be contacted regarding any problem situations.

Courts are split as to whether pregnancy is a nonoccupational sickness. Those decisions affect whether or not a pregnant employee can collect disability benefits while absent due to pregnancy. In some jurisdictions there are questions regarding entitlement to unemployment benefits.

Under equal rights laws there are legal questions as to whether husbands are entitled to leave while their wives are incapacitated at home and for how long.

No policy or procedure should be published without the review of corporate counsel.

GO BEYOND THE LAW

The pregnant employee is going through a difficult period. She is holding down a job while going through physical and emotional changes. This is not the time to appear callous or uncaring.

On the contrary, everything should be done to help the pregnant employee with her problems.

First, it is the correct thing to do. (All of the other considerations take a back seat.)

Second, it is good business sense. Organization morale suffers if the personnel think that the Company does not take care of its own.

Third, any assistance with her problems will also help her to be a more loyal employee.

WRITTEN LEAVE POLICY

Management can determine and write into the Company's policy and procedures with regard to maternity leave. However, the detail procedures should provide for some exceptions and flexibility according to circumstances. Some of the points to be considered include the following:

1. Application of the employee for leave.
2. Timing elements.
3. Medical department requirements (if any).
4. Notification of return to work or intention to resign.
5. Retention of job assignment after return to work.
6. Payroll arrangements and any disability payments.
7. Extended leave due to circumstances.
8. Other employee rights.

INTERIM PROCEDURE

The employee should be advised that the Company doctor and nurse are available to her for any further consultation that she may wish to have during working hours.

MANAGEMENT RIGHTS

While management has the right to fill a job vacancy due to an illness or pregnancy, it should have the policy of offering returnees equivalent work if their original job has been taken by someone else.

It is true that management has to get the work out despite absences of any kind. However, alternatives or partial solutions for getting the work out should be sought. Wherever possible, returning employees can be given preference with regard to their old job.

FRINGE BENEFITS

A pregnant employee should be advised of the insurance and other coverages that are available to her and the newborn infant.

One set of problems a pregnant employee or a new mother does not need are those snafus related to medical and hospital coverage payments. Yet, foul-ups in these insurance payments are a burden that a representative of the employer can straighten out much quicker than an unknowledgeable employee. Therefore, it behooves someone in personnel or elsewhere to be sure that good insurance premiums are not wasted and that payments are made when due.

CORPORATE ETHICS REVISITED.

Charles Dickens' Mr. Scrooge, before he reformed, would have laughed at employer attempts to be compassionate to pregnant employees. However, after he reformed, old Ebenezer Scrooge would have been the first to help an employee with a problem. If Mr. Scrooge can change his attitude, so can many other employers.

WHAT TO DO ABOUT THE BOTTLENECK SUBORDINATE

"If you want to know if the boss is stupid,
look at whom he hired."
UNKNOWN

"The work is not getting out and John is sitting on it."

Bottlenecks are a frequent managerial complaint, but the causes are attributable to either the design of the work flow or to the subordinate's habits. Poor design of the work flow can be detected by a simple test.

Have another subordinate assume the duties of the person in the problem area. If there is still a bottleneck (after a period of learning), then changes may have to be made in the work flow arrangement.

CHARACTERISTICS OF BOTTLENECK WORKERS

1. Too many items are held up because of relatively minor problems.

2. There is a low understanding by the subordinate of the exception procedures.

3. The subordinate has low decision-making capability.

4. There is low awareness of overall productivity requirements.

5. Team-member enthusiasm is low or the subordinate is a square peg in a round hole.

6. The worker has job or status insecurity.

7. There is an unusual fear of mistakes.

8. The subordinate is using "legal" countering of immediate superior instructions.

ORIENTATION RECOMMENDATION

Where there is no indication that the subordinate is being a deliberate bottleneck (as in "legal" countering of instructions), some additional job orientation is in order.

Some people tend to forget a good part of their training and education over a period of time. Therefore, consider giving the bottleneck some on-the-job *retraining*.

In order to reduce the time requirement, closely quiz the bottleneck on his or her understanding of the job. Then, fill in the gaps. Try some of the following steps:

1. Observe the subordinate's efforts.
2. Provide manuals or instruction sheets and sample finished items or reports.
3. Compliment him on parts of the job that he does well. (This step instills confidence to work faster.)
4. Show him some little techniques for improving his speed.
5. Explain methods for quickly catching his own errors.
6. Let him know that you have confidence in him to improve his performance.

The orientation and retraining can include a review of how the subordinate's efforts *fits into the total picture* and makes a contribution. If the subordinate is more aware of what functions are performed after his, he can use his judgment on the job with more knowledge of the consequences of his own performance.

USING THE TEAM PHILOSOPHY

In most cases, the slow performer does not want to be a slow performer. Nearly everyone wants to feel that he or she is cooperating in achieving common goals. The managerial ploy is to make everyone in the work force have a common goal. And, really, that is what it is all about—meeting and beating the competition.

The team in the work place is not a herd of animals who follow their immediate superior blindly. The team is a group of individuals, each trying to make his own contribution toward achieving the team's goals. The bottleneck employee, just like any problem employee, has to be shown how he can contribute to the team effort and just what are the group's goals.

Part of the front line manager's job is to so direct all of the employees, even those inclined to be slow learners, to best use their abilities to keep the work moving, moving, moving.

RECOMMENDATION FOR COACHES

Here is a way to cut down on the manager's time spent in training reinforcement. Have other employees be coaches to those subordinates who have a tendency to be bottlenecks. Have a try at something like this:

> "Say Joan, show Richard how you would move that project much faster."

> "Oscar, let Connie show you a couple of techniques for pushing the stuff through that we need now. Go ahead, Connie—show him how."

The slow poke may be more willing to learn from a coworker than a boss. For one thing, he wouldn't be embarrassed by any possible mistakes and might develop much more self-confidence.

Coach Benefit: As we have said, you can also learn a lot by teaching.

LONG-RANGE CONSIDERATIONS

An important element in eliminating the bottleneck situation is to make the problem employee want to put the work out faster. The longer outlook requires that the problem employee be treated as a team member rather than just one of the herd.

The paying of a few compliments here and there improves confidence among the slower employees. It permits them to have a greater feeling of job security and certainly reduces tensions. The bottleneck subordinate can become less fearful of incidental mistakes, thus reducing his own built-in need for more of his own excess controls on his own work.

THE BOTTOM LINE FOR PERFORMANCE

In short, job orientation, selective retraining, some coworker coaching coupled with a reduction of tensions about the job and status may free the problem employee to move the work faster.

HOW TO MINIMIZE RESTROOM BREAK ABUSES

"It is better to have loafed and lost than never to have loafed at all."
JAMES THURBER, 1943

"George went to the washroom."

"Sally is out powdering her nose."

There is no question that everyone has to take personal breaks during the day. Nature's call must be heeded—otherwise there could be a serious hazard to personal health. There is no way to avoid granting the privilege. However, some workers tend to abuse the accepted recognition of a fact of life.

Most employees will go to the restroom for a brief moment or two, while others will spend the better part of an hour a day in ostensibly honoring nature's call.

SOME TYPICAL GOLDBRICK ABUSES

1. Styling of hair (by men and women).
2. Reading the newspaper.
3. Chatting and lounging. "Meet you in the washroom and we'll talk about it."
4. Changing from or to street clothes.
5. Gambling and other prohibited activities.
6. Sleeping or cat-napping.

DIRTY WASHROOM TECHNIQUE

At one operation, the restroom facilities were deliberately left in an unrepaired and unsanitary condition. This ploy discouraged employees from using the restroom except for very pressing needs. Such measures reduce employee morale of the vast majority who are not goldbricks.

In addition, state and local inspectors can cite the employer for labor and building violations on inadequate restroom facilities.

ACTION THAT YOU CAN TAKE NOW

The purpose of the dirty washroom technique is to make the facility an undesirable place as a hangout. A similar result can be accomplished by removing some or all of the following: chairs, lounges, tables, sofas, large mirrors, and lamps. (It is interesting to see who would complain!)

The maintenance personnel should constantly remove and discard all reading material found in the washroom or rest areas such as newspapers and magazines.

Another ploy is to remove some of the lighting fixtures and to reduce the wattage of the remaining fixtures. A 25-watt bulb reduces reading capability.

Here is a ploy that is not recommended. One employer, who had more than his share of problem employees, went too far by shutting off the heat in the restroom radiators. One night, the water pipes froze!

SUGGESTED SUPERVISOR ACTION

The individual manager is responsible for the cost effectiveness and the productivity of his department. That is a basic management requirement. The front-line manager should be alert to those immediate subordinates who take advantage of any situation— including the right to a personal break.

Most of the time, hinting is all that is needed. If the abuse continues, the supervisor could try:

"Charley, would you like to see the Company doctor about any physical or medical problems that you might have?"

Some dialogue can be tried to let the employee know that the manager is definitely aware that the employee was away from his or her work station an undue amount of time:

"Richard while you were gone, we could not wait so we gave the job that you were working on to Jimmy to handle."

"Oh, Sally, while you were away, you had a call. Sorry, but we were too busy to get a message."

"Irma, your hair looks great. It would have looked better if you set it on your own time!"

"Warren, we were worried about you. I was going to send someone to the washroom to see if you were okay."

MAKING A POINT RECOMMENDATION

A front line manager does not become a manager by being a fool or even being perceived as a fool. And those in the work force who abuse personal privileges should be made aware that the boss has a lot of "street smarts."

If dialogue doesn't change the problem employee, try loading up his desk or workstation with plenty of work. Maintain tight and steady deadlines on almost everything. Let the culprit know that his productivity is being monitored.

An extension of this ploy is to assign a select amount of well-cultivated "dog" work to the problem subordinate. After a while, he may get the hint and reform.

HOW TO REDUCE CHECK CASHING TIME ABUSES

"I haven't had time to work in weeks."

JACK KEROUAC

"Sorry, boss, but there were long lines at the bank."

"I had to go cross-town to cash my check."

Experienced managers have heard every alibi for taking time off before or after lunch and even during the rest of the day in connection with payroll check cashing. The justification for the alibis can be varied but get down to the fact that as long as subordinates are paid by check, they have to take time to cash them.

In some states, and by some union contracts, the employees have to be given a designated amount of time off for the purpose of cashing payroll checks.

CASH PAYROLL IS NOT RECOMMENDED

Of course, the Company could meet its payroll with cash instead of checks. In some industries, the union contract or tradition requires that their payrolls be met in cash.

The drawbacks of a cash payroll are obvious to most management people. The disadvantages include the cost of handling cash, security requirements, vouching of the disbursements, and so on. Cash payroll services are provided by banks and armored car services. The cost of such service is significant.

CASHING PAYROLL ON PREMISES RECOMMENDATION

This method eliminates for the Company, the counting and disbursement of cash. It's an in-between approach. Have a check-cashing service visit the facilities on payday. Some of the employees will choose to endorse their checks and have the service cash them. The service is available from local banks, armored car companies, and independent check cashing firms.

For on-premises service, the service charge per check is either paid for by the employee cashing the check or as accommodation by the employer.

BETTER RECOMMENDATION

With regulatory permission, a nearby bank could set up a branch on the premises which is staffed on paydays. The branch would cash checks, sell money orders, and take deposits for employee checking and savings accounts. The on-premises bank branch reduces abuses of employees taking off excessive time to cash their checks.

Smaller operations will find it difficult to induce a bank to open a branch.

REDUCE CHANCES FOR ABUSE SUGGESTION

Start-up operations and others can reduce the number of paydays per year. By paying bi-weekly or semi-monthly, the number of times that there can be any abuse is reduced from 52 times a year to 26 or 24 times a year. Administrative and executive salaries could be paid monthly.

The reduction of the number of pay periods each year also reduces the loads of the payroll department. If the payroll is prepared off-premises by a payroll preparation service, then that expense is also reduced.

AFTER LUNCH DISTRIBUTION

If the employees were to receive their checks after lunch, they certainly cannot overextend their lunch break to cash checks (and perform other chores). If required, the employer could permit the employees to leave early for check cashing purposes. Some banks are open on certain evenings and even on Saturday mornings. There are 24-hour banking machines.

Permitting the employees to leave 20 minutes early for check cashing is sometimes less costly to productivity flow.

CHANGE THE PAYDAY

It is expected that banks and check cashing facilities are busiest on Fridays. If the payday were on some day other that Friday, bank lines would be shorter.

STAGGER THE PAYDAY

Not everybody has to be paid on the same day. By using various paydays, any possible abuses are spread out. Then, there would be more than a skeleton force to maintain some desirable level of productivity.

CHANGE THE LUNCH HOUR

Unfortunately, tradition frequently governs how often employees are paid and other factors. However, changing the lunch hour is usually possible. If the lunch hour was changed to closer to a time of the day when banks were least busy, there may be less abuse.

Some consideration can be given to staggered lunch hours. A front line manager could have staggered lunch hours even within a single department. In that way, he can have some kind of force meeting productivity requirements.

BASIC RECOMMENDATION

As with any opportunity for loss of productivity because of possible subordinate abuses, the manager could be sure that on payday, there is plenty of work for everybody. Tight deadlines and staying on top of the work flow are desirable.

THE JUSTIFICATION

In the business world, one has to set up the conduct their personal affairs for an absolute minimum interference with their work assignments.

HOW TO PREVENT EXTENDED COFFEE BREAKS

*"Work? I enjoy work. Why I could watch work
for hours at a time."*
UNKNOWN

Severe problems usually ensue when management attempts to cancel or curtail the coffee break. Yet, management has a basic right to manage the work force. Particularly vexing to many is the often forgotten fact that break time is paid time which is given away by the Company.

The break periods are a cause for reduction in productivity, and any unwarranted extension of the coffee break is further reduction of meaningful effort.

THE RANK AND FILE VIEW

Most employees tend to view the coffee break as a basic right. Some, including a few in management, believe that a break improves productivity. While there have been some studies that give support to this view, in the very real world of practicality such a contention is open to severe question.

As has been said, if the theory is carried to extreme, it suggests that unlimited breaks would cause unlimited increases in productivity. You do not have to have a rocket scientist's brain to know that such an outcome is impossible. Imagine a coffee break every hour!

TYPES OF ABUSES

1. Eating and/or drinking at work stations when or where prohibited.
2. Taking a coffee break away from work stations where prohibited.
3. Taking too many breaks.
4. Starting the break too early.
5. Stretching out the break.

6. Taking a break at the wrong time.

7. Engaging in a prohibited activity during the break.

WHY HAVE RULES?

The reliance on a rule of reasonableness is acceptable where there have been few abuses. The employees have an awareness of the importance of performance and productivity. The standard of reasonableness requires that employees enjoy the time that they need for actually having a cup of coffee and/or a snack and that they respect management's point of view.

However, for the few who are not reasonable, written rules, by which all are to abide, are required. It behooves management to make written rules with regard to the paid time for breaks.

LABOR DECISIONS AGAINST MANAGEMENT

Arbitration cases have gone against companies that discipline employees for overstaying coffee breaks where there is an absence of posted written rules.

ANOTHER REASON FOR POSTED WRITTEN RULES

Front line managers, who are required to get the work out, have to be *supported* by top management. Part of that support is the posting of rules which limit coffee breaks and other possible employee abuses.

EFFECTS OF SLOPPY MONITORING

The coffee break starts out at a plant or operation as a minimum interference in the work schedule. After a while, it grows to a 15-minute break. In time, 15 minutes becomes 20 minutes. Even at that point, which might be acceptable to some managements, some employees tend to further extend the break time.

THE BUZZER SYSTEM

Some companies install a buzzer which emits a signal at the start and at the conclusion of the break. The buzzer technique provides that the work is to cease on the first signal and to resume on the second signal. The elapsed time between the buzzer signals is supposed to be the full amount of the break.

The benefits of the buzzer system are that tight control of the time is possible and errant employees can be more readily discerned by the front line managers and subsequently disciplined.

DISADVANTAGES OF THE BUZZER SYSTEM

Some operations are not conducive to the use of the buzzer system. The most notable are those in which production cannot be entirely halted for a break. For instance, in process industries some coverage by employees is needed at all times. Where telephones have to be manned, a complete halt is not desirable either.

EXCEPTION BASIS

Where production can be continued with a skeleton staff, the buzzer system could still be used. The reduced staff could continue the operations during the main break and then take their break after the second buzzer. To accomplish this technique, explicit designation of the members of the skeleton staff is required. Otherwise, confusion can take place.

ADEQUATE FACILITIES RECOMMENDATION

Break time abuses could be the fault of management. There may be limited or inadequate break facilities. A typical symptom is the length of the lines at the coffee and other vending machines. Some operations can consider decentralized coffee and snack machines. Congregating and other abuses can be reduced by having the break facilities closer to the work stations of the greater number of employees.

BEST SCENARIO—AN EFFECTIVE MANAGER

Department managers, supervisors, forepersons, and section chiefs are fully responsible for the levels of productivity and performance of their personnel—at *all* times in the work situation. In short, they have to monitor and reduce coffee break abuses.

> *Front line managers and supervisors have to set meaningful examples by their **own** behavior at break time.*

All supervisory people should be prepared to remind subordinate supervision and the rank and file of the rules and to recommend or enforce discipline for those people who are unreasonable.

RECOGNIZING AND HANDLING THE DRUG ADDICT

"White rabbits, forced to smoke 87 joints a day, are
encouraged not to operate heavy machinery
or drive on freeways."
News Report, Saturday Night Live

Only the most efficient screening can detect the drug user prior to employment. Unlike alcoholics, the drug users have been successful in hiding their habits from relatives, friends, work associates, neighbors, educators, and former employers.

Because of this ability to conceal a drug dependency, it is difficult for managers and supervisors to discern which of their subordinates is a drug problem employee.

DIFFICULTY OF FIRING THE ADDICT

To fire an employee for drug use only is almost an impossibility. An ex-employee, fired for drug use, can counter with a wrongful discharge suit and have a good chance for success. He can win reinstatement, back pay, benefits, and damages. The employer could have difficulty producing proof such as an unbiased witness who is technically capable of discerning whether someone has been using drugs. "He looked high" and other such statements are conjectures and such opinions will not hold up in a court of law.

The results of medical tests are acceptable but are frequently too hedged to be of great help to the employer because "extent" frequently becomes a factor.

While the use of drugs will be difficult to prove, other problems created by the hard drug user will be easier to prove and can offer grounds for discharge. In such matters the advice of corporate counsel is highly recommended.

RECOGNITION OF THE DRUG ADDICT

As with many other types of problem employees, the frequent drug user will have poor, sloppy, or erratic work performance.

He will be tardy and/or absent frequently. He will share with the alcoholic employee the attributes of forgetfulness, disregard of safety and other rules, and marked indifference to production or work quality requirements.

Unlike many other problem employees, the frequent drug user will have a larger number of requests to leave work early and have more frequent sick leaves. He may be associated with areas of work where there have been instances of theft from other personnel as well as of Company property. There may be reports of attempts to involve other employees in drugs.

One reason for the attempts to involve other employees in drugs is that additional users become purveyors of drugs and thus reduce the addict's drug costs.

Employment Preferences of the Addict

Generally, drug users tend to restrict themselves to the kinds of jobs that lend themselves to compatibility with their habits. Demanding types of employment, constant observation jobs, those jobs that are restrictive or create emotional hassles, are usually not desired by the drug user. However, there are exceptions.

Resignation Possibilities

When the addict becomes aware that his immediate superior is suspicious of drug use, he may quit. After all, he does not want any possible accusation or a sermon on the evils of frequent drug use.

The usual history of employment of many frequent drug users, as well as other types of problem employees is choppy. This may be indicative of not only an inability to cope with social situations but also the incompatibility of the drug habit and a regular work environment.

Sale of Drugs on Company Property

All managerial personnel should be alert for any drug transactions on the premises. Remember, the pressure is on the police authorities to make arrests.

Any supervisor who becomes aware of the sale of drugs on Company property should report the discovery to the Company management. The corporate legal counsel can make any further necessary report to the appropriate police authorities.

HELPING THE DRUG ABUSER RECOMMENDATION

If the drug user is not selling drugs on the premises and is reasonably performing his work load with a minimum of problems, there is little reason why he cannot be treated just as any other employee. The manager has to recognize that curing the habit is difficult.

However, the immediate superior can recommend that the employee visit the Company doctor on a somewhat regular basis. In addition, in most localities, there are programs that provide assistance to the drug abuser who wishes to kick his habit and be a part of the conventional society.

THE BENEFIT OF HELPING

Former drug abusers have been known to be highly motivated workers who look forward to continuing opportunities for increased responsibilities and promotion. In part, it is reciprocity toward an understanding and helpful employer.

> *"The tragedy of life is what dies inside a man while he lives."*
> Albert Schweitzer

ENLISTING THE FAMILY'S HELP

"This is an absolutely fantastic, very fine elegant gold watch which speaks of breeding and was sold to me by my grandfather on his deathbed".
WOODY ALLEN

Individuals who may be very interested in the welfare of the Company include the immediate family of most employees. They are quite frequently willing to assist a manager or supervisor of a problem employee.

Whether the problem is alcoholism, drugs, tardiness, absenteeism, poor work performance, or whatever, an immediate superior has a willing ally in the employee's family in many cases.

ASCERTAINING EMPLOYEE BACKGROUND

The front-line manager can obtain the problem employee's personnel file and review his background. Areas of interest could include the following:

1. Marital status and the number and types of dependents.
2. Employment history and the reasons for leaving prior employments.
3. Any educational dropping out.
4. Frequency of address changes.
5. Fringe benefit claims and their nature.
6. Garnishees and Company loans.
7. Types of personal references submitted.
8. Person to notify in case of emergency.

From a review of the documented records and from general conversations, an immediate superior should be able to develop an insight into the home life of the problem employee.

Is the procedure justified?

Wanting to help a problem subordinate may or may not engender feelings of meddling. Intent is important. There has to be a desire to sincerely help the problem employee for *his* benefit.

First Attempt Scenario

In order to minimize any possible embarrassment, any meeting with a member of an employee's family should be out of the view of his coworkers. It could take place in the Personnel Department or after working hours in the manager's office.

In private, the employee should be asked to bring in his mother, father, or spouse. He is going to object. One could try the following:

> "John, you are a good worker—when you are here—but you have been absent too often. We would like to avoid having to fire you. We have tried every way that we can to get you to show up every day. You have refused. I either have to talk to your father and get his help or we have to let you go."

Stress can be placed on the fact that the meeting will take place away from the work area or will be held after working hours.

> "John, bring your father in on Thursday evening at six—well after quitting time—to my office."

Resignation Hazard

The employee could quit over the entire matter. (Whenever a boss wants to reform a problem worker into a productive one, there is some risk that he will resign.) However, he may realize that he will have difficulty in obtaining another job. Also, quitting, without good cause, will not readily entitle him to quick payment of any unemployment payments.

Using Your Best Shot

The boss can telephone the member of the employee's family who he wants to see and make an appointment. The reason for the meeting can be mentioned. The member of the family may be very interested in meeting the boss—out of curiosity, if for no other reason. Next, the employee must be told:

"John, I telephoned your father today. He is coming in to see me at six o'clock next Wednesday. We both would like it if you were there too."

There may be some subsequent discussion as to the need for the meeting. However, the immediate superior can stick to his guns. The chances are good that all of the parties will show up.

JUST THE FACTS AT THE MEETING

After complimenting the problem employee for his worthwhile attributes, it is best to "tell it like it is." Let the father arrive at his own conclusions. Listen to any possible recommendations that the family member might have.

"Mr. Kerr, John has good mechanical ability that we can use. However, he has been absent seven times in the last month."

In many instances, there will be an offer to render some assistance at home in curing the employee's problem. Certainly, there will be support for the boss's point of view.

DISLIKE OF SUCH PROCEDURE

Resorting to the use of a family member is frequently disliked by most managers and supervisors. However, if the employee is worth retaining, if his problem can be eliminated, and everything else has been tried, this last-ditch method can accomplish satisfactory results.

HOW TO ASSIGN OVERTIME WORK

"If you don't want to work you have to earn enough money so that you won't have to work."
OGDEN NASH

Where the assignment of overtime work is at the discretion of the manager supervisor, there is some advantage to this prerogative.

Even in a union shop, where the bargaining unit contract stipulates how overtime is assigned, there may be some discretion left to the front-line manager or supervisor. If in actual practice the assignment of overtime has been discretionary, then the practice, which had been accepted by all, may have preference over the contract wording.

RANK AND FILE PREFERENCES

Some subordinates will hardly ever refuse overtime.

Others, will hardly ever want it.

Factors that might affect an individual's inclination to accept the assignment of overtime could include the following:

1. Commuting and public transportation circumstances.
2. Company supper reimbursement policy and procedures.
3. Personal financial requirements and goals.
4. Holiday seasons.
5. Minor children at home.
6. Moonlighting and part-time jobs.
7. Job satisfaction.
8. Type of work performed in overtime.
9. The employee group (or clique) attitude.
10. Extent of prior notice.

11. Social and community activity commitments.

12. Premises and nearby area security in the evenings.

OVERTIME AS A REWARD (THE CARROT)

To those subordinates who perform well and want the overtime, it can be treated as a reward.

The department manager or supervisor may act as if he is distributing a major benefit. One way of encouraging employee work performance for those who want overtime is to withhold it from them when their job performance is less than satisfactory.

"Listen, Charley, you want overtime, but you have not been managing to hold up your end during the regular hours. Maybe when you can handle what you are supposed to during the day, you will get some overtime."

OVERTIME AS A PENALTY (THE STICK)

The other end of the ploy is to require overtime of those who do not want to work after quitting time but who have not been performing as well as can be expected.

"Roberta, you will have to put in some hours of overtime in order for us to get up-to-date. When you get caught up—and stay caught up—we will cut down on the overtime."

TIMING OF RESULTS

It is unlikely that the carrot and the stick approach will work right away. However, within a couple of pay periods, Charley, who *wants* overtime, may start applying himself more toward his boss's goals. Charley may have learned to live with the extra overtime money and now he may be running short on his cashflow budget.

For Roberta, who does *not* want any overtime, but has been "stuck" with it, circumstances at home or in her social life will start contributing pressures toward the elimination of the overtime responsibility. As her outside pressure problems increase, she may become a more productive employee during regular hours.

THE JUSTIFICATION

The manager or supervisor who uses the carrot and stick approach for overtime assignment is more accommodating to his people than outright fairness might be. Why? Their personal work objectives are more readily recognized by the manager. The manager and the company benefit also.

Charley, who wants, or needs the overtime, gets his overtime if he performs well. Roberta, who doesn't want overtime, is excused from overtime for her personal business, if she performs well during regular hours.

HOW TO CHANGE OR REDIRECT AGGRESSIVE ATTITUDES

"Egoist, n. a person . . . more interested in himself
than in me."
AMBROSE BIERCE, Devil's Dictionary

Without the use of any surveys, the experienced manager or supervisor has a "feel" for the employees' attitudes and egos. He can know how they regard their boss, themselves, the work environment, the duties of the job, the Company, and so forth.

In addition, managerial people can know which subordinates and employees have feelings of aggression toward their work situation in total.

The feelings which cause the aggressive attitude are detrimental to the usual goals of overall productivity and improved performance. Usually, these feeling are deep-rooted. The employee's immediate superior has the problem of either changing them (which, admittedly, is almost impossible) or redirecting them to advantage—not only for the Company, but for the employee as well.

THE JAPANESE ATTACK ON CONFLICTS

The Japanese method of handling the employee personality problems is to present the concept in the firm that nobody loses and everybody wins. All personnel (management and others) are expected to make sure that the organization is primary and *personal feelings are secondary*.

CAUSES OF CONFLICT

An interested manager or supervisor who is aware of a subordinate's problems need not search too deeply for the causes. The job-related causes of aggressive behavior on the part of the employee could include:

1. Insecurity on the job.
2. Job requirement inadequacies with regard to qualifications and credentials.
3. Low recognition of employee concept of achievements.
4. Underutilization of employee's ability.
5. Lack of identification with the work group (including racial and cultural differences).
6. Failure to feel settled in the occupation.
7. Career compromises.

PERSONALITY SQUARE PEG

In short, if Charley does not feel that he fits in, he is likely to have an aggressive attitude. That attitude can be directed toward Charley's immediate superior, others in management, top brass, coworkers, company contacts and so on.

If Charley doesn't feel that he belongs where he is at the moment, an attempt can be made to alter those feelings. Or, at the least, modify outward expressions of such an attitude. Some effort can be made toward directing the negative aspects of aggression toward a work-related goal if the overall attitude can not be changed.

HOW TO INSTILL CHANGES

The techniques that weld a section or department into a working group can be used on the problem employee by placing more emphasis on Charley's contribution to the group. For example, try some of the following:

1. Show Charley how his effort is needed by the group or his fellow workers.
2. Explain to Charley how his job is important to the Company.
3. Indicate to Charley how his skills, training and other qualifications can result in his doing a more satisfactory job.
4. Give Charley some recognition for his job accomplishments.
5. Use an occasional compliment for the work performed.

6. Bring Charley into group conversations; ask for his advice to the group or to his coworkers.

7. Carefully delineate Charley's work station and his job responsibilities.

8. Listen to more of Charley's problems

REDIRECTING THE PROBLEM EMPLOYEE

If an immediate superior indicates by his attitude that he feels that a problem subordinate is going to be counterproductive, that subordinate may continue being exactly what is expected of him—being counterproductive. However, if the superior's attitude indicates that he feels that the problem employee has much to contribute to the entire group's productivity, then the employee is more likely to assume such a role.

Positive thinking by the superior will tend to discourage negative thinking by the subordinate.

WHY BOTHER?

The importance of redirection is that frequently the aggressive attitude employee can direct his drive in very desirable ways. Redirected employees have a tendency to have above-average enthusiasm about their work loads.

If Charley is convinced that he can obtain some job satisfactions with his current job, he may adapt any feelings of personal frustration into attempts to do a better-than-average job. Most aggressive-tendency people are very success oriented.

Consider this: failures for aggressive attitude people increase their determination to avoid insecurity and any feelings of inadequacy.

The drive for recognition of performance could cause Charley to set high goals for himself in order to achieve further recognition. The inner dynamics and any frustrations can now be aimed at overcoming the real and imagined shortcomings through performance and subsequent recognition. Therefore, the redirected aggressive subordinate could be just what most companies are trying to recruit.

Long-range benefit

All organizations could use some more people who are personality square pegs, but who knock out the work and have push and drive to overcome obstacles. If any organization can get enough of these high-drive workers, then the front door key can be thrown away because those types have been known to work a "40-hour" day.

HOW TO RESCHEDULE THE LUNCH HOUR

"I never drink black coffee at lunch; it will keep you awake in the afternoon."
JILLY COOPER, *How to Survive from Nine to Five*

The determination of the time of the lunch hour should be largely influenced by business reasons. Very few managements give any real thought to the timing of the lunch break. However, several serious considerations do exist.

1. Delivery schedules of truckers and railroads.

2. Customary lunch break of suppliers and customers.

3. Cafeteria staffing for peak periods.

4. Nearby plant and facilities schedules and extent of available off-premises lunch facilities.

5. Overtime and supper break consideration.

6. State labor laws with regard to the number of hours that minors or women can work continuously without a meal break.

7. Collective bargaining contract limitations.

8. Check-cashing facilities on payday.

9. Power and other utility demands.

10. Change of starting hour to take advantage of hours of daylight.

11. Even flow of the workload or services.

12. Part-time workers and commuting schedules.

13. Coffee break arrangements.

14. Possibilities of a skeleton staff during lunch breaks.

AVOID SURVEYING EMPLOYEES

The institution of a survey of employees' preferences as to the timing of a lunch break may have a negative effect. Almost everyone will offer a different time (or so it will seem), and many of them will be unhappy that their particular suggestion was not adopted. It is really up to management to make the decision. The operating front line managers should have the most important input into the scheduling of the lunch break.

FREQUENT CAUSES FOR CHANGE

1. A high ratio of employees coming back late from lunch.
2. A large number of employees who have not returned to their workstation or desks promptly after punching in.
3. Productivity hindrances because a large number of employees are eating at their work stations during working hours.
4. Abuse of coffee break privileges.
5. A high volume of unanswered customer or other business calls during the lunch hour.
6. Some additional resistance of overtime.
7. Employee requests for extended lunch hours or additional time off.
8. Some uneven flow of the workload.
9. Low work attentive span prior to the lunch break.
10. Low work attentive span after the lunch break.

INSTALLATION OF CHANGE

Any change should not be made just to accommodate a few complaints but rather for the reasons that there is a general belief that productivity or performance will improve as a result of the change. Trading off one set of problems for another set is not necessarily desirable either. There can be overwhelming benefits to be achieved by making the change—but change for the sake of change is disruptive and can cause grumbling.

The notice of change can appear on the bulletin board at least one week in advance. It may contain a reference to the fact that the new lunch hour, while it is inconvenient to some and more convenient to others, is being accomplished for business or similar reasons.

DEPARTMENTAL CHANGES

Not every department has to schedule the lunch hour at the same time. There are advantages to staggered lunch breaks for various departments and even for sections. For one thing, congestion at lunch facilities is minimized.

TESTING

Changing the lunch hour around can be done on a test basis, and the announcement should state that it is a trial. It may well be that the new time for lunch has greater adverse attributes than the old time or than some other time that has not been tried which might be better.

If there are no major problems created by the new lunch hour, it will quietly slip into everyone's regimen within a few weeks. Then, further announcement is not necessary. After a while some of the old problems may start rearing their ugly heads, but it can he hoped that they will be minimal.

SUMMARY

1. The timing or staggering of the lunch hour should be in accordance with productivity or workflow requirements.
2. The pros and cons of any change should be reviewed with the front line managers and supervisors.
3. Improved control of time and other abuses by some employees is an important consideration.
4. Change for the sake of change should be avoided.

HOW TO HANDLE AN ETHNIC PROBLEM

"The fact that an opinion has been widely held is no evidence whatever that is not utterly absurd."
BERTRAND RUSSELL, 1929

Most of the individual work forces, if they are in compliance with the law or affirmative action programs, are a mixture of individuals of differing ethnic backgrounds. Turning the other cheek or tolerating an ethnic slur, whether against an employee, a supervisor, a customer, or even someone in the general public, is evidence of poor management.

An ethnic slur is destructive of the public-good portion of the company image.

IS IT A JOKE?

Jokes at the expense of someone else are not jokes at all. Sometimes, the "joke" telling gets out of hand. Another person's feelings are hurt and a fistfight or a pushing match can ensue. Managers would do well to discourage comments or "jokes" that could possible be ethnically related. One has to put the foot down when someone starts with, "Did you hear the one about a .....?"

Managers and supervisors should never joke about someone's cultural, racial, or ethnic background. Nor, should they condone such behavior on the part of their subordinates. One cannot judge how a comment or a joke in poor taste of any kind might affect an individual.

CAUSES OF PROBLEMS

Adverse ethnic comments stem from prejudice and not from the facts. Prejudice presumes that there is a stereotype of an ethnic group, and disregards members of the group as individuals with different characteristics. Personal insecurity is a major cause of most prejudice. For the front line manager, very little can be done to overcome insecurity on a short-range basis.

The slurs, comments, unkind names, and "jokes" are an outward manifestation of prejudice. Something *can* be done about the person who practices his prejudice by telling tales that hurt others.

RECOMMENDATION: A CALM REMINDER

"Charley, I don't think that was funny."

With *one* remark, Charley was put on notice. The manager has played down an ethnic slur. The ploy shows the manager's disapproval and makes the subordinates aware that the manager is monitoring them for such lapses in good behavior. To some employees, a manager's put-down of a slurring joke is indicative of the top management's attitude toward any manifestation of prejudice.

GOOD MANAGER ATTITUDE RECOMMENDATION

The front-line manager could convey the attitude that he or she takes exception to any adverse remarks or slurs against any person or group. The offending subordinate would get the hint from the content and tone of the immediate superior's comments.

Don't even attempt to counter argue. Logic did *not* create the prejudice nor is logic going to remove it. The manager should just repeat his position. Besides, the workplace or office is not the place for debates of any kind.

HANDLING HARD CORE OFFENDERS

Sometimes, a private session with the offender is in order. The superior can indicate his displeasure at any continuing offensive remarks. Any insistence by the subordinate that the remarks were "harmless" should be immediately overcome by the superior.

"Wendel, if they are harmless, then they are pointless."

Arguing is out. The boss is the boss. Adverse ethnic attitudes which have their outlets in the workplace defeat teamwork and are poor behavior patterns.

"Wendel, keep your thoughts to yourself, period."

WARNINGS AND THREATS OF DISCIPLINE

In serious problems, the manager can try:

"Wendel, a notation has to be made on your performance record as to how you get along with others. I would not like to put into your permanent personnel record that you don't get along. However, that is what I am going to do if you continue those remarks that I warned you about. Is that clear?"

JUSTIFICATION FOR DISCIPLINE

1. Discipline for continuing ethnic slurs is justified because it is the right thing to do.
2. The practice of ethnic slurs is detrimental to the corporate image of desirable human relations.
3. Displayed prejudice is adverse to teamwork in the work environment.
4. Infractions after a warning from a superior are deemed to be insubordination.

LOOKING OUT FOR NUMBER ONE

A manager, who is looking out for himself, should consider that ethnic slurs by himself or those under his control can be viewed dimly by the front office makers and shakers in his organization.

The higher one rises in an organization, the greater the need there is for contending and meeting people from varied backgrounds. If one's people-handling ability should be cramped by prejudice, there is a less of a chance of personal success. In addition, any manifestation of prejudice is highly indicative of a narrow mind incapable of broader responsibilities.

HOW TO REDUCE INCOMING PERSONAL PHONE CALLS

"Some are always busy and never do anything."
The Book of 1,000 Proverbs, 1876

Nothing is as annoying to a front-line manager as watching a particular subordinate receiving an excessive number of personal telephone calls. It is not just that the communication lines are being tied up, it is that the flow of work is being interrupted. An employee's personal phone calls should be held to a minimum. After all, he is at a place of business—his personal requirements should be able to wait until after work.

FACT 1: Telephone facilities are for business purposes.

FACT 2: Personal activity reduces productivity.

Because of varied types of operations, there isn't any single technique to reduce this problem. The combination of several suggestions are presented here.

COMBINED SUGGESTIONS

1. Reduce the number of telephone extensions which are available to the rank and file employees to a minimum. This step creates inconvenience for use of the telephone facilities.

2. Even where telephone instruments are required, "bridge" a number of instruments on the same extension number. "Bridging" means putting two or more telephone instruments on the same line from the switchboard. If it is necessary for each accounts payable clerk to have an instrument on the clerk's desk, then put a few of them on the same extension number. In this way, if one instrument is being used, the others on that line have to wait, but can proceed with their work.

   With this suggestion, anyone who monopolizes the line will not be appreciated by the other clerks who may want to use the phone. "Bridging" also makes the line busy for the incoming caller, who has to wait.

3. Stress to the employees that personal calls should be limited to two (or, whatever) calls and that these should be reserved for the more important and emergency calls. Ask them to advise their friends and relatives about the Company policy.

    The advantage of setting a numerical limit is that those who are inclined to abuse the privilege know where the line is drawn.

    Reserving the phones for important or emergency calls may not eliminate the frivolous calls entirely, but it will make fair-minded employees tend in that direction.

4. Require the switchboard operator to ask an incoming caller for his name and to say, "What company do you represent?" Nothing furthered should be ventured by the operator. The last question may be enough to embarrass the caller without being too nosy.

    Such a ploy tends to reduce the calls and their duration. The caller will undoubtedly relay the question to the employee receiving frivolous calls, and the culprit might take the hint that the phones are primarily to be used for business purposes.

SPECIAL TECHNICAL NOTE

If the operation has direct dialing (bypassing operator intervention), the central switching can be reprogrammed so that some lines would still go to an inside operator for call screening. This can be accomplished for both incoming and outgoing calls.

HANDLING PEOPLE WITH "TELEPHONITIS"

Unfortunately, there are some people who will disregard pleas and warnings to minimize personal use of the available telephone facilities.

Every operation has its share of people who are afflicted with "telephonitis."

Because of a few people, calls to certain areas or departments have to be screened. Sometimes, this has to be done on a temporary basis and at other times, it has to b a permanent step.

Part of the screening can be the taking of messages by an in-house operator or available receptionist. True, this is vexing and time consuming. However, in the longer run, some telephone abusers will shape up.

THE MANAGER'S RESPONSIBILITY

As with any time abuse by subordinates, the most corrective action can be taken by the immediate superior. First, the front line manager can be sure that those who would abuse the use of the telephone system would have plenty of work on hand. Second, let the culprit know that the boss is alert to such abuse.

"Charley, let's get some work out today."

It would seem like a good idea that Charley has medical insurance because there are times when the phone seems to be stuck to his ear.

A SMALL TRICK

A ploy that usually works well is for the boss to stand by the culprit's desk or work station when Charley is on a personal call. There is a tendency to shorten the call on the part of the culprit. Usually, he does not want everyone, especially his boss, to know his business.

EMPLOYEE PRIVILEGE VERSUS RIGHT

The employer generally grants the privilege of occasional use of the business phones for personal use. It is not a right of employment. Those who abuse the privilege are unfair to their coworkers who must carry a larger share of the burden of productivity and performance.

EXPLAINING AN UNFAVORABLE JOB RECLASSIFICATION

"A real diplomat is one who can cut his neighbor's throat without having his neighbor notice it."
TRYGVE LIE, Secretary General of the United Nations

A real challenge to a manager is to reclassify a subordinate downward and yet have that subordinate be committed to the job. And, if possible, enthusiastically.

Whether a reclassification is done by job ranking, a point or weight system, or whatever, the primary purpose is to align the job title (including possible pay scale) with the job. In this day and age of more job description changes, evolving new job requirements, shifting of personnel, reclassifications are becoming more frequent.

WARNING TO ALL MANAGERS

The manager who is not updating and increasing his or her own skills, is just as likely to become a victim of reclassification as any subordinate.

The multiskilled manager is more likely to have more job security and mobility than the single-skilled manager.

The trend in business is that people who have broad background (many skills) are better retention and promotion material. People who have fewer skills are more likely to be reclassified—downward.

REASONS FOR RECLASSIFICATIONS

Frequently, the original job classifications were performed on a helter-skelter basis—the needs of the moment made the orderly hierarchy of job titles a victim of expediency. In addition, mergers and acquisitions, departmental reorganizations and amalgamations, cutbacks, and technological changes increased the differences of job responsibilities. Top management wants valid and current job descriptions and titles to assist in making comparisons of their wage and salary costs with the labor market and with industry reports.

"DOWNGRADING"

All of these reasons are of little consequence to the fellow who has to be "downgraded." The shoe may look very nice, but he is the guy who has to wear it—even though it pinches only him.

"I was an assistant manager, now, I am a senior clerk."

He may have always been a senior clerk and may never have had the qualifications or performed as an assistant manager. Or, the definition of assistant manager may have been changed to be fairer to those who are really doing an assistant manager's job.

"Charley, an assistant manager has to be able to take over the department in the manager's absence - which you cannot do."

"Wilma, the difference between a secretary and a clerk-typist is that a secretary can take shorthand."

"Warren, can I classify you as a supervisor when you don't supervise anybody?"

HANDLE WITH CARE RECOMMENDATION

Reason or logic may play little part in the subordinate's acceptance of a changed status. To him, it is a large blow. No matter how undeserving his previous classification may have been, he does not have to view the change pleasantly.

It may be best for the immediate superior to promptly explain the change carefully before the subordinate hears it from the rumor mill or from some far corner of the operation. Blaming the Personnel Department, outside consultants, or anyone else is not desirable. There would be the implication that others are not familiar with the subordinate's qualifications, or who had concepts of their own and were working against the subordinate's interest.

The superior can state that he had a hand in the reclassification decision making and thought it would work out best for those whose classification did not change and for the orderly ranking for wage administration. (For these reasons, it is desirable that reclassification programs have the full input of the front line managers.)

HANDLING FUTURE PROSPECTS

Nothing lasts forever. Most organizations are dynamic; changes in methods, materials, products, types of services, and so on, are constant. Therefore, there will always be changes to some extent in job classifications. In meeting market challenges, duties change, new requirements have to be met, and, of course, job titles will change.

In addition, individual employees' qualifications can change for the better. As there is an upgrade of their abilities, there isn't any reason why a change in classification upward cannot be made at that time.

"Warren, when you get the required training time, I'll be glad to put you in for a reclassification."

"Wilma, when you pick up shorthand, we will reclassify you as a secretary with appropriate pay scale."

WARNING ON PROMISES

Experience indicates that any commitment made to change a classification has to be carefully worded. The required conditions that befall the subordinate have to be very specific. If a promise cannot be made safely as to the definite fulfillment of the classification change, it is best to avoid it as a topic of conversation.

THE LONG HAUL—CAREER WISE

Giving credence to job titles is only part of the picture. The more important aspect is payroll expense. Corporate emphasis is going to be more and more on cost effectiveness. It is less costly to keep (and promote) those who have a broader perspective of the overall workload.

Why the corporate push for cost effectiveness? Market challenge, paying off corporate debt, and "slimming" down to look attractive to others—including creditors, buyers, and merger candidates.

LOOKING OUT FOR NUMBER ONE—YOU

What is your personal goal? Learn, learn, and learn. The more practical and useful skills one has, the greater the job security. And, the easier it will be to walk across the street, across town, or to relocate elsewhere and get another (and maybe, a better) job.

A FREE INSURANCE POLICY FOR YOU

Learning is job security insurance. Just think, here is an insurance policy that does not have costly premiums. No payments of any kind are required. There is no medical exam or even a long application. Let's call it "job security insurance." To get this free very valuable coverage, one has only to learn all that one can while on the job.

INSURANCE CASH BENEFITS PAYABLE TO YOU.

If you are acquiring more practical and useful managerial skills, then you may expect the following possible cash benefits:

1. Regular dividends. Increases in your salary and/or bonuses.
2. Steady paychecks. Less and/or shorter periods of possible unemployment.
3. Higher salary levels. Promotion to new wage plateaus.
4. Greater lifetime earnings. Less chance of layoffs or unscheduled early retirement.

HOW TO MINIMIZE SICK LEAVE

"Hypochondria is the only sickness I don't have."
UNKNOWN

The largest element in the failure to control unwarranted sick leave is the lack of clarity in the language and preciseness of written policies and procedures.

Most abuses of existing policy can be traced to loosely worded or out-of-date written instructions regarding what constitutes justifiable sick leave. No effort to minimize or control the abuses can be effective without updated and very concise sick leave procedures.

RECOMMENDED CONSIDERATIONS IN THE PROCEDURE

Experienced front-line managers know that frequently, whatever is spelled out in the procedures is still subject to abuse. However, the written procedures is a starting point to curb abuse. Consider these attributes of a sick leave procedure:

1. Previous length of service. Part or full time?
2. Required notification to an immediate superior.
3. Doctor's statement after X number of days.
4. One paid day for every month up to 10 days in any one year.
5. Sick leave before and after a paid holiday.
6. Examination by the Company doctor upon return to work after X number of days.
7. Personnel Department to telephone the sick employee's home late in the day.
8. Sick leave during vacation or other paid leave.
9. Extent (if any) of accrual of sick leave to subsequent years.

10. Computation of overtime in weeks containing sick days.

11. How partial sick days are handled.

12. Partial return to work.

13. Job security after lengthy illness.

14. Handling of nonpaid sick leave.

15. Work-related illnesses and workers' compensation matters.

Maternity and paternity leaves would be covered in separate procedures. Alcoholism and drug rehabilitation programs would also be treated separately.

CONTROLLING ABUSE

Enforcing the procedure without bias puts those who abuse the privilege on notice that violations can result in a loss of pay while they are out. A written procedure provides the front-line manager with an equitable means of at least warning the problem subordinate that his paycheck can be cut.

THE CARROT APPROACH RECOMMENDATION

In some operations where absences cause serious disruptions in the flow of work and production and/or performance suffers, some benefit or recognition can accrue to employees who have favorable attendance records. While the truly sick people are not expected to show up for work, those who overcome minor ailments and put in a day's work should be additionally compensated.

The idea here is that since productivity did not suffer every time someone had a sniffle, part of that benefit to the Company can be awarded to the employee who managed to report to work.

One method is to pay, as a yearly bonus, 100% of the unused sick leave to each employee. Another method is to allow the accrual of sick leave up to X number of days. When an employee retires or leaves the Company, the departing employee would be in line for continuing salary until his accrued sick leave is zero.

RECOMMENDATION EVALUATION

The annual bonus may be more desirable as it is a "quicker" reward which may foster better attendance. Rank and file employees usually favor the annual bonus. However, managerial people may appreciate the year-to-year accrued method. If possible, there is nothing wrong with installing both methods—one for management and the other for the rank and file.

When an employee is out sick, while he gets paid for the day, he loses out in that his total pay for the year is reduced.

The Company benefits by paying the bonus. Why? There have been fewer disruptions in work flow, possibly less overtime to cover for sick employees, less resorting to temporary employees, and less shifting of personnel to maintain work flow.

LOWER TURNOVER BENEFIT

The payment of annual sick leave bonus can also reduce labor turnover to some extent. A written precondition to receiving the sick leave bonus would be that the employee has worked 12 months to qualify for the bonus.

If the employees are granted the bonus after their anniversary date, they are more likely to complete a full year before leaving the Company. Even after a number of years, they are more likely to remain after their anniversary date in order to receive the bonus.

YOU CAN'T WIN THEM ALL

Some employees will be out "sick" on almost any whim. No amount of incentive to report to work is going to be completely effective. Nor is an unlimited effort in making the job super-attractive going to be 100% successful. The supervisor would do well to keep in mind that there are many causes as to why an employee reports "sick," and that not all of the causes are created by the employer, his boss, coworkers, or anyone else other than the employee.

COMBINATION OF EFFORT

By having written and updated rules in the policy manual, by encouraging attendance with sick leave bonuses, and by continual follow-up on the causes for overall absenteeism, some reduction of sick leave abuse is possible. It is not improper to inquire of those who take sick leave as to why they did so. (Some will be quite frank.) Of course, one can expect all kinds of reasons. However, a good front line manager can get a better appreciation of who is sick and why.

SETTING AN EXAMPLE

No one has a right to expect someone to report to work when seriously ill. However, if managerial people report in with runny noses, using tissues, and popping cold pills or aspirin, it sets a good example of what may be expected of the rank and file.

Even if a manager or supervisor comes in for only the morning hours to get things rolling along for the day, it sets a welcome example for the subordinates.

EMPLOYEE EXAMPLE

The best examples are when rank and file people come in while feeling a bit under the weather. An immediate superior should not miss this kind of opportunity for a little recognition and encouragement.

> "Mark, I know that you are not feeling well, but I really appreciate your showing up to help us with the job (or to keep the wheels rolling)."

JUSTIFICATION FOR MONITORING ABUSE

Charley takes full advantage of sick leave. He uses all of his "days." However, if everyone was like Charley, costs would rise and the Company would have a rougher time staying in business or meeting and beating the competition. That would be the long-run effect.

In the short term, Charley, who regularly abuses sick leave privileges, is unfair to all of his coworkers. He is making them do more of his work.

PART 2

INCREASING SUPERVISOR AND EMPLOYEE EFFECTIVENESS

MOTIVATING THE EMPLOYEE

"Most salesmen try to take the horse to water and try to make him drink. Your job is make the horse thirsty."
GABRIEL M. SIEGEL

In a typical situation, the new employee comes through the Personnel Department where he or she receives some kind of orientation. Usually, the preamble to the job can be more or less summed up as follows:

1. This Company manufactures widgets (or whatever).
2. All of the employees are part of one big family.
3. Sixty-five is the retirement age.
4. Payday is every other Friday.
5. Welcome on board.

Such orientation may be termed as institutionalized motivation: not really inspiring; not enough of the nitty-gritty. In short, the orientation does not turn anyone on to do a better job.

For instance, it does not make the new employee understand that improved productivity can lead to job security, that better personal performance can lead to promotion, and that the Company's market position is threatened in a competitive world.

Typically, the new file clerk is escorted by a personnel assistant through the halls and introduced to the Central Files Department Manager.

"Roger, this is your new boss, Miss Jones."

WHERE TO START

Many managers and supervisors believe that if a new subordinate does not ask many questions about a new job, there may be a disinterest in the new work situation. Whatever the criteria or presumption, it may be best to assume that all new employees lack motivation, or at least a desirable higher level of motivation.

With such an assumption, it becomes easier to know where to start the attempts at proper motivation—at the beginning. And, even for those subordinates with some years' experience, who may need to be "re-motivated," a fresh start is recommended.

ON-THE-JOB MOTIVATING

No task should be explained to a subordinate without providing reasons as to why the task should be done well.

"Roger, you are in charge of filing in this group of files. Here is a copy of the index system for these file."

"Miss Jones, this is a great deal to learn."

"Yes, it is. Be sure to ask as many questions as you can think of. Okay?"

"Yes, I will."

"Good. You have an important job. If a customer contract is misfiled, it could cost our Company thousands of dollars in business. Together, let us look through each area so that you can become familiar with your responsibility."

SIMPLICITY FIRST RECOMMENDATION

Do not try "pie-in-the-sky" motivation. A file clerk is not going to be appointed president next week. No matter how well motivated, the best approach is to "Keep it simple, stupid (KISS)." And, that should be the approach on motivation. Stick to the nuts and bolts reasons for doing a better job.

SET AN EXAMPLE

The manager or supervisor who is well motivated will cause some of it to rub off on the subordinates. If Miss Jones wants to do a good job, that attitude may cause Roger to be well motivated. It is not always a matter of specifics but rather a combination of *displayed attitude and direction* that creates an environment that motivates subordinates. The boss has to project:

"Let us strive together to do a better job."

Give the new subordinate some easy tasks—ones that can lead to some early successes. The new person will gain immediate self-confidence. That should get his inner juices (dynamics) working. Top it off with some compliments on a " job well done." Now, the boss likes what he is doing. That's a double whammy of encouragement.

ANOTHER METHOD—USE A COACH

Let the new subordinate work for a few days with an experienced hand from whom successful techniques can be learned. This will help to achieve error-free work and a higher level of productivity. And, shortly after the subordinate has gone out "on his own," he can be told that he is picking up the job fast. A few compliments give the subordinate the self-assurance and some knowledge that his attempts are appreciated.

"On his own" means to an experienced manager that the new employee can now handle jobs that avoid the pattern of early mistakes which may necessitate criticism which in turn causes employee frustration and the resultant deterioration of motivation.

HELPFUL HINTS TO MANAGERS

1. As soon as possible, make new subordinates feel that they are a part of a winning team.

2. Arrange for a well-motivated subordinate to be a coach to new people.

3. Be quick to recognize special effort on the part of new subordinates.

4. Help subordinates to understand exactly what constitutes good job performance.

5. Make subordinates feel secure at their work stations or desks. (This is where you belong.)

6. Invite helpful hints from subordinates on how they can improve job performance.

SPEAKING PLAINLY

Some people are well motivated and some are not. Many books have been written on motivating employees and none of them have a guaranteed formula. What works for one manager may not work for many others.

An experienced manager can size up most of the attitudes of a subordinate. Then, the boss can take the desirable motivational attitudes and give them a push. It has to be done one subordinate at a time.

Each person is motivated by varying amounts of combinations of different stimuli: money, status, self-satisfaction, good job performance, praise, task difficulties, coworker relationships, and so on. The manager has a tough job in ferreting them out and making good use of these differing motivational stimuli.

HOW TO DETERMINE WHICH WORKER CAN BEST HANDLE EACH JOB

"My brother-in-law...I wish he would learn a trade,
so we'd know what kind of work he was out of."
HENNY YOUNGMAN

Major emphasis is put on the selection of the proper equipment or tools to do a job. Frequently, too little time is devoted to selecting the best available worker to do the required job. The fact that someone is sitting at a particular desk is no guarantee that person is the best person for the work that happens to cross that desk.

As in the selection of the best tool to do the job, a variety of factors exist in the selection of the best subordinate to do a particular job. The established criteria of experience and training are not necessarily the best factors in determining the potential for greater contributions to productivity.

USING THE OBJECTIVE ORIENTATION RECOMMENDATION

In determining which subordinate fits which position best, it is imperative to determine the requirements of the position. These requirements should state what objectives (not the type of work) have to be accomplished in that particular spot. Ignore all factors except what actually is to be done at that work station or desk! Here are some typical job objectives:

1. Completing certain reports by the end of each day.
2. Checking and correcting all of the computer input each day.
3. Supervising and keeping five clerks performing well.
4. Putting together 100 widgets, or whatever, each hour.
5. Answering all of the daily mail promptly.
6. Preparing 40 purchase orders each day.
7. Casting 200 parts an hour.

8. Collating 100 shipment documents a day.

POSITION EVALUATION

Once the objectives of the position are determined, some thought can be made as to which subordinate is likely to accomplish the objectives. Sure, training and experience are important—but not overriding.

Suppose a particular position is a high pressure slot. Who do we want there? Not someone who can fumble when thrown a problem. The brass would want someone who performs with grace under pressure.

In other words, if a new objective is to assemble 100 widgets a day, a profile of an acceptable candidate to fill the spot might include the ability to learn to operate a widgetmaker at the desired objective rate. By the way, the person, who has been operating a widgetmaker for ten years is not necessarily the fastest or least error-prone candidate for the job.

SWITCHING FOR MORE PRODUCTIVITY

If you have a hunch that someone could do a better job than the present incumbent in a job, then switch people. A manager cannot know who is best for the job until someone new is tried.

The downside: Loss due to a learning curve.

The upside: More productivity and/or better performance.

In many operations, employees go on performing for many years jobs that are not suited to their actual capabilities or temperament. The realignment of people and positions may be just as rewarding to the rank and file as to the Company. Chance plays a big part in the career selection of many people. Vocational opportunities are usually limited for those who have only complete minimal education and training. The neophyte in the job market, lacking any experience, has to start out in whatever is available. The choice is limited. However, the actual capabilities may warrant a different type of job.

UNION AND OTHER LIMITATIONS

Job switching is always difficult, particularly where there are administrative limitations. However, if the switch is considered desirable by both an immediate superior and the employee, progress toward the goal of fitting each worker where both the worker and the Company can benefit can be accomplished. No one says that it is easy—but it can be done.

MUSICAL CHAIRS

The constant switching around of workers from job to job may be harmful to employee morale. Using the old parlor game of musical chairs may demonstrate that management is not capable of making up its mind. Also, it is counter to higher productivity and improved performance because with each switch there is the loss encountered during the employee's learning phase.

However, in some operations musical chairs has worked wonders by bringing interesting and beneficial results. Hidden talents of some employees are brought into evidence, and new ways of doing things are discovered.

SUMMARY

1. Determine what has to be accomplished.
2. To some extent, ignore *how* it is to be accomplished.
3. Evaluate the skills inventory of the people on hand.
4. Develop some hunches about the subordinates.
5. Test your theories as to who can do what better.
6. If appropriate, use the musical chairs technique to discover some wild cards.

JUSTIFICATION FOR TRYING

Many of the people in our work force are "occupationally unsettled." Basically, that means that they do not really like their job (a serious drawback for motivation) or they are not using their best skills. Either way, they and their employers are not getting the full measure of work. In each case, the immediate boss has a problem subordinate.

Our management system works ideally when more people are doing the kinds of jobs that are reasonably best suited to them and to their organization. The task of the middle manager, who is in the front line of management, is to find which of his or her subordinates can do which job best.

HOW TO COAX AN EMPLOYEE TO CHANGE SHIFTS

"Leadership is the ability to get men to do what they don't want to do and like it."
HARRY S. TRUMAN

One of the most difficult chores for a boss is to get a subordinate to change shifts—particularly to a less desirable one. Changing work hours causes changes in the subordinate's life style. And that is good cause for employee resistance.

RECOMMENDATION FOR EARLY WARNING

"I wasn't told that I would be required to change shifts."

If the management foresees a possible movement, or if the Company has moved people from shift to shift in the past, then it is best to issue an early warning to subordinates of such a possibility. When an applicant is being interviewed for the job, the interviewer can ask the applicant if he has any objection to a change in shifts after he is hired. The answer can be specifically noted on the interview form.

Further, the job requirements can spell out that the prospective employee is expected to change shifts upon request.

For the employees who are transferred into a department that is prone to require a change in shifts, notice can be made of the possibility of shift changes prior to their transfer into such department.

WARNING: UNION CONTRACT PROVISIONS

In a union shop, shifting people is not very straightforward. The manager or supervisor would do well to become familiar with the collective bargaining provisions that limit management's authority to move people around.

Too many managers and supervisors rely on hearsay when it comes to knowing precisely what is in the contract. Careful reading of the important contract provisions will reduce misconceptions as to what are the rights that management has in making shift changes.

Questions of seniority, extent of notice, and so on, can be reviewed before an order is issued to change shifts. Otherwise, there can be a backfire produced by an employee who is more aware of his rights than his boss. Result: embarrassment for the boss, who may have to back peddle and retract an order.

CONTRACT NEGOTIATING VIEWPOINT

Management has the right to manage its work force. Part of that fundamental right is the ability to transfer personnel from one shift to another in order to maintain production or performance levels. Those who negotiate contract provisions can be made aware of the limitations, at times, severe, imposed by the inability of front line managers and supervisors to readily make shift changes. Who should make contract negotiators aware of the limitations? The front line managers and supervisors!

A WORTHWHILE TECHNIQUE: CITING ADVANTAGES

There are advantages to working late hours on a night or a swing shift. In order to get subordinates to like the idea, the following attributes of shift work should be kept in mind:

- The ability to rise late in the day.
- Time off during business hours in which to do shopping or other chores.
- Ability to attend vocational and other types of schools or colleges.
- Avoidance of rush hour traffic for commuters.
- Extra premium pay.
- Availability for a second job.
- Expanded opportunities for promotion
- Attendance at daytime sporting events.
- Increased transfer opportunities to other departments.

- More informal dress requirements.
- Generally lower administrative requirements (less red tape).
- Greater availability of employee facilities (less of a crowd in the cafeteria).

"TEMPORARY" CHANGE HAZARD

"I don't want to work days!"

Often, when people are transferred to the late shifts on a temporary basis, they tend to develop life styles that make them reluctant to transfer back to the day shift. And, how many times has an experienced manager witnessed that an employee, who strongly resists transfer to the night shift, ends up liking the new arrangement?

As a precaution, the manager or supervisor, when making a temporary change, should advise the subordinate that the transfer is strictly temporary—not permanent. This will help dispel possible resistance to a subsequent change back to the day shift.

An important point that a boss can make to encourage a subordinate to more readily accept a change to a late shift is that many people, who initially did not like the idea of working nights, now prefer to work nights.

"Roger did not want to work nights. Now, look at him—he won't give up staying in bed almost all day."

"Mary has become a night supervisor. She couldn't have gotten that promotion on days."

NIGHT PREMIUM BUCKS

"I don't want a cut in pay."

In operations where there is a significant shift pay differential, there is major resistance against transfer from the night shift to days. People seem to get used to the extra cash and do not want to take a cut back. The plus money becomes a part of their personal or family cash flow.

Rule 1: Shift differential attracts workers to night shift work.

Rule 2: Shift differential discourages night shift workers from wanting to work day shifts.

Extreme care has to be taken when transferring personnel to night shifts because of possible economic resistance to a subsequent move back to the day shift.

Therefore, an excessive shift differential premium pay can operate to offset management's capability of moving people around to meet changing productivity requirements.

STEPPING UP THE PERFORMANCE OF SLOWER PEOPLE

"Tomorrow is often the busiest day of the year."
ANCIENT PROVERB

Whether it is because of a lack of motivation or some inability to perform, some people will be slower than others. It is up to the front line manager or supervisor to bring the productivity and performance of each subordinate up to a meaningful level of output.

Of course, the superior can set the example with regard to motivation. The boss can find substitutes in shortages, develop new techniques to bypass roadblocks, and be constantly alert in overcoming all sorts of operating problems. Such a prominently displayed attitude can inspire subordinates to a higher level of performance.

TEAM EFFORT RECOMMENDATION

A group of almost any subordinates could be thought of as a team with the boss as a coach. The boss might have trained the group to work as a team. It is his team, with objectives that he has selected. As in team play, the boss (coach) assigns to each team member his required contribution to the overall team effort.

While it is the herd instinct, most people like to feel that they are a part of the team, that they belong to a group. It makes them feel more secure—both personally and professionally.

When the team approach is stressed, each "team member" may consider it important to do their fair share of the team's workload. If the team spirit is properly developed among subordinates, other members of the team may provide an emotional push forward to anyone who may need some prodding or assistance. Therefore, the slower worker may get some prodding from other workers.

WORK TEAM BASICS VS. MR. SLOPOKE

Why is the team concept important in some types of operations? Consider this. Mr. Slopoke, who is not willing to knock himself out for the Company, the boss, or the brass, may have a different attitude toward colleagues. The trappings of authority are one thing, but the relationship with coworkers is sometimes quite another matter.

Mr. Slopoke may not be able to let his fellow teammates down. While grudgingly acceding to any authority, he may have a high performance drive in supporting the people around him.

OLDER-HAND RECOMMENDATION

If Mr. Slopoke is a new employee, there is another technique which can be useful. For new personnel, those who are learning new techniques, or those who are more prone to have low levels of productivity, some industry situations lend themselves to having two subordinates work together. If such is the case, the manager or supervisor can select someone who has comparatively a higher level of productivity to work with someone who has a lower level.

> *The slow performer can pick up some methods and techniques that will improve his speed and abilities. Some of the motivation of the older hand may rub off on the slower worker.*

An experienced boss can pair together workers with differing abilities and motivation or inspiration rather than those with approximately equal abilities and drive.

THE JOB TITLE INCENTIVE RECOMMENDATION

Frequently, objectives or goals are stated to subordinates, but there is a failure to indicate the rewards that can occur when a subordinate achieves the desired goal. As always, the monetary reward of a pay raise is sufficient incentive to some. Promotions or other forms of recognition may be more of an inducement to others.

A CASE IN POINT

Here is ploy used in one plant. The Company reclassified all of the *assemblers* to *assembler trainees, junior assemblers,* and *senior assemblers.* You may have guessed what happened. Few employees liked the designation of "trainee," and therefore many put forth their best efforts to reach at least the more advanced classification of *junior assembler* And, of course, the "juniors" wanted to advance as well.

A possible improvement in job title, sometimes no matter how slight, could be a very large encouragement for slower performers to improve output. In addition, those employees who have the more senior designations, which have been earned over a period of time, frequently feel that they have something to live up to.

NONOPERATING PEOPLE

Clerk, junior grade is quite different from *clerk* and certainly a lower status than *clerk, senior grade.* Using a job title reclassification system can provide impetus for improved performance. Why have all the clerks rated as "clerks"? They do not all have the same performance. Salary ranges is an additional side issue.

PERSONAL TALK RECOMMENDATION

Disparaging talk to Mr. Slopoke about his performance cannot be expected to bring results in most instances. If there are any positive results, it is usually for only a short period of time. However, offers of assistance and assurance can make Mr. Slopoke feel more responsive about poor performance on his part.

> "Mr. Slopoke, is there anything that I can do to help you get the work out faster?"

> "Mr. Slopoke, I know that you are capable of handling more work. What can be done to help you?"

> "Mr. Slopoke, you are doing a good job at what you are doing, and I think that you have the ability to handle this additional work."

YOU ARE NOT GOING TO WIN THEM ALL

Some people are slower than others, for a variety of good reasons: job insecurity, fear of error, low learning ability, personal problems, and so on. The boss who does not try to reform the slow poke is being unfair to the other subordinates who have to carry more of the workload. Further, the boss who has failed to reform the slow poke and does not want to do something about the situation is equally unfair to others.

Failure to reform a slow poke but continuing his retention is adverse to good employee morale.

Everybody has to produce their fair share. Otherwise, the system will not work. Keeping people who, after attempts at reform, cannot carry their fair share of the load is not taking on full managerial responsibility and there is a loss of cost effectiveness.

WHEN TO COMPLIMENT AN EMPLOYEE AND HOW

Fan: "You were superb in 'Romeo and Juliet.'"
Actor: "I bet you say that to everyone who's superb."
ANONYMOUS

Everyone likes to have some applause now and then. The right timing and the selection of the accolade can certainly make a boss's job easier. The purpose of the compliment in the work place is to encourage continuing improved performance.

"Being nice" is not in lieu of promotions, merit pay increases, or other forms of recognition. It can be more useful than a plaque for an attendance record or a savings bond for a worthwhile suggestion. Those more material items are reserved for special events. The occasional compliment by a boss can overcome the nitty-gritty of the daily grind, and, it can be done right away.

OCCASIONS FOR A COMPLIMENT TO IMPROVE PERFORMANCE

- Discovering a minor hidden error.
- Completing a new and difficult job.
- Handling a customer well.
- Putting in some offtime on the job.
- Improving relations with a supplier.
- Obtaining agreement on a new procedure.
- Selling a new product for the first time.
- Redesigning an old form.
- Using a substitute supply item.
- Keeping the work moving under adverse conditions.
- Simplifying a small work technique.
- Improving a work tool.
- Restoring small equipment into working order.
- Doing well on a Company community project.

- Getting favorable mention in a local newspaper.
- Giving another employee a hand.
- Finishing a rush job on time.
- Finding a new use for the computer terminal data.

THE DERIVED BENEFITS TO THE BOSS

When an employee's day is brightened by the recognition of some minor achievement, that employee becomes a happier participant in even the more difficult chores. He develops the feeling that his effort is being appreciated. He knows that his worth to the Company or his boss is being noticed. His contribution to the day-to-day operations of his department will be increased.

WHY BOTHER?

It is much easier to be a boss of a group of subordinates who are appreciated for their special effort than to be a boss of a department where the boss does not take occasional notice of some additional effort.

A boss, who is a stick-in-the-mud, has a much tougher time running a department than one who does not have that image.

CAUTION FLAG—LIMIT THE APPLAUSE

Overdoing compliments is as adverse as giving no compliments at all.

After all, everyone is paid to do a job to the best of their ability. A significant extra effort is worth saying something about, and has the added bonus of boasting morale. However, one cannot cheapen the compliments by making them too frequently.

An exception: To new employees, a boss may be a little more generous in the dispensing of compliments so that they may gain some more added confidence about their new job. Older hands may be expected to perform above average anyway.

THE TIMING RECOMMENDATION

As with other job rewards, a compliment should be given as soon after the good performance as possible. This cause-and-effect relationship leads to good feeling on the part of the subordinate who has turned in an excellent performance which has been noticed and remarked on by the manager or supervisor.

"My boss liked the way I handled that job today."

If more employees could say that when they get home when their families or spouses ask, "How was work today?" then more employees would like their job better and be more motivated into doing a better job.

BREVITY RECOMMENDATION

The compliment should be direct and to the point. Brevity is best and avoids the danger to the boss of sounding somewhat insincere.

"That was fast thinking in switching terminals."

"Good salesmanship in selling the ABC Company."

"It is a well thought-out procedure!"

"It was smart to use iron oxide parts."

GIVING RECOGNITION TO EMPLOYEES

"I offer neither pay, nor quarters, nor provisions; I offer hunger, thirst, forced marches, battles and death."
GIUSEPPE GARIBALDI, Italian Patriot

Supposedly, Napoleon said that a man would give his life for a little piece of blue ribbon. Wait a minute! No one expects rank and file employees to make any such extreme sacrifice. However, some sort of "little piece of blue ribbon" is due on occasion.

The college athlete, the actor in an amateur theater production, the volunteer in a community activity have little thought of any financial gain for their effort. Yet, these people frequently devote their entire energies to such work and stand to receive only a small amount of recognition.

BACK TO BASICS

If people will work very hard, and in wars, even try to kill themselves for a little piece of blue ribbon, why not use this motivation in the workplace? Actually, the workplace is an ideal environment for the granting of recognition.

Any laurels given to an employee should be as EXTRA recognition rather than as a substitute for raises, bonuses, or promotions that may be due to a subordinate. To give a certificate of appreciation for good work instead of the raise that was anticipated usually only works the first time out. After that, nobody wants the certificate; everyone will say:

"Give me the raise instead."

If the award is made in addition to all of the other things that may be due to the employee, it can work wonders. The recognition has to be a sign of real appreciation rather than a substitute for the coin of the realm.

Quick and Effective Recognition

One way to convey recognition is to provide it verbally at the time of the superior performance or reasonably shortly thereafter. A boss can ask the subordinate to come to the office, and say:

> "Well, Gloria, you certainly saved the day on that job!"

> "Wilbur, you managed to take care of that situation very well. Thank you."

Sometimes, verbal recognition is more effective when done where others can overhear the commendation or possibly join in the applause. If the sentiments are expressed at the subordinate's work station or desk, where others can overhear, it may be more appreciated. Each situation requires a little managerial finesse.

There may be expressions of sour grapes by others, but usually the recognition will last longer than the detractors' comments.

Is Recognition an Effective Motivator?"

Just how much recognition does the average worker receive in his or her entire lifetime? Think about it! A high school diploma, a bowling trophy or two—and what else? Very little. What achievements can an average worker discuss with family and friends? The comment attributed to Napoleon may be of some real significance.

"At least, my boss appreciates what I am doing."

An employee who can make that statement to himself or to others will be better motivated toward doing a more conscientious job. Therefore, a little pat on the back once in a while can do wonders for productivity or performance at little to no cost or effort.

How to Give Recognition

- A handshake by the top mover and shaker in front of others.
- An engraved certificate.
- Mention or an article in the Company publication.
- A press release to the local newspaper.

- A plaque or desktop pen and pencil set.
- A savings bond.

OPPORTUNITIES FOR RECOGNITION

- Achieving a particular production goal.
- Reaching a sales quota or breakthrough.
- Submission of a cost-cutting suggestion.
- One year of perfect attendance or on-time record.
- Community service work.
- Suggesting a new product or service.
- Praise from a customer for service.
- Completion of a trainee program.

MR. SCROOGE LOSES OUT AGAIN

The manager or supervisor who cannot, or will not say "thanks" once in a while is not in a happy situation. He has subordinates who are NOT fully motivated. Mr. Scrooge may say, "Well, that's what they are getting paid to do." Let's accept that he is right—the paycheck is the sole motivator. But why not have work atmosphere that is pleasant?

People work best when they believe that their work is appreciated. The department head, who may believe that employee recognition is "kid's stuff," is not fully aware of people motivation. He is actually making the supervisory aspects of his job much more difficult.

HOW TO MINIMIZE THE EFFECTS OF RED TAPE

"One way to get high blood pressure is to go mountain climbing over molehills."

EARL WILSON

The purpose of management policies and procedures is to create uniform handling of situations and to accomplish overall Company objectives. However, at times those policies and procedures are adverse to the stated objectives.

When there are sufficient exceptions to, or problems created by, the procedures, they should be changed—maybe eliminated.

In the interim, front line managers and supervisors have to use some judgment in bypassing the required paperwork or procedures that tend to prevent or delay the overall objectives.

WHAT IS RED TAPE?

Red tape may be defined as unnecessary procedures. However, in each instance, who is to decide what is unnecessary? Is the writing of a supply or parts requisition form unnecessary? To the floor supervisor, it may well be. After all, it does not accomplish any part of the floor supervisor's job. However, how else can one expect the terminal cost input clerks to charge supplies or parts to jobs or budget areas accurately? How can one maintain cost or budget analysis?

It becomes clear that what may be red tape to one manager or supervisor is absolutely necessary to another.

LOOK TO THE TOTAL PICTURE

An accident report may be just so much red tape to a Company driver. To the insurance or claims manager it is a vital document—one that can mean many thousands of dollars to the Company.

Therefore, procedural requirements of any kind have to be viewed with the overall objectives in mind. (Otherwise, how can the truly unnecessary procedures be selected for bypassing?) Judgments as to necessity have to tempered by consideration of the intended purpose and just what overall requirements have to be met. A supervisor can ask, "Why was this procedure installed?" If not satisfied, a check can be made with higher or other levels of management as to the purpose of the procedure.

SOLUTION BY EXCEPTION

Those who developed the procedures tried to cover every base that they could think of at the time. Of course, situations change and new problems arise. The supervisor has to recognize situations where an exception has to be made to the procedure. The criteria for departing from the procedures include:

- Obvious jeopardy to the health or safety of personnel or others.
- High adverse impact on productivity or performance.
- Extraordinary increase in costs.

An exception to a policy and procedure may be warranted because the consequences, which have to be readily evident, are clearly detrimental to the overall Company goals.

REDUCING DAY-TO-DAY RED TAPE

Ignoring the highly unusual sets of circumstances, there are elements of red tape in daily operations where such effort has to be minimized in order to accomplish the job on hand. Some successful techniques for reducing daily problems include:

- One procedure is coordinated or combined with another to reduce possible duplication.
- A lesser-skilled or nonproductive subordinate is used to fulfill the routine procedural requirements. (This saves higher-skilled people for the more important jobs.)
- The procedures requiring excessive time are postponed to a slacker period in productivity or performance requirements.

- Several departments combine resources or alternate the responsibility with regard to certain procedural requirements.
- Part-timers or temporaries are used during periods of higher or more unusual requirements, permitting the regulars to maintain production or performance.
- Repetitive data is mechanically reproduced or photo-copied on forms and reports so that the completion of the forms takes a minimum of time.

AGE-OLD RECOMMENDATION TO REDUCE RED TAPE

Without going through the training to become an efficiency expert in reviewing procedures, consideration can be given to the following scenario:

1. Can any of the procedure steps be eliminated?
2. If not eliminated, can any of the steps be combined?
3. If not eliminated or combined, can any of the steps be more simplified?

Mr. Blockhead is going to say "no" to all of the above three queries in most instances. "That's the way we have been doing it for years." Well, he has forgotten an important managerial rule that is older than he is and that is:

"There is no best way, only better ways."

HANDWRITING ON THE WALL

Those organizations that permit Mr. Blockhead to ravel the rest of their people in red tape are sending an invitation to the corporate undertaker. Unnecessary procedures are NOT cost effective. Companies that become slowly less cost effective have to ultimately close their doors.

No buyer in the market place wants to pay for red tape. Generally, consumers will pay well for products and services and the more-or-less direct effort that goes into them. That is, more or less a given. However, any unnecessary effort is not for their account. Woe to the company that thinks otherwise.

HOW TO INSPIRE A TEAM EFFORT

"The Pentagon is like a log going down river with 25,000 ants on it, each thinking he's steering."
HENRY ROWAN

In many industries and organizations there have been changes in how the work is accomplished. Computers and other technical innovations have brought about more occupational specialization in which each employee is trained for a specific set of operations.

Due to these changes, the work of the individual has to blend in more with the work of the group. Front line managers and supervisors have been quick to realize that the individual initiative has been made to conform more to a group goal.

EXCEPTIONS TO GROUP ACTIVITY

Not all types of work are handled best in team fashion. In each operation, evaluation has to be made as to whether productivity or performance improves by making individuals part of the team or by making each of them responsible for their own workload.

For certain types of operations, the competition between individuals is more desirable than welding of the individuals into a workteam.

OVERCOMING A DRAWBACK

As enterprises become larger and more complex, there is a growing requirement of specialized skills in the workforce. Automation, robotics, new materials, and careful engineering of the workflow have reduced the need for the unskilled or semiskilled employee.

A drawback to this trend is becoming evident in most plants and operations. Wilbur, a skilled worker, has been looking only to his part of the workload—his contribution to the overall payoff. Wilbur's outlook may not be consistent with interdependence of the workgroup.

Wilbur's supervisor has to integrate Wilbur's efforts into the team efforts. He has to be made partially responsible for the section's total workload.

THE BENEFITS OF TEAMWORK

Less supervisory effort is required where members of workgroups are more or less supervising each other. Ned can spot Bill's lathe motor overheating and do something about it. Mary can show Wilbur how to replace a die. Joan can instruct Oscar in how to bring up new data on the computer terminal. The department manager or supervisor then has more time to handle the more difficult problems and to coordinate with other groups.

The superior can find that with group support, the chance for achieving production or performance goals is improved. The mob does not always do what the mob leaders want and on occasion will even turn on their leaders. However, the team will usually support the team captain.

HOW TO SHARE THE BURDEN

Here is what a front line manager or supervisor can do fairly quickly:

- Increase the responsibility of the individual for the group's performance.
- Assign a complete unit of work to the group.
- Remove some controls so that individuals can act for the group.
- Grant more freedom to the group as a group, permitting group discussions on alternative work methods.
- Discuss new assignments with the group.
- Require group members to coach each other to learn new skills or to handle new problems.
- Report and comment on group performance rather than on any individual effort.
- Reward the entire group for any outstanding performance.
- Lead group discussions on problem areas.

GETTING THE SQUARE PEG INTO THE ROUND HOLE

Not every subordinate wants to work within a group. The manager or supervisor has to make the square peg fit into the round hole—and like it. Some employees want their own assignments and want to have individual recognition for a job well done. Sometimes, it will take some buttering up.

> "John, you are an expert in what you do, but the others in our group need your knowledge, and more important, your support. Give them some of your expertise."

> "Gunther, the big boss likes your work. Keep it up. But I have a problem with the others in the group. Can you lend them a hand to keep them on the straight and narrow?"

> "Mary, why don't you give the others some help in figuring out that new job?"

GETTING UNEXPECTED HELP

In any group of people, there may be one or two subordinates who, on their own, want to make team activity work. Avoid standing in their way. Let them do most of the coaxing for team effort. And, let them push other members of the team to perform well on group work.

Allowing these sparkplugs to encourage team effort, makes the job of the boss easier. First, because the sparkplugs are a grass roots effort. Second, coworkers provide a different type of persuasion than a boss does.

BIG ADVANTAGE OF TEAMWORK

A surprising outcome of the replacement of individual assignments with group assignments has been that skilled employees have a greater varied work exposure. They learn how their part of the work fits into a larger picture. And, they can anticipate more of the problems that they may create.

What happens? In group work there is less potential for errors and poor quality. It is a big plus benefit that was not anticipated.

How it works

Charley was responsible for assembly of one part of the refrigerator door. Now, he and others are responsible for the assembly of the entire door. In the past, he may not have cared about what problems there were in the total door assembly. After the door assembly became group work, Charley had to change his outlook.

Multiskilled force benefit

When employees work in groups there is a tendency to learn each other's skills. Those subordinates, who acquire additional skills, are of greater value to their immediate superior and to the Company.

Generally, unions are opposed to such tendencies.

However, in industries or operations that have more multiskilled workforces there is more job security for the rank and file. At least, for those people who become multiskilled.

In nonunion foreign countries, our competition has an edge. The managements there do not concern themselves as to whether their employees want to become multiskilled or not. Either a worker becomes multiskilled or it's back to the back-breaking work under the sun. There is no third way!

CHOOSING WHEN TO REWARD LOYALTY

"Loyalty is like love, you have to give some in order to get some."
UNKNOWN

Personal loyalty by subordinates is difficult to come by and, at times, any rewarding for loyalty can backfire. A subordinate who performs a loyal act will frequently be downgraded by coworkers as an apple polisher. Then, any reward would only confirm some opinions of the coworkers.

However, acts of subordinate loyalty should be rewarded—whether the acts were committed for reward or not.

EXAMPLES OF SUBORDINATE LOYALTY

- Coming into work while suffering from illness although paid sick leave is available.
- Last minute change of vacation plans because of work requirements.
- Going into work on a day off or after hours on short notice.
- Volunteering to assist on a Company community service project.
- Commendable (loyal) actions during a regular or wildcat strike action.
- Boosting the Company's products or services away from work.
- Recruiting new employees.
- Participating in after-hours training programs.
- Rendering first aid to an injured employee.
- Foregoing lunch hours or breaks during peak production periods.
- Preventing theft or damage to Company property.

WHY SUBORDINATES ARE NOT LOYAL

Many people in management complain that employees no longer perform as many acts of loyalty as they did years ago. Managers complain there is a general reluctance on the part of members of the workforce to step forward and to help their employer. Maybe so.

The other side of the coin is that some managements contribute to the discouragement of such loyal acts. How often is an employee thanked for coming in sick when he or she was needed?

In one instance, an employee came from a hospital bed to help out the supervisor, who not only did not thank him but did not even ask how he felt.

In another case, during a wildcat strike, a union member crossed the picket line to go to work. She received jeers and an unkind name. For years afterward, some management people kept referring to her, in her presence, by that unkind name. She smiles—but her loyalty is forever faded.

PERSONAL THANKS RECOMMENDATION

Few people want to be paid double for coming in when they are ill or altering their vacation plans to meet problem requirements Nevertheless, some sign of appreciation is in order. A personal "thank you" is in order for at least two reasons:

1. It is the right thing to do.
2. Appreciation encourages such commendable action.

   "Thanks for coming in while you are sick. Can I have someone drive you home after work or can I call a taxi for you?"

Appreciation does not have to be big, like a three-foot high loving cup. It can be as simple as saying, "Thanks a lot for helping out on this." Most people are not loyal for some kind of reward.

Loyalty is not bought, otherwise it wouldn't be loyalty but rather services rendered for payment. Supervisory people can learn to say thanks more often, even if they do not think that it is completely in order. In other words, say "thanks" in marginal cases as well.

Using timing effectively

As with any kind of recognition, formal or informal, the timing is important. (No one likes after-thoughts.) Signs of special recognition for outstanding performance can be made as soon after the event as possible. However, it need not be done within earshot of all of the subordinates. If nothing else, the employee being recognized could be embarrassed. The opportunity need not be used to show other employees how they should behave or could have behaved in similar circumstances.

Sometimes, public appreciation cheapens the situation by making the loyal act as an example for the behavior of others. The others may see it as a cheap shot at them.

The expression of appreciation is frequently best performed in privacy. It avoids embarrassment to the loyal subordinate and accomplishes just as much.

"Hank, thanks for coming in on your day off."

Making old mr. scrooge look better

There is nothing wrong with sending flowers or a box of candy to an employee's home according to a given situation. It is a nice touch to reward a loyal subordinate. If the Company does not buy that sort of thing, brown bag your lunch one or two days and spring for the gift yourself.

Getting back to "people-smart"

Do you show that you care about your people? If you do, then chances are that they will put in that extra effort for you.

No one is saying that a boss should become wishy-washy. The boss can remain very authoritarian and still obtain loyalty from the subordinates. We all know a number of bosses, who are as hard as nails, but their people are devoted to them. Somehow, these bosses convey that loyalty works both ways.

HOW TO GET YOUR CURRENT STAFF TO RECRUIT NEW EMPLOYEES

> *"A good secretary is worth killing for."*
> MARY ANN ALLISON & ERIC ALLISON

Where you have found one diamond, you just might have additional good fortune and find another. Frequently, employees know about friends or relatives who are in the labor market and who might make good employees.

Not only does this source cut down on recruiting costs, but also the present employee may have some worthwhile knowledge as to the capability of the prospect or how he or she might work out in a particular job situation.

USING EMPLOYEE RECRUITING

1. *Special responsibility.* The recruiting employee may feel that any poor performance of the recommended recruit would be a reflection on the employee. Therefore, the existing employee will likely render every assistance possible to make the new employee succeed. A part of this effort will be job coaching, Company orientation, and so forth.

This induced responsibility on the part of the recruiting employee may motivate him to a more outstanding performance in his own work. The motivation that he is attempting to instill in the new employee may rub off on him.

2. *Gratitude.* The new employee may feel that he has a special debt to his friend who recommended him for the job. This debt may be paid off by attempting to perform very well on the new job. He may apply himself to learning the new tasks or to having a good attendance record, and so on.

In short, he does not want his performance to be an adverse reflection or embarrassment to the friend who recommended him for the job.

3. *Community relations.* Such recruits are generally from the surrounding area and not from far afield. The more local employees that a plant has, the better the chance for improved plant-community relationships. There is also the desirable conveyed attitude that "the plant looks after its own."

4. *Expense.* Word-of-mouth advertising is far less expensive than newspaper advertising and is also more convincing. While the newspaper reaches more people faster, the other help-wanted ads involve more competition.

KICKING THE HECK OUT OF THEORY

The theorists and their in-house followers believe that advertising brings people to the door who are screened and then hired. But what kind of people read and answer ads? Those looking for jobs! Sometimes a really good candidate is not looking for a job—not even reading the ads. Yet that person who is *not* looking may be just the ticket.

Roger is a good programmer—one of the best. However, there is a need to increase the programming staff. Roger has many friends who are programmers elsewhere. The computer department manager engages Roger in conversation.

"Roger, we have a couple of programmer openings."
"Is that so?"
"Yes. If you know of any possible candidates that want
to listen to a good offer, have them call me."

NOTICE OF OPENINGS

The use of the Company bulletin board is an effective way to convey the existence of openings to the present personnel. The Company newspaper is an effective media as well. The cost of such effort? Very low.

However, one of the best ways is—again—word of mouth. The manager or supervisor tells the subordinates about the openings. First line supervision is the best contact for any questions that employees may have regarding the openings.

"If anyone knows of a good word processor, let me know."

USING INCENTIVES

Many operations dispense savings bonds or bonuses to any employee who recruits another employee. The award may be given after the new employee is on board for 30 days or so.

The effect of the incentive award is to increase both the new employee's and the older employee's sense of responsibility for the good performance of the new worker. After the award has been given, no one wants it to develop that a dud had been recommended!

Sometimes more useful than the monetary incentive is the use of a little verbal recognition. Words tend to show a less perfunctory attitude than the awarding of a savings bond. A personal appreciation can be indicated:

"Joan, many thanks for bringing Gloria on board. She is working out very well."

To further reinforce the sense of responsibility for the recommendation on the part of the recruiting employee, a few more words can be added such as:

"I hope Gloria continues to knock out the work."

ANOTHER GOOD RECRUITING SOURCE RECOMMENDATION

Employees are not the only ones who can recruit by word of mouth. There are salespeople, vendors, customers, and so on, that call on your operation. Let them know what kind of people you are looking for.

New Times, New Methods

Every operation has its fair share of slow pokes, error prone, political sharks, clock watchers, nitpickers, deadwood, rip-off artists, red tape dispensers, trouble makers, nervous nellies, complainers, social lions, goof-offs, and bottlenecks. Some operations have more than their fair share. Your operation does not need any more of those people.

Today, it takes a great deal of effort to acquire good people—the right stuff. More effort and new methods are required. Making everyone a recruiter is a start.

LISTENING TO BECOME A MORE EFFECTIVE MANAGER

"I not only use all the brains I have,
but all I can borrow."
WOODROW WILSON

How many times have we all heard the following:

"I told them that last week."

"No one is going to listen anyway."

One of the corporate maladies of today is that within each organization there is a certain amount of failure to listen. A competitor could not have picked a better ally. Some management personnel can be accused of not listening to employees, customers, contractors, suppliers, staff specialists, consultants, other managers, supervisors, competitors, and so on.

PROVEN SIGNS OF FAILURE TO LISTEN

Here are the symptoms of the organizational malady of failure to listen:

- New products or services offered by competitors come as complete surprises.
- Few worthwhile suggestions from employees.
- Duplication of administrative effort.
- High scrapping costs and error rates.
- High product returns by customers and service complaints.
- High labor turnover.
- Few changes in equipment—slow to computerize.
- Few changes in production techniques.
- New advanced materials are not used.
- Large number of industrial relations problems.
- Uneven or unpleasant supplier relationships.

How Management Becomes Deaf

Most managers contend that they have an open-door policy. That is if someone has something to discuss, the manager is available at almost all times to listen.

> *Having an open door policy and having an open door are two different matters.*

"Listen, Willy, not now. I have to get out the monthly report and there is not time right now. I will get back to you."

"Yes, Willy, I know that you wanted to discuss overtime, but I want to ask you about the inventory levels now."

"Willy, I discussed that with Jim the other day. Forget it."

An open-door policy means *not* putting off what one may not wish to hear at that particular moment. And it also means having an open mind.

The Big Drawback of an Open Door

Even if a manager feels that he has heard every possible suggestion or complaint that there could ever be, it is advisable to listen once again.

First, a manager can make some evaluation, which could be helpful, of the person who is speaking. It rounds out the knowledge that a manager can have of a subordinate.

Second, the speaker is encouraged to be alert on the job because the speaker believes that in the future someone will listen again.

Third, the speaker has gotten something off his chest. Even if the discussion matter is a well-repeated gripe. Just listening may prevent the matter from going any further.

It just may be that after scores and scores of experiences of fruitless listening, one good idea may come in through the doorway. That one valid suggestion may make everything else worthwhile.

ASK QUESTIONS

In order for the manager to benefit from the person who has something to tell him, he should draw him out. Typical questions, which indicate interest as well as arriving at a possible point of benefit, can include:

- What is it that should be accomplished?
- Why should we want to accomplish that?
- Where are we going to do this?
- When should we do this?
- Who is to be involved?
- What is the cost effectiveness of doing this?

CONCLUDING THE DISCUSSION

The fact that there is an open-door policy does not mean that any topic should be jawed to death. However, in concluding, some appreciation for the effort can be shown.

"Willy, I have reviewed this suggestion before. The answer was 'NO.' However, I certainly think that you were alert in grasping the situation. And, I appreciate your attitude in trying to do a better job. Thanks."

"Willy, thanks for telling me about this matter. I will try to handle this the best way I can."

GAINING INSIGHT

Even if a good idea never comes through the door, there is a benefit of the open-door policy to the manager. By listening, a manager can gain some good information about the subordinate. Work attitudes, personal goals, job skills and other characteristics of the subordinate come into the open. A psychological test could not be more revealing.

WHAT TO DO

1. Be willing to listen to almost anyone.
2. Use questions to show interest and to draw out the more important points.

3. When the conversation gets repetitive or pointless, try to conclude it—but not abruptly.

4. Be appreciative of the fact that certain matters were brought to someone's attention.

5. Consider that, once in a while, someone will have a good idea that you ought to listen to.

HOW TO PERK UP YOUR PEOPLE WITH JOB ROTATION

"The people who get into trouble in our company are those who carry around the anchor of the past."

JOHN WELCH, CEO,
General Electric Company

Musical chairs is a very interesting children's game, but when applied properly to work situations, it can relieve boredom while improving productivity or performance. The key phrase is "applied properly."

Fundamentally, job rotation is when John does Mary's work, Mary is working at Charley's desk, Joan has taken over Wilbur's chores, and so on. The workflow remains the same, but the people are changed.

No one should be exempted from job rotation. The benefits of job rotation are not restricted to blue collar workers, but are available to white collar, managerial, and professional employees as well. The more sophisticated the skills, the more interesting the benefits of job rotation.

GIVING THOUGHT TO ACTION

Blindly throwing people up into the air to see where they will land can be disastrous. Job rotation is a technique that requires analysis of the jobs to be performed and an inventory of skills that are available. Switching your subordinates from one boring job to another provides only short-range benefits frequently not worthy of the effort required to explain and to install the change-over.

Undoing a job rotation scheme can lead to increased work disruptions and overtime.

127

MAKE SOME BASIC ASSUMPTIONS

Many jobs are more demanding than others, regardless of the amount of training or experience required to do them effectively. Some jobs are more rewarding to the average employee than others. That is they offer more of the various types of rewards that most employees seek. So, there are jobs that are more demanding and others that are more rewarding.

Many employees have an "owner" fixation about their particular jobs. Most rank and file people and even many supervisors view their jobs as their personal property. No matter how beneficial a move might be, they refuse to consider making a shift. They are deep rooted in their job and only extensive spade work will pry them loose to at least try something else.

USE OF VOLUNTARY METHOD

A job exposure program permits the employees to be loaned out to other departments where there are vacancies. Openings can be announced on the bulletin boards. Permission for the loan-out has to be approved by the employee's regular immediate superior. After a limited period, application can be made for permanent transfer or a return to the original department. Benefits can accrue that outweigh potential disruptions to productivity.

NONVOLUNTARY METHOD

Most job switches are inspired at the immediate supervisory level, whether the employee volunteers for the change or not. The immediate boss believes that John can handle Bill's work more effectively and makes the switch. However, in addition to meeting the superior's immediate needs, a program of cross-training has been started.

Cross-training provides greater flexibility in the event that a group is short staffed. Another quick benefit of job rotation is that employees can learn what problems the other person is facing and therefore be more accommodating in meeting the overall problems of maintaining or improving productivity or performance. If Rona, a chief inventory clerk is switched to being a chief production control clerk, then she will gain broader background in the bigger picture.

SWITCHING NEW PEOPLE

At the practical level, the job switching of new employees in the operation will help them find what kind of work that they like to do best and where the Company can make the most use of their potential talents. While a recent school graduate might think that he or she prefers the purchasing function, some job rotation may reveal to the neophyte that some mechanically oriented job is even more desirable.

New people cannot be expected to know where they will be happier or work out best for the Company.

Rotation programs for the junior levels of experience tends to reduce employee turnover which is all too common at those levels.

Think about this: people who have little work experience, frequently have to be assigned where there are vacancies for the inexperienced—even though they may NOT be suited for that job. Then they work 40 years at an occupation that is not ideal for them *nor* for their employer.

QUICK STEPS YOU CAN TAKE NOW

1. Who is needed where—compare requirements with your skills inventory.
2. Gamble on somebody else's being able to do the job better than the present incumbent in the job.
3. Increase cross-training for more assignment flexibility.
4. Try "temporary" changes for switch-resistant subordinates.
5. Move junior level people around until there is mutual job satisfaction.

THE BENEFITS

Job rotation makes employees learn new responsibilities and improves production methods and performance. ***New minds are being applied to old problems.*** Aggressive and hard-working subordinates tend to look forward to being able to handle new challenges. For them, it is a relief from boredom.

ONE OF THE REWARDS OF BEING A MANAGER

No manager is going to make every subordinate happy with his or her job. However, once in a while, a manager can shift somebody to a job slot where there is greater personal life long *occupational satisfaction* for that subordinate.

That kind of a good deed makes all of the long hours, weekend work, shortages, snafus, nosy outsiders, unrealistic budgets, unappreciative superiors, union aggravation, red tape, tight deadlines, uncooperative colleagues, short lunch hours, political infighting, ivory tower edicts, people problems, low pay, stress, and lots of hard work *worthwhile* for most managers.

There is a reward that will never be in a paycheck.

HOW TO CHOOSE THE BEST NIGHT SHIFT OR WEEKEND PEOPLE

> *"Most people like hard work, particularly when they are paying for it."*
> FRANKLIN P. JONES

Many companies view their operations during night shifts or weekends as supplemental and not as fully rewarding in terms of productivity as the regular day shift. In selecting which employees to assign to the nonregular shifts, a little understanding of the reasons why these operations are not as productive as they can be is in order.

THE CAUSES FOR REDUCED EFFICIENCY

Admittedly, each industry differs. However, there are some adverse circumstances, which are corporate maladies, that are common to many operations on their night or weekend shifts, including:

1. Less experienced supervision.
2. Absence of review by top levels of management. (Few top managers and executives visit their operations at night or on weekends.)
3. Fewer technical and professional personnel are available who can supply certain capabilities to operations.
4. The more capable personnel are promoted to the regular shifts.
5. Lower experience requirements for nonregular shifts.
6. Fewer or lower nonmonetary incentives for improved performance on nonregular shifts.
7. Apprehensions that nonregular shifts will be terminated if volume requirements decline.

SUGGESTION: CONSIDER LIFESTYLE OF EMPLOYEE

Some employees do well working nights because they enjoy the freedom of personal activities that is not available to workers on day shifts. For instance, day college students can meet necessary expenses while continuing their education. Working on the 4 P.M. to midnight shift gives them these advantages.

Older persons who wish to have a short workweek in order to maintain benefits or for other reasons may be ideal for weekend-only work.

Older persons can provide experience and skills which may not be available at nonpremium wages.

Senior citizens, who are seeking to supplement social security and pensions, usually have a great deal of desirable expertise that can be made available on nonregular shifts.

Handicapped people, who may have transportation problems during normal commuting hours, are frequently ideal for nonregular shifts. Often, they appreciate the opportunity to be part of the productive workforce.

LOOK FOR SELF-STARTERS

Employees, who can lay out and proceed to do their own work with a minimum of supervision, are desirable on the night shifts. As supervisory effort is spotty or light and as technical assistance is limited, those workers who can apparently maintain significant levels of productivity without the aids that are available to the regular shift can be expected to perform well at times other than on the regular shift.

Those employees who are not self-starters to any extent, who require more than a minimum of supervisions, can be left on the regular day shift where these characteristics are not as much of a drawback.

Rule 1: People who need more supervision should workdays.

Rule 2: People who need less supervision should work nonregular or night shifts.

PICK PROMOTION MOTIVATED

Those employees who are aggressively motivated to move up the ladder to supervisory or managerial levels are also ideal candidates for the nonregular shifts. First, there is usually greater opportunity to move to foreperson or section leader because there are fewer supervisory personnel on the nonregular shifts.

Second, many in supervision on the nonregular shifts want to transfer to the day shifts. This increases workforce flexibility. Third, a high promotion motivation worker on the nonregular shift may be a spark in encouraging others on the shift to improve their performance.

DANGLING A CARROT TRICK

Those employees who complain of a lack of promotion opportunity can be reminded that much more opportunity for advancement exists on late shifts and that superior performance can become more readily obvious.

Many a middle and higher level management person got their initial start in management by working nontraditional hours.

USE A TESTING PROCEDURE

A self-starter or promotion-motivated employee can be asked to try a temporary transfer to another shift. If it is mutually agreeable, the transfer can be made permanent. The effect of this technique is to give the employees, who are likely to be more of an asset to the nonregular shift, an opportunity to see if they like or can adapt to a late shift.

IMPROVING PRODUCTIVITY AND PERFORMANCE

There are types of employees who, for economic or other reasons, or because they are self-starters or are well motivated, would be valuable additions to the usually more undesirable shifts. By careful people selection, the performance of the late or weekend shifts can be improved. Diligent recruiting and reviewing of possible transferees will upgrade the quality of off-shift personnel and increase nonregular shift productivity.

Just Where Is Siberia?

Relegating people on whim or without forethought to nonregular shifts is counterproductive. Nor, should transfer to nonregular shifts be for some punitive purpose. The managerial purpose in having shift and weekend work is to make further use of existing facilities and equipment. The objective is to lower costs on total production.

That cost-effective objective is sidetracked by having people in the off-hours who are not fully productive.

Foreign competitors do not have similar problems. Their facilities and equipment have to have full utilization. No shift is an "also ran." There is complete performance accountability for every production hour—days, nights, weekends and 2 o'clock in the morning. There is no shift differential pay, overtime wages, incentive pay, nor does the boss have to be nice about transfers.

HOW TO USE MORE EFFECTIVE NONMONETARY INCENTIVES

"Be nice to people on your way up because you'll meet 'em on your way down."
WILSON MIZNER

When a corporal becomes a sergeant, he receives not only a monthly pay increase but also another stripe on his sleeve. The additional stripe is a readily obvious sign of his change in title, relative position to his associates, added responsibilities, and so on. The new stripe is as much sought after as the increase in pay; and by some people, more.

Why? Perhaps it is because most people like to feel that they are succeeding in what their endeavor is and that some apparent recognition of their abilities was made.

IMPORTANCE OF NONMONETARY ACHIEVEMENTS

Mountain climbers endure fantastic hardships and risk injury and loss of life just to attain some summit. Few receive any monetary gain from such endeavor and hardships. They do it for the satisfaction of achievement.

In the business and industrial world, few are expected to endure such hardships. However, there are interesting goals that can be set to motivate employees to a higher level of performance. The nonfinancial rewards for those achievements can be as much sought after by many employees as any in the nonbusiness world.

SOME NONMONETARY INCENTIVES TO CONSIDER

One has to consider which nonmonetary incentive works best with which subordinates. Here are a few ideas:

1. Change to a better job title.
2. Change in desk or workstation location.

3. An article or a mention in the Company publication.
4. A certificate or a plaque.
5. Congratulations by the Company president.
6. Granting of signing or authorizing authority.
7. Name on Company letterhead.
8. Company business cards.
9. Name on door and/or building directory.
10. Inclusion in higher level meetings.
11. Appointment to committees.
12. Ability to delegate certain tasks.

DANGLING THE SUGAR PLUM

Complete disinterest in nonmonetary incentives is unusual. Most persons feel that the incentive award is worthwhile at least —even if it does not result in more money in the pay envelope in the near future. In addition, it is a form of recognition of performance or some accomplishment:

> "Oscar, if you round out your knowledge of purchased parts buying, you can be given authority to sign purchase orders in the future."

> "Helen, if you show that you can get the computer report out daily, you can assign the requisition analysis work to Alice."

> "John, if you can keep the flow of work up to last week's level, I'll change your job title."

> "Marsha, as facilities manager you could be handling the facilities budget preparation. If you take it over, I'll pencil you in for the budget committee meetings with the brass. Okay?"

USING STATUS SUCCESSFULLY

Unlike a corporal promoted to sergeant, Roscoe cannot wear a pay raise on his sleeve. However, Roscoe wants to show his improved status. His boss has to figure out how to increase Roger's status within the operating limitations.

The important thing to remember is that most people *want* their achievements to show. A bigger paycheck is nice, but for most people it is not enough. A supervisor would do well to inventory just what "goodies" are available to dispense to worthy subordinates.

A PLUS FEATURE

An additional status achievement is granted when some kind of fuss is made over the announcement of a change in status. Therefore, when an award or change is made, it should be properly announced. This announcement of itself is a recognition symbol that is very well understood by the recipient and the coworkers.

Look in the financial section of the papers. Every bank announces promotions to vice president, and so on, in the press. Why do they do it? Because it is a double whammy of status achievement.

PERFORMANCE IMPROVEMENT GOAL

Those operations that do not use nonmonetary incentives have to try to use the costly substitute—money. And that does not always work. Increases in financial incentives do not necessarily result in higher production or performance. In some instances, the improvement can become cost prohibitive.

If an employee is able to attain all of the creature comforts and a few luxuries through performing the minimum effort, then what else is there? Status symbols, awards, personal gratification for a job well done are the currency with which performance can be improved.

PERSONAL GOOD FEELING—A TEST CASE

Suppose the mail room supervisor was called "Director of Communications" and the supply room manager was called "Director of Supplies" and the switchboard operator was called "Communication Coordinator." Chances are that these people would like their new titles.

One computer software company did just that. As a result, many people were made happy almost overnight. The long-range important benefit for that organization was that employee turnover was sharply reduced.

The theorists say that such a ploy cheapens titles. Could be, but it makes people happy and reduces costly turnover. What about raises to go along with the titles? This is not hard to accept by people that have been around—there are many people who would rather have a title than a pay raise.

Here was another big plus. A better than expected title in a job vacancy makes it easier to recruit people for that vacancy.

PEOPLE ARE FUNNY ABOUT NONMONETARY AWARDS

Would a corporal take a promotion to sergeant without a pay raise? Would he accept the extra stripe with nothing to go with it? Changes are, yes! And, so would most people in the business world, because *most people are status seekers.* It remains for middle managers to figure out how to use that drive.

BALANCING METHODS AND PEOPLE TO IMPROVE PRODUCTION

> *"Will you tell me who did win the battle of the Marne?" "I can't answer that," said Marshal Jofre. "But I can tell you that if the battle of the Marne had been lost, the blame would have been on me."*
>
> *Newsweek*

Front line managers and supervisors know that when productivity and performance become poor, they are faulted. When things go well, nothing is said.

At the beginning of this century, methods were more important than people in the race to improve productivity and performance. Frederick Taylor, the supposed father of scientific management, said:

> "Each man must learn how to give up his own particular way of doing things, adapt his methods to the new standards..."

For decades, this thinking prevailed. Most tycoons considered that workers were economic animals with strong muscles and weak minds and that workers would and did accept 50% wage incentive increases while increasing productivity 300%.

ADVENT OF MECHANIZATION

When the more labor-intensified jobs became mechanized and when greater skills were needed in the labor marketplace, the emphasis began swinging around toward the importance of the employee. Not for his muscle, but rather for his mind. Mechanization also brought about a much greater volume of consumer goods—which labor wanted and which management was then able to supply at reduced competitive costs.

RISING EXPECTATIONS

The labor force organized and kept improving its objectives. Mere wages were insufficient. Fringe benefits, which were not based on productivity, were included in organized labor demands. Now, product and service labor costs were increasing.

To meet the challenge of increased labor expense per unit of goods or services produced, industry turned to automation. The automatic equipment reduced labor requirements and became a way of industrial and business life. However, with fewer jobs, came the requirement for a greater skilled workforce.

With more efficient equipment, the skills requirement becomes more intensified.

First, there was mechanization and then automation. Then came computerization and robotics. With each step in the process, more emphasis is being placed on how to best use the equipment and what kind of worker is required.

THE TREND FOR PEOPLE MANAGEMENT

Most jobs today require comparatively little physical effort, as the physical portion of the operations is performed by the equipment. More and more jobs require higher and higher levels of skills to operate the equipment.

Here is the outlook today. Effective managements turn aside the emphasis on methods, which can for the most part be accomplished by machines, to concentrate on people who have the skills necessary for the determination of which set of instructions to give to the machines.

Train people, not to operate machines, but to instruct the machines.

Industries that are bucking the trend toward greater use of equipment to perform and even control the work will soon be in the same category as the buggy whip manufacturers.

SUCCESSFUL EXAMPLE

There is a nylon producing plant that turns out millions of pounds of nylon each month, using only 27 employees on each shift. Most of the employees, by virtue of their training and experience, are equivalent to chemical engineers.

As the methods and equipment become more improved, there is a greater need to upgrade the skills requirements of the operation:

"Wally, we need personnel who understand our system and can program the equipment."

POOR METHODS—HIGH PRODUCTION

It hasn't all happened yet. Without citing exceptions, there are many instances where operations with inadequate equipment and inefficient work flow can meet production requirements. Usually, the employees and middle management are well trained and have above-average motivation. Tight schedules are taken in stride.

WHICH ORIENTATION TO USE

The technical and professional personnel are not as reliant as blue collar workers upon methods. The job functions that require less equipment and are thus more demanding on individual know-how are more people oriented than methods oriented. Those people are definitely more important than methods, if for no other reason than that they usually select the methods of their own operations.

THE NEW CLASS OF WORKER

There are an increasing number of people in the workforce who are not blue collar or white collar workers. They are what have been called "gold collar" workers. These people earn the pay of a middle manager but actually work on the production floor. They are capable of programming or instructing several machines which are working in unison performing a number of operations with no human operators.

OUTLOOK FOR MANAGERS AND SUPERVISORS

In time, fewer people will be needed to do more of the work. For the front line management, that means acquiring more skills and having greater flexibility in the use of methods. There will be more of a delicate balance between methods and people. Greater challenges will evolve.

The way widgets were made yesterday is not necessarily the way that they are going to be made tomorrow. Nor is the way we keep records, answer mail, or any administrative chore going to be the same. The trick to be on top of all of the possible innovations, and to stay ahead, is to pick up new skills.

EFFECTIVE USE OF THE AFTER-HOURS MEETING

*"I always keep a stimulant handy in case I see
a snake—which I also keep handy."*
W. C. FIELDS

Not everyone likes to talk business after working all day. However, there are times when it is desirable to get a few things squared away over a drink far from the work-a-day world. An after-hours drink with one or more associates at the Blue Bird Tavern or another place of relaxed atmosphere can establish a rapport that is completely unavailable during regular business hours.

There is a sign under the mounted moose head on the far wall of the tavern and it says, "Drink is the Curse of the Working Class." It's always good for a small laugh.

Laughter is common at the Blue Bird Tavern and an antidote to the large problems that come into the tavern. There are problems of managerial personality conflicts, interdepartmental turf battles, missing reports, rhubarb about red tape, he-said-she-said arguments, and so on. All of these large work problems become much smaller or nonexistent later in the evening.

SALES MANAGER AND PRODUCTION MANAGER

Each member of the management team has his own job to do. Sometimes, difficulties can be made a little easier for two managers to meet after work, away from the work environment, and discuss mutual problems over a couple of martinis or mugs of beer.

A lunch meeting is acceptable but the time confinement and the inner feeling of still being involved in the workday might prevent a more developed rapport.

After work, people are more likely to let their hair down and to seek empathy for what is really bothering them:

"Roger, the Production Department has been doing an outstanding job on deliveries except for the new product line, and I have some old customers who are screaming."

"I didn't know it was that bad."

"It sure is. Can anything be done?"

"Maybe. Warren, if you agree to let us cut back the standing inventory levels on some of the shelf items by about 25%, we might be able to clean up the back orders on the new product line. What do you say?"

"It's a deal. The next round is on me."

CONSIDERATION TIME

An advantage of after-work shoptalk is that new ideas or suggestions can hit upon more fertile soil. Further, there is more opportunity, free from work pressures, to give the matter greater consideration during the rest of the evening and someone can even sleep on the new idea overnight.

Too many drinks can be as bad as not being reasonably sociable at all. Reputations can be easily smashed by participating in too many "happy hours" or having a few too many. An occasional drink after work should not be overdone.

OTHER LOCALES

After-hours shoptalk need not only be conducted at a bar. Company bowling nights are ideal times in which to review matters with various individuals. In between spares and an infrequent gutter ball, some serious problems can be broached or discussed in a cordial and informal atmosphere.

RECOMMENDATION: LIMIT THE PLOY

Like any technique, talking shop after hours can be overdone. Continuous attempts at the ploy will arouse irritation in someone who may feel that he has become a captive audience. Being recognized as a bore will not solve problems at work and may create a limited social life with regard to coworkers.

How to Pick a Topic

No one wants to be a bore and take too much advantage of a social occasion. Before discussing shop away from work, some useful considerations might include the following:

1. Is the topic of interest to the other party?
2. Will the discussion of the topic be productive for both parties?
3. Is the topic boring to the other people present?
4. Can the discussion be limited to brief important points?
5. Are the regular Company communication channels more efficient on the desired topic?
6. Can the discussion be cut short when there are signs of disinterest in the topic?
7. Are you appearing to be too much of a political animal?

Handling Problem Subordinates

When there is a personality conflict or other problem with a subordinate that cannot seem to be resolved during working hours, it may be advisable to ask the employee to have a drink after hours. In a nearby bar, some of the tensions of the work situations are missing. The atmosphere may be ideal for a heart-to-heart talk on mutual problems. It may be worthwhile to try it once or maybe twice with an individual employee.

Such invitations between members of the opposite sex are usually not advisable.

Romance or Work?

Any invitation for an after-work meeting off premises with a member of the opposite sex—no matter how harmless—is cause for concern. The reputation of both parties is subject to rumor and gossip inside and outside of the organization.

HOW TO BE SURE THAT AN EMPLOYEE UNDERSTANDS ORDERS

"Too bad all the people who know how to run the country are busy driving taxicabs and cutting hair."
GEORGE BURNS

In the mail room and on the shipping dock, there are people who "know" how to run the Company—or at least a large part of it. Their problem is that they may not know how to give explicit orders and instructions. That is something that comes with a great deal of experience.

In the charge of the Light Brigade in the Crimean War, 600 British troops went into the valley of death against overwhelming Russian forces because of a misunderstanding of orders by their superior officers. If well-trained, highly disciplined officers could misunderstand their orders, there is good reason to suppose that almost anybody could misinterpret orders in the everyday business world.

PUTTING THE BLAME WHERE IT BELONGS

If Charley misunderstands his instruction, is it his fault? Probably not. First, his superior may have incorrectly evaluated Charley's ability to comprehend a certain level of instructions. Second, the instructions could have had more than one interpretation—or a misleading single interpretation.

Instructions or orders have to be given with due consideration of the experience and the level of comprehension of the subordinate who is on the receiving end.

FOLLOW A SIMPLE RULE

Of course, excessively detailed instructions are too time consuming for the boss. However, a presumption has to be made with each order or instruction:

If an instruction can be misinterpreted—it will be.

That premise can too often be true whether the subordinate is careless or conscientious in complying with the superior's orders. Therefore, before issuing an instruction, consider if there are any possibilities for alternative reactions on the part of subordinates.

ACTUAL CASES OF CONFUSION

With regard to instructions that are not followed, attempts have been made to discipline employees for alleged insubordination. In the case of Ekco Housewares Company versus the Steelworkers Local 5391, an arbitrator found that the orders to a cleaning person were confusing and therefore her job suspension was revoked. She had been requested to clean a larger area than usual and she did not comprehend those instructions.

Another case that went to arbitration over confusion was one where a supervisor instructed an employee to report to work on a certain day. However, the bulletin board had a notice that the plant would be closed on that day. Despite the confusion, this ruling went against the employee for failure to clear up the matter.

Despite the favorable ruling, which is always nice, the employee did not come in on the day in question, industrial relations suffered, and it was not worth the effort which the supervisor could have forestalled if he had read his own bulletin board.

GUIDELINES FOR INSTRUCTIONS TO SUBORDINATES

Here is a fast action checklist for reviewing instructions to subordinates:

1. Who is to perform.
2. What is to be done.
3. When is it to be done.
4. What are the exceptions.
5. What is to be done with the exceptions.
6. What are the alternative methods.

7. When are alternative methods to be used.
8. Who has additional know-how.
9. When should advice be sought.
10. Where are written instructions to follow.
11. Which equipment is to be used.
12. What tools are available.
13. Which examples should be followed.
14. What follow-through is required.
15. What checking should be done.
16. How are errors to be handled.
17. When is the task considered to be completed.
18. What is to be done with the finished product.
19. What is to be done after the task is over.

DAY-TO-DAY OPERATIONS

"Get this report out today!"

Naturally, the more repetitive chores require little explanation of "how and where." The boss could assume that the subordinates should have grasped how to maintain the normal flow of work.

On new or special jobs, the boss should not make any assumptions on the comprehension of instructions. The hazards of making assumptions as to instruction comprehension include having to re-start the job from scratch. Lost time, lost effort and lost patience can be the result.

SOME LEARN FASTER THAN OTHERS

In most operations there are people who are quick to comprehend less-than-detailed instructions. Show them the end product, a sketch, or an outline and they are on their way. These people are sparkplugs.

Use the sparkplugs with slower people.

"Ask Gunther how to get that done."

By using sparkplugs, less supervisory time is required. Let's face it. No boss can stand over everyone's shoulder to be sure that instructions are followed. The more effective way is to use those who know how to do the job guide those who have less experience or are slower in understanding instructions.

TRAINING IS EVERYTHING

Every front line manager and supervisor has a side job: being a teacher. A boss has to train people in how to do their job and how to follow instructions. If the boss is a successful teacher, he or she will have more time to concentrate on the bigger problems of managing a section or department.

HANDLING PASSED-OVER EMPLOYEES

"The fault, dear Brutus, is not in our stars,
but in ourselves that we are underlings."
WILLIAM SHAKESPEARE

One of the most difficult things for a manager or supervisor to do is to explain to an employee why he has been passed over for promotion. Not only does this effort require tact, but there also has to be a dialogue that continues to seek the employee's best effort in his existing job.

PRESERVE THE EMPLOYEE'S FEELINGS

Being passed over for promotion can be an emotional shock. Regardless of how valid the reasons may be, the subordinate's feelings may be deeply hurt.

Wendel may have been expecting the promotion for some time, believing that he had committed quite a bit of effort toward meeting the requirements for promotion. His ego has to be handled with care.

Furthermore, Wendel may have told others of his expectations, including coworkers, family and friends. He will have to face these people and try to explain to some extent the reasons for the disappointment.

EXPLAIN PROMOTION REQUIREMENTS

Much of Wendel's disappointment could have been avoided if his expectations were kept within reason. One technique is to have the requirements for promotion completely understood by any likely candidates for promotion. Formally documented, written guidelines are preferable to informal methods. Position job descriptions, which are kept up-to-date are helpful.

SOLUTION FOR INFORMAL PROMOTION SYSTEMS

In smaller operations, where position documentation requirements are minimal, the recommendation of a key manager is the usual technique. The manager's evaluation of know-how, problem-solving ability, and accountability within the organization is crucial. Accordingly, it is desirable that those supervisors and managers who govern promotions make their criteria known to possible candidates for promotion, even on an informal basis.

Dissemination of requirements provides job motivation to all eligibles, and there is a reduction of over-expectation on anyone's part.

WARNING: MINIMIZE PERSONAL PREJUDICES

If a manager or a supervisor permits excessive personal prejudices to interfere with the promotion system, he is likely to reduce motivation for some qualified people. Further, the boss will be faced with more subordinates who are unhappy about being passed over for promotion. While it is true that a boss is more aware of the capabilities of those employees with whom he has a greater contact, he may be shutting out those employees who are more qualified or entitled to the promotion.

USE DIPLOMACY

> *"Diplomacy is the art of letting somebody else have your way."*
> DAVID FROST, 1983

When an employee is passed over for good cause, the supervisor has to be very diplomatic. He must avoid being brutally frank—even when asked for a frank opinion. Yet, he must convey valid reasons. Being overly frank will not change anyone. Nor will it add to a two-way discussion.

Being totally frank will lead to an argument or a scene. That kind of reaction is to be avoided.

One technique is for the supervisor to recite the qualifications for promotion—whether formal or informal to Wendel. Then,

Wendel can be asked if he thinks that he measured up satisfactorily to each requirement. Wendel's own appraisal, even if completely less than candid, may make him see his own shortcomings.

If Wendel exaggerates his own qualifications, the supervisor can matter-of-factly cite exceptions and should be able to provide ready documentation or proof of the more salient points.

The supervisor should not argue the facts—simply state them just as they exist.

RECOMMENDATION: MAKE "NICE" AT CONCLUSION

The conclusion of the session may be a vote of thanks on the part of the supervisor. After all, Wendel did try to meet the requirements. The supervisor's recognition of this fact may keep Wendel well motivated, since his attempts have warranted recognition.

"Wendel, I want to thank you for your efforts in trying for the new job. You tried very hard and I appreciate that."

"Wendel, it's too bad that you didn't make it. You certainly deserve an 'A' for effort and I appreciate your trying."

WHAT TO DO

1. Promotion requirements should be documented or well explained to possible candidates.
2. Promotions must be based on a number of factors but personal prejudices (likes and dislikes) should have no effect.
3. Diplomacy is important to keep subordinates well motivated.
4. Good points of the subordinate should be enumerated.
5. Thank the subordinate for trying hard. Appreciate the effort.

MANAGERIAL DUTY AND PERSONAL SUCCESS

A middle manager is rated by the higher levels of management. One of their criteria is how well the middle manager selects people for promotion. Does he reward friends or does he consider the Company's objectives *first.*

Sure, there are "teacher's pets" and "apple polishers" who get promoted. However, the person who does that type of promotion may be limiting his or her own chance for moving up. In addition, those people who are qualified but who are not promoted lose a certain amount of job motivation. That means that such a department can have less productivity or performance. Maybe not right away, but certainly down the road.

A PERSONAL WARNING

Here is something else to try for size. If a middle manager is "unthinking" about his departmental promotions, how can the front office makers and shakers rely on him about *other matters*?

WHEN AND HOW TO DISCUSS PROMOTIONAL OPPORTUNITIES

"I started at the top and worked my way down."
ORSON WELLES (1915–1985)

Whether it is to the presidency of the Company, or from a trainee to junior salesman, a promotion is an event that most of the workforce looks forward to.

The enlargement of job responsibilities is a recognition which can also mean an increase in pay, rank, prestige and all of the features of status symbols. In addition, privileges and comforts can accrue with increases in rank. Because of what promotion can mean, and since promotion is a vital incentive to improved performance and productivity, subordinates should be made keenly aware of how they can obtain promotions.

The improvement efforts of subordinates can be more intensively directed if discussions with them are properly timed for effect and directed toward being of assistance to them.

RECOMMENDATION FOR NONCAREER ORIENTED

Not every employee is career oriented. That is, their planning is at best intermediate rather than geared toward a longer view of constant promotion up the ladder of success. They may have taken their present job just to fit in with more current financial plans. Or, they may not have invested in college or the necessary training to pursue much higher goals than their present positions.

However, even noncareer oriented employees or even those with seemingly dead-end occupations could look forward to various types of promotions. Therefore, promotional incentives can be directed toward the noncareer oriented. Typically, they can at least look forward to changes in job title, if not in job responsibilities.

AVOID OVERSELLING

The front line manager or supervisor who oversells the promotional opportunities to subordinates may enjoy short-term productivity increase. In the longer term, there can be an adverse impact on productivity in addition to a general credibility gap between the boss and the subordinates when reality creeps in.

> *Some subordinates can become skeptical almost immediately and short-term increases in productivity may not materialize either.*

"There is no limit as to where you can go from here."

Even if such a claim could be true, it may seem excessive, particularly if there are only a few obvious examples of rank and file employees who have moved up into the higher levels of management.

"The president started out in the mail room" speech does not always work to increase motivation for improved performance. It's nice, but it seems more like "pie in the sky." It is overselling because it is not more fundamental or a near-term possible reward.

DISCUSS MORE IMMEDIATE POSSIBILITIES

It would seem more realistic to discuss only the next step in the promotion ladder rather than "the pie in the sky" with employees. Of course, each employee would like to become president. However, the employee expects to discuss only how to get to the next rung on the ladder. The subordinate would like to know what he or she has to do in order to move up one notch. Therefore, the discussions on promotion can center on that more immediate goal:

> "Kathy, in order for you to become section chief, you can start by learning about everyone's job in the section."

USING CARE ON CONDITIONAL PROMISES

The wording on any promotional promise has to be carefully thought out. If it is conditional, the terms of the conditions must be plainly understood so that no subordinate will even think of saying, "But, you promised me that job and I didn't get it."

There are times when it is necessary to "keep a promise" even though all of the conditions for promotion have not been met. A section chief may be needed immediately and the only likely candidate is not fully qualified. A conditional promotion can be made thus:

> "Kathy, I'm moving you up even though you have not learned all of the required operations. It will be a temporary promotion until you pick up on all of the other operations."

The beautiful double-whammy benefit is to reward Kathy for her prior and continuing efforts and still provide plenty of incentive for her own occupational improvement.

TIMING OF DISCUSSION

If a subordinate comes forward and asks about the promotion opportunities, he or she has to receive a complete answer as soon as possible—preferably in private.

> *Some qualified employees are timid about asking and may have to be prompted.*

When a superior believes that a subordinate is possible promotion material (as when the subordinate takes on additional responsibilities or makes an effort to learn about the jobs of others), the boss should have a frank discussion with the promising employee. There may be an attempt to determine the subordinate's job goals.

After an assessment of the subordinate's potential and attitude toward promotion, the immediate superior can discuss the possible opportunities and the necessary qualifications:

> "Ms. Robinson, you may have what it takes to get ahead. You have some leadership ability and a willingness to learn. We are opening a new section for consumer products. If you can learn that product line completely, we might be able to put you in charge of it."

SUMMARY

1. Don't promise the moon.
2. Stick to more likely immediate promotion goals.
3. Be sure that any conditions are fully understood.
4. Make conditional promotions where required.
5. Evaluate which subordinates are promotion material.

THE TOUGH SHOTS TO CALL

Casper Milquetoast or Susy Quietone may lack the outward signs of leadership. They may lack confidence for being assertive. However, either one of them may be ideal for promotion on other grounds. In such instances, a boss has to help out with a friendly talk that is intended to instill leadership confidence.

And, why not? We all had help from someone in the past. We learned some little techniques and tricks from an old hand. Now, it may be payback time. Besides, it is a wonderful feeling to help a subordinate to succeed.

GETTING A SUBORDINATE TO WORK OVERTIME AFTER HE REFUSES

> *"Hard work never killed anybody, but why take a chance?"*
> CHARLIE MCCARTHY (EDGAR BERGEN)

Even where the Company may have rules for compulsory overtime, a certain amount of resistance to overtime on the part of individual employees may exist. Such resistance may not only be in the form of squawking, but may be evident in reduced performance by the reluctant employees.

OLD IDEA: CARE DURING RECRUITING

When interviewing to fill a vacancy, whether overtime is eminent or not, the job prospect can be advised that overtime might be expected:

"By the way Mr. Hanson, the job may entail about 10 hours a week of overtime and about one Saturday each month. Would there be any objections on your part to the overtime?"

The applicant's answer may be noted on the interview sheet. Later, the answer could be a useful reminder if the employee becomes reluctant about overtime.

MERIT INCREASE PLOY

Here is a technique that can be helpful. A part of the criteria for the justification of a merit increase can be the subordinate's willingness to work overtime. The willingness to work extra hours is highly indicative of an employee's commitment to the job.

"Charley, one of the factors for approving a raise is the extent to which you are willing to cooperate when overtime is required."

"LOW MAN ON THE TOTEM POLE" PLOY

Nowhere is it written that one has to be overly nice to someone who does not care to help his or her boss and the Company with some overtime.

> "Charley, several people requested the same vacation time that you did! In all fairness, first choice has been given to those who have been putting in most of the overtime. I'm sorry, but you need to choose some other time for vacation."

Fair is fair. Somebody has to be the lowest person on the totem pole. For the sake of department morale, if Charley has less commitment to the job than others, then Charley is low man.

THE IMMEDIATE NEED SOLUTION

The above ploys are drawn-out techniques that will help over a period of time. What if you need somebody *now*? Consider this. Find out the reason for any employee's refusal to work overtime on short notice. Perhaps the reason can be readily overcome. Maybe it is as simple as the employee's needing a ride home after work because of commuting or car pool problems. Or, a telephone call can be made to change an appointment for the employee.

The superior can try to help the subordinate solve the subordinate's problem so that the subordinate can solve the superior's problem—getting the work out on time.

"DON'T LET THE COACH DOWN"

Appeal to the team spirit. No one likes to be a slacker or a stick in the mud in matters concerning the team. If everyone is chipping in and helping out, then why can't the recalcitrant employee? The supervisor can put emphasis on the sacrifice that others are making.

> "Charley, everybody is doing their best for the department to get this job out on time. You can help too."

REPAYMENT OF FAVORS SOLUTION

Many a subordinate received special consideration when he or she needed Company support. The supervisor can gently remind the employee of backing that was provided in time of need:

> "When you had personal problems, we were able to arrange time off for you. How about helping the Company out now with some overtime?"

> "The Company stood by you when you had a financial crisis. How about lending a hand now?"

The more such reminders that there are, the more difficult it will be for an employee to refuse working overtime—even on short notice.

OTHER QUICK SOLUTIONS

The front line manager or supervisor may have eliminated many of the reasons for refusal and reminded the employee of past favors. Still, the employee may continue to be reluctant to put in the overtime. At such point, it may be time to warn the problem employee that documentation of such refusals may be kept on file.

> "Charley, I will have to write a memo for entry into your personnel folder that you have refused to work overtime upon repeated request."

> "The shipping department has asked us to send over an input clerk for temporary duty. You're it this week."

> "Someone who does not share the load is setting a bad example for the rest of the department. You have been warned that I need people who can share the load. Sorry, Charley."

SETTING THE EXAMPLE

> "35-hour week? Heck, I put in a 40-hour *Day!*"

On the run, seldom taking a break, skipping or cutting lunch short, in early, and so on, are the working conditions of most managers and supervisors. To top it all off, they frequently put in PLENTY of overtime.

"Are you married to the job or me?"

It goes with the territory. Almost everyone in front line middle management signed up for a long hard day—almost every day. The rewards: stress, high blood pressure, ulcers, back aches, and near nervous breakdowns. But, it is worth it. It is a challenge to learn how to handle people—even those who are problem subordinates.

HOW TO GET A SUBORDINATE TO WORK ON SATURDAY

> *"Many people quit looking for work when they find a job."*
> ANONYMOUS

There is little question that almost everyone likes to have a maximum amount of time off. However, occasionally, business cannot take a day off and there is need for an extra workday.

Years ago, it was assumed that Saturday work was not to be questioned. However, over the years, the lifestyles of the workforce have changed. More employees have homes of their own, which creates more chores to be accomplished at home than ever before. There are many leisure-time activities that are enticing and have become more readily available.

With higher wages and a better standard of living, fewer workers are quite readily interested in working a sixth day.

EARLY EXPECTATION SOLUTION

When an applicant is being interviewed for a job, the prospect can be asked the question:

"Do you have any objections to working Saturdays when requested to do so?"

The answer can be noted. The job applicant can be told the extent to which Saturday work is expected:

"You may be expected to work at least one Saturday during every month."

"You may be expected to work every Saturday during our busy season, which is....."

Of course, experienced front line managers and supervisors know there is a difference between a promise at hiring time and the reluctance that begins to occur down the road. However, it is certainly best to be able to say, "you were alerted about Saturday work."

THE DISTINCTION WITH AFTER-FIVE WORK

Many employees do not mind as much putting in some time after normal quitting time but view work requirements on Saturday quite differently. Evening work is not as much of a sacrifice as it permits the accomplishment of many personal chores on Saturday. An employee already at the work premises does not seem to mind as much putting in a few hours overtime as giving up a day off.

Many people like to have time during daylight hours in order to be with their families.

CITE ADVANTAGES OF SATURDAY WORK

There are some distinct advantages for employees to work on Saturdays and they should be enumerated to reluctant subordinates. These include the following:

1. Overtime pay or a compensating day off.
2. More informal atmosphere at work than during week days.
3. Easier commuting—no rush hour traffic.
4. Reduction of pressures of backlog during the rest of the workweek.
5. Less crowded employee facilities.
6. Easier atmosphere for training purposes
7. More opportunities to learn other operations.
8. Lower administrative pressures, less red tape.
9. Less top brass on the scene.

Each business or type of industry can cite other advantages. For some employees, Saturday work is more desirable than evening overtime because of commuting or other conditions. In addition, some personnel who care for youngsters or who keep house would like to be home in the evenings to prepare meals, and so on, and would rather work on Saturdays if given the choice.

Reimbursement of Saturday Expenses Solution

As further inducement and in order to make the Saturday overtime pay as fully rewarding as it is intended to be, there can be reimbursement of certain employee expenses connected with Saturday work. Carfare or commuting expense and lunches can be reimbursed out of petty cash within certain defined limits. This relatively small payment is a very definite incentive to many employees. If coupled with prompt payment, it is very effective.

Putting-Them-Down Solution

"Charley, others will be in on Saturday and I cannot make an exception for you to the rest of the team."

"Charley, when you were hired, you were told that you would be expected to work on Saturdays when requested. You agreed to that."

"Charley, you know our workload and your own responsibilities. If you don't show on Saturday, I'll have to put a memo to that effect in your personnel folder."

Summary

1. Know the lifestyles of subordinates and what their attitude is with regard to working on Saturdays.
2. Cite the advantages of working on Saturdays.
3. If possible and as an inducement, consider granting Saturday expense reimbursements.
4. For diehards, let them know what remedies are available to the supervisor.

The Manager's Obligation

Those employees who refuse consistently to work a sixth day upon request are not only reducing their own productivity but are adverse to good department morale. If the front line manager or supervisor has welded the section or department into a team, then a slacker is undoing all of this good work.

Business does not stop because someone would rather go to a ballgame. The competition prevents that. The rush or special jobs that have to get out—have to get out. There is no alternative.

MAKING MEN ACCEPT WOMEN EMPLOYEES AS A PART OF THE TEAM

*"Whatever women do, they must do twice as well
as men to be thought half as good.
Luckily, this is not difficult.*
CHARLOTTE WHITTON, former mayor of Ottawa

Despite many programs and serious efforts to fully integrate women into all of the workforce, the female employee frequently feels that she is not being treated on an equal basis.

An adverse attitude of any group toward their work situation can lead to lower performance and productivity levels and resentment against the management.

Some of this feeling of resentment is caused by unwritten policies and attitudes formed and nurtured by male-dominated managements.

WRITTEN POLICIES VERSUS UNWRITTEN RULES

A good percentage of most policy manuals can be discarded. Not because they are just red tape, which they frequently are, but because actual practice may widely differ. The written policies usually state that there are no "second class" workers. yet, the number of males outnumber women in the executive suite, middle management and almost all areas of authority.

In most operations there is a wide gap between the stated corporate objectives and what is actually going on. One can be cynical about the contents of policy manuals.

MORE COST EFFECTIVENESS

Job commitment is a tough thing to quantify—even for the theorists. However, one thing is granted by any experienced manager or supervisor—lower commitment to the job and the Company means lower productivity generally.

In order to increase commitment and motivation, all of the workers have to feel as if they are a part of the team. Anything less results in less commitment.

Subordinate Created Problems

"I don't want to work for a woman."

"Mr. Macho, that's the way it is."

It is of little point to argue. Mr. Macho has his viewpoint which logic will not readily change. His viewpoint may be prevalent among other males. However, he should have been around enough to know that times are changing. Whether he accepts a woman as a boss is going to be *up to him.*

Chances are that Mr. Macho will not be ready to take a walk off the job. What can he say to a subsequent job interviewer, "I didn't like who they picked as my boss?"

What Mr. Macho might be ready to do is quite different from resigning. For one thing, he could try to undermine his new boss. His sly attempt may be to make her fail as a boss. The stunts that he could pull might include:

- "Legal" countering of instructions.
- Professing lack of knowledge of certain areas or skills.
- Going over a boss's head, bypassing channels.
- Pointing out any of the boss's supposed failures.
- Bad-mouthing the boss to others.
- Borderline insubordination.
- Unwilling to work overtime.
- High absenteeism and lateness.
- High error rate.
- Missing deadlines and ignoring schedules.
- Encouraging others to also do all of the above.

All of Mr. Macho's ploys are obvious to experienced middle and upper managers and can be readily exposed. A warning will usually shape up Mr. Macho. If the warning does not work?

In a sea of changes, Mr. Macho is a fish out of water because more and more companies realize that to obtain full commitment from all of its workforce, *there can be no auxiliaries*.

PRECONCEIVED NOTIONS

The idea that women cannot do this job or that one is fast falling away. Even the fallacy about more rigorous work is becoming history. Sound management dictates how a Company should be run on a business-like basis.

MAKING WOMEN A PART OF THE TEAM

When women feel that they belong to the Company, that they are not just being used in the low-priced unattractive jobs, they will participate more as team members. It is good management not only because it is the law, but because it is good business. Why? Because more people can be doing more for their Company.!

If job barriers are reduced, more women will feel equal to the task of competing with male coworkers and increasing performance levels all around. Even Mr. Macho might say, "I have to try harder because Gloria might beat me out as section chief."

DETERMINING THE BEST TIME TO GIVE A RAISE

"Live within your income, even if you have to borrow money to do so."
JOSH BILLINGS

Some managements look upon the granting of merit raises as a management requirement rather than as a *management tool*. A narrow view is to keep raises down and thus retain lower costs. While it is true that there has to be a balance—continuous raises can increase costs without increases in productivity—there can be an overreluctance to grant wage increases at the expense of the bottom line.

Wage increase policies are a management tool. As with any management tool, the question is when to use the tool and how. The purpose of any tool is to increase or improve the product. As a good craftsman knows when to use his tools, a manager should know when and how he can use the raise most effectively.

TRADITIONAL SOLUTIONS

1. Salary reviews are made on each six-month anniversary of the employee's joining the firm.
2. Annual anniversary date reviews.
3. Only in January or some one month of the year.
4. Only in January or July.
5. When the employee applies pressure.
6. Combination of any of 1 through 5 above, plus exceptions.

THE DRAWBACKS

"Give him twenty (or forty, or whatever) dollars and he will be happy."

First, the employee will not necessarily be happy. The employee recognizes that it is a perfunctory amount and that the timing is statutory. Worse still, the employee can arrive at the conclusion that the raise had little to do with his performance.

A perfunctory raise may be money down the drain as far as any incentive for improvement in performance is concerned.

Avoid the Christmas raise syndrome. The Christmas raise syndrome is the use of a fixed date for a raise. It does not improve performance, which is what a raise is supposed to do. Consider this. Little Bill will be a "saint" in the expectation of a new bicycle on Christmas Day—but only before the big day. For the rest of the year, he may be his old self. This Pavlovian conditioning will not be a stimulant for improved employee performance at other times of the year—EXCEPT when nearing payoff time again.

Some typical conditioning ploys that are used prior to raise-granting time might include the following:

1. Perfect attendance record for a month prior to the date.

2. Good on-time reports.

3. Taking work home.

4. Working more overtime, whether paid or not.

5. Meets more deadlines.

6. Gets along with everybody.

Of course, shortly after the raise, like little Bill, some employees revert back to their old work habits. The size of the raise may not tend to delay the return to those more consistent work habits.

THE BEST COUNTER PLOY

Avoid fixed dates for awarding raises. If someone does not know when they are to receive the carrot, there is more of a tendency to try to earn it over a longer period of time. The real trick is to avoid a consistent pattern of raises.

"Charley, I like the way that you are taking care of that project. That's why I put through a raise for you, starting on Monday."

Charley does not know when the next raise might come along—so, he may try to keep up his performance.

The policy of granting more raises but of lower amounts can permit more prompt rewards after some kind of unusual effort on the part of the employee. The small lead time will cause the employee to more quickly associate his raise with more superior effort.

THE BIG ADVANTAGES

Random raise granting eliminates fixed dates and the Christmas type of syndrome. It rewards superior performance quickly.

If the employee has not asked for a raise and there is not fixed time for raise granting, he will be pleasantly surprised—almost no matter how little the raise. It is a good feeling to be recognized unexpectedly.

Unexpected raises generally do not engender feelings of disappointment over the size of the raise that can be possible when an employee looks forward to a fixed date and develops an estimate in his mind of what he thinks he deserves.

In other words, expectations and chances for a likely disappointment are reduced.

SUMMARY

1. Evaluate the benefits derived from fixed-date rate procedures.
2. Is the current raise granting method encouraging superior performance all year long?
3. In the existing circumstances, can a random raise policy improve performance?

OPPORTUNITIES FOR RANDOM RAISES

- New procedure which improves work flow.
- A special job was handled very well and on time.
- New uses for computerized data.

- A cost saving technique.
- Greater control of errors.
- Elimination of some red tape.
- Higher production rate.
- Improvement in communication.
- New uses for scrap.

THE BOTTOM LINE BENEFIT

Economically speaking, raises cannot be made unless there is improvement in the organization's profitability. Without performance improvement, unjustified raises can make the product or service offered too expensive for the marketplace.

The trick for middle managers is to develop a balance between raises and improvement in the bottom line. Random and prompt raises for superior performance can help to maintain that balance.

GETTING THE MOST FROM SUPERVISORS

> *"Here lies a man who knew how to enlist into his service better people than himself."*
>
> ANDREW CARNEGIE, requested epitaph

No organization can expect to do well unless it recruits and retains the best possible supervisors. Part of the function of higher levels of management is to be instrumental in being sure that supervisors are as free as possible to supervise.

Section head, chief, foreman, or by whatever name he or she is called, the supervisor is in the very front line of getting the job done. Let's face it, getting the job done pays for all of the other nonsense.

WHAT IS A SUPERVISOR'S JOB?

The supervisor maintains Company policy at the lowest level of the organization's chart. In addition, the supervisor is a feedback to top management on how their policies are working or perhaps not working. Besides being a channel of communication, an average supervisor must do some or all of the following:

- Plan a group's workload.
- Seek the best possible workflow.
- Be a leader or coach in the assignment of work.
- Provide information on how to do the job.
- Coordinate the group's efforts with other groups.
- Mediate in small crises.
- Inspire improved subordinate performance.
- Conduct personnel administration.
- Train and increase subordinates' skills.

Most supervisors have all of these qualities to a major degree. It is not by accident. Over a period of years, supervisors acquire the necessary skills and techniques for doing their job.

Too often, little recognition is given to these people. Often, the top management has not permitted the supervisor to emerge as a part of the management team. Yet the supervisor is the most important member. Just review the qualities that an average supervisor has to have!

SUPERVISORY QUALITIES TO LOOK FOR

People on other levels of management are gifted with their talents. However, a supervisor has to do the following well:

1. Select and instruct new employees.
2. Make minor repairs on equipment.
3. Obtain parts and supplies when they are short.
4. Coax personnel to work overtime and on Saturdays.
5. Motivate personnel to greater productivity and improved performance.
6. Advise and discipline employees. Keep subordinates reasonably happy.
7. Coordinate productive efforts with other groups.
8. Improve production or workflow procedures—frequently, on the spot.
9. Detect and control errors. Reduce waste of all kinds.
10. Act as an arbitrator between groups of employees or individuals.
11. Recommend changes in production equipment and install accepted changes.
12. Recommend and install changes in overall workflow procedures.
13. Maintain and monitor safety standards.
14. Make product or service change recommendations.
15. Interpret management policies—and quickly.
16. Handle on-site union relations.
17. Increase his or her own skills.

It is no wonder that good supervisors for any type of operation are more difficult to find; think of the standards that are imposed! Many upper level management people are not fully aware of the complexities of a supervisor's job.

Where there are accurate and up-to-date job descriptions or write-ups of the supervisory function, there is a greater understanding and appreciation of the supervisor's role in the organization.

NEITHER FISH NOR FOUL

Despite an increasing awareness of the supervisor's job, some higher level management people retain the idea that supervisors are not a part of the management. The real drawback to that kind of thinking is that supervisors tend to become less than well motivated.

If a person supervises even one employee, then that person is in management. This is not only true in labor relations but as a practical matter. After all, if a person is enforcing management policies by use of discipline, that person is a part of the management.

HOW TO INCREASE SUPERVISOR MOTIVATION

By recognizing supervisors as part of the management team, the front line supervision is reinforced. Rank and file personnel will also be more aware that these people are really bosses and are not just running errands for the top brass.

Any increased supervision status will make the supervisor's job of getting the work out easier. The supervisor will then be recognized as being a part of the command structure because the supervisor's orders and instructions will seem to carry more weight of authority.

The beneficial spinoff of such recognition and increased status will be that supervisors will have a greater chance to carry out the mandates of the management more completely. After all, they, themselves, are a part of management.

RECOMMENDATIONS FOR IMPROVING THE MANAGEMENT TEAM

If supervisors are *de jure* (by law) part of the management team, let's also make them *de facto* (in fact) part of the team. Here are a few of the simple steps:

- Include supervisors in management meetings and conferences.
- Memos that concern their areas of responsibility should include them in their circulation.
- Change some titles to provide additional management status.
- Provide additional managerial training to supervisors.
- As often as possible, promote supervisors to higher levels of management. (Promote from in-house.)
- Seek to obtain supervisory opinions on front line operations.

None of the above costs a lot. However, the bottom line rewards of such effort can be large.

CREATING A MIDDLE MANAGER POOL

Sure supervisors are not fully experienced as middle managers. However, they have individually a lot of experience in the present operations. Therefore, they may be ideal candidates for moving up in responsibility.

Increased in-house recruiting for middle level managers creates incentive for improved supervisor performance.

Promotion possibility is one of the best of job incentives around.

In most operations there is a great deal of in-house talent. Much of this available managerial potential is in the ranks of the supervisors. For continuing good performance, it just has to be discovered and encouraged.

A MONEY INCENTIVE THAT WORKS WONDERS

Ralph Kramden: "Before I let you go to work, I'd rather see you starve. We'll just have to live on savings."

Alice Kramden: "That'll carry us through the night, but what will we do in the morning?"

THE HONEYMOONERS

Most of the gags about money (or, not having money) seem funny because there is an element of truth in them. For most people in the workforce, they never seem to have enough.

That's why money is still one of the best work incentives. Nonmonetary incentives such as status, job satisfaction, appreciation, and so on, work and always will. However, money can have a special incentive—especially when money is applied in a different way.

RAISES ARE OUT

Wage raises do not always work as an incentive. They become expected. Sometimes the raise is a little more. At other times, it is a little less. As an incentive for improved performance they have lost their glow.

Give bonuses instead of raises.

THE SCENARIO

Many operations have eliminated the granting of raises. Instead, before December 25th of each year, a bonus is granted to individual members of the entire workforce.

The individual bonus can range from a few hundred dollars to many thousands of dollars.

THE DETAILS

Instead of a salary review, the employee is subjected to a bonus review sometime in November. The boss decides if the subordinate has improved his performance during the past year.

If the subordinate is a hot shot at his work, he is advised that he will receive a substantial bonus in the thousands of dollars. If the subordinate's performance has been lack luster, he may receive only a few hundred dollars—or even no bonus at all.

Marginal performers can be advised to work harder to achieve a larger bonus next year.

THE EMPLOYEE VIEW

A large bonus check can be ideal. As most household budgets are stretched at holiday season, the timing (December 15th) is a natural.

A big chunk of money that is not spread out seems bigger.

Typically, a raise becomes a part of the worker's ordinary cash flow; a bonus is different.

THE CORPORATE COST JUSTIFICATION

Bonuses are cheaper than raises.

What's the cost difference between giving a raise spread out over the year or a one-time bonus check? A raise becomes a part of the worker's salary. The regular salary is the basis for determining many benefits such as pension contributions by the employer. A bonus is not usually included in that calculation, or in other calculations of benefits.

Another plus feature for the Company is that the Company hangs on to the money longer. That feature can be worth a great deal in interest and other funding opportunities.

Anti-turnover Benefit

As an employee must be on board in order to receive the bonus, labor turnover during the year is reduced. As turnover can be extremely costly, the bonus system produces a large savings.

Turnover costs money in terms of recruiting, hiring, training, learning curves and an uneven flow of the work.

Benefits to the Frontline Management

At a raise review there can be a discussion between the boss and the subordinate about absenteeism, tardiness and other employee-created problems. Some of the points made by the boss will sink in and the subordinate may tend to reform.

However, at a bonus review, more immediate bucks are at stake. There is a greater likelihood that a subordinate may take the boss's observations and/or comments more to heart.

How to Install the Bonus System

In January, the Company can announce that instead of raises during the year, except in unusual circumstances, the employees will receive a merit bonus in December.

The size of the individual bonuses will be determined at an evaluation session that each employee will have with his immediate superior in November.

Warning: the typical controls that exist on raise requests will lap over into the bonus granting process.

Exception Circumstances

There will be instances where raises will be granted. For the new techniques to work, these should be held to a minimum.

An exception might exist where an employee completes a course which makes him immediately more valuable to the Company. And, his new salary would likely prevent him from jumping ship to a competitor.

Another exception might be for an employee to whom a previous promise of a raise had been made.

INCENTIVE FROM EXPECTATION

There are credit card balances, past-due auto payments, holiday shopping, buying a refrigerator, and other cash requirements that can play havoc with an ordinary paycheck—even a raised pay check.

That is why the bonus system can work wonders for employee work incentive: not only for debt catch-up time, but for other expenditures such as a down payment on a new home, and so forth.

THE ETHICS OF A BONUS SYSTEM

For the employee, the bonus system is a "forced savings" plan which helps in a material way. For the employer, there are cost benefits and a workforce which has better work incentive than mere raises can provide.

There are few techniques which are of benefit to both employee and employer. The bonus system is one of them.

PART 3

HOW MANAGERS BRING WASTED EFFORT UNDER CONTROL

HOW TO CUT DOWN ON THE MISTAKES OF ERROR-PRONE SUBORDINATES

"Only the mediocre are always at their best."
ANONYMOUS

Just as auto insurance companies recognize that some drivers are more prone to having accidents than the general population of drivers, so some recognition must be given to the fact that some subordinates are more likely to make mistakes than others.

Of course, deliberate mistakes are a cause for discipline up to and including the discharge of the culprit subordinate.

However, most mistakes are not intentional. They are caused by a variety of reasons, including the errors of judgment on the part of management. For instance, inadequate training may be a large cause for errors.

EVALUATION OF MISTAKES

It may be said that there are two types of mistakes, systems and human mistakes. Consider each one.

SYSTEM MISTAKES. These types of errors result from flaws in the design of the system. The methods and techniques used permit a certain number of errors. Constant improvement of the system design tends to keep reducing the error rate.

HUMAN MISTAKES. No matter how well the system is designed, there is a certain reliance on the human factor. That factor is the one to which line management people have to apply a great deal of attention.

THE TOTAL SYSTEMS SOLUTION

It may be desirable to consider that human mistakes are after all just system mistakes. How can that be? Well, the reasoning is that the system should have had the provisions for checks that catch (and possibly correct) the human mistakes. Who is to blame? The systems designer may be at fault for omitting routines that control "human" error.

GETTING PRACTICAL WITH SUBORDINATES

All of the systems theories are nice, but what can the front line manager or supervisor do to control errors? The human factor is what should be of practical interest. In error-prone situations the following conditions may exist:

1. Inadequate or incomplete job training.
2. Scarcity or out-of-date written instructions.
3. Excessive number of subordinates reporting to one supervisor.
4. Too few intermediate levels of supervision.
5. Dull work environment.
6. Job boredom or lack of obvious job enrichment.
7. Low analysis of error causes.
8. High employee turnover and low morale.
9. Failure to use self-checking methods.
10. Omission of cross-checking techniques
11. Imperfect exception handling procedures.

PRIDE OF WORKMANSHIP IS ALIVE

Most employees like to feel that they are earning their pay. Part of that feeling of pride stems from their opinion that their own work has few, if any, errors.

> *Many subordinates appreciate help, when offered gracefully, in improving their own image of pride in their work.*

"Wilbur, I know that you can do better that this!"

ADDITIONAL PLOYS

Here are a few additional techniques to make subordinates more conscious of error control:

- The frank admission of mistakes by the boss (That encourages others to admit errors as well.)
- Improve and tighten up techniques for quick detection and correction of mistakes.
- Provide some recognition to those subordinates who perform well.
- Provide a working climate which suggests that quality is of equal consideration as quantity.

CONTROLLING THE ERROR-PRONE SUBORDINATE

One method of attack is to provide an employee-coach for the error-prone subordinate. The senior employee, who is proficient on the job, should be able to isolate the causes of the problem employee's errors. In addition, the coach can provide instruction in special techniques to either avoid such errors or to be able to catch the mistakes and then know how to take corrective action.

Error control is reduced when the problem subordinate does not know the proper corrective action.

To further minimize carelessness, the problem subordinate has to be shown at which points or steps in the job or work process some additional attention must be applied.

"Wilbur, always re-check yourself right here."

Some discussion of the problem with the employee may be desirable. Warning: watch out for the ego. The boss can approach the topic gingerly in order to prevent the subordinate from acting defensively about the mistakes. Such a reaction closes the subordinates's mind to the problem and the desirable possible solutions.

THE APPROACH

"Alan, I need your help on a problem ..."

"Nancy, your attitude is pretty good on the job ..."

MUTUAL PROBLEM

"Alan, you and I ought to be able to ..."

"Nancy, the group has improved productivity ..."

SUGGEST A SOLUTION

"Alan, can you spend a little more effort on ..."

"Nancy, can you follow up on these areas ..."

MANAGER RESPONSIBILITY

An old management hand once asked, "Why is it that we always have time to redo a thing, but we never have time to do it right in the first place?" The answer might be a misconception of "pressure" that considers speed as a higher priority. Actually, speed and quality are a dual priority requirement—even under extreme pressure.

An inaccurate report submitted on time is as valueless as a correct report submitted very late. Likewise, defective widgets, or whatever, delivered on time may be as useless as good widgets that are delivered too late for customer use.

Most managers would agree that taking extra time to do something right the first time is the best short cut in the long run.

HOW TO OPTIMIZE THE SPAN OF CONTROL FOR BETTER PERFORMANCE

"I was to learn later in life that we tend to meet new situations by reorganizing...and a wonderful method it can be for creating the illusion of progress while producing confusion, inefficiency, and demoralization."
PETRONIS ARBITER, Roman administrator, circa 60 A.D.

The managerial "effective span of control" may be defined as the optimal number of people a manager can successfully supervise directly to achieve a certain level of performance of subordinates.

A minimal span of control exists where a manager or supervisor has too few subordinates. A maximum span of control exists where a superior has too many subordinates and actual control of the operation becomes spotty.

Clearly, an optimal number of reporting subordinates is the desired aim in an organization.

HOW TO IMPROVE THE EXTENT OF CONTROL

Certain methods and techniques can be installed or improved upon which can increase the number of subordinates who are more effectively supervised. Here are some considerations:

1. Examine the extent of similarities of the functions of subordinates. The greater the similarities, the greater number of people that can be effectively supervised by one person.

2. Look for ways to channel the dissimilarities so that their effects are minimized. The existence of large volume of dissimilarities of functions requires more divergence of a supervisor's time and a greater variety of skills—which one supervisor may not have.

3. Reduce the geographical separation and increase work proximity of subordinates. (Keep them closer together.) Side benefit: work flow is improved.

4. Improve the training of subordinates. Training should emphasize "minimal supervision" requirements.

5. Reduce the number and frequency of outside contacts with subordinates. Have outside contacts coordinated by one person in the department rather than several. Fewer interruptions in the work flow.

6. Reorganize the work flow to provide for increased stability of operations. Functions that are simple, stable, routine and patterned after models require less of supervision time.

7. Simplify, wherever possible, complex functions. Simplification makes it easier for subordinates to recognize and solve their own problems. By eliminating variable work characteristics there is less of a demand on the time of a supervisor.

8. Increase specialized training for areas which require a higher consciousness of quality control. Backtracking and rework effort is reduced for the manager or supervisor.

9. Make sure that verbal and written communications and instructions are clear and easily understood by the subordinate recipients. Work is more likely to be done right the first time.

10. Improve the internal control and security procedures to minimize the need for supervision in these areas.

11. Allow subordinates to do more of the checking of their own performance to reduce supervisory effort on quality control considerations.

12. Assign the more routine chores to subordinates relieving the supervisor of these tasks and permitting more time for direct supervision.

13. Train clerk and administrative assistants to handle more of the supervisor's chores to decrease supervisor time requirements in non-supervisory areas.

14. Provide more manuals and written instructions to more of the subordinates to reduce the need for supervisory overview or assistance.

15. Permit service groups to handle more of the internal department workload to free up more personnel.

16. Assign other subordinates as coaches to slower people or those who have greater job problems in order to make more time available to the supervisor.

17. Cross-train more subordinates so that they can help each other in problem situations and provide less reliance on supervision.

IMPROVING MANAGER PERFORMANCE

Each person is competent to a different extent with regard to the number of subordinates that he or she can supervise effectively. What may be a large number for one supervisor would be a small span of control to another supervisor who may be more competent in that regard.

However, there is a clue as to this type of competency. It is this: in most cases, the manager or supervisor who can more *effectively use* his own time can handle a larger span of control.

QUERY: WHY BOTHER?

The number one answer to that query is "look out for number one—you."

A manager or supervisor who can successfully and effectively supervise (control, if you like) a large number of subordinates is more likely to have greater job security, promotion potential and job mobility.

The number two answer to that query is "that you can do a better job." Which leads back to the number one answer!

WHY IS OPTIMAL SPAN OF CONTROL IMPORTANT TODAY?

Top management is under the gun to trim the management layers. In order to do that middle managers have to be spread even more thinly. With fewer bosses directly controlling more of the work. However, the work is becoming more complex—requiring a greater variety of skills in the work force *and* in all levels of the management. Therefore, a greater span of control becomes more difficult.

In this squeeze, those front line managers and supervisors that can handle a more varied skilled work force (larger span of control) are more valuable to the organization.

HOW TO REDUCE VACATION BACKLOGS AT LOWER COSTS

"Oh, vacation—that's when daddy works harder than
he does at the office."
UNKNOWN

Some more obvious solutions to the problems of vacation production and performance backlogs are authorizing more overtime, hiring of temporary personnel and increasing incentive. There is one big trouble with all of those types of solutions—they cost money. That is; they add to production or service costs.

The extent of these increases in expense added to the cost of the vacation payroll can decrease or wipe out the profits for the Company.

Viable solutions have to solve productivity or
performance problems without putting the company in
the red.

RECOMMENDED STEPS TO TAKE

If an unplanned backlog occurs during a "vacation season," consider asking employees who have not taken their vacation as yet to reschedule their time off to a more advantageous moment as concerns production scheduling. Caution: The rescheduling will only reduce *current* bottlenecks. Some care has to taken so that the vacation problems are not as vexing in future months.

Many employees are willing to make some sacrifice
during peak periods.

Here is a cost-saving ploy that works! Those employees, who are currently on vacation but are at home, can be asked to come in and to help out. If the employees have not made plans to go away, they may be willing to punch in and lend a hand. Their remaining vacation can be rescheduled to a more mutually advantageous future date.

It is worth a try. A call by an immediate superior, explaining the problem would cause a number of subordinates to consider at least a slight change in plans—perhaps even for a few days.

While last-minute rescheduling of vacations is not completely desirable, it is a limited-cost solution up to the extent that employees are willing to make changes.

"I got a call from the office, they need me tomorrow."

CUSTOMER PRIORITIES SOLUTION

However, there are always a certain number of customers who can be contacted by the sales force for a discussion of their needs and considerations of mutually agreeable delayed deliveries. Some of the customers will help out automatically. They have had similar problems of their own and can understand that any operation can develop a backlog.

Even customers who are in a tight corner because of their own time-frame requirements, might agree to partial shipments on a mutually agreeable *dependable* schedule.

"Mr. Customer, we have your order for 10,000 widgets to be delivered on September first. Instead, can you use 2,000 widgets a week for five weeks starting on that date?"

MATERIALS AND PARTS SHORTAGES

Shortages of any kind will add to the problems of vacation backlogs. Suppliers can be canvassed by the purchasing people and requested to move up their shipment schedules.

"Mr. Supplier, we need another 500 wire harnesses a week."

QUICK STEPS TO MINIMIZE DISRUPTIONS

1. Usually, vacation time is selected for making changes. However, if there is a production backlog, plans to make any work flow or equipment changes can be postponed so that disruptions, however minor, do not contribute to the backlog problems. While the changes ultimately may be beneficial,

a decision to delay them will work to the current advantage of minimizing disruptions.

2. The training programs provide long-range benefits, but the short-range requirements may outweigh such benefits. If the effort or the goal is to reduce vacation backlogs quickly, then training programs have to be interrupted or stretched out until the backlog is reduced. Trainees and instructors could become more available for operations.

3. In the same manner, any job rotation or cross-training programs can be delayed until a more acceptable schedule is devised.

WHERE TO GET EXPERIENCED HELP FOR ANY BACKLOG

More companies are using their own retirees as stand-by help. Why? Because these people frequently have the necessary experience. Not only that, many retirees are more than willing to work part time or for a partial year. They still get their pensions and most of their social security benefits.

Here is how they do it. The Company sends out an explanatory letter and a form. The form includes indication of desirable working hours and periods of time that the retiree is available. The returned completed forms are subsequently forwarded to middle managers for their consideration.

The middle managers review the forms and then to ask to discuss reemployment with certain retirees. Acceptable retirees then become a part of a stand-by work force.

WATCH FOR ATTITUDE

Many operations have the preconceived notion that vacation season is time for a slump in productivity, performance and the bottom line. That need not be the case. A primary requirement for improvement is to *change that attitude.*

"Hey, it's July, what can we expect?"

Well, if expectations are low, then productivity, performance and profits are going to be just that, low. However, if expectations are higher, all of the personnel can be oriented toward looking for ways to maintain improved levels.

WARNING: LOOK OUT FOR POST-VACATION TRAUMA

"We have got to play catch-up."

Fine, but that costs a lot of money. Overtime, use of temporaries, and all of the other costs of panics do not make the Company any more cost competitive.

Experienced and cost effective managers can find ways not to have the problem in the first place—not only because it is cheaper, but because that is what management is all about. If nothing else, ***good management means planning***. Now, planning can include reducing the peaks and valleys of volume requirements as can happen with vacation considerations.

GETTING MORE PRODUCTIVE TIME OUT OF THE WORK WEEK

> *"There cannot be a crisis next week. My schedule is already full."*
> HENRY KISSINGER, former Secretary of State

One company had a divisional manager that top management thought was the "greatest" for that particular division. Year after year, the division performed excellently. There was good productivity at relatively low cost and with on-time deliveries—an admirable record.

Then one day, that divisional manager became seriously ill and had to be hospitalized for an extended length of time. A ready replacement was not available. The only person who could be entrusted with the job was a line supervisor who was technically capable but who was a neophyte to the top position. Top management anticipated a slack period for the division.

The manager's sudden illness was not the only surprise for the brass. The first reports from the division were unbelievable. That neophyte was outperforming the old divisional manager. The division was becoming even more profitable than it was before!

"LET'S TAKE A LOOK"

Top management went out to the division for a peek. It developed that the new manager had had little experience in administration, so throughout the division he sidetracked those administrative functions that he thought did not relate to getting the job done. He didn't know which functions were important or which were unimportant, and only concerned his people with minimal requirements.

The replacement manager's instruction to the production people had been to "Do what has to be done to get the work out quickly, nothing more."

194

APPLICATION OF THE SOLUTION

Many management experts can provide "good" reasons as to why such an attitude is unrealistic. However, because one extreme may be unrealistic does not mean that one has to go to the other extreme either. The "no-nonsense" instruction worked and will continue to work in some places. Of course, the management has to be result (or objective) oriented. Every operation (direct and indirect) has to be viewed critically with such queries as these:

1. If this operation is eliminated, will the product or service still get out on the shipping dock or out the door?
2. If this operation is needed, can it be simplified?
3. If the operation is needed and it has been simplified as much as possible, can it be combined with another operation?
4. If we had to, is there another way of doing the whole thing?
5. Is what is being done getting product or service in the hands of the customer?

RECOMMENDATIONS FOR INCREASING PRODUCTIVE TIME

1. In a comprehensive survey, it was found that front line managers and supervisors spend over 25% of their time in personnel administration. This effort can be reduced by having the personnel departments pick up some of the chores and eliminating, simplifying and combining others

2. A typical complaint by front line management is the extent of time that is spent at meetings. (Meetings are not locations where jobs get out of the house.)

   One executive found that management meetings that started at 4:30 p.m. did not tend to drag. In addition, much of the work force were completing most of their job assignments for the day by that time and fewer managers were required on the floor.

3. Another way of cutting back on management meeting time while increasing the time available to managers to be at their stations is to have business dinner meetings at a

nearby restaurant. A cocktail, some steak, dessert—and then a meeting which does not interfere with productivity.

4. One suggestion is to cold-shoulder time-wasters. These are people, subordinates included, who have to interrupt a hard working manager to recite all kinds of nonsense. "Send me a memo instead."

5. The "clear the desk" ploy can work for a busy manager. Merely shift the paperwork on to capable subordinates. Sure, they are busy. So what? Better them than the boss. "From now on, you handle these requisitions."

IMPROVING SUBORDINATE PRODUCTIVITY

1. Old trick: reduce the time away from work stations or desks. For instance, have one subordinate be responsible for gathering supplies, parts, reports, and so on instead of everyone being their own "goffer." In addition, have only one fast subordinate deliver finished materials, reports, and so on instead of everyone providing their own delivery service.

2. Whenever possible, remove administrative functions from the operating personnel. For instance, have a capable section clerk handle as much paperwork as possible. Or, in the worst case, permit only one operating subordinate to handle the paperwork for all of the others.

3. In certain situations, require that subordinates have their coffee break at their work stations or at least in the work areas. (This reduces wandering or, more aptly, socializing.)

4. Increase individual backlog. Example: instead of putting 100 reports to be checked out in front of a subordinate, try putting 110. This technique tends to reduce coasting and "day end" slacking.

5. Move timeclocks, coat racks, and so forth, to the more immediate work areas. Then, there would be less strolling around by clock watchers.

6. Provide alternative workloads. This technique keeps the subordinate busy even if he should come to some stopping point in his regular work.

TIME IS AN ASSET

Organizations spend a good deal of money to prevent any manager or employee from stealing property or money from the Company. Yet, while it is not a piece of office furniture or a Company check, valuable time is taken away from front line managers and supervisors.

There is a difference between stealing inventory from the Company and stealing (or misusing) an operating manager's time. Maybe the difference is one of intent. But the results are exactly the same—an increase in the Company's cost of the end product or service. Any time taken away from an operating manager is that much less effort which can be devoted to getting the work out.

WHEN AND HOW TO INVITE SUBORDINATE COMPETITIVENESS

> *"Bloke at work, went in for a competition and won a trip to China. That's right, to China. Fantastic. He's out there now trying to win a trip back."*
> JERRY DENNIS

Generally, employees like to be competitive, even if such competitiveness is only within their narrow part of the entire operation. While not every operation in varied areas lends itself to employee competition, where it is possible, it has proven to be a big help in improving productivity or performance.

Competition among employees, properly fostered, can lead to greater productivity without the use of more costly incentives and with a certain amount of quality control improvement.

DIRECT COMPETITION TOWARD A GOAL

Even where the work may be described as very routine, if each employee is shown what is expected of him or her and of the others in the group, the employee is more than likely going to try to achieve the objective that has been assigned.

There are some techniques for instilling a more competitive spirit including the following:

1. Permit subordinates to maintain their own production or performance records. The posting of each record on a nearby bulletin board may be desirable.
2. Advise each subordinate of the overall plan and his or her part in that plan.
3. Let each subordinate know exactly what is expected of each of the coworkers.
4. Permit individual subordinates to establish which alternative techniques that they may want to use. (Avoid being too rigid in suggested methods.)

5. Give individual subordinates some freedom to set their priorities within the overall plan.

6. Seek agreement on deadlines and on rush or special jobs. Let each subordinate estimate time requirements

7. Develop methods for attributing defective work or errors to individual subordinates.

8. Have cross-checking done by others in the group. Reduce reliance on self-checking

9. Recognize superior performance—either publicly or privately, depending on circumstances.

10. Give extra work to those who "eat it up."

    Competition frequently brings out the highly motivated and the recognition drives aggressive workers.

11. Avoid giving extra work to those who break under the stress of competition.

GROUP VERSUS INDIVIDUAL INITIATIVE

Not all types of industries or operations lend themselves to the fostering of individual competition. There are many types of situations that require group participation. That is, it takes many hands to complete an operation. For instance, an assembly line discourages individual initiative. All of the workers have to group together to meet production requirements. In such instances, reliance is placed on teamwork.

RECOMMENDATION: REWRITE JOB DESCRIPTIONS

Written job descriptions with proper grading of jobs by productivity, performance and quality characteristics can cause more employees to set and achieve higher work goals

For example, if a job write-up states that a Grade B Order Picker has to complete 100 orders per day, there is a target for the employee to shoot at. Otherwise, there is no quantitative goal for such a classification and less reason to improve performance.

How the boss can help

The front line manager or supervisor can provide one of the best impetus for employee competition. First, a boss can set one subordinate against another with regard to productivity or quality or whatever.

By being partial to the performance of one subordinate and then switching loyalties to another, the boss can keep several subordinates on their toes. And, if the boss avoids choosing a "teacher's pet" there will be attempts to gain the boss's recognition and approbation.

"Nice try, John, but Nancy finished her job 20 minutes ago."

"Good work, Wilbur, you did more than Waldo, but less than Oscar. How come?"

"Keep at it; you are improving."

Putting a little "grease" in the competitive gears doesn't hurt. It also means that the manager or supervisor is giving some recognition to the competitive spirit. Some subordinates may come around to the boss and ask for hints on how they can improve their performance. Others may try to pick up some short cuts on their own.

Why instill competition?

We are accustomed to competition and even enjoy a certain amount of that spirit. We competed in school for grades and even teacher recognition. Many of us, who are sports minded, appreciate the role of competition in self-improvement. Even in pursuits that do not involve a competitor, we try to improve our own abilities—competing against ourselves—constantly measuring our own performance.

Why not bring that spirit to the work situation? There are some subordinates who will be inflexible. That cannot be avoided. However, for many, even those with the more routine work, there will be a remarkable acceptance of the challenge.

It is the easiest way to make work exciting at minimal cost.

PERSONAL ADVANTAGE

The big plus of competition in the work place is that frequently the boss is no longer a boss. He or she has become, of all things, a coach—whether the competition is individual or group. It is much harder for a subordinate to let the coach down. One just does not do that sort of thing.

By accepting the role of a coach, the front line manager or supervisor enjoys greater subordinate esteem and, most important, the supervisory work is made easier.

OVERCOMING THE SHORTAGE OF GOOD SUPERVISORY PEOPLE

"Some men are born mediocre, some men achieve mediocrity, and some men have mediocrity thrust upon them."
JOSEPH HELLER, *Catch 22*

The hiring of new supervisors from outside of the Company can frequently help in a crunch situation. However, the drawbacks of going outside could include the following:

1. While the new leader is an experienced person, that person may know little about the Company and its business.

2. An outsider will be unfamiliar with in-house methods.

3. The neophyte to the Company will not have an immediate rapport with other supervisors with whom there has to be coordination.

4. Subordinates will be less familiar with the neophyte.

5. Additional training and orientation may be required.

THE OVERPROTECTIVE SUPERVISOR ROLE

Many a supervisor is reluctant to train an assistant. The sometimes unadmitted justification for the reluctance is job security. (Just suppose the assistant works out too well!) However, that rationale deters the supervisor from getting promoted. The top movers and shakers dialogue could be:

"Wilbur is a good stockroom supervisor but no one in the stockroom can take over his job. So, he is not a viable candidate for promotion to the new purchasing slot."

A lack of an understudy reduces opportunities for personal promotion.

Without a pool of assistant supervisors, the Company has to go outside for supervisory help.

STANDBY SUPERVISOR TRAINING

The major benefit of cross-training subordinates is that if one is out, another can take his or her place or pinch-hit so that production and performance levels can be maintained.

The same is true for supervisors. Wally Hotshot is not going to be out for any minor reason, but sometimes it happens that Wally has to be away from his supervisory job. Of course, another supervisor could cover for Wally, but that could be spreading the supervision too thin.

"Who have you got to cover for you?"

It may be advisable for Wally to have some subordinate within the group get some on-the-job training as a standby supervisor. That person could be someone who shows leadership ability, has an overall view of the requirements of the group, and has a potential for developing into a management person.

The supervisor should review the potential of all of the persons in the group. Likes and dislikes should be minimized. The reason? One measure of the supervisor's own management potential is the ability to select competent intermediate supervision.

SUGGESTION: GIVE THE STANDBY A SLOW START

One way of testing the candidate for standby supervisor is to try that person out for short periods. If the supervisor is called away, the candidate can be told:

"Nancy, I am going to a meeting. I want you to cover for me while I'm gone."

"When will you be back?"

"In a couple of hours. You can hold the fort until then."

"What do I do?"

"Just keep the work moving. The new motors are coming directly from Receiving. When they get here, have the crew start slapping them into the B assemblies."

"I can handle it."

"Good, you should have no problem."

THE STRAW BOSS SOLUTION

The other employees will come to recognize Nancy as the straw boss. Some will try to be helpful. Others may try to undermine her limited authority; that would be a good test for Nancy.

The backup effort will enhance Nancy's authority as a straw boss because her instructions in the future will then seem to carry the weight of the supervisor.

SUCCESSFUL TRAINING

As time goes by, the standby supervisor is given more responsibility for longer lengths of time. That is reinforcement of prior training. Eventually, the standby can evolve into a well trained full-fledged supervisor. And, at some point, the bird can be encouraged to leave the nest and take on a supervisory job.

> *WARNING: If a straw boss is not working out, try someone else. Being a straw boss is not a lifetime commitment for anyone.*

UNION SHOP PROCEDURES

Where a potential supervisor is a union member, additional steps may be required. *Read the union contract.* The candidate may want to resolve the duties as a straw boss with union loyalty requirements. Unless the candidate clearly wants to take advantage of the opportunity, there may be difficulties.

However, an aware supervisor should be able to determine where the difficulties lie and who within the group is willing to meet the challenge of moving up.

SUPERVISION IS NOT FOR EVERYONE

There are people who have leadership ability, technical know-how and other supervisory qualities. For good reason, they do not want the additional responsibility of supervision. It is best not to oversell the opportunity—it can backfire. It is best that a candidate, not only have ability, but innate willingness as well.

MANAGER'S RESPONSIBILITY

"I wish I had another section chief like Gloria."

To develop an available pool of potential supervisors takes a great deal of work. Careful recruiting of even rank and file, training, encouraging people, and prodding existing supervisors is part of the effort.

Is the effort to have a good supervisory staff worth it? Yes, for two reasons. First, the manager's job is made easier. Second (and maybe just as important) is that the manager becomes better promotion material. Being able to recruit, train, and keep a good supervisory staff is a big personal plus. Consider this: a winning team is deemed to have a good captain.

MORE CONTROL AND REDUCTION OF MISTAKES AND SCRAP

"This sounds corny as hell, but everybody in an organization has to believe that their very livelihood is based on the quality of the product they deliver."
LEE IACOCCA

The army that makes the fewest mistakes wins the war. And, in industry, the business that makes the fewest mistakes beats the heck out of the competition. Let's face it—mistakes cost companies money. Some say that the other side of the coin is that zero defects cost money, and that a perfect end product would be price prohibitive.

The cost versus profit dilemma may be expressed as a formula which is simply something like this:

"Would the cost of catching (expensive) and correcting (also expensive) the mistake be less than the penalty suffered (yes, lower profits) by letting the mistake go?"

THE BIG THREE MISTAKES

1. INHERITED ERROR. This is a human or systems mistake that was made in an earlier operation. It was uncovered in a subsequent operation down the line or in final assembly.

This type of error is very costly because additional operations and materials have been added after the mistake was made. By remaining undetected, the subsequent operations and/or the entire product became significantly valueless.

Example. If the main frame was defective, all of the operations and materials added to it increased the cost of the one error.

2. PROPAGATED ERROR. This mistake occurs when an assumption is made that is based on incorrect facts or inferences.

Example. An error in the summarization of customer orders by product line resulted in an error in the production forecasting for the next month. (production forecasting was in error caused by an error elsewhere.) As a result, for a whole month, a plant will be building fractional horsepower motors when it should be building multiple horsepower motors.

3. SYSTEMS ERROR. This mistake occurs because of the methods selected to accomplish the work. The fault lies not with the individual employees but rather with the one who designed the system or methods used.

Frequently, when a set of procedures is tested, not all of the ramifications are included in the test—even where the test is performed in a live situation. Thus, when a new set of circumstances enters the production or process, a great deal of scrap and wasted effort is created.

A PARTIAL ANSWER TO SCRAP COSTS

Prior to the addition of any major material or labor cost to a product in process, the product should be tested at that point.

To test after the addition of a subassembly results in adding the cost of the subassembly (plus labor and overhead) to the scrap cost. For some unknown reason, some plants will spend more money on quality control after assembly than before. They fail to realize that if parts and subassemblies test well prior to assembly, there is a greater likelihood of favorable final inspections.

HOW TO CATCH UNREALISTIC INSPECTORS

How much smaller would the scrap pile be if it was located "up front?"

Middle managers should, once in a while, take a stroll and examine the scrap piles. Are the scrap items mostly parts, subassemblies, or completed assemblies? If a major assembly is scrapped because of parts defect, find out why the parts were not inspected or tested. The only assemblies that should be in the scrap heap are those that were defected in the assembly operation. An example of this would be a main assembly that cracked during an assembly welding operation.

Employee Orientation Solution

If there are many mistakes that are caused by people rather than be equipment or the system, a certain amount of emphasis must be placed on improving job orientation with regard to error-free work. During training and other sessions, the importance of self-checking procedures should be emphasized. Correction and rechecking methods should be reviewed with the lowest level of clerk.

Supervisors and managers can make informal studies as to just where and how mistakes within their own areas are being made.

Steps to Take Right Now

1. Reassign inspection stations in the work flow to catch errors before major additions are made to the product.

2. Train inspectors to analyze not only the where and how of mistakes, but also just how the self-checking failed.

3. Occasionally, check the inspectors' understanding of their jobs.

4. Use blind receiving. Preconceived notions on purchased parts are reduced.

5. Constantly review the costs of scrapping versus reworking the material. Rework can be scheduled for lulls in the production flow when much of the labor and overhead costs continue anyway.

6. Reassign the error-prone subordinates either to less critical areas or to spots where checking is intensified.

7. Revise the organization chart so that inspectors, and so on, report to higher authority other than any immediate geographical supervisor. IT'S BEST THAT THE KING'S FOOD TASTER REPORTS NOT TO THE CHEF, BUT TO THE KING.

8. Review employee training programs with regard to the self-checking procedures, and so on. Increase quality orientation to include the job security target.

9. Bring suppliers and subcontractors to the premises to observe operations with a view to improving their product.

10. Check out the scrap heap now and then and try to assess the causes of the scrap.

THE DUAL PRIORITY

If we accept that the customer is the king of the market place, we also know that the customer can curtail or close any operation for less reasons than shoddy merchandise. You can't goldplate everything. However, he does have reasonable expectations of the products that he buys for what he pays for it. And, there's the rub. He insists on getting what he thinks is his money's worth.

The customer is willing to pay a certain price for a certain level of quality. It is up to the people at the producer to deliver that. If the production or service people can not meet end-use quality expectations, then call the auctioneers because another operation or plant closing is inevitable.

"They are not even making plastic like they used to."
Quality control department graffiti

USING SHORT-INTERVAL SCHEDULING TO IMPROVE PRODUCTIVITY

"So much of what we call management consists in making it difficult for people to work."
PETER F. DRUCKER

One of the facts of industrial life is that the attention span of a subordinate is considerably reduced when the time necessary to complete a job is very extensive. It would seem that the longer it takes to complete a task, the less likelihood there is that the worker will be well motivated toward the realization of a goal.

In the same manner, if the time required for the completion of a job is too short, completion of the task itself becomes a meaningless goal. For example tightening a nut on an assembly line is a short-range accomplishment. The short-range type of tasks does not invite the sense of significant accomplishment that most workers would like to obtain from their jobs.

*Tasks have to be of **optimum** size.*

SHORT-INTERVAL SCHEDULING SOLUTION

The tightening of nuts or doing the complete assembly are examples of assignment extremes both of which tend to rule out significant favorable job satisfaction for the average worker. However, putting parts together for certain major assemblies may be in the order of "bite size" (optimal) assignments.

Short-interval scheduling (SIS) is a technique which is possible in many operations by redesigning the workflow. Instead of emphasizing daily or weekly job assignments, work is assigned within a series of **short-term performance** goals. The production engineer has to consider limiting or building up of job assignments where the production worker can have more of a sense of job completion.

"Bite size" jobs are easier to monitor from a supervisory point of view.

ATTACKING THE DEMON—MONOTONY

SIS also tends to relieve the production worker of the more monotonous aspects of the job. Instead of doing just one function all day long, short-interval scheduling makes it possible for a production employee to perform several functions of a differing nature in order to complete one assignment.

"Marlow, instead of just attaching the name plates to the front assemblies, from now on you will handle the entire front panel assembly."

HOW SIS PROVIDES ACCOMPLISHMENT

Previously, Marlow attached 100 name plates an hour—boring work, which leads to absenteeism, and so on. After training and redesigning the work flow, Marlow can be expected to do all of the tasks required for the assembly of a complete front panel.

When Marlow completes a job assignment (a finished front panel assembly) in less than the scheduled time, which should happen from time to time, Marlow will have a sense of accomplishment. That "job reward" is quite different from attaching name plates almost all day long—it creates more work incentive.

INCREASING PRODUCTIVITY QUICKLY

The SIS workflow technique can permit more meaningful monetary rewards for the higher performance worker.

Under the old system, Marlow received incentive pay when more than 100 nameplates were attached. (Small potatoes—and difficult to keep track of.) A plus feature of SIS is that the larger assignments allow for the establishment of larger incentive pay bonuses than those set for the smaller and more routine types of jobs.

You are not giving away the store or killing the bottom line. The bonuses are being rearranged to be more meaningful as a real incentive. (Instead of pennies, the worker is looking to dollars.)

A STEP TOWARD MORE QUALITY CONTROL

Forgetting that the reduction of monotony leads to improved quality consciousness, there is another big factor. After switching to assembling of the front panel, Marlow can draw greater satisfaction from the work.

A worker can feel more satisfaction from a complete job.

That attempt at satisfaction leads to improved quality control. The front panel assembly can more easily represent Marlow's contribution to the end product than a much smaller or almost insignificant step in production. Marlow may feel more responsible for the quality of the product.

STEPS TO TAKE

1. Review the production techniques.
2. Combine small or insignificant tasks.
3. Define optimum size jobs.
4. Restructure the workflow around "bite size" jobs.
5. Devise new incentive scales based on optimum jobs (like subassemblies) rather than on production steps.
6. Retrain production workers to increase their skills for larger tasks.
7. Improve equipment to be more multi-functional.

OVERCOMING UNION OBJECTIONS

There will be union resistance to changing occupational requirements of their membership.

A dramatic change in the workflow is going to require union agreement. In the short run, it is going to be tough to gain acceptance. However, when each union member realizes that his or her job is being expanded and that each union member will acquire new skills it may be an easier selling job.

In the long run, improvements in productivity increase job security and mobility. Why? The Company can more readily compete with those organizations (foreign and domestic) that have already improved their productivity. Ultimately, without needed productivity improvements, there will be no jobs in the plant or office for anyone—union or management.

All around us there are reminders of what happens when productivity cannot be improved. Many plant gates and office doors are closed permanently because of a lack of cost effectiveness. Many of the good and experienced people, who worked at those very installations, are out flipping hamburgers, peddling insurance to relatives, standing in job lines, pumping gas, throwing newspapers on front lawns, washing cars or trying to get by on a monthly early retirement check.

SELECTING THE RIGHT DAY OF THE WEEK AS PAYDAY

"Do you hear about the mint employees who went on strike to make less money?"
JACK HERBERT

Friday, although somewhat traditional, is not always the most desirable day to pay the employees. There are many factors which should be involved in the selection of some other day of week. In addition, there are many considerations as to why many firms are paying other than weekly.

Some of the factors for the selection of which day to use as payday include the following:

1. Union contract requirements.
2. Evening hours schedule of nearby banks.
3. Absenteeism experience on Mondays and Fridays.
4. Lunch hour check-cashing facilities. Proximity of nearby bank branches.
5. Required lead time for payroll preparation.
6. Overtime pay inclusion requirements.
7. Differing paydays for various departments.
8. Abuses of time off for check cashing.
9. Workload and peaks in the payroll department.
10. Reliability of outside payroll services.
11. Interim problems of changing paydays.
12. Special problems in computing gross pay.
13. Difficulties of promptly paying for week-end work.
14. Required tax reports and payments.

A CAUSE OF ABSENTEEISM

In many operations there is some sort of correlation between Friday payday and the extent of absenteeism on Monday.

One cannot know for sure just how much payday can be blamed for absenteeism on a subsequent work day. Many employees, even those who may be deemed as critically ill, manage to come in on payday but seem to lack the same enthusiasm to make it on the following work day.

A number of organizations in order to reduce the propensity for this type of absence, pay their employees once every two weeks.

A by-product cost advantage to paying every second week is the reduction of the work load of the payroll department. Biweekly payrolls result in 26 payrolls instead of 52 to get out each year. Biweekly payrolls result in 50% less check cashing excess time abuses.

THE OVERTIME REWARD

It is easier to motivate the personnel to work overtime if the reward for that overtime is quick in coming. Someone who may be required to work on Saturday, is more likely to volunteer to work the sixth day when he believes that the extra remuneration will be prompt.

However, some companies choose to pay for the current overtime in the following pay period. The benefit is that the lead time required to compute the current gross pay can be shorter. For gross payroll, the overtime of the previous payroll period is added to the current regular pay. Therefore, there is always a delay of one payroll period in paying the reward for overtime. Where the overtime requirements are more or less consistent, the effect of the delay may be of small consequence.

SPREAD OUT THE PROBLEMS

By staggering the payroll days for different departments, the workload of the payroll department is also staggered. If some of the production departments are paid on Wednesday and the others of Friday, for instance, then the deadlines are also spread out for the payroll department.

Any fallout of the problems or absenteeism, check-cashing time abuses, and so on, are spread out through the other days of the week.

Spreading out paydays does not eliminate the problems. However, it does isolate the problems and make them more manageable.

One further step would be to pay the executive and administrative personnel every other week, semi-monthly, or monthly.

COORDINATE WITH CHECK-CASHING FACILITIES

If the day that is selected as payday does not coincide with the days that the local banks are open late, or if there is a lack of check-cashing facilities on that day, a check-cashing service can be requested to come to the premises to accommodate those employees wishing to cash their checks or to buy money orders.

The service can be paid by the employee, or the employer, on a per check basis. In addition to check-cashing firms, others that offer similar services include local banks and armored car companies.

This technique reduces the abuses of granting time off for check cashing.

COST SAVING SOLUTION

More than half of the social security recipients do not receive checks. Their payments are made directly to their bank accounts via direct deposit.

This technique has been adopted by big pension funds and many large employers such as Sears. It provides that the paying (employer's) bank remit the funds to the payee's (employee's) bank for credit to the payee's bank account.

The benefits to employees include the following:

1. Immediate availability of funds. (There is no waiting of days for a payroll check to clear.)

2. No standing in line at a bank waiting to deposit his or her paycheck.

3. No possibility of a lost check.

The benefits to employers include the following:

1. No check-cashing time abuses.

2. No effort in the preparation of checks.

3. No effort in the distribution of checks.

4. No effort in the handling of canceled checks.

5. No effort in replacing lost checks.

Some employers report a net cost reduction benefit of over $1 per payroll check. (That takes into account the interest on P/R account balances.)

How to Install Direct P/R Deposit

The company's financial people have to confer with their banking people. Bankers favor direct deposit activity because they have cost savings in such a method. Employees have to provide their bank and their bank account number to the payroll department for inclusion in the payroll computer run. Weekly, or whenever, the run is submitted to the employer's bank who makes the timely transfers to the various banks for further crediting.

Why Bother?

For one thing, lost time is lost profits, even for seemingly valid reasons. There is no known survey as to cost of payroll-related absenteeism, and so on. Let's say that it is as little as 5% of the productive time. (In some operations, it's a great deal more.) That 5% would still be significant because the 5% plus overhead is added to the cost of widgets, or whatever. That margin can be viewed as a big costly leak in what might be otherwise a tightly run ship.

Second, payday abuses, of one kind or another, are adverse to good employee morale. Most employees are committed to their job. They do their fair share and more. For those people, considerations have to be made that will result in more fairness to them.

WHEN TO BUTT INTO PERSONAL PROBLEMS OF A SUBORDINATE

"There's no problem so big or complicated that it can't be run away from."
GRAFFITI

Personal problems of various kinds interfere in many ways with a subordinate's performance at work. Some of the repercussions, which directly affect the front line supervisor or manager, include the following:

1. High absentee record.
2. Requests to leave work early.
3. Lateness at the start of the work day.
4. Lateness upon returning from the lunch break.
5. High number of personal telephone calls.
6. High error rate and improper handling of corrections.
7. Oversight of safety and health rules.
8. Reduced production or performance goals.
9. Increased or lengthier fatigue.
10. Reduced willingness to work overtime or weekends.
11. High "sickness" days out.
12. Loss of work initiative or incentive.
13. Expressions of irritability to coworkers.
14. Requests for irregular vacation time.
15. Antipathy toward immediate superior.
16. Anti-company attitude.
17. Lower training capability.
18. Slow or "legal" countering of instructions.
19. Higher grievance rate or general complaining.
20. Low willingness to install changes.

21. Abuses of break time.

22. Poor housekeeping around desk or work station.

No one subordinate is going to have all of the above attributes. However, a discernable change in the work situation attitude does become prevalent when a subordinate is more preoccupied with personal problems.

Avoiding Embarrassment

Whatever Charley's problem is at home or elsewhere, he does not want it to follow him to work—even though his work might be affected by it. Charley can be expected to have general resistance to discuss the matter with his boss or others who just may be able to help him.

Charley has to be convinced that his personal problem will not be a source of embarrassment to him on the job before he will seek any help with the problem.

Requirement: Maintain Confidentiality

The supervisor's tone should be that of a Dutch uncle, even if the subordinate is an older person. The subordinate can be advised that the matter will go no further than the supervisor. Expressions of discretion are advisable to instill confidence.

The efforts of the supervisor should relate to *personal* problems only and not to legal matters or related entanglements. Any problem involving legal issues should be referred to an attorney promptly.

In the handling of personal problems, the supervisor can point out the extent to which the subordinate's performance is below average. Comparisons to previous records can be made. The supervisor may suggest that the problem has to be at least mitigated in order for the subordinate to function properly at work. And that the supervisor is available to render any possible and proper assistance.

When to Stay Out

The supervisor would do well to avoid interfering in the personal problem if the subordinate indicates a negative reaction to offers of help, such as:

"I'll handle it myself, thanks anyway."

The supervisor should be concerned with the problem only if it is the express wish of the subordinate. The supervisor can continue to hammer away at lateness and other adverse work behavior and symptoms of the problem, but there should be no interference with the problem.

SELECTING THE RIGHT MOMENT

In a private conference, the supervisor can point out the deficiencies in the subordinate's performance. If there are no work-related causes, the following can be put forth:

"Miss Mason, we both know that you are capable of better work. Is there some way that I can help you get back on the right track here at the plant?"

"I do not know."

"Well, if you'd like to talk about it, it will just be between us; it will go no further than this room. It might be that I can suggest something. Or, at least, I will understand what is happening."

THE IMMEDIATE BENEFIT

Upon becoming aware that the supervisor has noticed an adverse work attitude or lower subordinate performance, the subordinate may push to solve his or her own problem—or at least learn to live with it so that work is not affected.

BOSS'S DUAL OBJECTIVE

The supervisor's duty is to assist a subordinate who has a personal problem—providing such assistance is wanted and is possible. Equally, there is the obligation to the company, which requires the best possible performance from each of its employees

WATCH THE LIMITATIONS

Not every problem is solvable by a boss. Sometimes, providing a sympathetic ear will do wonders. A little caution is suggested;

the supervisor would do well not to become directly involved in the subordinate's affairs other than as a possible source of advice.

> *"No good deed goes unpunished."*
> ANDREW MELLON

For the supervisor, being a Sigmund Freud or Advisor to the Lovelorn is one thing. But supervisor involvement in someone else's personal problems may deteriorate the supervisor's own work capability.

TIME TO CALL IT QUITS

If a subordinate is continuing to permit problems to interfere with work performance, a supervisor has to recognize where further effort would be more rewarding.

There is a limit to the supervisor's available time. If a subordinate cannot shape up to the demand of the job within a reasonable time, then that may be the moment to decide to part company. Other subordinates can use the supervisor's time for improving their performance.

HOW TO SPARK NON-CREATIVE SUBORDINATES INTO CREATIVITY

> *"A camel is a horse created by a committee."*
> UNKNOWN

Even many seemingly dull jobs require employees to use a portion of their creative ability or at least some initiative. The end product of many jobs is not the assembly of 100 widgets, or whatever, a day. It is also judged by the more nonquantitative measures of reports, design, problem solving, and ideas. The employees who work in the less mundane areas are expected to be more creative.

TOP BRASS OUTLOOK

As one executive remarked, "A new type of wheel is not going to be designed every day, but at least some new uses of the wheel might evolve."

Whether it is a new advertising slogan, design of an improved assembly line, or a new type of accounting report that quickly pinpoints cost overruns, the front line supervisor or manager is faced with the problem of being able to instill creativity.

CREATIVITY AS A REQUIREMENT

First, there is the "institutionalized creativity" in an organization. Generally, this is confined to the product development function. Within this function, the same types of resources are made available for creativity as for the manufacture of products or the rendering of services. There are trained personnel, specialized equipment (including computers) and sufficient organization.

The product development function involves people, who have a good track record in developing new products, equipment to make and test new products and ideas, and the procedures to recommend, test and evaluate their creativity.

Many worthwhile innovations were not attributable to the product development function.

Second, creativity arises in the operational function. Actually, the people who are not in the labs have the greatest opportunity at innovation. Because of proximity to live situations, operating people can initiate and develop more ideas on how to make a better widget, or whatever.

Provide fertile soil

The new ideas that are needed in every organization are more likely to be advanced if the reception to them can be compared to fertile soil. If there is likely to be resistance to change, few new ideas will be put forth to rock the boat. If the Company, every once in a while, tries out a "crackpot" idea, then more of its personnel will be inclined to advance or suggest a new and different concept.

Unusual ideas have included the airplane, the horseless carriage, the electric light bulb—and probably even the wheel.

Advancing new techniques

When an employee, who may not have been too creative in the past, does offer a suggestion—for no matter how useless it may seem—the front-line manager and supervisor should listen. The creator of an idea or a suggestion likes an audience and is more encouraged to pursue and advance other ideas as long as he or she believes that someone will listen to another proposal.

WARNING: One way of turning off creativity is to turn a deaf ear.

Try this attitude. Almost every serious suggestion has some merit; that does not mean that it is usable, but it does have some merit. In order to keep personnel from being disheartened or discouraged about creativity ability, the boss can compliment the subordinate for those portions of the idea that do have merit.

Stimulate new ideas

When an idea or suggestion is used, appropriate credit to the subordinate is desirable. This recognition can stimulate the subordinate to keep trying for further improvements.

"Wally thought this out and we are going to try it."

"That's a good idea, Wilbur. Do it."

"Nancy's new method works. Congratulations."

REWRITE JOB DESCRIPTIONS

"Part of the task is to find better ways of doing ....."

"And to make suggestions for improving ...."

Frequently, the job descriptions, whether formal or informal, fail to state to what extent the subordinate is expected to be creative. Is the subordinate expected to develop new methods of doing the job or seek out workable cost saving ideas?

Increase expectation of creativity.

If the manager intends that a subordinate find new and better ways of doing the job, it is best that this intention is not left to assumption. The immediate superior should confirm the fact that creativity is part of the required job and is a measure of subordinate performance.

THE SQUARE PEG IN A ROUND HOLE

There are some people, who can develop new and worthwhile ideas despite organizational resistance to change, their boss's attitude, the adverse remarks of coworkers, and so on. They have to be found out and encouraged. Why? Someone across the street might steal these assets away. These nonconformist types, who do not use "tunnel-vision" and are not victims of "Gestalt," can make large innovative contributions.

Tunnel-vision is the capability of applying attention solely in a frontal or expected direction.

Gestalt is the capability by reason of the expectation of the mind to discern an "A" when in fact the "A" is really "B."

*"I suddenly realized that anyone doing anything weird
was not weird at all and it was the people saying
they were weird that were weird."*
PAUL MCCARTNEY, musician and songwriter.

THE MANAGER'S DUTY

At every moment, there is somebody in an office or on the
plant floor who is fumbling with an idea in the dark recesses
of their mind. It remains for that person's boss to maintain an
attitude and environment where that idea can be expressed and
maybe even tried out.

HOW TO GET YOUR PEOPLE TO TAKE ON MORE RESPONSIBILITY

"There are not enough competent people in the world to go around; somebody must get the incompetent lawyers and doctors."
GEORGE BERNARD SHAW, author and playwright

One of the chief purposes of getting subordinates to accept more responsibilities is to require them to solve their own working problems. The benefit of that switch is to free the manager or supervisor for more important chores. The goal is for the subordinate to work independently of higher supervision and control and to meet the performance requirements of the job.

The acceptance of more responsibility by subordinates can be accomplished by a training process. After each step is learned, the subordinate is given another area over which he or she will have additional responsibility. Or, there is a substitution of responsibility to a higher or more sophisticated level.

IMPORTANCE OF UPDATING JOB FUNCTIONS

Whether formal or informal, the job write-up should be revised periodically to include broadened areas of responsibility that the boss wishes to delegate.

"Gloria, you have been handling the requisitioning quite well. Now I want you to take on the expediting effort on requisitions."

"Bill, you are doing a good job on coding. Starting today, input the coding directly into the terminals."

CAN YOU ACCEPT EXCUSES?

"Boss, I can't do that and get my job done too."
"Charley, that is part of your job."

One of the reasons subordinates use for declining more responsibility is that the subordinate believes he or she will not have enough time to do it.

Try this approach: Tell the subordinate to do it anyway and wait and see if it can be handled by the subordinate.

"Waldo, just start doing it and we will see what time or other problems, if any, you run into."

There is little point in discussing the addition of responsibility with the subordinate. If such a debate has to take place, it can be after the subordinate starts on the new responsibility. Of course, there is a limit on how many pounds you can put into a five-pound bag!

On responsibility limits, who should be the judge—the boss or the subordinate? By virtue of training, know-how and commitment, the boss has a far better grasp as to a subordinate's capabilities to handle additional responsibilities.

MAKE THEM TROUBLE SHOOTERS

There isn't any reason as to why every subordinate cannot be his own trouble shooter. In many instances, a supervisor can quickly throw the problem-solving effort right back at the subordinate.

"Waldo, you do not want me to handle that problem when you know when and just how to solve it yourself!

"Come on Gloria, why don't you research that out?"

"You can take care of that call."

If the subordinate cannot handle the problems that go with his or her function, then maybe the wrong person has been selected for that function. In any event, the extent of incompetency can be measured by the inability to solve job-related problems.

TURN THEIR COMPLAINTS AROUND

When a subordinate complains that he or she is not getting the right data or required materials or that the same is not being handled properly, the boss has an unparalleled opportunity to grant additional responsibility to that subordinate.

"Roscoe, you are right! From now on, take charge of getting the proper materials."

"Zachary, I have noticed that too. From now on, you can expedite that data."

QUICK STEPS TO TAKE

1. Assign tasks to subordinates that have a nearby geographical locale.
2. Consider reassigning vertical or lateral operations to existing tasks.
3. Increase self-checking steps and procedures.
4. Install *automatic* cross-checking techniques.
5. Have subordinates initiate more of their own workflow. (Let them learn to start their own jobs.)
6. Encourage subordinates to solve their own job-related problems.
7. Make subordinates get their own proper materials or accurate data. Let them follow up on shortages.
8. Increase subordinate understanding of overall production and performance requirements.
9. Permit subordinates to select their own work methods.
10. Redesign a group's workflow for minimum supervisory intervention or effort.

INCREASING PERFORMANCE

It has been said before: "An average team is deemed to have an average captain." The front line supervisor or manager, who wants to "look" better to the corporate makers and shakers, has to increase his or her department, section, or group's performance. One way of doing that is to increase each subordinate's responsibility.

AVOID OUT-OF-DATE THINKING

"If you want something done right, you have to do it yourself."

The more efficient attitude is, "If something has to be done right, ***get the subordinate*** to do it right." The boss cannot and should not do everything.

Admittedly, the supervisor has to pitch in now and then. But that expedient is only an expedient. Supervisors and managers are not doing their required jobs when they are doing the work that can readily be assigned to subordinates.

HOW TO CRACK DOWN ON ABSENCES DUE TO PHONY ILLNESSES

"The rule of thumb in the matter of medical advice is to take everything any doctor says with a grain of aspirin."
GOODMAN ACE

A large contributor to the breakdown of employee morale is the fact that some employees get away with calling in sick, get paid for the day, and were not ill.

While it is difficult to determine completely who is truly ill and who is not, steps can be taken that will tend to assure that the privilege of sick leave with pay is not completely abused.

REASON FOR CRACKDOWN—THE AVERAGE GOOD WORKER

Wilbur will show up for work even with a runny nose and a fever and refuse to take advantage of the sick pay policy. Wilbur, and others, feel that they do not wish to take sick leave for minor ailments because they may need the leave when they are "really" sick.

Marvis will show up because he feels that no one else can handle his job as well. There is some responsibility for performance. For many others, it is a part of the work ethic of being a good worker to avoid being out for minor ailments.

When those types of employees are out sick, it is generally because they are really ill and cannot perform any work.

An experienced boss can recognize who makes sacrifices and who does not.

WATCH SUBORDINATE ATTITUDE

"I've got eight days coming to me."

There are some employees who will be out for any and every minor ailment. They view sick leave as a right and want to take full advantage of any accrued leave. They may demonstrate little responsibility for any required productivity. The fact that coworkers will have to carry a larger workload or that their Company will suffer economically is of little concern to them.

THE CHRONIC ABSENTEE

"Sorry, boss, but I can't make it in today."

How many times a year does an employee pull that line before he or she is considered a chronic absentee? One company says that eight or more absences of one or more days each during a twelve-month period generally indicates a problem employee.

WHAT'S THE LAW?

First, generally, management has the right to require proof of an employee's claim of sick leave.

Second, the sick proof policy has to be applied equally to all employees. In actual practice, there can be no picking and choosing as to who has to comply.

A MANAGEMENT SUB-RIGHT

Under the right of requiring proof of illness, the employer has a subsidiary right. The employer may require proof that the employee is fit to return to work! This can be very interesting if the employee has used, or is about to use, all of the available accrued sick leave.

WARNING: With exceptions, the policy of proof of fitness has to be applied equally to all.

"Exceptions" would include the stated policy that fitness proof is required only after a certain number of days absent for illness.

QUICK ACTION RECOMMENDATIONS

When a subordinate calls in and says: "Sorry, boss, but I can't make it in today," a seemingly good reply may be: "Sorry, Jimmy, but stay out until you feel better."

Do **not** say that. Don't worry; chances are that Jimmy Sicklie, the chronic absentee, will stay out until he feels much better. Why should Jimmy knock himself out? Probably, he views sick leave as his right.

One of the better responses, with a slight tone of sarcasm, is to say, "Jimmy, get well fast, we miss you here."

In the interim, consider moving his desk or work station down the hall or in an uninspiring corner. When he returns to work Jimmy may notice that he has become the low man on the totem pole.

Here is another ploy to consider. Near the end of each work day, require the Company nurse or the immediate supervisor to call the problem employee at home to ask:

"Jimmy, how are you coming along? I'm calling to see if you expect to come in tomorrow."

Two spinoff benefits can result from that call without much effort. First, it has been determined that the absent employee is really at home. (Of course, Jimmy could have been out to the doctor.)

The second benefit has a more hidden advantage. The employees, who become aware of this procedure, may be discouraged from taking sick leave for seemingly minor ailments or to accomplish some personal chore.

Here is another good shot at the perennial goldbrick. The late-in-the-day telephone conversation can include the query:

"Jimmy, shall I send the Company doctor over to your house to offer any possible assistance?"

HARD LINE RECOMMENDATIONS FOR TOUGH SITUATIONS

In operations where absenteeism is a large disruption in the workflow or in service to customers, management has to rely on some stiffer illness verification procedures, including any of the following:

1. Returning employees must produce a doctor's certification for three or more sick days in any one period.

2. After a certain number of days out, a returning employee must report to the Company doctor first.

3. After a certain number of days out, the employee must provide his doctor's certification as to fitness to return to work.

4. A doctor's certification is required for any absence due to illness before or after a holiday weekend.

5. After a certain number of days in any one period, the Company doctor or nurse is to visit the employee at home.

6. An employee, who is out more than 7 (or whatever) days in any one year, is required to submit to a complete physical examination by the Company doctor.

7. Any employee who falsely claims sick pay is subject to discipline including dismissal.

Dismissal is a tough remedy. However, merely as a stated policy, it can be a serious deterrent to sick pay abuse or, to call it more plainly, cheating.

All such policies have to be in writing and in application, applied uniformly.

CUTTING DOWN ON EMPLOYEE DAYDREAMING

"It is impossible to enjoy idling thoroughly unless one has plenty of work to do."
RALPH BORSODI

We all daydream, but some people do it to excess—to a point where it interferes with work or the quality of the work. Some jobs lend themselves more to daydreaming than others and have to be monitored carefully.

IS IT THE JOB OR THE SUBORDINATE?

Charley does some daydreaming at work. Should we blame him or the job that we have him do? His job may be so boring that Charley cannot keep his mind on it. If Charley does nothing all day long but tighten nuts on widgets, or whatever, on an assembly line with a pneumatic wrench, he is going to be inclined to daydream.

Where greater worker attention is required, daydreaming (the result of boredom) can result in the loss of productivity, errors and even accidents. The problem may not be the worker, but rather the way the job was designed.

WORK ENVIRONMENT RECOMMENDATIONS

Daydreaming and boredom can be reduced by the use of selected piped-in music that provides a faster tempo which in not conducive to encouraging wandering thoughts.

The design of the workstation can reduce the tendency for a worker's mind to wander. Operations that must be performed while standing tend to discourage daydreaming.

One company has specially designed work stools for people on their assembly line. The seat of the stool is tilted at about a 30-degree angle. That makes the stool slightly uncomfortable for complete sitting purposes but has the feature of keeping assembly line people in an alert position.

Work area decor is of prime importance in providing some relief from boredom. Bright and unusual and varying color schemes are more desirable than dull ones without any contrasts.

Consider this arrangement. Do not use the same color for all of desks and workstations. Eliminate the appearance of monotony in the workplace.

Those work situations that require a higher degree of creativity or attention span on the part of the workers should have a colorful an "nonplain" environment that is indicative of some expression of creativity.

MODIFY THE WORK FLOW

Where different and varied types of work proceed through a work group, there is likely to be less daydreaming and more responsiveness to work requirements.

The use of alternate flows of work in many instances provides increased productivity, as many employees can express greater personal interest in a work situation that has some elements of occasional change.

The side benefits. The use of alternate workflows provides some cross-training (more people know different jobs). That workforce feature can give supervisors a greater flexibility in the assignment of their subordinates to various jobs.

CHANGE OPERATIONS SEQUENCE

A useful technique is to allow Charley some flexibility in sequencing his operations. This method allows him to decide how and when to handle particular steps. The decision process will tend to keep Charley more alert to the work situation. Operation descriptions have to be rewritten to permit this flexibility.

Side benefit. By being permitted to select alternative steps, the worker can become more proficient in varied techniques and may provide additional skills which improve productivity and performance.

CHANGE PRODUCTS OR GOALS

By allowing some flexibility in the products or results to be obtained, boredom can be reduced. For instance, instead of requiring 100 pieces of A, then 100 of B and finally 100 of C—open the doors for a breath of fresh air. Let Charley have some decision making in how many A's he can produce before he turns to do some B's or C's.

> *Try to give overall assignments in overall time frames to each subordinate or group.*

If subordinates are allowed to make some decisions about what they are to produce that day (or week), they may become more interested in their work. **Learning drawback:** providing overall assignments, rather than handing them out piecemeal, may require a little more supervisory effort—at least in the beginning. After the learning curve, the advantages could be worth the effort.

> *If the technique of overall assignments is successful, a long-term advantage is that such a method requires less continuing supervision than individual assignments.*

HARD CORE PROBLEM SUBORDINATE

No matter what efforts are made in dispelling the daydreaming potential, some employees seem to be lost in the clouds. Only constant supervisory effort can dispel the problem and make such employees have a higher attention span.

For a particular problem employee, sometimes, a short discussion between the boss and the subordinate, with specific reference to the problem, may be in order. After trying almost everything a manager or supervisor has to consider that the continuing problem employee may not be suited to a particular work situation.

QUICK STEPS TO TAKE

1. Evaluate the work environment. Make changes to relieve as much monotony as possible.
2. Revise the workflow to increase alertness.

3. Allow employees, at their discretion, to use alternative methods to accomplish the work.

4. Permit employees to work on overall assignments allowing them to decide what to do that day or week.

5. Increase cross-training of subordinates so that each of them has more skills.

6. Recognize which subordinates have lower attention spans and discuss the problem with them.

7. Be prepared to acknowledge that some employees might be daydreaming no matter what is done.

MANAGERIAL REQUIREMENT

Not every job is going to solve the problems of the world. Many jobs can be deemed as having potential for daydreaming. Throwing one's heart and soul into many jobs can be difficult. However, the front-line manager and supervisor can try to make each job as interesting as possible. It is not always easy, but what choice is there? As a minimum, the boss can show the subordinate how the job contributes to the total picture.

HOW TO INTEREST A BORED SUBORDINATE IN DOING A BETTER JOB

"Any idiot can face a crisis—it's this day-to-day living that wears you out."
ANTON CHEKOV

Boredom is a larger corporate malady and supervisory problem than most knowledgeable management people care to admit. Specifically, it causes other problems, the cause of which is not easily recognized. A dull job can be an underlying cause of absenteeism, lateness, alcoholism, drug addiction, insubordination, and other problems and abuses.

High error rates (or scrap costs) can be indicative of low interest on the part of bored subordinates.

QUICK JOB ENRICHMENT STEPS TO TAKE NOW

By making the job more fulfilling for the subordinate, even the more repetitive tasks can be made to seem more interesting. Some steps that the front line manager or supervisor can quickly take to increase job interest would include the following:

1. Explaining to the subordinate how the job contributes to the final product or service.

2. Having the subordinate handle more of his own supervision.

3. Interspersing the more interesting tasks among the more boring chores.

4. Developing alternate methods for performing the same function and permitting the subordinate to select the work method to use.

5. Installing subordinate self-checking techniques.

6. Training subordinates to do minor equipment repairs and maintenance.

7. If possible, alternating the workflow through various sub-ordinates.

8. Give overall assignments rather than piecemeal chores.

9. With individual subordinates, discuss their suggestions for making their jobs more interesting.

10. Test their suggestions, even when it does not seem sufficiently justifiable. (They may come to believe that the supervisor is seeking to improve their lot.)

11. Offer recognition for particular milestones of productivity and performance achievements.

12. Encourage any superior performance.

13. Make a "nice" fuss over a subordinate who found a new way to do some particular task.

14. Get one of the sales executives to visit the area and comment on the favorable quality of the products or services.

15. Increase cross-training so that subordinates can acquire other interesting skills.

16. Do some job switching.

SUBORDINATE WORK STATION CHANGES

While the work stations have to be functional with regard to productivity and workflow, some subordinate discretion may be in order.

Allow work station creativity to flourish. A quick fix is to allow the subordinates to make and carry out some changes in layout and the decor of their own immediate working surroundings. There are limits in taste that can be suggested, such as a prohibition against hanging nude pictures.

If the subordinates are permitted to make a few additions, such as plants, posters, and so forth., or alter the immediate layout of their work stations or office arrangement, they may take more of an interest in their work.

A little raid on petty cash for potted plants (selected by subordinates) might be helpful.

Supervisor Interest Increases Subordinate Interest

Expressions of *express* interest on the part of the supervisor encourages more interest in the work on the part of the subordinate. Even if the subordinate assembles 100 widgets, or whatever, every day, week in and week out, and nothing unusual seems to happen, the supervisor can inquire about the work periodically.

"Paul, how are we doing on the widgets?"

The supervisor can then engage in conversation about the work, any particular problems, and so on. The display of any interest may be welcome.

A Little Caution

It is always a good rule not to argue with subordinates—especially as to whether a particular job is boring or not. If the subordinate considers the job dull, accept it at that. It is pointless to argue.

While the supervisor can point out the more interesting or challenging aspects of a job, the determination as to how dull the job is can be left to the opinion of the person who is doing the job every day.

Do Not Work Against the Subordinate

The supervisor should be prepared to admit the facts as the subordinate sees them and to start from there. The boss can take the subordinate's suggestions for making the job less boring, and add more ideas.

The supervisor can compliment the subordinate for a job well done—even though the job is boring to the subordinate. A show of appreciation of the subordinate's handling of a boring job will indicate understanding and be generally helpful.

"Wilson, you have been handling the job well, and I appreciate what you are doing."

"Simon, I am very interested in the work that you are doing. Keep it up."

QUICK ACTION STEPS TO TAKE NOW

1. Acknowledge that some other subordinate problems may stem from job boredom.
2. Install programs of job enrichment.
3. Give more meaning to accomplishment rather than the function performed.
4. As far as possible, permit work station or office layout changes.
5. Have subordinates participate more in possible changes.
6. Provide more supervisory interest in even dull jobs.
7. Recognize some milestones in subordinate achievement.
8. Avoid arguing as to whether a job is boring.
9. Show appreciation for a job well done as an offset to boredom.

HANDLING THE COMPLAINT ARTIST

There are some employees who will offer complaints about the boring aspects of almost any type of job. No matter what the supervisor does, there is still grumbling. An experienced supervisor knows that some people are never satisfied. There are times when the supervisor has to have a "deaf" ear. That is, listening does not mean agreeing. It is best to remember that every operation has its fair share of complainers.

HOW YOUR SUPERVISORS CAN REDUCE EMPLOYEE WASTE

"I would [that] I could stand on a busy corner, hat in hand, and beg people to throw me all their wasted hours."
BERNHARD BERENSON

There are four areas of waste: (1) product materials, (2) supplies, (3) labor, and (4) services. The misuse of any one of these items increases costs and harms the competitive position of the Company.

Excessive waste leads to the loss of jobs. While the rule seems extreme, almost anyone in business and industry knows of companies that "bellied up" because of competition in the marketplace. Plants and operations that could not cut production costs, of which waste can be a large element, are now forever closed.

There is a difference between waste and other production or operational costs. Waste can be more readily controlled and minimized by the efforts of all of the employees. Other costs frequently come under only limited control.

SUGGESTION: MINIMIZE THE TYPICAL PROGRAMS

The usual (institutionalized) anti-waste and cost control programs include wall posters, management pep talks, notices on the bulletin boards, articles in the Company paper, and the use of the suggestion box system. These endeavors tend to make the employees conscious of only the management program. Some inroads are made—but not nearly enough.

These programs lack rationale and the affixing of responsibility.

A BETTER WAY

One of the best rationales for the control of waste and costs is that such effort makes the Company more competitive and thus provides greater job security to all levels of personnel.

The basic responsibility for the control of waste and costs belongs to front-line supervision. It is the supervisor who can monitor subordinates in order to improve cost effectiveness.

Consider this: The reason that the traditional types of waste and costs programs are not fully successful is a lack of reliance placed on the one-to-one relationship of the supervisor and the subordinate. Most of the typical programs by-pass the front line management.

CURING THE CORPORATE MALADY

Successful operations view their line management not only as a means of maintaining a certain level of productivity but also as a means of minimizing costs of that production. And, cost includes waste.

Mr. Fred Sparkplug is a gung-ho department manager. He knows exactly what is going on in his area and what he has to tolerate as waste in order to maintain the desired level of productivity.

Posters are nice, but they do not exert control. A program geared to the placing of the burden on the front line managers and supervisors, who have to carry it back to their subordinates, is more likely to meet success in the company's attempt to keep waste to a minimum.

CRUNCHING WASTE

The manager or supervisor can set an example to the rank and file, not only by turning the light out at the end of the day, but by some effort all through the day. The boss can make constant reminders while observing almost any operation. Here's how:

"Johnson, that part does not need that much grease."

"Frank, what about shorter wire leads?"

"Rosa, use non-plated screws instead of oxide plated ones on that interior assembly."

"Walter, only order the paper that you really need."

"Conley, shut off that idle machine for now."

"Arnold, do not call them. Let's fix it ourselves."

"Angela, do not rerun the report but show the corrections in red."

Waste does not necessarily improve the product or customer service.

FRONT LINE RECOGNITION AND ENCOURAGEMENT

The employee need not recommend a large cost-cutting measure in order to obtain some sort of commendation. In day-to-day activities, the front line manager or supervisor can notice and comment favorably on the small efforts of waste control. This recognition encourages many in the rank and file to look for little things (and some big ones) that help keep cost down.

"Wally, that was clever of you to repair that equipment by yourself."

"Nancy, the way you saved and reused those scrap pieces shows good thinking."

"Waldo, that's a time-saver cutting down on that daily report. Keep it up."

NICKEL NURSERS TO THE RESCUE

Anyone who thinks that GM does not want to save a nickel on every car it sells or that GE does not want to save even a penny on every light bulb it produces is not realistic. Many play down small savings, but the small savings do add up.

IMPORTANT. A workforce that is conscious about pennies, nickels, and dimes is becoming wary enough to also keep an eye on the bigger bucks.

MANAGERIAL RESPONSIBILITY

Cost control does not start with the cost accountant or other numbers crunchers. It starts with the front line manager or supervisor who initiates costs. That person puts labor expense on the job or project, causes materials and supplies to be used and requests supporting services. Usually, that person is capable of controlling and minimizing those costs—including waste.

To a large measure these front line management people are responsible for whether the bottom line is good or bad. In order for them to do a better job of cost control, they need the support and confidence of the higher levels of management.

WHAT IS THE BEST NUMBER OF SUBORDINATES FOR EACH SUPERVISOR

> *"Why only twelve?"*
> *"Sir, that's the original number."*
> *"Well, go out and get thousands,"*
> SAMUEL GOLDWYN, when filming *"The Last Supper"* and asking about the number of Apostles.

Selecting what would be the optimum number of subordinates a supervisor can handle most effectively is difficult. Primarily, it depends on the type of work being done. Workstation or desk location is also an important factor.

A widely disbursed operation requires more communication effort on the part of the supervisor and therefore lessens the number of people that he or she can control. Workers performing dissimilar functions require more of a supervisor's time, thus reducing the number of subordinates that can be effectively supervised.

The ratio of subordinates to direct supervisors is affected by the amount of supervision each subordinate requires.

There are no subordinates/supervisor ratios which are engraved in stone. While there are some industry and occupational guidelines, they are suspect. For the same reason there are no two operations (even while similar in function) that are exactly alike.

USE SPECIALIZED SERVICES

If the effort is to free front-line managers and supervisors for more supervision, then greater support services are suggested. Increased support services permit the front-line management to handle more personnel.

Example. In a relatively smaller operation or plant where there is only a limited size Personnel Department, a supervisor may have to spend a great deal of time on matters that relate to the personnel function. The supervisor has to recruit, conduct interviews, complete various types of personnel forms, and so on. Or, where there is a limited size Purchasing Department, the front-line manager is concerned with the purchasing function in addition to the duties as supervisor.

The *primary* duty of front-line managers and supervisors is to get the work out. The more administrative chores the front-line managers and supervisors have, the less time is available for direct supervision. Therefore, the smaller the number of subordinates per supervisor is the result.

CONSIDER THESE SPANS OF CONTROL

White Collar. For the professional, staff, or administrative functions, a supervisor can *generally* supervise four or five subordinates. For instance, a purchasing manager can effectively supervise four or five buyers, each of whom might have his or her own assistant or clerical support personnel.

Or, a chief engineer can supervise four or five lead engineers who individually may have designers or other personnel who report to them. A senior accountant could be expected to handle four or five accountants reasonably well.

Blue Collar. In a production situation, where the work is rather routine (few work-related problems) and confined to a relatively small area, a supervisor should be able to manage up to 20 people. Where the type of products vary and/or the operations are subject to various changes, the optimum number can drop dramatically.

In large metal fabricating and assembly work, a supervisor may be able to handle up to 10 people. Where highly technical personnel are concerned, as in electric subassemblies, the optimum number might be 8 people.

QUICK HINTS TO IMPROVE THE OPTIMUM NUMBER

1. Reduce the number of administrative chores of supervisors.
2. Decrease the work scope on remaining administrative chores.
3. Provide more training to rank and file personnel in order to reduce their reliance on supervision.

4. Have operating procedures updated and revised in much greater detail. (Make the assumption that no supervisor is available for explanations of operations.)

5. Immediately reduce any geographical dispersion of any subordinates who report to the same supervisor.

6. Realign the production flow by types of products, services or functions to be performed. Avoid using a mix of required subordinate effort.

7. Provide part-time administrative assistants where possible to increase supervisor's available time. (Why have high-priced managers doing low-paid clerk's work?)

8. Develop a system of straw bosses. Assign some supervision functions to a lead machine operator, lead engineer, or chief clerk.

9. Post signs that contain generalized instructions.

10. The front or the back of forms should bear the instructions for the preparation of that form.

11. Reduce the number of required supervisor meetings and their length. (Keep supervisors and managers in the front lines.)

12. Increase managerial training of managers and supervisors. (Place more emphasis on time management techniques.)

13. Have service groups supply more on-the-spot services.

14. For many supervisors, reduce the required number of outside contacts. (Channel inquiries and so forth to one area of responsibility.)

NEW INTERMEDIATE MANAGEMENT REQUIREMENTS

Today, in most industries, the attempt is to reduce the layers of management. The benefit sought is not merely the reduction of overhead expense. The better benefit is the improvement in communication. If there are less management layers to go through, then communication is easier, and more importantly, faster.

"Fast throughput" is the new norm. Speed and more speed. Meeting new market challenges, customer demands, consumerism, newly required services, and competitive attacks are causes for the new emphasis on fast through-put. "We can't wait a month to get the project out."

Companies are requiring more managers and supervisors to have more varied operational concerns.

The new approach: training of more managers and supervisors to handle a **greater variety** of functions, sections or departments. Just as there is cross-training of rank and file to increase the pool of available functional skills, then management people are to be cross-trained.

ADVANTAGE: Cross-trained managers and supervisors can be more valuable to the Company.

SIDE BENEFIT: Multiskilled managerial people have the potential for a greater span of control.

YOUR PERSONAL CONSIDERATIONS

Due to the trend in increased managerial span of control, managers and supervisors would do well to protect their personal economic interest by learning more skills. It is a matter of job security and mobility. The person that is merely content to know how to supervise a single type of function may be shortening his or her stay in any one place.

MAKING ALL EMPLOYEES MORE AWARE OF COST CONTROL

"You do not need an MBA from Harvard to figure out how to lose money."
ROBERT LITTLE, Chairman, Textron

While many employees may be frugal at home in order to cut their own living expenses, the same attitude does not seem to occur on the job. The sparing use of electricity, water, and so on, the reworking of tools for continued use or doing without or finding adequate substitutes seem to be admirable personal traits. Somehow, while at work, these very same people will not display any such nickel-nursing qualities.

Most of the people are not deliberately wasteful. It is just that, at work, they are not as deliberately cost conscious as they can be.

AVOID MANAGEMENT'S COSTLY WAYS FIRST

The example set by the management people is often a key to many of the attitudes adopted by all of the other personnel. Frequently, there are indications of adverse management performance and even waste. More often than not, these will come to the attention of the rank and file personnel. Some of the points that are raised by the rank and file include:

1. Excessive expenditures for top managerial travel and entertainment.
2. "Luxury" cars for certain management people.
3. Management failure to limit inventory deterioration.
4. Low training emphasis on preventative maintenance of machinery or equipment.
5. Excess expenditures on executive office decor and facilities.
6. Heavy budget for management staffing.

7. Lack of managerial planning. Panic situations arise fairly frequently.

8. Management "over-obsession" with administrative chores.

9. Duplication of effort. Excessive red tape.

10. Failure to adopt good cost-saving ideas.

These are common complaints. Whether they are justified or not is immaterial. The facts are that these "presumptions" (as they frequently are) can be a basis for a lack of cost consciousness on the part of the nonmanagement employees.

Everyone should cut costs because costs cost money.

Today, that old comedy line put another way is that more than ever before, excessive costs can cost jobs.

WHAT TO DO RIGHT NOW

1. Try to make *every* employee feel that he or she is a part of our Company.

2. Have all of the managerial people set a proper and readily obvious example of cost consciousness.

3. Encourage the rank and file personnel to help reduce expenses and costs.

THE MANAGER'S TASK—COST-AWARENESS

The front-line managers and supervisors can readily encourage their subordinates to think in terms of how much a particular operation or action will cost "our Company." Even if only some of the subordinates will go along with the concept, that is still a partial victory. Another technique is for middle managers to stress the very real threat of competition.

THE COMPETITION THREAT—A SELFISH REASON

An aspect of any cost-awareness effort that is receiving much more consideration is the resort to the threat of foreign and domestic competition. Foreign-made products have lower pricing in the marketplace and thus reduce job security. Even unions have joined in the effort to minimize the inroads of imported low-priced goods.

THE SUPERVISORY VIEWPOINT

The supervisor, foreman, department head, and section chief have to be introduced to an "owner's" attitude. That is in all situations, he or she can approach the creation of new costs by asking:

"If this were my money, would I spend it this way?"

The rationale is to use the same frugality initiatives on the Company's money as one does on his own!

QUICK COST REDUCTION MEASURES

Any managerial or employee orientation or training toward more effective cost reduction can indicate the areas likely to encourage suggestions for savings or immediate on-the-spot actions. Some of these measures could include the following:

1. MATERIALS. Consider the substitution of less expensive materials which can continue to maintain a certain level of quality; review undue specification requirements, and so on.

   Also, give thought to using more costly materials that reduce labor effort and result in overall savings.

2. DIRECT LABOR. Reduce the number of production steps to an absolute minimum and simplify or combine the remaining required steps. (Make one operation do the work of two.)

3. INDIRECT LABOR. Try to keep any support services to a minimum and combine certain activities.

4. UTILITIES. Power costs can run high. Shut down any equipment when it is not in use. Simplify and/or combine certain operations.

5. DEFECTS. Follow up on claims to equipment and material vendors; increase the returns to suppliers, develop alternative uses for defective parts. Investigate and reduce the causes of scrap.

6. SUPPLIES. Requisition only the likely necessary quantities from the supply room; return excess amounts promptly; find desirable substitutes. Low-priced supplies do not require excessive controls.

7. SMALL TOOLS. Install written controls; return even broken tools to the tool crib supervisor for possible rework; eliminate certain controls for the low-priced items.

8. EQUIPMENT. Prevent overloading; use slack periods for rebuilding or maintenance; buy good used equipment; train operators in minor repairs.

9. CLERICAL. Reduce duplication and red tape; install self-checking procedures to minimize errors.

10. SKILLS. Provide more cross-training for a greater talent pool; have more people learn about automation and computers.

11. INVENTORY. Spot check computer listings with actuals; use more care in inventory area housekeeping.

Varying kinds of operations have other areas where there can be other types of cost reduction initiatives. The point is to start in each area of the operation. *No area should be off limits.* Any such limitation can reduce cost control consciousness for most of the Company people.

HOW TO CURB THE OVERLONG LUNCH HOUR

> *"Minister of Labor: The workers of Freedonia are demanding shorter hours."*
> *"Firefly (Groucho Marx): Very well, we'll give them shorter hours. We'll start by cutting their lunch hour to twenty minutes."*
> ARTHUR SHEEKMAN and NAT PERRIN,
> from the movie *"Duck Soup"*

Whether there is a bell or buzzer system or an informal method for indicating the beginning and the end of the lunch break is immaterial for some of the employees. Actually, it is not the period of time taken for the lunch break itself but the **total** amount of time that certain of the employees can be away from their workstations or desks that is of significance.

TYPICAL ABUSE

Washing up and preparing for the lunch break and getting re-organized after the break can add up to a great deal of lost productive time. Ten minutes lost slides into twenty minutes over a period of time—especially if there is no monitoring of the abuse.

DRAWBACKS OF THE INFORMAL METHOD

TYPICAL POLICY. "We adopt the attitude that our employees are mature and that they will not take advantage of the time assigned for lunch."

ACTUAL PRACTICE. In many operations, if there is no bell or buzzer or some other formal method for indicating the starting and ending times, some of the employees will extend the lunch break. While managers may close their eyes to this lost time as being of small consequence, the few employees who get away with extended lunches will cause adverse effects on employee morale.

Where an informal method is used, any attempts to monitor for abuses are also informal and very difficult to sustain.

THE EMBARRASSMENT PLOY

"Our people have a staggered lunch hour so that we can keep the work moving."

Of course, the staggered break arrangement keeps more personnel at their work stations or desks and there is coverage in order to maintain the workflow or service. Under any system, without the vigilance by the operating managers and supervisors there are lunch break abuses and reduced productivity and performance.

Being alert is one thing: handling the abuses is another. One of the better ploys is to embarrass the errant subordinate. This is especially effective under an honor system. Try any of the following dialogues:

"Scott, I was looking for you right after lunch to handle a special job for me. It's too late now."

"Smedley, while you were out, you had a call, but I was too busy to get a message."

"Wingate, I thought you were going to handle that letter before lunch. What happened?"

"Whipple, you missed a section meeting after lunch!"

"Warren, who got your work out after lunch?"

HOW TO AVOID PRE-LUNCH SLOWDOWN

Some employees will start preparing themselves for the lunch break as much as a half hour before. These culprits start to make arrangements with coworkers, get their hair combed, put work aside, stop answering the telephones, and so forth. Production and performance suffers.

First, it's five minutes, then, ten, and soon it seems automatically to be fifteen minutes. After a while, the lengthened lunch period becomes a part of the established practice.

Things left to themselves go from bad to worse.

To counter the pre-lunch slowdown, front-line managers and supervisors should be readily evident in the department. They can be handing out assignments, monitoring the workflow, getting reports, asking questions, and generally keeping their subordinates alert to the required work load. This type of effort can be maintained right up to the designated lunch break.

How to Avoid Post-Lunch Tardiness

Likewise, after lunch, managers and supervisors can give out instructions for the afternoon workload, follow-up on earlier assignments, and generally be very obvious as to an interest in getting the work moving quickly.

Several discipline possibilities exist, including docking for lateness, withholding the granting of desirable projects, minimizing overtime, and changing the hour for lunch for some of the problem subordinates.

"Remco, I note that you have difficulty in getting back to the job at one o'clock. So, starting tomorrow, your lunch hour will start at twelve-thirty."

Understanding the Need for Discipline

How can anyone expect the more conscientious subordinates to be attentive to the lunch hour time requirements when others, who are less conscientious, get away with extended lunch hours?

On an overall basis, discipline is difficult to administer and maintain in all other areas because of the excesses of those who get away with even minor transgressions. There can be an accusation of unfairness.

A hallmark of poor overall discipline and the lack of acceptance of the rules is the disregard of time abuses.

WHY DO THEY VIOLATE THE RULES?

Frankly, we will never know completely why some subordinates choose to violate the rules or abuse privileges. One can say that it could be an anti-management attitude, antagonism against the Company, ill-feelings about the boss, or even a combination of all three.

One experienced manager contends that it would seem that such problem subordinates want to get away with something.

Another well-versed manager presumes that the cause is an outgrowth of sloppy work-related habits. The contention is that time abusers and other rule violators are not necessarily the best of workers to begin with anyway.

INSTILL COMMITMENT

It is best for the managers and supervisors not to have to be the police officers on the beat. Sure, they have to enforce the rules. However, that job could be easier if subordinates were *instilled with commitment* to the job. That effort takes a while and the benefits are more long range. Nevertheless, the technique can be very worthwhile. Instilling job commitment into subordinates starts at the job interview.

LONG-RANGE METHODS OVERCOMING REFUSALS OF OVERTIME WORK

Employee with both feet on desk: "Overtime?
Sure boss, why not?"
Cartoon on office wall

In the past decade there has been a large increase in leisure time activities. The life style of millions of workers has been changing each year—from urban confinement to a suburban setting. The desire to enjoy the benefits of leisure time and to fulfill a defined role in suburban life has cause otherwise hard-working employees to consider any requirement above the normal work week as a severe limitation on their enjoyment of their potential role.

THE SECONDARY PROBLEM

Too often, with top management's unwilling support, overtime is made to appear as a chore—even a form of punishment. If a section is not producing up to par, a threat frequently used is the fear of overtime for those who may lag behind. Semantically, "overtime" has become a negative term.

LONG-RANGE SOLUTION

Starting at the employment interview, the following dialogue may be ideal:

> "Before we hire anyone, we have to tell you about the required overtime."
> "Okay."
> "We consider overtime as a part of the job. Of course, you will get time and half pay."
> "Sounds fine."

"Is there any reason to believe that you will not be able to work about 10 to 15 hours of overtime during the week and a couple of Saturdays each month?"

"None."

"May I note in your application's comments section that you are prepared to work overtime?"

"Sure."

The effect of this and similar dialogues is to put the prospective employee on notice that a condition of employment is that there is no compunction against overtime work. The awareness that overtime is part of the job is reinforced upon the actual hiring as follows:

"Congratulations. Report on Monday morning to this office."

"Thank you."

"By the way, I want to remind you of the understanding."

"Oh?"

"That overtime is expected of you—right?"

"Sure."

During the job orientation, even though it may be informal, the new employee can be made aware once again of the overtime commitment.

UNION WARNING

If there are any collective bargaining stipulations regarding overtime, they should also be brought to the attention of the new employee.

REINFORCE THE COMMITMENT

Many people tend to "forget" the promises that they made— particularly those made at interview time. At least, no matter what ensues, the supervisor's mind is clear—there was a commitment.

The new employee has to be reinforced on the commitment in the early training and further orientation. Later on, when the subordinate is obtuse about working overtime, the commitment can be run up the flag pole.

"Mr. Weasely, you knew about the overtime requirement when you took the job."

A GOOD TOOL—A COMPUTER REPORT

Have the computer department or outside payroll service run a report listing the employees and cumulative overtime hours worked.

Nothing fancy, just an alphabetical periodic listing by section or department. It can be a by-product of the payroll processing.

Running and distributing the report is not enough. The rank and file must know that such a tabulation is being kept. One way of achieving this awareness is to discuss the report at the salary raise review time with each subordinate. During the review discussion, the dialogue can include the following:

"Weasely, I have a report that you worked only 30 hours of overtime since the beginning of the year. Is that correct?"

"Well, I guess so."

"We consider overtime as a part of the job. That's why we keep the records."

"How does that affect my raise?"

"Very directly. Because the extent of overtime is indicative of job commitment and that affects the considerations for a merit raise."

"It seems unfair to me!"

"Unfair? You had the lowest number of overtime hours. That means that others in the department had to carry an *unfair* part of your burden."

AN ADDITIONAL TOOL

The computerized report of cumulative overtime is a double tool. Not only can it affect considerations of merit raises and even promotions, but it can be used regularly to aid the front-line manager or supervisor.

Here's how. In the selection of which employee to work overtime currently, the boss can approach those with the least cumulative number of hours. A dialogue could include the following:

"Weasely, I see by the latest report that your overtime is below average for the department. Let's bring yours up."

FACING REALITY

When someone is forced to work overtime, it does not mean that they are going to knock themselves dead after five to maintain productivity. The Company could be wasting money.

It is up to the front-line supervision to be sure that goldbricks, slow pokes, work shirkers, red tape artists, day dreamers, bottlenecks, clock watchers, socializers, and so on, are not a part of the team. Overtime is only valuable to the organization if there is *comparable* productivity and performance.

WHY HAVE OVERTIME?

Despite the overtime and/or premium pay expense, the costs of equipment, facilities and certain overhead items are being spread *out* over more productivity or services. The unit costs may be reduced with overtime work and the Company can be more competitive in the marketplace.

The subordinate who contends that overtime "does people out of jobs" is not increasing employment. Nor is that short-range-view person protecting even his own job. More jobs and job security exist where costs per unit or service are lower—period.

SHORT-RANGE METHODS OVERCOMING REFUSALS OF OVERTIME WORK

"The students react to my praise of toil with great applause and loud demands for a holiday from work."

JOHN KENNETH GALBRAITH

Admittedly, the long-range methods for overcoming resistance to overtime require considerable time to install—and a bit more time until the benefits are achieved. For the operating supervisor who has to face the problem this afternoon, here are some solutions that he or she can try immediately.

THE INDIVIDUAL BIG STICK SOLUTION

Each employee who has refused to work overtime, or who wishes to work only a limited amount of overtime, should be spoken to separately. The dialogue can be as follows:

> "Mr. Weasely, we have spoken about your unwillingness to put in overtime before. Now, this Thursday, you will be required to work late."
>
> "You know that is difficult for me."
>
> "Your personal affairs are your problems. We have already entered in your personal file your past two refusals to work overtime. You are warned that a third refusal may be cause for suspension or dismissal."

It is really unfair for the other people in the section who do work overtime and carry an unfair share of the load when requested.

At times, the big stick approach can be more effectively used by the Personnel Department. There may be a greater feeling on the part of the problem employee that the threat will be carried out!

Other threatened discipline can include change of shifts, relocation of work station or desk, departmental transfer, and so on.

Threats have to be viewed in the light of possible grievances and other ramifications. However, despite a contemplated grievance, the use of threats may produce the desired overtime.

If nothing else, the supervisor can make written notes of each refusal to work overtime. This procedure, while it may go no further, may instill a fear in the subordinate that something "bad" can come of these written notes.

SIDE BENEFIT. The written notes can be saved as a reminder to be flashed when the problem subordinate has a request (like for a raise) to be made of the supervisor.

> "Mr. Weasely, you picked a good time to talk about your commitment to the job (or, whatever). I have these memos about your refusal to work overtime twice last month."

UNUSUAL CARROT APPROACH

How about offering some goodies just when the supervisor is really in need of overtime help?

WARNING. Giving away goodies on a steady basis cheapens the reward and can result in having to up the quantities over a period of time.

Consider this instance. Overtime is required at unusual hours and with very little notice. Then, try this dialogue:

> "Winslow, you have come through for us in the past."
> "Come on, boss; I have something to do."
> "You can have double compensatory time off next week if you lend a hand tonight."
> "I get double time off with pay?"
> "Yes, listen—you can use my office phone to call anyone you want to in order to change your plans for tonight."

JUSTIFICATION. The double time off is not as expensive as it sounds as overtime requires time and half pay anyway. However, when is the subordinate more critically needed—tonight or next week? During next week, some personnel substitutions can be made and the current workflow is maintained.

BREAKING THE RULES

The best managers and supervisors are "horse traders." Once in a while, a boss has to give a little in order to get a lot. To maintain productivity or to handle special or rush orders, you have to come up with a carrot—even when you do not want to and when it is against the rules.

"I do not care about procedures, Smedley got the job out."

Trading goodies for favors is one way of getting people to do what they do not want to do.

WHAT'S THE LAW

It's tricky, but the law comes down on the side of the employers who do their homework. First it is a "given" that the employer complies with all of the wages and hours laws and regulations.

Then, it is a matter that the employee undertook the job knowing that he or she may be required to work overtime (including the maximum number of possible required hours) and the possibility of weekend work. All of that extra work is not guaranteed but subject to employer request.

Next, the Company policy with regard to overtime has to be applied evenly and fairly. The employees have to be aware of the extent of discipline and the disciplinary procedures.

Anticipated legal problems with a disgruntled employee or ex-employee have to be referred to corporate counsel.

WATCHING UNION CONDITIONS

In a unionized operation, the management has agreed (in the union contract) to certain procedural steps with regard to overtime of union members. The first and repeated recommendation is to read the union contract first hand.

Too many lower and middle level management people rely on stewards, work shirkers, rumor spreaders, and other partially qualified or biased sources for information on contract overtime provisions. If the written word is unclear, and that happens too often, then request additional insight from higher levels of management or the industrial relations people.

Know management's rights with regard to overtime.

In addition to the overtime procedural steps, the contract also provides for disciplinary action upon refusal of a proper order or a refusal to work overtime when properly requested. Check it out!

OVERTIME AND JOB COMMITMENT

It is a great deal easier to get people to work all kinds of hours and days when they have job commitment. It falls on the shoulders of the front-line managers and supervisors to instill job commitment among their subordinates. It is not easy to do, but the benefits are obvious. Look at it this way; willing workers are the best people to have on overtime.

HOW TO INTRODUCE NEW TECHNIQUES MORE SUCCESSFULLY

> *"In the fight between you and the world,*
> *back the world."*
> FRANZ KAFKA

In the business and industrial world, change has become a constant pattern. Not only is there more change, but the rate of such change is in upward momentum. That is, new products and services are coming into the market much faster than previously. It seems almost pointless to fight change.

"You can't teach an old dog new tricks" may be true because the old dog does not want to learn new tricks. If Fido wanted to, you could probably teach the dog a lot.

Experienced managers know that subordinates resist training in new methods for a variety of emotional reason. People get "locked in" on certain ways of doing their job and will stonewall any attempt at change.

Frequently, even learning a comparatively new function is resisted by employees because they may have a concept of how they *think* the job should be handled. There may be little interest in someone else's ideas on how to perform the new duties.

PRECONCEIVED NOTIONS PROBLEM

People like to see things as they think they are. They have preconceived notions which conflict with reality. They "know" how a job should be done even though they may have never done that job before.

This natural inclination to resist learning new ideas can become a nuisance in many cases. There are instances where secretaries had their training and experience on a particular model of typewriter and do not wish to learn more about, or to use, a newer advanced model. It would seem that if they were not so messy, some clerks would still be using quill pens!

RECOMMENDATION: CREATE CLIMATE FOR CHANGE

In spite of the natural resistance, employees do learn how to use new equipment and to master new techniques. One basic method is to provide the right working environment for the attitude that, generally, change is for the better.

An organization that can have the attribute of being among the leaders in its industry, particularly with regard to innovations, is ahead of the game. Others have to catch up by providing the environment in which the employees become eager to learn how to do their particular job better. The benefits could include the following:

- Training is easier. (Willingness to learn makes a better trainee.)
- Cross-training programs can be more readily installed. (More people want to learn new skills.)
- Innovations are more readily installed. (Smaller learning curves.)
- Employees are looking for better ways to do their job. (No suggestion is considered "ridiculous.")
- Supervision time for training is reduced.

CONVERSION SOLUTION

All around us there are examples of how computers have changed out lives. However, in each installation, there probably was a certain amount of resistance to computerization. Yet, it was overcome. Even the top managements had to go out and learn to use the new tool. Roscoe had always operated the crimping machine. He knew how to set it up, how to affix the various dies, and even how to keep it running despite its age. Roscoe was a better-than-average employee.

Out of the blue, a methods engineer came across a new machine that was faster and had less potential for down time. No one could convince Roscoe even to go see the new machine. Roscoe offered a variety of reasons. Few of the reasons were valid, and all of which did not outweigh the benefits of the new crimping machine.

THE ACTUAL TECHNIQUE USED

First, Roscoe had to be made to feel that the work he had done for the Company over the past years is appreciated. Anyway, a loyal and true blue employee should be appreciated. (Not every organization has its fair share of loyal and true blue people.)

Second, Roscoe was given some say about converting to the new machine. Here is a frequent corporate malady; higher levels of professional and staff people or the front-office movers and shakers do not consider the input from the rank and file who have to live with the decisions that they make.

The rank and file can come with some useful suggestions. More important, they feel that they have participated in the changes. There is no question that participation encourages acceptance and a willingness to train for the changes.

OVERCOMING RESISTANCE

Roscoe has been brought into the picture. He has seen the proposals for the new equipment, the sales literature, the operating manual, and so on. He was asked for his opinion and points of contention were resolved.

Even if Roscoe should turn out to be negative, his feathers have been smoothed down. He has participated in the decision. That alone provides some level of acceptance.

SOLUTION FOR A LARGER ORGANIZATION

Even where individual conferences are not practical because there are too many Roscoes, some measures can be taken to assure some participation in changes. One useful idea is that a methods engineer conduct a survey of reaction to the proposed changes. That step implies that "everyone's" pros and cons have been cranked into the decision for the changes.

A SURPRISE BENEFIT

Amazing but true—sometimes someone on the floor or at some remote desk has an outstanding valid reason why the proposed change will not work. It does happen in the best of managed operations. While the industrial engineer or other expert may have egg on his face, an expensive mistake has been averted as a result of the survey.

SOME HINTS FOR MANAGERS TO CONSIDER

- Do not change for the mere sake of change.
- Do change for the sake of improved productivity, performance, cost reduction, error or waste control, and so on.
- Experimentation with possible changes is "in."
- Do not make changes that are not well organized as to implementation. (Disruptions can excessively postpone payoff.)
- Do monitor to insure obtaining the goals of the changes.

EXPLAINING WORK STANDARDS TO RANK AND FILE

"Never ask of money spent / Where the spender thinks it went.

Nobody was ever meant / To remember or invent

What he did with every cent."

Robert Frost, poet, *"The Hardship of Accounting"*

The average person understands the ramifications of a budget for a household. The wage earner brings home paychecks which are allocated to meet certain expenses such as rent or mortgage payments, food, clothing, paying creditors, utilities, and so on. Any excess is further allocated to savings for rainy days, a new car, or a larger home.

The same thing happens in business. Customers' checks are allocated to every day type to expenses, paying creditors, and provision for new equipment, rainy days, and the like.

In business, there are three types of expenses: labor, materials, and overhead. These are the elements for a budget. When the expenses are broken down by product, they are called the product cost standard.

ANALYZING OVERHEAD

The overhead expenses are associated with the plant operation. Such expenses include utilities, maintenance costs, services labor (such as the accountants), and others that are not directly associated with the volume of production. However, the budget or standard for each unit produced contains a portion of the overhead (indirect) expense.

As more units are produced, the overhead is spread out over more units (less overhead cost per unit.)

ANALYZING MATERIAL COSTS

The material portion of the cost standard has two variables. One is how much material is used to make each product. (Any excessive use of materials increases actual costs.) The other variable material costs is how much is paid for the materials used in each unit. (Any increase in the purchasing price of materials causes a standard overrun—at least in that variable.)

Therefore, every attempt is made to control the amount paid for raw materials put into the product and also the amount of materials used in the product. These twin variables are the material standard (or budget) for the manufacture of the product.

WHAT ABOUT LABOR COSTS?

Just like the materials standard, the labor standard has two variables that are very similar. One is the number of hours of labor that was used in the product. The second is the cost of such labor. A high number of direct labor hours for each product or paying more than the budgeted labor rate causes cost overruns.

HINTS TO BEAT THE BUDGET

1. Use supplies, utilities, and services (controllable overhead expenses) in a sparing manner.

2. Look for ways to decrease the amount of direct materials used in a product.

3. Minimize scrap and rework costs.

4. Reduce the number of labor steps used in production steps. (Find procedural shortcuts.)

5. Develop faster production techniques and use equipment that can do more steps per operation.

6. Use lower level skilled employees in more steps.

7. Train and use more multiskilled employees which may eliminate or reduce labor steps.

QUICK COMPARISON

As with the household budget, if the elements of expense (labor, materials and overhead) get out of hand or are disproportionate to the income, some of the rainy day money has to be used.

TOOLS FOR MONITORING ACTUAL COSTS

In each area of expense, management has to have certain controls that emit a signal when the expenses that are actually incurred are over budget (standard). The standard is analyzed down to each step in production. Each step's cost contributes to the total product cost and is compared to the standard.

If attaching part A to part B is supposed to take ten minutes of labor (the standard) but actually take longer, then that is a signal that the labor expenses are running over the standard (budget).

The work standards are developed by the management and the numbers crunchers in order to indicate just where and to what extent expenses are becoming excessive. The significant overruns of costs are cause for seeking ways to reduce costs.

THE SHOE ON THE OTHER FOOT

What happens when actual costs are under the standard? Well, that seems favorable. It could be. But there are two possible causes for being lower.

The first possible cause is that the standard was estimated incorrectly. That happens all too frequently. The budget for the various elements of cost could have been set too high. Therefore, the actual costs "look" better than expected.

The second possible cause is that the actual operations were more efficient than had been planned. For instance, it took less time to perform a particular step.

In either case, somebody goofed in estimating or in planning.

UNDERSTANDING STANDARDS

1. The need for standards may be difficult for the rank and file to comprehend.
2. A simple explained comparison to home budgets may create more of an appreciation of standards (budgets) at work.
3. The explanation of the elements of costs aids in the acceptance of standards.
4. The comparison of actual costs to the standard (budgeted) costs is a cost control technique.
5. Cost reduction efforts can be accomplished more readily if there is an acceptance of the purpose of standards.

SUBORDINATE ORIENTATION

Cost accounting **has always** been plagued with systems errors, human mistakes, computer snafus, unreliable overhead rates, estimating goofs, price increases, volume fluctuations, incorrect instructions, misunderstandings, wrong codings, invalid input, product or service changes, and so on.

Front-line managers and supervisors have a tough time selling the cost accounting system to their subordinates. However, budgets are way of life. Even the government has to have a budget. Because a budget or a cost standard is *a plan of action.*

MORE EFFECTIVE USE OF EMPLOYEE ON-THE-JOB TRAINING

"Hiring and training are costly, but it is infinitely more costly to have a marginal or barely average on the company rolls for 30 years."
GORDON W. WHEELING, Beckman & Whitley

The purpose of the on-the-job training programs is to provide additional skilled personnel quickly and with a minimum of economic costs of training. Many such programs do not accomplish their purpose because of poor structuring of the program and the attempt to acquire a quicker-than-should-be-expected payoff in increased production and performance.

CHECKLIST OF CAUSES OF FAILURE

1. Inadequate pool of personnel who are suitable for training. (Low emphasis on training capability in recruiting.)
2. Improper selection of trainee candidates.
3. Use of good supervisors and managers who do not necessarily have a flare for training.
4. Failure to develop a realistic training schedule.
5. Insufficient motivation provided to the trainees.
6. Low effort to obtain cooperative efforts of other talented rank and file employees.
7. Small training budgets and few desirable training tools.
8. Inadequate or minimal space devoted to training.
9. Low managerial support for training effort.

CENTRALIZED VERSUS DECENTRALIZED PROGRAMS.

Not every industrial or service operation lends itself to having special instructors, a training room or area, books and training tools, and many of the other characteristics of a vocational school. A decentralized program permits the immediate supervisor to work with each subordinate, giving that person the benefit of good experience and helping the subordinate to become more fully productive.

The reasons for centralized training programs include the following:

1. Large required increase in the workforce.
2. Insufficiently skilled people in the labor market place.
3. New and complex skills are required of more people.
4. A dramatic increase in cross-training effort. (Giving more personnel more skills.)
5. Operations requirement of multiskilled personnel.
6. Small O-T-J training efforts are proving too hectic and/or disruptive of the workflow.
7. Lack of sufficiently qualified personnel with training skills.

   Every graduate of any training program still requires additional training or reinforcement of job function fundamentals.

EVERY BOSS, A PROFESSOR

Despite training programs and inherent employee skills, *all* bosses have to devote some time to at least further training. Forgetting for the moment existing requirements, there is new equipment, new methods, new materials, differing end products., special jobs, and so on. Besides all of that, there are ways that each boss wants things done.

HOW TO TRAIN FASTER AND BETTER

Usually the immediate supervisor has some innate knowledge of which of the subordinates can learn fastest with a minimum of problems. Therefore, the boss can select the best material for training purposes.

Few managers and supervisors were fired for their teaching ability.

The boss's instruction techniques may be deficient. A knowledge of the job requirements is good, but getting it across is another matter. Here are some good background hints in getting the training lessons across:

1. Keep the employee-student well motivated. (Results are always better when the pupil wants to learn.)

2. Provide pep talks (within the training) sprinkled with a few compliments as to progress.

3. Illustrate only the right methods which produce the desired results.

4. Stay away from examples that display the wrong method as they may stick in the employee's mind and/or create confusion.

5. Recognize individual differences in learning ability. Some additional push for slow learners may be worth the effort.

6. Let the bird leave the nest. Trying to do the job is one of the best "self-teaching" techniques.

7. Divide the body of knowledge or techniques into key areas. Break the areas down into several pieces, making each piece a concept that can be grasped in one training session. "This afternoon we are going to learn how ....."

8. Impart an understanding of the total job. Explain how each learned concept or technique fits into the whole story and therefore is not disjointed or perplexing to the student.

9. Permit lots of questioning by students. Besides the answers being of help to the students, the questions may indicate weak areas of training.

10. Monitor (testing?) student performance. This effort provides insight into where additional training may be required.

11. Make comparisons between students. Those trainees who are more capable can earn the more challenging work assignments. Those who are not, would earn the more routine work.

12. Provide practice for the subsidiary skills. If someone fully understands the concepts of bookkeeping, but cannot add, then what?

13. Expect low-volume and high-error rates. For training rein-forcement, let the student find what he or she is doing wrong. Remember, self-teaching is a good training technique.

14. Distribute manuals and instruction sheets *after* class. If they are distributed during class, students will provide divided attention to the instructor. Also, they are not as likely to take notes—another reinforcement tool.

FOUR EASY STEPS FOR THE MANAGER-PROFESSOR

1. SCHEDULE. Write down a plan of learning. What should the trainee have learned the first week, second week, and so on?

2. JOB ANALYSIS. List the most important things a trainee should learn. Underline the key items. (By the way, the list is your teaching objectives.)

3. MATERIALS. Have instruction books, operating manuals, materials, parts, reports, supplies, and so on readily available to the trainee. (Be sure that everything is *current*.)

4. WORK STATION. Have the trainee's area set up exactly as the trainee is expected to maintain it. This will not only improve productivity but will also ease the instruction process.

BEING A GOOD TRAINER—A SELFISH MOTIVE

Do not forget that being a good trainer of subordinates makes a manager or supervisor better promotion material. It is an *important* personal advantage that we lay aside only for the moment. There is a more immediate personal benefit for any good manager or supervisor who also happens to be a good trainer.

"Smith can handle that chore because I trained him as to how I want it done."

Those supervisory people who are poor trainers unfortunately have to work harder. The key to success is to work less harder but smarter. Part of the effort is to be a better trainer.

HANDLING THE SQUARE PEG IN THE ROUND HOLE

"Nothing is ever accomplished by a reasonable man."
J. FRED BUCY, Texas Instruments

One of the toughest subordinates to handle is the nonconformist—the square peg in the round hole. Not that he may not be worth the effort, but it is tough.

The subordinate who does not "fit in" is not every hard working manager's cup of tea. As distinguished from most other problem employees, he is not only a challenge to his boss but to the other subordinates as well.

EASY TO RECOGNIZE PROBLEM EMPLOYEE

Rodney Noway will wear narrow ties when everyone is wearing wide ties, bow ties when all are wearing narrow ties. Rodney dons cowboy boots when everyone is sporting loafers.

His wardrobe is of minor concern compared to his work habits. Mr. Noway's work habits have a consistency pattern. At times, the consistency is infuriating. He is absolutely opposed to the way things have been done. Mr. Noway wants to change the way things are done every time.

It may be said of his religious convictions that Rodney Noway is an orthodox nonconformist. Rodney views himself as a bona fide contrarian—one who does not want to run with the herd.

CHANGING TIMES

At one time, it may be said, that a three-headed frog had a better chance of getting by the personnel department than someone like Rodney Noway. Not so, today, People like Mr. Noway are in high demand by organizations faced with a changing business environment.

The biggest and best of managed corporations are looking for square pegs. They exude change. And "change" is the new managerial commandment.

> *"We're trying to change the habits of an awful lot*
> *of people. That won't happen overnight,*
> *but it will bloody well happen."*
> JOHN AKERS, CEO, IBM Corporation
> *Business Week* Magazine 2/15/88

THE ADVANTAGES OF THE NONCONFORMIST

There are changing markets, materials, financing techniques, methods, and equipment. There are moments when the business world goes topsy-turvy. Yet, there are people in the workplace that are stuck doing some operation over and over again the same old way because that "is the way it was done last year."

Along comes Rodney Noway. He does not want to do some process the way that it was done last year—he does not even want to do it the way it was done yesterday. He takes a hard look at everything and asks, "why not do it a different way?"

"Do they really need this paperwork?"

One of Mr. Noway's advantages to his employer and boss is that he is *always* looking for short cuts. He does not want to perform any effort which does not immediately lead to the objective of the work. Unnecessary effort is not his bag.

Rodney likes work, particularly accomplishment type of work. When he completes an assignment or is at a stopping point, he inquires of his superior, "boss, what else have you got?"

THE DISADVANTAGES OF THE NONCONFORMIST

Non-conformists are not ideal team workers.

Usually, other workers will resent someone who is always questioning work techniques and methods. In addition, the nonconformist frequently is productivity and/or performance oriented.

Often, in order to justify the label of nonconformist, this type of worker does not accede to lower productivity goals of his coworkers. *He does not follow the herd.* To identify himself that he is not in the herd, he will have a high work drive.

IMPORTANT. It may be said that a nonconformist's natural enemies in the work jungle are red tape artists and make-work stiffs.

NONHERD CREATIVITY ADVANTAGE

Mr. Noway's penchant for doing things differently can lead to more innovation in the workplace. New methods, products and services can evolve in a creative-permissive work environment.

"Boss, why not pre-stamp the part number on the obverse side for ready identification?"

"Boss, I talked to the computer people, we can have backlog status on the terminal screen by next month."

Sure, these efforts rock the status quo boat and make waves for those people who feel uncomfortable with some progress. In some circles, the nonconformist with his contrarian ways is viewed as a threat.

THE BOTTOM LINE

While a certain amount of conformity is required in most organizational operations, the fresh air brought in by a nonconformist can bring ready improvement.

The nonconformist also instills a willingness on the part of many others to have another look at the way that *they* are doing things. In addition, others may want to emulate a higher work drive.

The square peg in the round hole may be just the ticket where there is an overemphasis on corporate conformity. In those operations where stagnation has taken hold, a contrarian, with rough personality edges, could be a sparkplug.

BEYOND THE BOTTOM LINE

Innovation research is an investment in the future. It either protects market portion or provides new markets, but it rarely helps the *current* bottom line. However, bringing potential innovative people into an organization now can help the bottom line currently and in the future.

PART 4

HOW MANAGERS IMPROVE INTERNAL CONTROL AND SECURITY

SELECTING THE BEST PLACE FOR A TIME CLOCK

"Work expands so as to fill the time available
for its completion."
C. NORTHCOTE PARKINSON, *"Parkinson's Law"*

Frequently, time clocks and time card racks or computer time terminals are put wherever a blank or unused wall is available. However, the available space is not necessarily the most advantageous location. To avoid certain abuses, a certain amount of thought should be given to the selection of the location of time recording devices.

Depending upon the time recording location, a certain number of employees will punch in and then avoid proceeding directly to their work area. Or, near the end of the shift, they will leave their work area well in advance of normal quitting time in order to be on their way as soon as possible.

SOME LOCATIONS TO AVOID

1. Rest Room Area. Employees could punch in and then proceed directly to the rest room, with a resultant loss of production time. Near the end of the shift, some employees will hang around the rest room awaiting quitting time.

2. Lunch or Snack Room Area. After punching in or before punching out, some employees may be inclined to have another coffee or snack.

3. Exit Areas. One of the worst locations. An employee can punch in and then immediately leave.

4. Remote Corners. Locations that cannot be readily observed by supervisory personnel invites "ghost punching" in and out. Ghost punching occurs when one employee punches in and/or out for another employee.

RECOMMENDATION: Time fraud artists and their ghosts should be subject to severe discipline including immediate discharge. Payroll theft is a crime.

5. Supply Areas. Employees could steal supply items that could be concealed in their lunch boxes, newspapers, or in their clothing while punching out on their way off the premises.

6. Near Stairs. This is a potentially big accident location. Occasionally, there is pushing and shoving when employees are in a rush to punch in or out.

AFFIXING MANAGERIAL RESPONSIBILITY

Front line managers and supervisors bear the ultimate responsibility for their subordinates being at their work stations or their desks as much of the time as possible.

A certain amount of dawdling after punching in will exist no matter where time recorders are located.

Employees can still punch in and then proceed to rest room, snack areas, or wherever—no matter how far removed. As has been said, every organization has its fair share (sometimes, even more) of goldbricks.

Luckily, it is just a few people who do not put in the time expected of them—or the time for which they are being paid. By monitoring abuses, the operating manager or supervisor is being fair to the other subordinates. How? By being aware that most subordinates are conscientious. They put in a full day's work in order to get a full day's pay. Anyone, who is doing less is passing more of the work load unto them.

"Boss, I punched in at 9 o'clock."
"You weren't at your desk until a half hour later."

CENTRALIZED VS. DECENTRALIZED

An advantage of the centralized time recording is that the Company's policies on clocking in and out can be more easily monitored.

The additional cost of decentralized time recording can be offset by having the clocks or devices closer to the work stations of the employees. In this way, there can be less abuses because an immediate supervisor can spot his or her subordinates who may wish to abuse the situation.

THE SPOT CHECK PLOY

Once in a while, the immediate supervisor can review the "punch-ins" with an actual count of the subordinates. It can be done in as full a view as possible of subordinates so that they know such a check is occasionally made. (It is part of the games that all supervisors have to play now and then.)

GETTING BACK TO BASICS

In most operations the primary method is that the immediate supervisor can account for all of his or her people and that, to a great extent, they are all working as hard as anyone can be expected.

Admittedly, that is not always easy. Nevertheless that is the basic function of front line and operating managers and supervisors.

HOW TO MAKE MATTERS EASIER

One method for making supervisory life easier is to avoid disbursing a section or department in more than one geographic location. If that in unavoidable, local chiefs may be created to help in the supervision.

Another way of making life easier for the front line supervisor is to hire more people with the right stuff—people who want to do a day's work for a day's pay. Then, petty subordinate abuses fade as a problem.

FRONT-LINE MANAGEMENT MAINTENANCE OF COMPANY POLICIES

> *"Of course they're out of date. Standards are always out of date. That is what makes them standards."*
> ALAN BENNETT, *"Forty Years On"*

Written and informal policies are labor-saving techniques for the management personnel. Every time a new set of circumstances has to be resolved, a policy is established. The procedure for establishing a policy may be complex. However, once determined, very little new effort is required when a particular circumstance arises again.

> *Policies or standard operating procedures are what the top brass wants accomplished.*

AVOID IGNORANCE OF POLICIES

Any professed ignorance of corporate policy is not only a poor alibi, or excuse, but raises certain questions of competency on the part of the manager or supervisor.

"I didn't know there was a policy."

The errant manager or supervisor should have known. Experienced middle managers would know that certain sets of circumstances probably happened before—or that such circumstances would have been anticipated.

Even where there is ignorance of the stated policy, a well trained manager or supervisor should inquire—either of a fellow middle manager or the immediate superior. Anyone taking an action without knowledge of the stated policy can be in trouble.

MISINTERPRETATION—ANOTHER POOR ALIBI

Failing to understand a policy properly, whether intentionally or not, opens almost the same questions of competency as ignorance does. If there is a possibility of "getting a wrong reading" of a policy or procedure, it behooves the manager or supervisor to make inquiries.

Admittedly, sometimes something has to be done very quickly and without sufficient time for consultation with anyone else. In a well-managed situation, this should be a seldom thing. With proper planning, most sets of circumstances can be anticipated. If not, then the planning was at fault. Either way, it does not look good for the middle manager.

OVERCOMING POLICY PROBLEMS MORE EASILY

Management meetings are opportunities for top makers and shakers to make known and to explain the policies that cover various aspects of the business. Also, they present an opportunity for the operating managerial levels to inquire about the policies and their application.

IMPORTANT. Of even greater importance to the line managers and supervisors than the clarification of certain policies is the opportunity that such meetings provide to learn the intent behind policies that affect their operations.

SMALL WORD—BIG MEANING

The key word is *intent*. It is important for the operating levels of management to fully comprehend what is *intended* by a policy. The front-line manager and supervisor can then know when to make exceptions, while still maintaining the intent of the policy.

Line managers and supervisors can make very important suggestions in the formulation of policy because they are the ones who have to carry out the nitty-gritty aspects of the policy. In most operations, such advice and insight should be well received.

SPEAK UP

Even in the best of managed operations, there are policies occasionally formulated which are counter-productive to the overall organization objectives. Front-line people can readily spot them because they are living with them.

Grumbling or calling them "ivory tower edicts" is just as counter-productive as the poorly devised policies.

The better way is to bring such policies, which may be adverse to productivity, performance, regulation compliance, cost effectiveness, sound ethics, good morale, etc., to the attention of the powers that be.

Constructive comments of corporate policy are made by good managerial promotion material.

THE DUTY—ENFORCEMENT

If we do not like a policy, it's up to us to get it changed. Until it is changed, we are required to enforce those existing policies. When we signed on into management, we agreed to do that.

Most of the rules, explanatory memos and procedures are developed from Company policy and are intended to assist the operating managers and supervisors in their effort. There is some leeway granted to middle managers. For instance, let's say that it is the Company's policy to discipline employees who are late for work. Usually, the immediate superior has some discretion as to the type of discipline with regard to each case.

The worrisome thing of policy enforcement in the work place is "fairness." While managers and supervisors have to play it as they see them, they have to avoid the charge of any unfairness. Unfortunately, frequently even the appearance of unfairness can bring reproach.

No one said that being a manager or supervisor was an easy job.

TOP MANAGEMENT RESPONSIBILITY

In an operating situation, decisions sometimes have to be made very rapidly—without further consultation. If these decisions are fair and follow the basic policy intent, then the top brass has to support the decision maker.

A failure of support is a downgrading of local management authority.

Top brass support tends to uphold local on-the-scene leadership and the power to discipline. With regard to the maintenance of organizational authority the front office has only two options. Either to fully support its front-line management or to replace them with people who have front office confidence.

There is no third way. Barring replacement (good people are difficult to find), the proven battle-tested choice for most organizations is option one, full support to the members of the front-line management.

HOW TO GET PEOPLE TO TIDY UP THEIR WORK STATIONS

"Happiness is an untrained puppy at home and a cluttered desk at the office."
UNKNOWN

Many think that good housekeeping is not an indication of an efficient operation. They consider it window dressing, for they believe that an operation can be just as productive no matter what housekeeping conditions exist.

LOSS OF EFFICIENCY

Poor housekeeping at work stations or desks can cause inefficiencies and waste. Some of the resulting attributes include the following:

1. Missing records, files, floppy disks, reports, and so on.
2. Lost or misplaced tools and equipment.
3. Unscheduled computer down time.
4. Delays in the workflow.
5. Errors and incomplete information.
6. Improper mix of parts inventory.
7. High contamination of product.
8. High scrap and rework costs.
9. Poor balance of finished products inventory.
10. High machine down time.
11. Low employee morale.
12. Employee disinterest in working overtime.
13. Discipline problems and labor turnover.
14. Poor response time for customer services.
15. Lower safety record.
16. Fraud and theft—poor internal controls.

17. Confusion on instructions.

Depending on the nature of the operation, there can be many more adverse attributes of poor housekeeping.

LOOK TO MANAGEMENT'S RESPONSIBILITY FIRST

Part of the poor housekeeping problem may not be the fault of the employees, but rather would fall on the shoulders of the management.

Let's consider this: to the extent that there is an unwieldy layout of the workflow, few intermediate storage facilities, faulty equipment, and so on, there will be reduced employee enthusiasm toward keeping neat work stations or areas. Once the managerial defects have been cured, chances are that there will be less reluctance (or excuses) on the part of the rank and file to maintain their work areas in an orderly fashion.

INSPIRATION SOLUTION

One way of motivating the subordinates to maintain tidy work areas is to set very *clear examples.* If the executive, administrative, and other offices are neat and organized, and if the managerial and supervisory work stations are well maintained, then good housekeeping habits are more easily encouraged among the rank and file. Many of them will be impressed by the good example.

CONSTANT REMINDER APPROACH

Subordinates who have poor housekeeping habits may change their ways in response to constant pressure and reminders such as the following:

> "It is no wonder that you can't find the production report considering the way your desk is organized."

> "The missing clamp is probably in those tote boxes that are improperly stacked in your area."

> "Tripped over a carton? Sorry! But your area looks like a hurricane hit it."

"The cleaning people complained about the trash around your immediate area."

CONFRONTATION APPROACH TO THE HARD-CORE

As with many other types of problem employees, a private conference may be in order for a discussion of the problem.

"Larry, you're one of my best workers, but your work area makes it look like you are the worst. Take some time and get it squared away by . . ."

ENCOURAGING DAILY CLEAN-UP

One way of maintaining good housekeeping is for the manager or supervisor to be sure that all workstations and desk areas look neat at the end of the day. If Rodney is heading home, stop him if his workstation is messy. When others become aware of the practice, they are more likely to organize their areas before quitting time. Chances are that they might keep their areas more organized during the day.

Does a cluttered desk mean a cluttered mind? Could be! There is a tendency toward lower efficiency for those people who maintain any kind of sloppy work habits including poor area housekeeping.

UNION OBJECTIVES

"I'm not on the cleaning staff."

Unions should not be opposed to good housekeeping as it improves employee morale, group solidarity and safety. Some crafts might resist certain clean-up chores as not being consistent with their job descriptions.

Read and know the contract.

Chances are that Charley is wrong again. Most contracts provide provisions for housekeeping effort at workstations. If Charley resists, he may be insubordinate. Once again, check the contract.

CHECKLIST SOLUTION

For the more difficult problem operations, a written checklist of housekeeping activities is advisable. The checklist may be posted, made a part of the training manual, put into the operating manual, and distributed to the employees. The list can offer a guide of what is expected of the employees with regard to good housekeeping.

PRESSURE AND MORE PRESSURE

We return to one of our favorite old stories of the woodchopper who made his living by chopping wood for the villagers. One icy cold winter, he had plenty of orders for firewood. But, he could not find time to sharpen his ax. As he worked harder, the ax got duller, and duller, and duller. The poor fellow didn't have time for sharpening the ax. The dull ax made him work harder and harder to keep up with orders.

The analogy in any operation is this: expediency in the workplace frequently prevents us from doing the chores (like keeping our areas organized) that we should be doing all along. Sloppiness makes the work that much harder to do.

CONTROLLING WHITE COLLAR CRIME

> *"Any company executive who overcharges the government more than $5 million will be fined $50 or have to go to traffic school three nights a week."*
> ART BUCHWALD

We are going to call him, Mr. Willy Wilely. That wasn't the name that he had used at his place of employment, or at the job before that, or even the one before that. Mr. Wilely doesn't use his own name but has used other peoples' names quite regularly.

Supposedly, the last time that Mr. Wilely used his own name was when his mother checked him into elementary school.

Mr. Wilely works pretty much of the time. His job? Let's put it this way, his occupational skills—the way that he makes real money—is *not* taught at any vocational schools or colleges. Despite the job descriptions imposed by various Personnel Departments, his true vocation is being an impostor.

WHY BE AN IMPOSTOR?

Being an impostor allows Mr. Wilely to gain work at a Company fairly quickly—which by itself is a nice reward. When inside of the organization, if the opportunity exists, he can proceed to try his more unsavory skill. He will attempt to ransack the Company's bank accounts.

GAINING ANOTHER IDENTITY

Mr. Willy Wilely hangs around employment offices, puts help wanted ads in the newspapers (replies to the box number, please), and generally looks to acquire current resumes and completed job applications.

He screens them as well as most personnel people do. What is he looking for? An identity. One that closely resembles what he can handle and fits in with his goals—a job entry as a senior clerk or equivalent position in some purchasing section or an accounting department.

He prefers identities of people who do not have current jobs. (Nobody would call him at work!)

GETTING PAST PERSONNEL

No sweat! He looks good, has the required amount of experience, and is within the salary range. Only in rare instances does Mr. Wiley get ruled out because of some inconsistencies in the background checking. At the level being considered, few interviewers are going to conduct an FBI investigation.

GETTING HIRED

Mr. Wiley has a lot of experience in surviving interviews.

In the interview with the immediate supervisor, he speaks well, provides a good first impression, displays self-confidence, dresses okay, and has good grooming. In addition, he is able to answer most of the technical questions, has an understanding of the overall systems, wishes to learn, and not only all of that, he can type. Chances are that he is the best candidate for the job.

"Welcome aboard, Mr. Wiley."

IS IT THAT EASY?

Unfortunately, it is being done and fairly often.

Mr. Wiley, as an impostor, adds a little "insurance" to his technique. To avoid or minimize any identity problems through coincident circumstances, and to reduce possible checking, Willy takes only jobs that are out of town.

"I just relocated here so my wife can be near her parents."

Coincident circumstances would include that someone at his new place knew someone at his old place of employment. That might unravel the identity.

WILLY WILELY BECOMES A HARD WORKER

To seemingly justify hiring, Mr. Wilely is quick to take on a great deal of responsibility. He likes a lot of work. For one thing, he wants to work overtime and Saturdays. In addition, Willy wants to learn the existing systems.

HIS GAME PLAN

1. Increase other people's confidence in him.
2. Learn the internal controls. Which people can sign which documents?
3. Find out where blank checks, purchase orders, vouchers, and so on, are stored.
4. Know the computer reporting system. Get copies of computer expense coding lists.
5. Determine how in depth are controls during evenings and weekends.
6. Find glaring weaknesses in the reporting methods.

TESTING THE WATER

During overtime or on a weekend, Mr. Wilely, with the aid of a typewriter, a pen, and a good copying machine produces a doctored set of documents. He checks and rechecks his work for every possible inconsistency. If blank checks are not available for forgery, Willy puts the set of documents in the "in" basket to be paid.

Previously, Mr. Wilely has had the foresight to set up drop addresses and bank accounts all seemingly legal.

Mr. Willy Wilely has gone into business for himself.

MILKING THE CASH COW

Willy rechecks what he has done, looks through reports to see how the transaction appears and smiles at his handiwork. He considers some improvements, and proceeds to make unnoticed raids on one of the Company's bank accounts.

The job hazards

If caught, Willy Wilely will be fired. There is a chance he will be arrested. If he makes some restitution, any charges may be reduced or forgotten. The criminal matter is a long drawn out situation for the Company which at times it would rather scatter under the rug. (After all, it is embarrassing and bad press for the Company.) In the usual worst case, the culprit serves six months.

For the skeptics

"Willy Wilely can't exist in our Company."

Mr. Wilely and others (some better and some worse) like him have burrowed into and ripped off the most renowned and best managed companies. If there is any doubt, investigate.

RECOMMENDATION: Find out what your employee bonding insurance company underwriter can tell you.

The total extent of employee defalcations are in the hundreds of millions. Rest assured that Mr. Wilely is a nickel and dime artist. However, by being that, he gets around more. As a matter of fact, "Willy" could be in your personnel department reception area right now, or maybe working down the hall.

IN GOD WE TRUST—USE INTERNAL CONTROLS FOR ALL OTHERS

"I generally avoid temptation unless I can't resist it."
MAE WEST

It is only the most trusted that are going to accede to temptation as they frequently are endowed with the opportunity. We do not have to worry about the temptation of those we do not trust as we avoid giving them a chance.

Frequently, we place trust in certain management people because we think that the risk of exposure will keep them on the straight and narrow path. That is not always possible.

First, the trusted person tends to ignore risk because he may feel that the trust placed in him may avert a possible review and exposure. Second, there is a tendency to overrely on trust which we developed by some instinct.

FALSE HOPE

Avoid the "too-much-to-lose" syndrome.

We tend to think that people in positions of trust are not going to steal from their company because that could ruin their career, and they could go to jail and pay heavy penalties. They would end up with a life in tatters.

A white-collar management criminal has *two* rationales for his actions. One is that because of his "trustworthiness" there is not likely to be a check. The other rationale is that he believes that his particular scheme is "foolproof."

"Trust everybody, but cut the cards."
FINLEY PETER DUNNE

TESTING A "FOOLPROOF" SCHEME

Typically, the white collar criminal does not try to rip off *all* of the company's bank accounts in one fell swoop. He stages a test. If that initial comparatively small rip off does not cause queries, he can replicate his action again and again.

Big numbers can draw unusual attention and then possible exposure. So, rather than try for any one big defalcation, the culprit pulls a number of smaller rip offs over a period of time.

FEEDING THE HABIT

One of the reasons that apprehended white collar criminals cannot make major restitution and pull some chestnuts out of the fire is that they no longer have the loot.

Significant restitution is a seldom thing.

The culprit has absorbed the increased cash flow into his budget. As a matter of fact, he is almost forced to continue with his rip offs in order to support his new increased level of spending.

The culprit has invented a cash machine which he cannot stop.

POTENTIAL BACKFIRE

When the culprit is caught, the shortage of available cash or equivalent does not prevent the court-ordered loss of the culprit's other assets including his home.

A CASE OF TRUST

We are going to call him Joe Honest, because he has more than enough trouble already. All of it brought on by himself.

At 27, Mr. Honest went to work for a giant financial services institution. He had also passed the bar exam.

In the 11 ensuing years, Joe Honest worked his way up the corporate promotion ladder very well. One promotion after another. A really great success story.

Before his undoing, he had become a senior vice president. A fast track manager in a fast track company.

Joe married, had three children and lived in a nice well-to-do community.

Why not trust honest Joe Honest? After all, he had a lot to lose by pulling any stunt whatsoever against his company. He was a top mogul at work, an attorney and was enjoying a good life.

STATE COURT RECORDS

Mr. Honest was found guilty of stealing $186,000 from his employer. The same company where he had earned a living for 11 years and which had given him a high position of honor and trust.

His "foolproof" ploy? The former senior vice president had misappropriated funds into fraudulent corporate bank accounts that he had set up and had personally controlled.

SENTENCING SCENE

The court had ordered restitution. Mr. Honest had a partial amount available for such purpose.

The defense attorney argued against a jail sentence for his client. The judge listened very carefully but sentenced the former executive to five years in jail.

A CAREER DOWN THE TUBES

As an attorney, Mr. Honest knew the risk of committing fraud possibly more than most people. So risk was not a great deterrent as against temptation. At age 38, with a lot going for him, a promising career comes to a screeching halt.

INTERNAL CONTROL LESSON

We have to accord people a certain amount of trust in order to accomplish much in the business world. However, we do not have to rely on trust alone. Remember, usually it is someone else's money that we are trusting someone else with.

There are other people who may be guilty of improperly handling other people's (the company's) money. Those managers who are lax in installing and maintaining internal controls may be permitting temptation to run its course.

Overreliance on trust and/or the concept of fear of exposure may be excuses for the departure from good business practices.

Most managers recognize that duty. (Otherwise, defalcations and embezzlements won't be the exception, but the rule.) Each major procedural step in any system has to be viewed with the concept of adequate managerial and financial control.

REDUCING EMPLOYEE GAMBLING ACTIVITY

> *"If there was no action around, he would play*
> *solitaire and bet against himself."*
> GROUCHO MARX (of his brother, Chico)

From time to time, almost anyone will make a small wager on the outcome of a Saturday or Sunday football game, the American League playoffs, or even on the Company bowling tourney. Such wagering is trivial and largely of no consequence to management.

However, where individual employees pursue an avocation of distributing football cards, collecting bets, or disseminating gambling materials, or conducting any other wagering activities—whether during working hours or at any time on Company premises—such activity should be stopped.

WATCH COMMUNITY RELATIONS

If any gambling becomes common knowledge in the community, then community relations may be adversely affected. Many persons, who have moral or religious views against gambling, may be opposed to any community support for the Company in municipal zoning or other situations that require a measure of local support.

THE OTHER ADVERSE CONSIDERATIONS

1. Gambling is not an innocent employee hobby. There have been instances where it has grown severely out of hand.
2. Gambling is a significant distraction from productive effort.
3. Gambling encourages borrowing among employees and requests for advances against salary.
4. Gambling can lead to the increased use of the telephones for nonbusiness purposes.
5. Gambling can increase the potential for white collar crime among those who handle Company transactions.

6. Gambling can cause disputes and even fights among employees.

7. Gambling may attract unsavory characters to the premises.

8. Gambling is a distraction which can reduce quality and performance.

9. Gambling can bring the authorities to the premises.

CASE STUDY

Every Friday, during the season, Charley came to work with football cards—a listing of the games to be played that weekend with an indicated point spread. He distributed the cards in the morning to interested employees.

In the afternoon, after most employees had cashed their payroll checks, Charley collected the bets. Every Monday, Charley went around and paid off the winners. It seemed innocent enough to Charley's boss and no attempt was made by the boss to curb the activity.

One day, an employee's wife called the plant manager. She told him that her husband had lost quite a bit of money on the football cards. She had talked it over with her minister, who recommended that she promptly call the plant manager.

There was a real threat to the Company image in the local community.

Charley's boss, who did not profit from Charley's gambling activities, was called into the head honcho's office for some explanation as to what is going on in the department—and whether there was enough work in the department to keep everybody busy.

No front-line manager or supervisor can come out of such a meeting looking good.

Charley was given a written warning about the gambling activity with a threat that a recurrence can cause his discharge. The losers? Charley and his boss, who, by the way, never gambled.

It's 8 to 5 that managers and supervisors will lose if serious gambling activity exists among their subordinates.

QUICK STEPS TO TAKE NOW

1. No significant gambling activity can take place without the knowledge of the immediate supervisors. At any time, top management can survey the supervisors in order to determine if any gambling activity is taking place.

2. A written policy can be developed, stating that gambling activity is prohibited on the premises at all times. Any proved infraction of the policy could cause suspension or dismissal. Further, it is understood that the Company can ask the local police for assistance in curbing gambling activities.

3. Front-line managers and supervisors should keep employees from other departments out of their departments if they have entered for the purpose of gambling activity.

4. Most union contracts provide for disciplinary action for illegal activities. The contract terminology usually has to be broadened to include all such activities whether there is a prosecution or not.

5. Any gambling paraphernalia that is discovered should be trashed. Any widespread gambling that is uncovered should be referred to the corporate counsel for action.

WARNING AGAINST LACK OF WRITTEN PROHIBITION

In the matter of General Cable Corp versus IBEW, Local 1800, an employee was fired for operating a football pool, among other things. He openly distributed football cards and collected the bets. There was little question on the evidence.

However, the discharged employee was returned to his job by the labor arbitrator. This was largely because there was no anti-gambling provision in the union contract nor did General Cable have a written prohibition against such activity.

WARNING AGAINST LACK OF ENFORCEMENT

Let's see what happened in a case where there were written Company policies. In the matter of Fargo Rubber Company versus Rubber Workers Local 141, eight employees were discharged. It seems that they were rolling those 7-11 cubes until the early hours of the morning in defiance of written policies.

The labor arbitrator's verdict? Reinstatement. Fargo Rubber had failed to enforce the anti-gambling policy in the past. Therefore, the sudden enforcement was on unsuspecting employees.

THE TREND AND THE BOTTOM LINE

With exceptions for good reasons, as indicated above, labor arbitrators and courts support employers in their quest to reduce gambling activity on their premises. Gambling is not just a matter of whether it is a crime or against public policy, which it is, but more than that.

Serious gambling is a distraction from productivity and performance. It can and does disrupt the workflow. In addition, employee gambling could lead to personal financial problems for which the Company might surreptitiously end up paying the bill through theft or fraud.

REDUCING SUPPLY THEFTS—A PETTY NUISANCE

> *"Conscience gets a lot of credit that belongs to cold feet."*
> ANONYMOUS

Without a doubt, one of the aggravations of being a manager or a supervisor is contending with the theft of supplies. It is not just the loss of the dollar value of the thefts that is annoying, but also the constant reordering of items that usually have just been restocked.

ANYTHING GOES

Any experienced facilities manager or office supervisor can relate that the varieties of items that are constantly stolen is remarkable. Included in any list would be paper and pencils from the office supply closet, salt shakers from the cafeteria, toilet paper and towels from the washrooms, and so forth.

It would seem that a few people have the following creed: "What is loose is mine, what's nailed down, becomes loose."

WHO IS THE CULPRIT?

The executive who takes home a few colored markers in order for his child to complete a coloring book is setting a bad example in attitude. Nor is the executive, who takes a staple gun home for his hobby, helping matters much ether. This type of minor pilfering engenders an attitude of, "Why not?"

A few employees in most operations do not require examples of poor attitude toward the property of others.

Good example does not eliminate ALL petty supply theft.

WHY THE RIPOFF?

Here are some of the possible reasons for employee-stockpiling:

1. Anti-company attitude.

2. Anti-managerial attitude.

3. Sniping at authority.

4. The thrill of getting away with something.

It comes down to this: the hard core petty thief generally has a low regard for the work situation. Usually such a person is not the best of workers.

In addition to all of the above, the hard core petty thief is a coward. Such a person usually has cold feet—if he had the nerve, he would rob banks.

It is not economically justifiable to lock everything up. (Besides, most employees are honest.) The problem employee is a sneak thief and the chance of catching such a person in the act is low. Simple security measures will reduce some supply inventory shrinkage.

CASE STUDIES

1. One company kept the supply cabinets in the hallways which made for easy access by all of the employees without any observation. To remedy this, they moved the cabinets into office service areas where they were in direct view of supervisory personnel.

2. At another company, the supplies were divided into two categories, high priced and low priced. The lower priced items such as pencils, paper clips, rubber bands, and so on, were kept in unlocked closets. The more attractive items such as staple guns, reams of bond paper, and so on, were kept in locked cabinets for which only the supervisors had keys.

THE BENEFITS OF CONTROL

Without a lot of red tape (avoidance of requisitions), a certain amount of theft reduction is possible. Relocating supply cabinets, putting them under observation, and segregating items by their cost are steps that reduce the nuisance of theft without unusual effort.

THE OPERATING SUPPLIES

Almost any employee will take home some nuts and bolts. Write it off to the cost of doing business. However, parts bins can be centralized and controlled to some extent if they are under supervisory observation.

Getting caught

Finally, someone has been caught! The tough question is, what should the penalty be?

In the old west, horse thieves were hung by the neck until dead. Cattle rustlers faced the same fate. Why? Not to get the livestock back or to teach the dead thief a lesson. The purpose of that extreme and barbaric penalty was further prevention.

Discharge or lengthy suspension is very drastic, usually when compared to the value of the theft. The justification is not that the penalty fit the crime but that the penalty serve as a deterrent to others.

In the matter of Kaiser Aluminum and Chemical Corporation versus Steelworkers, Local 5124, an employee had been caught stealing a small drill. After a fuss, the union persuaded the company to agree to reduce the penalty to a 51-day suspension without pay.

It is not for the value of goods that the punishment has to be severe, but for the nature of the act.

How tough is tough?

Discharge is drastic. Such a separation can ruin a career and/or another chance for a job. Few organizations would want to hire someone who has been discharged for stealing!

A better way

The discharge penalty may be as bad as hanging. A more suitable penalty may be suspension. For one thing, when the culprit does return to work, he or she becomes a living, walking example to others—more constant reminder of the folly of theft from the Company. That advantage is not derived by discharge.

The length of the suspension can vary with the nature of the act and other circumstances. Such other circumstances could include the current need for tighter discipline.

HANDLING THE DISGRUNTLED EX-EMPLOYEE

*"Revenge, the only debt that people wish
to pay promptly."*
MAX GRALNICK

One of the toughest assignments any management has to face
is the handling of the problems that are created by disgruntled
former employees. Make no mistake, it is a sticky mess.

Look at it this way. As an employee, there was a relative
give-and-take relationship which provided for some sort of desirable
solution to a problem. Now, after the separation, any possible
reins on the employee's behavior that existed before are more
or less eliminated.

TYPES OF DISGRUNTLED EX-EMPLOYEES

PASSIVE. This disgruntled ex-employee sulks. Mr. Wimpy shoots
off his mouth on occasion, but that is the extent of his adversarial
behavior. Nevertheless, Wimpy is harmful as he can create a
bad image for the Company by word of mouth although the
effect is usually very limited.

LEGAL BEAGLE. This upholder of the law will go to every
governmental agency, seeking assistance in righting the "wrong."
"The law is on my side." Attempts can be expected at trying
to obtain an attorney to help in the "crusade."

VIGILANTE. This ex-employee would like to take the law
into his own hands. Usually, there has been a marked failure
of governmental agencies and/or an attorney to help render "justice."
While rare, arson, vandalism and sabotage are potential hazards.

LONG-RANGE SOLUTIONS

1. SCREENING. Pre-employment interviewing techniques and
   careful screening can provide an insight as to the psychological
   attributes of potential employees. Applicants with a history

of having difficulties with employers or who evidence adverse situations in schooling or even in home life may have tendencies that, while not necessarily anti-social, might indicate the possibility of their being problem employees.

While almost everyone has emotional problems of one sort or another, a large majority of people have learned to cope with their problems—at least to the extent that they are capable of being good employees.

Careful screening of applicants for those who are adverse to the work situation may reduce the potential for disgruntled ex-employees.

2. GRIEVANCES. Every relationship between people produces problems. In the interest of productivity, management has to try to resolve the problems between subordinates and itself. Grievance procedures that permit a full airing of problems can tend to reduce employee dissatisfaction—at least to the extent that the grieving employee has heard the other side of the story.

Front-line managers and supervisors who are patient listeners let unhappy employees get a lot off their chests.

BENEFIT 1: Reasonably happy subordinates are easier to work with.

BENEFIT 2: Reasonably happy subordinates are less likely to be disgruntled ex-employees.

3. EXIT INTERVIEW. Many organizations require that every departing employee go through the procedure of having an exit interview, usually with the Personnel Department. In addition to the perfunctory matters such as turning in credit cards, manuals and tools, address updating for W-2's, and so on, any possible grievance can be discussed with the departing employee.

Some of the dialogue can include the following:

"Charley, you worked for Mrs. Norman. How is she as a boss?"

"Willard, what is the real reason that you are leaving our Company?"

"I see that Mr. Shawne is letting you go. What is *your* side of the story?"

Exit Interview Advantages

A dialogue with a departing employee can serve two purposes. First, the employee has a chance to air his or her gripe. Getting the gripe out into the open might prevent some sulking about it later on. Second, the interviewer can become aware of which of the departing employees could become problems after separation. Then, at least, management can be alerted to a potential adverse situation.

SIDE BENEFITS. The exit interview can provide some insight as to why employees are leaving and what their gripes are at that time. This effort could lead to recommendations for improvement in employee-management relations.

Quick Short-Range Solutions

1. Ask the disgruntled ex-employee to come into the Personnel Department (or to see the ex-supervisor) to discuss the grievance.

2. Avoid blackmail. "If you do not . . . then I'm going to file a complaint." Advise the ex-employee that he or she has every right to go to the appropriate agency to complain. Gather documentation and organize the facts in order to be able to demonstrate the Company's viewpoint at any possible hearing or litigation.

3. If there is a legal issue involved and/or as soon as the ex-employee engages an attorney, notify the Company counsel and bring the matter up to date.

4. If the ex-employee should threaten sabotage of any kind or bodily harm to anyone, the police can be notified. Once again, seek the advice of corporate counsel.

Would-Be Whistle Blowers

There is a public perception that whistle blowers of one kind or another are good for the public interest. Frankly, that has not always been the rationale for someone to be a whistle blower.

*Experienced managerial people can attest that, more
often than not, some whistle blowers are out for revenge
of some sort over a personal grievance.*

Proof? Why does the whistle blower live with the adverse
situation for 5, 10, and sometimes 15 years before coming out
of the closet and hollering? Obviously something else triggered
the "expose."

Of course, some whistle blowers are true reformers. Their
value to society can be immeasurable. However, many are not.
They have embroidered a would-be, one-side-of-the-facts case and
have stepped into the limelight. Their tools are incomplete or
slanted information. Their motivation may be revenge for some
kind of slight which they may be slow to admit to.

*It may be desirable to handle any kind of whistle
blower as one would handle any other kind of
disgruntled ex-employee.*

HOW TO CONTROL EMPLOYEE SABOTAGE

*"The guerilla must live among the people as the fish
lives in the water."*
Sayings of MAO TSE-TUNG

There is probably more sabotage going on than most managements would care to admit. Frequently, the sabotage is identified as "accidents" or, more often, "vandalism by outsiders." It is true that there is a certain amount of "outsider vandalism." As a manager, compare the motive for vandalism against the penalty for getting caught.

How many people would risk iron bars and gray walls for the thrill of vandalism. Not too many! Sabotage is sabotage.

Quick Steps to Consider Now:

1. Are the front-line managers, supervisors, forepersons, and so forth on the floor most of the time during business hours?
2. Are burglar alarms tested regularly?
3. How about the sprinkler system? Could your premises pass a fire marshall's inspection?
4. Have passes, badges, and keys been returned by ex-employees?
5. Have former security personnel returned uniforms, and so on?
6. Is an updated current list maintained of premise's keys holders?
7. Are there supervisory people who have the responsibility to check that "exit only" doors are always secure?
8. Do housekeeping procedures prevent the accumulation of trash and flammables?
9. Are the roof exits secured?
10. Are production mishaps and other accidents reported and analyzed as to the causes?
11. Do guards or other security personnel report all suspicious incidents? Is there a written incident reporting system?

12. Are parking lots and outside areas sufficiently secured?

13. Is there a periodic check of any vandalism to outside fences?

14. At night, are outside areas sufficiently lighted?

15. Is the computer department a highly restricted area?

16. Are back-up or "grandfather" files maintained for all computerized information?

17. Are the back-up files periodically moved to more remote locations?

18. What is the extent of screening of job applicants?

19. What is the procedure for the analysis of high cost scrap items?

20. During collective bargaining periods, are additional guards and security procedures in use?

21. If outside guard service is used, has anyone reviewed their union contract?

22. Do the switchboard operators, receptionist, and so on, have the telephone numbers of police, fire departments, and ambulance services readily available? Is there a procedure for the reporting of extraordinary telephone calls.

23. If operations are in a multitenanted building or industrial park, is security coordinated with these other tenants or operations?

24. Is security coordinated with other nearby Company facilities?

25. Can unauthorized personnel be readily denied access to the more critical areas?

26. Are boiler rooms, utility closets, wire rooms, and so on, always locked? Who controls access?

27. Are ALL locks and keys occasionally changed?

28. Are the managers and supervisors knowledgeable in the handling of trespassers?

29. Do the visitors' procedures need some tightening up?

30. Do the executives, and middle management personnel provide "look in" visits in off hours and weekends? Are such visits on a *nonregular* timing basis?

THE LONGER RANGE SOLUTIONS

Frankly, most companies are vulnerable to the employee who in *dedicated* to commiting an act of sabotage. (Even the army is vulnerable and they have three million rifles and a half million machine guns.) Putting a police officer next to every machine, desk, utility locker, or whatever, is cost prohibitive.

At best, management can only reduce the opportunities for sabotage by use of the quick solutions listed above. The longer-range solutions require some additional effort but are, in part at least, effective in that potential saboteurs are reduced to a possible few.

1. EMPLOYEE MANUAL. Whether the manual is distributed only to supervisory personnel or to the rank and file as well, it can contain the admonition that any employee who is caught damaging Company property *deliberately* is subject to discharge.

2. IDENTIFICATION. The use of colored identification badges is suggested. The color is indicative of which department the employee reports to—the purpose being that anyone who is wandering around can be more immediately identified as not belonging to a particular department.

3. FIRE REPORTING. All fires, no matter how small, should be reported to the local fire department—even if they are extinguished almost immediately. Management may request a copy of the fire marshall's report in order to ascertain the cause of the fire. Suspiciously started fires may be reason for further concern.

4. POLICE ASSISTANCE. All acts of wanton destruction to the premises should be reported to the local police immediately. In this manner, they are put more on the alert and usually will provide sufficient additional patrolling.

5. STRIKE PROBLEMS. In the event that a strike might be considered, supervisory personnel should be advised in advance as to what extra precautions should be taken. A written strike-prepardness procedure for supervisory people can include the following:

   a) A list of emergency phone numbers.

   b) The location of fire alarm stations.

c) The home phone numbers of managerial personnel.

d) Reporting methods for "accidents" and incidents.

e) Location of standby facilities and equipment.

f) Use of alternative production or service methods.

g) Emergency equipment repair methods.

h) Warning to be given to nonstriking personnel.

i) Premise entrance procedures.

j) Required attitudes toward strikers and pickets.

k) Special requirements for company and other vehicles.

PROFILE OF THE SABOTEUR

As with other similar problem employees, the saboteur is a sneak. He is more cowardly than the petty supply thief because his risks are greater. The saboteur is prone to cause destruction at long range—far from his home base.

A saboteur usually avoids his own immediate work area because he might be readily suspected.

The saboteur is usually not a loner. He favors "action committees" and seeks people like himself who favor "doing something" instead of "just talking." A reason for seeking the sympathetic colleagues is that if he does commit an act of sabotage, he desperately does want someone else to know what a "hero" he really is.

Usually the saboteur is anti-authority—not only against the Company and/or its management, but sometimes even against his own union and/or its officers.

"The union isn't doing enough."

Because of cowardice, simple precautions against acts of sabotage are cause for the commensurate reduction of such acts. Frankly, my dear, the industrial saboteur is not the type to charge up San Juan Hill or to volunteer to be dropped behind enemy lines.

Where security precautions exist, the "hero" backs away.

IMPROVING COMPUTER DATA SECURITY

*"Our computer system is very updated. It gives no
information to those who need it, and plenty to those
who do not."*
UNKNOWN

No sooner was the commercial computer age upon us then we
became aware that computers were also a tool for misuse. Not
just innocent errors on the grand scale but actual pilfering of
information and outright fraud.

Today, there is a quiet "war" going on all around us. On
one side there are many brainy technicians figuring out how
to make computer systems and their contents more secure from
misuse and intrusion. They are constantly revising both the hard-
ware and the software.

On the other side of this battle zone, there are equally
brainy people trying to figure out how to undo what the other
side is doing.

INVENTING A BETTER LOCK

The most common lock and key method for the remote use of
computer systems is the granting of identification numbers and
pass words (keys) to legitimate users. The use of a look-up
table (a lock) in the computer system security software containing
valid ID numbers and passwords.

The result is that someone who attempts to gain access
by using an invalid ID and/or password would be denied access
to the computer stored files.

WARNING: LOOK OUT FOR COMPUTER NUTS

There are people who surreptitiously develop programs which
have "hit and miss" routines. Upon gaining entrance to the first
security level of a computer system, these routines try various

combinations of numerals and characters in an attempt to come up with a valid ID and password (a hit).

A high speed remote computer and an efficient "hit and miss" routine can develop and test millions of possible combinations in minutes. Therefore, computer systems which have minimal security can be vulnerable to intrusion by this subculture of computer nuts—illegal hackers.

RECOMMENDATION: ALLOW ONLY THREE STRIKES

The most common way of defeating the "hit and miss" programs is the use of a maximum number of permitted entrance attempts. After three invalid attempts at an ID and password in a single connection, the computer software will disconnect the incoming call from the computer system.

DRAWBACK. Of course, the "hit and miss" program can have a subroutine set of instructions which will automatically redial any number from which it receives a disconnect—a new dial tone.

However, the disconnect procedure will dramatically increase the telephone toll time it takes for the "hit and miss" program to work. We are talking months and/or years, instead of minutes to test the millions of sets of ID and password possibilities.

Some disconnect software routines will invalidate an ID upon receipt of a flawed password.

SHORTCUTS

The illegal hackers have not thrown their "hit and miss" programs away. Instead, they have developed subroutines which try to first approximate the size of a valid ID and password. Size information can dramatically reduce the number of permutations that a "hit and miss" routine has to go through to obtain a valid ID and password.

SOLUTION: USE CALL BACK PROTECTION

Let's get back to the look-up table. The security program can be designed so that upon receipt of any ID and password, the computer refers to the look up table for validity. If valid, the computer system disconnects and automatically dials a telephone number or extension that is on the look-up table next to the valid ID and password.

Here's how it works. A user makes a call into the computer, enters his or her ID and password, gets a validity signal and then hangs up. A moment later, the phone rings, the user answers and has electronic entrance into the computer files.

This procedure eliminates the possibility that someone with valid ID's and passwords, who is not at a previously prescribed phone or extension, can gain computer file entrance.

ANOTHER PLOY

Back to the look-up table. In addition to the other security steps, one more can be provided. Its purpose is largely to reduce the efforts of nosy people. Next to each valid ID and password we can insert an access level or storage area code.

This feature means that a valid ID and password can only gain entrance (access) to a limited number of computer files. For instance, a manager wouldn't want an inventory clerk (or even an outsider) to roam around the computer files related to the payroll processing.

The inventory clerk's ID and password would permit only that party's entrance to the inventory and related files—nothing more. However, the payroll people's ID and password would have an access code permitting entrance to the payroll files.

SEPARATED AND DISCHARGED EMPLOYEES

For any person leaving employment, his ID and password would be promptly killed on the look-up table.

IMPORTANT. When any of the programmers leave the Company, there may be a need to significantly change the entire software security system.

RECOMMENDATION: SUNSET ROUTINES

The look-up table can contain one more important feature. Each ID and password would have a kill date and time. In other words, after midnight on March 23rd, a particular ID would become invalid. The user would have to apply for a new ID.

If each ID and/or password has its own particular sunset date, then, this procedure keeps the look-up file current and also permits review of access levels upon granting of a new ID or password.

A further security angle is that if an outsider has the old entree into the computer, it has become dead.

THE ENEMY—COMPUTER SECURITY COMPLACENCY

Illegal hackers have gained entrance into security-conscious governmental agencies, banks and other types of seemingly secure operations. They have committed fraud, obtained commercial secrets and planted computer viruses and Trojan Horses.

Nosy employees have been able to gain important data, commit embezzlement, tamper with files, and render computer systems useless.

One thing that illegal hackers have taught us is that in the matter of computer system security, we have to keep *improving* our electronic locks and keys. What could be an airtight security precaution today may be just quaint history or only false hope after tonight.

REDUCING INVENTORY THEFTS BY PERSONNEL

"Thief, one who has a habit of finding things before people lose them."
JOE E. LEWIS

There was a time when thefts from inventory only affected industries that had "attractive" types of inventory—that is, items that could be readily sold by the culprit or used at home. Not so, anymore. Increasingly all types of inventory are becoming subject to theft—not only completed assemblies, but parts, supplies, and even raw materials are constantly being stolen.

EVERYTHING IS SUBJECT TO THEFT

At one electrical assembly plant, certain employees were constantly stealing copper wire. The material which had cost the company a good buck was being sold below scrap prices by trusted employees.

At a metal fabricating operation, an "enterprising" employee was taking good parts from the shelves and putting them in the scrap pile. When the scrap dealer came for the pick-up, the employee received a cash kickback.

SOME QUICK MEASURES TO TAKE NOW

1. If not installed, then initiate a property pass procedure. Nothing is to be removed from the premises or out of the building without a written pass. The pass completely describes the property being removed.

2. Outgoing shipments can be held open until the contents are compared with the shipping ticket, invoice, bill of lading, or other document by someone other than the person who packed the shipment.

3. Inventory items that can be readily concealed in clothing can be removed to areas that are more likely to have supervisory observation.

4. A notice on the bulletin board can state that lunch boxes and other packages can be examined at any time. Likewise, lockers, desks, and so on, are subject to inspection.

5. Material requisitions can be reviewed for inconsistencies, such as parts and/or assemblies being ordered in unusual quantities or by a section that does not have a required need for such items.

6. Scrap piles can be inspected by the Quality Control Manager or the Assistant Plant Manager for any unusual items.

7. Outside contractors can be required to submit monthly inventory lists of the completed and unfinished items over which they have custody.

8. Identification serial numbers can be permanently embossed on major or significant assemblies. (This is largely a psychological step. A potential culprit would have reason to believe that the serial numbered item could be traced.)

9. Computerized inventory usage reports can red flag items that have fluctuating or unusual usage.

10. Items which incur significant difference between the book (paper record) inventory and the actual physical count can be thoroughly investigated.

11. Shipping and receiving areas can be restricted to shipping and receiving personnel only.

WHO IS STEALING?

Experienced security people relate that almost any type of rank and file and managerial person is capable of stealing. How about trusted people? Usually, they have the greatest opportunity.

Strange, but true. Even security guards have been caught loading up their car trunks!

MORE MEASURES TO CONSIDER

1. Slow moving inventory items are good theft possibilities. If usage of an item is slow, it should be marketed the best way possible. At times, it is even desirable to sell such items as scrap. Why? It is better to realize some income than to watch the items slowly disappear.

2. Perpetual inventory systems are useful. However, an increase in the frequency of cross-checking with the physical counts will tend to reduce shrinkage. At the very least, items of very great theft attraction should be reviewed on a more current basis.

3. Reduce employee traffic near inventory bins or shelves. Re-route the flow of traffic or move the material to least trafficked areas.

4. Assign inventory accountability requirements to inventory personnel. Jones can be responsible for 1 through 25, while Smith can be responsible for 26 through 65, and so on. Or assign the responsibility by areas. They have to account for any discrepancies for their control areas.

5. Require managers and supervisors to report suspicious activities and observations to the management. The top brass must support the action of supervisory personnel who apprehends an employee caught stealing.

6. Shipping and receiving areas should not be used for entrances and exits of nonshipping and receiving personnel.

7. The written stated policy of the Company should indicate that the theft of Company property is cause for discharge.

8. Vendors, suppliers, and sub-contractors should receive annual warning notices regarding kickbacks in cash or goods.

WHY HANG TOUGH—A CASE HISTORY

One company pressed charges against a trusted employee who was caught putting two dollars worth of gasoline from the Company gas pump into his own car's gas tank.

The rationale for the legal effort was twofold: first, no one knew how much gasoline had been stolen before the apprehension

Second, the Company wanted to demonstrate to other employees what it thought of such an act—deterrence.

BETTER BET—REMOVE OPPORTUNITY

Arrest, discharge and suspension are tools for deterrence. However, these recourses are not for all of the personnel.

In most operations there is no sure fire way of completely stopping all inventory theft. If there was, it would be too expensive. A better way is to simply reduce the opportunities for theft.

PREVENTING AND CATCHING KICKBACKS TO EMPLOYEES

"We often buy money very much too dear."
WILLIAM THACKERY, 1852

Thackery was right. The price that one pays for accepting kickbacks can be very high—especially when caught.

Among the more distasteful problems in every company are kickbacks to employees. There is almost little question that millions of dollars find their way from suppliers into the hands of some employees—even very trustworthy employees.

This really should come as no surprise. After all, is not the most trusted employee the most likely to get away with kickbacks? The junior level purchasing agent may not have the opportunities that his superiors would have!

PRICE AND QUALITY COST

The Company can lose in two ways. First, the cost of the kickback plus usually more is packed into the price that the Company is paying for the product or service.

Second, the other more concealed economic cost is the lower quality standards of the material or level of service purchased when kickbacks are involved.

INCREASED COMPENSATION FOIBLE

Higher salary levels are generally not the answer to the kickback problem. Excluding situations where the salary is extremely low (an incentive for the employee to seek kickbacks), a more than adequate wage will not necessarily reduce the climate for the acceptance of gifts by employees.

As a matter of fact, one can point to extremely well-compensated senior management personnel who are occasionally uncovered accepting kickbacks.

THE PENALTY POLICY

A very real deterrent is the stated policy, whether formal or informal, that those employees who are caught accepting kickbacks will be promptly dismissed and/or criminally prosecuted.

INCREASING THE COSTS OF KICKBACK ACCEPTANCE

Here is an additional deterrent. The Company can commence civil suit against an errant employee for the refunding of kickbacks, overcharges by suppliers, damages from the acceptance of substandard products, and penalty damages. The stated policy can also indicate that the Company has that recourse.

> *The corporate counsel can offer the desirable legal methods for obtaining such compensation to the Company.*

SOME RECOMMENDED STEPS TO TAKE

1. Suppliers can be informed that the Company views any bribe-taking by its employees as unethical and possibly illegal. The suppliers can be put on such notice when they begin doing business with the Company, either directly or via circular notice periodically sent to all suppliers.

2. Employees with purchasing authority could be required to report all the gifts that they have received which exceed a certain minimum. Some companies require the reporting of ALL gifts that are received.

3. It is desirable to switch purchasing assignments around every so often. If Jones has been buying sheet metal for the past six months, change his area of responsibility to electrical parts.

4. While competitive bidding is not always feasible, the buyer can at least report prices in catalogs that are available from other suppliers as backup data to the purchase order.

5. The purchase order requisition can recommend two or three possible suppliers from whom the purchasing agent is required to obtain bids.

6. The Company can maintain alternate supplier sources on as many purchased items as economically feasible.

A supplier with even a small percentage of the total business may keep chief suppliers AND the buyers on their toes.

7. On large purchases or those of long-term duration, more than one purchasing agent can be used. Then, opposing buy recommendations can be considered.

8. Some operations do not permit purchasing directors or managers to do any buying. Their main function is that of reviewing the purchase recommendations of subordinates.

   NOTE. That technique provides a checks and balances system.

9. The quality control manager can report to the plant manager (rather than to the production manager) the more serious departures from quality control standards of purchased parts and materials.

10. Production supervisors can occasionally visit nearby suppliers and maintain a liaison outside of the purchasing channels.

11. Overstocked items can be investigated for undue volumes of ordering.

12. Unusual or nonindustry paying terms for certain suppliers or vendors can be reviewed as to required purpose.

13. Lateness of credits or refunds for returns or merchandise claims can be investigated.

STRIPED SUITS AND BARS PAYOFF

Not only are civil suits possible against the errant employee but also against the supplier. In addition, the proven acceptance and payment of a kickback are hard-time crimes for both parties in every jurisdiction.

The fact that the kickback was voluntary is immaterial in court. If the kickback was an employee requirement (under duress) in order to continue to do business, then the employee may also be convicted of extortion (more hard-time).

There is bigger trouble for the errant employee who does not report the kickback income on his or her tax return. That's a big jailable offense (concealed gross income) under the tax evasion laws. The punishment includes a stretch in the federal penitentiary in addition to paying the income tax, hefty penalties and interest—not to mention the criminal fines and monumental legal cost.

RISK TO REWARD RATIO

Let's face it, not everybody gets caught. Let's assume that even one in a hundred get caught. Is it worth the risk? A crashed career is minimal and then the stakes get higher.

First, it's a few easy bucks in kickbacks, then a few hundred and pretty soon it's a few thousand. Stack that against lifetime earning and potential bankruptcy.

By the way, when it gets to a few thousand, too many people get to know about the kickbacks. A definite increased danger. (Greed seems to have its own set of limitation rules.)

NEW CONSIDERATIONS OF ARREST RECORDS OF JOB APPLICANTS

*"A personnel officer should possess a sensitive ear,
a caring heart and the skin of a rhinoceros."*
PRISCILLA GROSS, Vice President, AMA

*WARNING: Unless there is a valid reason for knowing,
the employer would do well to avoid inquiring about a
job applicant's arrest record.*

"Arrest" does not mean "conviction."

LANDMARK COURT CASE

One employer had a policy of requiring job applicant to complete an employment application which in part required information indicating the arrests of the applicant for other than minor traffic violations. Evidence was produced that showed to the court that the employer did not hire applicants who had been arrested on several occasions even though the applicants had not been convicted.

FINDINGS

1. The employer had failed to demonstrate that there was good business reasons for the requested information.
2. Even though the employer applied the hiring practice to all applicants, the policy was unlawful. The reason? Statistics show that blacks are arrested more often without convictions than whites.
3. Though the policy was evenly enforced, it had the effect of denying black applicants an equal employment opportunity.

VERDICT. Based on the evidence and findings, the court determined that the employer had unlawfully discriminated against blacks under the Federal Civil Rights Act. (*Gregory vs. Litton Systems,* Inc., DC, Cal.)

POLICY GUIDE

*If there is not a clear need to know, **do not ask**.*

Unless the employer can prove in court or at some kind of hearing that the question of an arrest record is material in considering an applicant for a job, it is probably best to leave it off the application. If it is left on the form, it may influence a hiring decision by an interviewer although it is not directly relevant to the job requirements.

WHAT ABOUT A BACKGROUND CHECK?

Once again, unless it is essential in the job requirements, any background check, conducted in-house or by an agency, should omit the request for an arrest record.

WARNING: There is the further legal jeopardy that an applicant may sue for undue invasion of privacy on questions of unrelated arrest records.

The Company's legal counsel can be consulted with regard to how far, and under what circumstances, such inquiries could be made without further legal entanglements.

A POSSIBLE SOLUTION

It is difficult to run a business without some control, at some levels, over inquiries into a job applicant's prior character. Many companies have two different types of employment applications.

One form is used for functional and/or operating personnel. The other form is used for administrative and professional staff. The questions on the latter form deal with elements of character predictability.

As it is more likely that administrative and professional staff personnel are required to have a different type of background and character profile that rank and file personnel, deeper background checking may be in order.

The requirements with regard to prior character may be material to the job and the nature of the business

Once again, legal opinion before action is desirable.

A MANAGERIAL RIGHT

If it is discovered that an employee lied on his or her application for with respect to an arrest record or conviction, and that employee is not fired immediately after the discovery, the Company's option to fire that person later is foreclosed.

Here is the logic. An employee can only be fired for a material misstatement on an employment application. It would be obvious to the court (or at some hearing) that the misstatement was not material. Why? Because the employer kept the employee after knowing of the misstatement and therefore, it was not material.

Keeping an employee after discovery of a "material" misstatement means that the employer recognizes and acknowledges that the employee can do the job—despite the fib.

BASIC DOCTRINE

PUBLIC POLICY: An employee should be fired only for good cause.

"Well, a year ago, we knew that he did ...."

What may have been good cause a year ago when it became known is of no consequence currently. By not doing anything, an act of omission, the employer **accepted** what was known then.

SUMMARY AND CONSIDERATIONS

1. Information about arrest records may be immaterial as to whether an employee can do the job.
2. Arrest record information may be material for certain types of jobs.
3. A second type of employment application, which is used uniformly for certain types of positions, may seek such data that is indicative of character.

4. Criteria for any position have to be applied uniformly and fairly.

5. Material misstatements on applications have to be acted upon as soon as they are known or not at all.

6. It is generally public policy that employees should be fired only for current good cause.

7. Employment interviewers should be briefed on the Company's policy position and the law.

8. Company counsel should review employment application forms and hiring practices for comparison to the latest court or governmental agency decisions.

THE LEGAL TREND

At times, it would seem that the court opinions are like a pendulum swinging from one position to another. However, there is a trend. The trend is one of further protection of a job applicant's rights. Correcting imbalances of various kinds is another part of this trend. In the end, all of these matters (some of which are conflicting) will sort themselves out. In the meantime, managers and supervisors will have to be patient.

WHEN TO PASS A TROUBLEMAKER ON TO PERSONNEL

"If you pick up a starving dog and make him prosperous, he will not bite you. This is the principal difference between a dog and a man."

MARK TWAIN

A manager who is spending a large amount of time trying to straighten out a troublemaker subordinate is cheating not only the employer, but the other subordinates as well. There are times when a manager has to draw the line, discontinue efforts to reform the problem employee, and permit others, who may have a better or different approach, to try to handle the problem employee.

The effort that can be wasted in attempts to reform one employee may be better spent on improving the productivity and personal accomplishment of other more worthwhile subordinates. Giving up on a problem employee should not necessarily be considered a failure but an opting for more important alternative requirements of the manager's job.

FACE IT—YOU CAN'T WIN THEM ALL

While every employee can make a valuable contribution, and there is a desire to protect an investment of time, the manager has to draw an imaginary line.

That line is the extent of commitment one has to a subordinate who respects and reciprocates that commitment. If there is a continuing failure to reciprocate, then the manager has to recognize the situation and accept it.

The jails and reformatories are full of incorrigibles, and society does not necessarily bear the blame in every case. Nor is the manager to blame for every subordinate who does not work out as expected.

*The manager may be at **fault** if he or she continues to put off seeking a solution by others.*

The perennial troublemaker, the constant critic, and the recurring problem employee has to be accepted as the one who cannot be won over by any manager.

Reinforce Employee Orientation

During training and beyond, a subordinate is oriented toward what is expected in the way of discipline and behavior. That is in addition to learning how to perform.

Before the employee can become of value to the Company, he or she has been told what is expected, what authority the boss can exercise, the required behavior pattern, and the working of the system of rewards and disciplinary action.

THE UNWRITTEN CONTRACT. The employee has accepted the job under the prescribed circumstances, and continues to accept a defined employee-employer relationship on each day that he or she reports to work.

Excuses

"Charley is a good worker, but . . . "

Why make excuses for the problem employee? Charley has been told about his faults before and he knows how to make attempts to compensate for those faults.

Many front-line managers and supervisors would rather have a less competent subordinate but have fewer problems so that their group's overall effectiveness is higher.

Personnel Department Recourse

A preliminary discussion between Charley's boss and a staff member of the Personnel Department can lead to their acceptance of some responsibility for the troublemaker employee.

Employee turnover is a partial reflection on the personnel policies and their enforcement. Therefore, if the Personnel Department believes that they can resurrect a problem employee with a minimum effort, they should try.

If not, it is better for the Company, the immediate superior, and the other employees in the department to let Charley go. And, maybe, just maybe, Charley can fit in elsewhere and even like his new job better.

PERSONAL RESPONSIBILITY

It is an occupational thing; most managers and supervisors like to help their subordinates. For many middle managers, someone, somewhere (way back in the past) lent a helping hand in their career efforts. Some old "coach" provided some job insight and/or some hints on how to get along.

The difference between then and now is that the help given then was appreciated and there was probably a favorable response and heeding of the advice.

A boss, who has tried every technique to turn someone around into being a productive and cooperating team member, has to know when to give up. After all, there are other subordinates who need a conscientious boss's help. Above all other management rules, for the sake of that old helpful coach, "It is always pay back time" for the conscientious subordinates.

ISOLATING AND HANDLING THE COMPLAINING EMPLOYEE

"There was nothing wrong with her that a vasectomy of the vocal cords wouldn't fix."
LISA ALTHER

Every office, plant, warehouse, or any other type of operation has its fair share of critics. (Some have a little more.) They know how to do everything better than the way it is being done—and, of course, most important, better than their immediate superior.

An experienced boss can discern between the complaining subordinate and the individual who sincerely wants to do his or her job a better way. The sincere employee usually acts through channels, understands why certain changes can not be effected right away, and is usually diligent (willing to work overtime, and so on) about his or her job.

NOTE THE DIFFERENCE

Now, let's look at the other fellow. The chronic complainer is more disruptive, sees "evil" in every new management directive, and readily spreads his or her adverse opinions among other employees. The reasons for the chronic complainer's existence are varied. Maybe the complaint artist is transferring his personal problems to the employer or seeking recognition from peers.

DILIGENCE VERSUS DISRUPTIVE

Take a long look at MOTIVE

The immediate manager or supervisor has to evaluate whether a subordinate, who has a complaint, is being *disruptive* or is being *diligent*. The diligent employee generally wants to improve matters. The disruptive worker is not necessarily looking for improvement in conditions and may have few, if any, constructive suggestions.

Either the chronic complainer has to be changed quickly or he or she has to be fired. There is no third way. Any attempt to live with a disruptive complainer is not warranted. The effort of putting up with a complainer could be directed more beneficially to encouraging the sincere employees to do a better job.

A LITTLE EASY CONVERSATION

An older superior might have a Dutch uncle talk with a younger employee who is a habitual complainer. On occasion, it is worth the effort for reform. Sometimes, the problem employee can see through the gambit and can embarrass the superior.

RECOMMENDATION: TAKE A GOOD SHOT

If the superior is interested in reforming Charley, the constant complainer, the boss should wait for an opportunity. Let Charley continue to voice complaints. Wait until there is a complaint about which Charley is absolutely wrong. Then nail Charley to the wall with a severe counter attack. This may cure Charley of complaining.

ONE-TO-ONE RECOMMENDATION

When Charley has opened his mouth once too often, his boss can ask Charley to discuss the issue in the privacy of an office. After the boss has demonstrated that the complaint is groundless, the conversation might be as follows:

"So you see, Charley, you have nothing to complain about."

"All right, so you are right."

"This is not the first time that you have had a groundless complaint. However, it is the last time that we are going to have a discussion about your complaints."

"What do you mean?" (As if he didn't know.)

"Your complaints have been getting my goat. You do not have helpful suggestions—only complaints. Just as in this case; they were without foundation."

"So?"

"So, no more complaints—of any kind—or out you go."

"What if I have a good idea?"

"You haven't had one yet. So keep the 'good ideas' to yourself. Understand?"

NO SECOND CHANCE

If Charley shapes up and is no longer a problem employee, great. Otherwise, it is best to part company. Further time and effort could best be directed to more fertile areas of subordinate improvement in productivity, performance, and their personal achievement.

DIRE WARNING

If the problem employee stays and continues the complaining ways, it will encourage others to become complainers. The immediate superior will be faced with having decisions and instructions doubted by a whimpering department or section.

Complainers encourage others to complain.

SUPPORTING REFORM

Frequently, the complaining employee, who has been shown the error of his ways, reforms and becomes a productive part of the organization. When Charley does, he should be noticed and encouraged. After all, recognition may be all the Charley is after.

CURBING 900 CALLING AND OTHER TELEPHONE ABUSES

"Alexander Graham Bell did not invent the telephone,
he invented a source of entertainment."
UNKNOWN

There is fun and information available on 900 access telephone numbers. It is too bad that some employees feel that dialing a 900 or similar number is a good fringe benefit to use during working hours—sometimes excessively.

PHONE SEX AND THE DOW JONES

When some employees should be knocking out the work, here is a sample of what they could be listening to: sports news, Hollywood gossip, stock market reports, sexy voices (of both sexes), "dating" services, Elvis recordings, horoscopes, religious inspiration, personal lucky number for today, and so on.

TELEPHONE ADDICTS

A once-in-a-while call is not the end of the managerial control world. The real concern is the employee who is addicted to making these calls. Some people have run up personal telephone bills in the hundreds of dollars—a small few into the thousands.

The 900 or similar calling is not a ten-cent call. The people who provide these call-in services charge a high rate by the minute. The charges are relayed through the local phone companies to appear on the telephone owner's monthly bill.

COMMUNICATION TARIFF REGULATION

The presumption made by the regulatory agencies is that the party that has the phone also has control of those who use that phone. Unauthorized use is of little or no concern to the local or long distance phone companies.

339

"Business office manager, I didn't authorize such calls."

It's a no-win situation. Unauthorized calling on the Company's phone system is for the account of the Company. If there is any misuse of an employee privilege, then it is up to management to curb such abuse.

AN EMPLOYEE PRIVILEGE

A certain amount of personal phone calls is almost unavoidable. However, a line has to be drawn. Otherwise, some personnel will definitely abuse the privilege. The control of abuse of any privilege is highly dependent on how conscientious is the workforce and the management's efforts at control.

WARNING: ANOTHER COST LEAK

The toll charges are only a part of the total cost of 900 and other dialing and other telephone user abuses.

Consider this: while the employee is running up nonbusiness toll charges, he or she is distracted from the workflow. The result is a loss of productivity and performance.

Twenty minutes a day of nonbusiness telephone calls is almost 5% of a typical worker's daily productive time.

And, 20 minutes is sometimes on the low side of an average estimate, while 7 hours of daily productive time is frequently on the high side.

A case in point. One enthusiast of the financial market spent a couple of hours a day on the telephone checking up on the status of this "big" stock plunger's investment. He was quick to put the phone down when his boss appeared.

RECOMMENDATION: TELEPHONE SWITCH MODIFICATION

Many in-house telephone switches today have features which permit calling limitations. (The switch is the equipment in that hall closer or separate room which control the Company's telephone equipment.)

The local telephone company or the outfit that maintains the switch may be able to modify the switch so that no 900 call can be made on the Company's telephone system. Remember, there is seldom any valid business reason to call a 900 or similar number.

ANOTHER LIMITATION POSSIBILITY

In certain areas, the local telephone company has a restrictive feature on their customer service switch equipment. By calling the local telephone company business office manager, one can determine if 900 calls can be prevented.

Telephone companies make money on such calls.

If the local telephone company has the limitation feature, one might have to get a little pushy to get the limitation installed on the Company's line.

(If you have children at home and you wish to restrict any 900 calling, the same phone company limitation in certain areas can be imposed on home phones.)

BETTER RECOMMENDATION

As with abuses of other employee privileges, the front-line manager or supervisor can best handle the situation. By monitoring employee activity and keeping the work flowing as much of the time as possible, telephone and other abuses are reduced.

THE RIGHT OF PRIVACY IS LIMITED

There is no question that an individual has a constitutional right to privacy. However, like many other rights, this one has its limitations. For one thing, this right and other certain rights are waived by the acceptance of employment.

Generally, an employer can eavesdrop on in-house incoming or outgoing telephone calls. (Outside of the premises, such action is a jailable offense.) It is proper for an employer to know how the business (or lack of business) is being conducted on his telephone lines.

If there is a doubt as to the propriety of listening to calls, corporate counsel should be consulted.

THE TOTAL PROBLEM

Telephone misuse and other employee privilege abuse can be a much smaller problem when there is greater care in hiring and orienting the workforce.

> *By definition, the **conscientious** employee does not abuse privileges.*

Fortunately, most employees recognize their responsibilities and do their own thing on their own time. Because of these people, there has to be some control effort on the abuser of the telephone privilege.

AVOIDING AND MINIMIZING UNDESIRABLE SITUATIONS

HANDLING SUPERVISORS WHO DON'T WANT TO SUPERVISE

"You cannot make a crab walk straight."
ARISTOPHANES, c. 448–380 BC

There are some managerial people who would rather be "doers" than managers. They show it in many big and small ways.

In most job situations, there is a "mix" of managerial and nonmanagerial functions. That is, certain duties require the direction of others and certain duties are concerned with the actual performance of the work. If the mix of duties becomes such that the direction of subordinates is lax, then productivity and performance suffers.

Whether one person can do both kinds of work is a fruitless argument. Let's say that a person can. The real issue is this: "Should one do both kinds of chores?" That is the question. The answer, for better productivity, generally, is "no."

If any managers take a hand in the regular chores, they may be doing so to the detriment of their main function, which is the supervision of subordinates.

DON'T RELIVE THE PAST

Fred Fixit is a manager who rose from the ranks. He frequently likes to continue his fascination with the functional job that he had years ago. He likes to "keep his hand in." That fascination is keeping Mr. Fixit from being a complete manager.

In another case, the president of a beer distribution company used to like to go out with the new junior salesmen, "to show them the ropes." This executive started as a salesman and as president still enjoyed going into a territory. An outside consultant convinced him that the company's performance would more likely be improved if the president was where he was needed more frequently. (The stockholders had brought the consultant in when the profitability of the company was dropping.)

345

WARNING: For some managers, the fascination with the functional jobs is an evasive action intended to escape their managerial responsibilities.

UNUSUAL SKILL RATIONALE

"I'm the only one that can line up the machines (or program the computer) as they should be lined up."

One person may be very skilled. However, someone else, with adequate training and experience, can learn those skills.

One of the desirable attributes of good managers and supervisors is their ability to train their own subordinates. If Fred Fixit is reluctant to adequately train subordinates, he may be saying one of two things that provide insight.

The first thing that Mr. Fixit may be saying is that he does not have the ability to adequately train subordinates. That possibility is to *his* inherent disadvantage as a manager.

The other possibility is that Fred Fixit does not want to train others—which is the Company's loss.

If Mr. Fixit is not a good instructor, he can be given assistance in training subordinates in a particular function. (After all, managers and supervisors are not hired as much for their training ability but rather for their ability to get the work out.)

The goal is to relieve managers of functional duties in order to meet managerial responsibilities.

EXPEDIENCY—SHORT-RANGE SOLUTION TO LONG-TERM PROBLEM

In an emergency, a manager or a supervisor has to pitch in to get some work done or a particular job out of the house. However, emergency conditions have to come to an end.

In a strike situation, managers and supervisors may be expected to perform the more routine jobs as best as they can. As a matter of fact, it is ideal that they have training to be able to handle those routine chores.

Pitching in is one thing, but continuing to pitch in on the routine chores is wasteful. The manager has to manage, the supervisor has to supervise—that's what they are earning their paychecks to do.

No question, expediency is a justifiable cause for breaking all sorts of rules—except *one*. That is, expediency is *not* justified once expediency starts turning counterproductive.

TENDENCIES TO ERR ON EXPEDIENCY

Every operation likes to run a tight ship. However, putting managers on the production line continually or having them more constantly answer customer service calls is counterproductive and wasteful. It is a short-term solution (expedient) to a longer-term problem (short staffing).

> *Overall (total) performance is improved where there is less reliance on a manager who pitches in on the functional jobs.*

RECOMMENDATION: AVOID PART-TIME MANAGERS

If the supervisor is doing many routine jobs that are properly assignable to subordinates, the supervisor's performance as a supervisor has to suffer. A supervisor's value is diminished when he or she is not concerned with the real test of the job—being a full-time supervisor.

The supervisor frequently refuses to admit that apples and oranges are being mixed and finds excuses for the mix of duties. While some supervisors like being advanced into management, they may truly prefer to be doing the rank and file work or just being in the rank and file!

That condition of occupational preference may not be recognized, much less readily admitted, by the supervisor. The supervisor's superior has to acknowledge the situation, possibly reorient the supervisor as to duties, or find a replacement supervisor.

Being a boss is not everybody's bag. A good supervisor has to be emotionally settled in the job, otherwise he or she is not going to be happy (or successful) in the long run.

> *"If my boss calls, try to get his name."*
> Old office graffiti

DECIDING WHEN TO "REQUEST" AND WHEN TO "COMMAND"

> *"He's fair. He treats us all the same—like dogs."*
> HENRY JORDAN

If orders are disguised as suggestions or requests rather than commands, some subordinates are more likely to use initiative and to be better motivated to accomplish their part of the job. However, there are times when a command is more effective in getting things done.

A request is less downgrading to many people than a command. The informality of a request allows a certain amount of willingness on the part of the subordinate to accomplish the task at hand.

CREATING FERTILE SOIL FOR REQUESTS

A semblance of authority is desirable before there is a climate of ready acceptance of requests. If subordinates know that they could be ordered to do a certain chore, they are more likely to go along with and even approve of the requesting technique.

In the heyday of the British Empire, a British colonial administrator was asked how he was able to do his job and to govern so many people without the use of constant force. He replied, "Sir, I stand in the shadow of British bayonets."

STAND IN THE SHADOW OF AUTHORITY

If a front line manager or supervisor making the request is cloaked with sufficient authority and there is little reason to believe that there are any cracks in that authority, everyday requests can suffice in place of commands.

RECOGNIZING THE PROBLEM AREAS

"Requesting" does not work in every operation. Only distinct commands are possible for some operations. Subordinate acceptance attitudes will not favor the use of the requesting technique where the following conditions prevail:

1. Discipline has been lax in the past.
2. There have been instances of the unfair application of discipline.
3. Top management support of front line authority has been minimal or uneven.
4. A high level of turnover of managers and supervisors.
5. General employee morale is low.
6. Excessive changes in operating methods.
7. Countermanding of instructions and orders.

It is simple. If the observance of explicit orders is difficult to maintain, then there is a greater likelihood that any request will be, at least partially, ignored.

CASE STUDY OF AN EXCEPTION

In one operation where employee morale was low, a supervisor was able to show higher productivity and quality by using the requesting techniques despite the adverse circumstances.

How did he do it? He did not request anything of his subordinates that they could not truly handle or that he was not willing to do himself. He carefully explained the purpose of the request before making it. No one was berated for misunderstanding the request; he spent time reviewing unfavorable situations with his subordinates and assumed all responsibility for errors or differences.

INITIAL APPROACH RECOMMENDATIONS

Explaining the situation before making any request is worth the extra time. Basically, that ploy reveals whether the subordinates are on the defensive against any request. It is a sounding out process which brings any possible emotional resistance to the forefront.

Another good initial approach is for the supervisor to state what the objectives are to be accomplished. Then, delay any requests for action until everyone has been heard from. This ploy tends to reduce technical or side issue objections because the supervisor is the arbitrator on how to do the job. It also follows that the supervisor would know who would be best able (the fellow with the fewest objections) to handle a particular job.

Last Recourse

A manager or a supervisor can rely on ordering rather than suggesting that something be done. In an "ordering" situation the element of willingness on the part of the subordinate is missing.

There are some subordinates who would not look upon a request very seriously. Others can recognize that they are being treated like members of the team.

The immediate boss has to be aware of subordinate attitudes and play the game accordingly. Some subordinates, who are borderline with respect to the use of commands versus requests, could tend to go along with requests if that is the way that most of the other employees (peers) are treated.

Improving Your Leadership Qualities

"Can you get this out tomorrow?"

By experience, a manager or supervisor can acquire a talent to know how firm an instruction to a particular subordinate need be. It is a talent or capability that is not developed over night. Frankly, it takes a great deal of work. Here are some helpful hints for being a "requesting" supervisor:

1. Have an air of confidence in your technical skills.
2. Listen carefully to objections. They also provide insight into the emotions of subordinates.
3. Admit you are wrong when you have been caught.
4. Try to let your authority be understood rather than voicing it. (Stand in the shadow of your power.)
5. Act as if subordinates are as conscientious as you are.
6. Take care in your use of words—they trigger seen and many *unseen* responses.

7. Engender and encourage a cooperative feeling between subordinates.

8. Avoid shouting, banging desks, bad language, or any other obvious loss of your personal control.

9. Be quick to smile, even in adversity.

10. Always be fair. You can be firm with some subordinates and still be fair.

WHY GO FOR IT

Leadership is a very sketchy, somewhat murky attribute. No one can put his or her finger on it. It is a quality that you cannot buy but which you can develop.

Part of the leadership quality has to do with how subordinates react to a request instead of a command. Inspiring leadership seldom has to command.

As we mature in our management careers, we slowly improve our leadership ability including how to get subordinates to respect our work requests.

HOW TO IMPROVE MINORITY EMPLOYEE RELATIONS

"I am free of all prejudices. I hate everyone equally."
W. C. FIELDS

In order for productivity to be maintained, all employees have to work together in required groupings of functions. The technological age requires that work is to be accomplished with a pool of various skills.

If some of the workers do not feel that they are a part of the group or team, or worse, if there is resentment, productivity suffers.

Anyone who has a feeling of being an outsider in the work place is going to be less of a contributor to comparatively higher levels of productivity.

INSECURITY IS ADVERSE TO PRODUCTIVITY

Who is a second-class citizen? Anyone treated as an outsider in his or her own land. Outsiders have less reason to be loyal to the Company, the management, their superiors and to fellow workers.

Being the last to be hired and the first to be fired, or not being considered a member of the work team, can lead to an attitude that results in lower performance.

THE GOOD NEWS

Attitudes in all areas are changing. Feelings of insecurity are less common and minority workers are beginning to feel more and more that they are a part of the team.

AVOID CODDLING

Most people want to earn the money they make. It may be embarrassing to some employee if they are given soft assignments. Work should be distributed without regard to the color of skin, national or cultural origin, or sexual preference of subordinates.

When all of the employees are treated equally as to job assignments, they come to believe that they are each a part of the work team.

INSTILL JOB AWARENESS

Some people in the workforce do not have the same early job orientation that others do. Their orientation to the job situation has to be reinforced as to the environment of the employer-employee give-and-take. For instance, they have to be shown the benefits that can accrue to them through improved performance.

That effort is additionally beneficial for all of the employees.

IS FAULT IMPORTANT?

When employees do not work as cooperative team members, both management and employees suffer. The results are the same—lessened productivity—regardless as to whose fault it is.

In most work situations, employees want to do and react just as they are expected to. The management, at all levels, has to show the way. Favorable results (in any type of situation) are more important than trying to place the blame for poor work relationships.

TRAINING SUGGESTION

With any new employee, regardless of background, the supervisor has to break the person into the supervisor's own way of doing things. Even the most skilled of new people require some orientation.

Now the nitty-gritty. This effort should be applied evenly. Then, there is less of a chance that someone may feel like an outsider.

The next step is to provide an employee-coach. This ploy is more likely to make the new person feel that they are a part of the team right off.

"Wendell, this is Rodney. You will be working together."

KEEP DISPLAYING TEAMWORK

The supervisor can demonstrate how the new subordinate's effort contributes to the whole output (the big picture orientation). Further, there can be explanation of the possible rewards of team effort and personal achievement.

It is difficult for an accepted member of the team to be insensitive to the needs of the team.

APPLY SUFFICIENT EXPLANATION

As with any trainee, care can be taken to point out the cause of any error and what can be done to minimize mistakes. Remember, errors can be expected of anyone who is new to a situation. They are not necessarily a reflection of ultimate competency.

Similarly, when there are some early job successes, a supervisor can be *quick* to apply a little applause. Appreciation reinforces the status as a team member.

GETTING TO BASICS

If a subordinate is being treated fairly, understands the reasons for discipline when necessary, and has an awareness of what is expected personally (regardless of background), the subordinate can function in a job environment without any chips on the shoulder and with an even temperament.

MANAGER VIEWPOINT

A "good" manager or supervisor can effectively handle subordinates of the same or similar racial or ethnic background. However, a "better" manager or supervisor can effectively handle subordinates of differing backgrounds. It takes greater leadership ability.

In the changing world of the work place, middle managers that can lead subordinates of varying background are better suited as managerial personnel.

TOP BRASS VIEWPOINT

Our system works best when everyone has an equal chance. It makes for a level playing field. There has to be some correction of prior inequities.

If discrimination is poor management on the assembly line, then it is also poor business to practice it at higher levels—even on the executive floor.

ASSESSING OLDER JOB APPLICANTS

"I refuse to admit I'm more than 52, even if that does make my sons illegitimate."
LADY ASTOR

A popular misconception is that older employees are slower to learn how to do new chores or are slower at job performance. Many firms that hire older applicants consistently do not find this to be true.

What they do find is that older applicants are more business-like in their approach to the job situation. Their maturity tends to make them more responsible.

LIKE LADY ASTOR

Older applicants at times hesitate in stating their correct ages or resent detailed questioning leading to an age determination. The fears are based upon the suspicion that the potential employer will discriminate against them because of their age.

KNOW THE LAW

Generally, no distinction in hiring practices can be made with the intent to bar older persons from employment. Governmental agencies will readily make an issue of any complaint that they receive which indicates that there was any discrimination against older applicants.

Any query on an application about age can only be justified in certain situations.

As regards fringe benefits and certain required governmental reports, inquiries about age can wait until after the applicant is hired—not one minute before.

If due to the nature of the operation, there is a doubt about pre-employment queries about age, consult the corporate legal beagle.

How old are you, anyway?

Actually, a question about age *after* hiring may elicit a more truthful answer. However, even then, the employee may be concerned about the effect that an accurate age may have on any opportunities for retention and/or promotion.

Make older applicants feel at ease

If the job applicant is at ease during the interview and throughout the screening process, the interviewer can make a more accurate assessment of the applicant's abilities. An applicant's concern about age being a limiting factor can cause an uneasiness or apprehension which may cloud the real issue—the applicant's ability to do the job.

The wrong techniques

The interviewer should avoid stressing, or even noticing, the fact that the applicant may be significantly older than the interviewer. Over respect for age, discussions of very early work history, and so on, tend to make the applicant aware that his or her age has been noticed (and possibly noted).

While such conversations may, at first, seem harmless, they are not calculated to make the applicant feel that his age is not a factor in the firing process considerations.

The applicant could be so offended that a complaint would be filed with a governmental agency citing possible discrimination based on age.

Good old fashioned basics

As in any interview, a job applicant wants to feel that abilities, not age or other factors, will govern the hiring procedure. If applicants are concerned that age is a factor, they may hesitate to supply completely frank answers. Such reluctance (or nervousness) prevents the interviewer from gaining more accurate insight into an applicant's work potential. The recommendation that works best is to try to handle all possible applicants uniformly—stick to basics.

WHY SOME FIRMS LIKE OLDER WORKERS

Absolute rules about any group are difficult to sustain. However, there are a number of factors favoring the hiring, rehiring and promotion of older employees including the following:

1. Very familiar with employer-employee give-and-take situation requirements.
2. More likely to comply with rules and have less discipline problems.
3. Less abusive of employee privileges.
4. Understand overall corporate objectives.
5. More businesslike in dealing with outsiders including customers.
6. Higher reliability on assignments.
7. More likely to work overtime and weekends.

The above is not always true for every older worker and certainly not in every type of operation. There still has to be a certain amount of care taken in the firing and screening process for any would-be worker at any age.

PROS AND CONS—GRAY HAIRS AND GRAY MATTER

Anybody can rely on stereotypes or point to a bad example. However, examples are not the general rules. Good management requires that each situation be judged on its own merits—or drawbacks. That's using evaluation.

"We don't hire older people."

Any attempt to bar people for employment or promotion strictly on age (besides being against the law) is cutting off a source of potentially good people. They are not all the best of workers, and neither are all of the "nonolder" people the best of workers. However, the fact is there is talent everywhere.

THE SHORT-SIGHTED

It happens all over. Sam works 30 years and the front office choppers put him out on the street. What about all of those years of loyal and faithful service? "We have to make room for new blood." Frequently, Sam has the experience that cannot be bought or even found.

If Sam is not doing his job, then light a fire under him. If he responds, great. If he doesn't then consider letting him go. (Some companies are too quick with the pink slip.) In this competitive world, it is wise to run a tight ship, but the tighter the ship is, then the greater the need for a more experienced and multitalented crew.

> *"Retirement at 65 is ridiculous. When I was 65*
> *I still had pimples."*
> GEORGE BURNS

WHAT TO DO WHEN AN EMPLOYEE GETS SICK AT WORK

"To avoid delay, please have all of your
symptoms ready."
Sign in a doctor's reception room

Fast thinking and action are the strengths of front line managers and supervisors. This ability comes greatly into play when a subordinate becomes ill or injured in the workplace.

Quick assessments have to be made. Comfort has to be supplied, and some kind of remedial action or emergency steps have to be started.

It is a good asset to be able to apply first aid as the need arises. However, there is no substitute for professional help. More damage can be done by ignorance.

First aid, at best, is intended as a momentary recourse and not as a complete approach to an emergency health situation.

WHAT CAN HAPPEN?

Someone who is not properly diagnosed and treated could become further ill or injured—sometimes it could be permanently. No one would want that on their conscience.

Another aspect of "doing the wrong thing" is that if there is further damage sustained, the ill or injured employee and the family have grounds for legal suit against the good samaritan supervisor. That is in addition to a suit against the employer.

WARNING: There are possible legal repercussions in
providing aid to someone in distress.

Unfair? Maybe. However, the courts have held that people who have gone to someone's aid to be *responsible* for their action. They can be responsible for large money damages as a result of what some expert doctor on the stand says was improper care.

360

Good intentions are of little consequence.

FIRST AID LESSONS FIRST

You are on the scene. You have compassion for the ill or injured subordinate. You want to do something.

The best approach is to have had first aid lessons provided by the Red Cross or some other organization long before any need for such training may arise. The training is also valuable if you should become ill or injured.

FIRST AID EQUIPMENT

A well-stocked first aid cabinet is a good precaution. Unfortunately, it cannot be locked because in an emergency, it will take too long to locate the key. (First aid supply pilfering is part of the game.)

In special types of situations, as in many chemical operations, antidotes and other special types of first aid supplies have to be readily available. Posters illustrating first aid procedures are highly desirable as well as first aid manuals around the work area.

WHEN AN ACCIDENT OCCURS

There are always slight injuries connected with most jobs. It is part of the territory. However, when a subordinate has some sort of condition or injury above the very commonplace, it is best to rely on others.

First Recommendation: Promptly, call any in-house medical personnel for assistance.

Second Recommendation: In the absence of in-house assistance, promptly call emergency medical services or an ambulance.

Even if the subordinate is showing some signs of recovery or relief, do not hesitate to call for medical assistance.

WARNING: One never knows when there may be a relapse or some other hidden condition which is not readily discernible.

A LARGE HAZARD

"Myrna fainted, but she is okay now."

"Okay now" is a diagnosis that only a sufficiently trained doctor can make. Even then, they are, regrettably, sometimes wrong!

Fainting and other similar circumstances may be caused by something that is not in any first aid manual.

One of the larger hazards in a suit for health or injury damages is the failure of the good samaritan to obtain professional medical help.

"He should have called an ambulance."

ASSUMED DUTY

With exceptions, if you step forward to help somebody in distress, their well-being is in your hands. If you should make an error while that person is in your care, you may be held financially responsible for that error.

Let's look at intention. "Trying the best that you can" includes seeking competent help for the ill or injured on a timely basis.

ON THE PRACTICAL SIDE

In today's litigious society, almost anyone can end up in court for almost any matter. One experienced manager handled the situation this way: as soon as any subordinate was ill in the workplace, he called an ambulance. He was taking no chances. His objective was to let a doctor release the employee to go back to work.

Once an employee was sick to his stomach but was recovering. The manager, who took no chances, called an ambulance anyway. It turned out to be more serious than at first thought. The employee had ingested "some bad lunch" and a stomach pump and other medical procedures were required promptly.

CONTROLLING EMPLOYEE ABUSE

There are problem employees who will pull a "sick stunt." Either they want to take it easy for an afternoon or they may want sympathy.

In any event, sick or playing sick, it is a good ploy to call an ambulance in all cases. First, the truly sick are going to get the help that they really need. Second, the malingerer is getting more than he or she bargained for, which is a good deterrent to false claims of illnesses.

THE BEST WAYS TO DENY UNJUSTIFIED WAGE REQUESTS

"In order to be a diplomat one must speak a number of languages, including double talk."

CAREY MCWILLIAMS

Excuses, alibis, delaying words, weasel phrases, fibs, outright lies, forgetfulness, busy signals, acute deafness, and even double talk, have to be used by the diplomatic manager or supervisor to put off a subordinate's unjustified request—especially if the request is for a pay raise that may not be such a good idea.

KEEP THE TWIN GOALS IN MIND

In the handling of an unjustified wage raise request made by a subordinate there are two goals to keep in mind:

1. For good management, an unjustified request has to be denied.
2. Despite denial, the subordinate's motivation for doing a better job has to be increased.

ORGANIZATION PROBLEMS

Justified salary increases are the rewards for higher levels of productivity or performance. Without improvement there cannot be continuing wage increases.

In our competitive society, product and service cost limitations form a lid on excessive expenditures. There is a fine, fine line between what a business can pay employees and what that business can recover in the market place.

Even in government organizations, the outlay for salaries is limited by what the government can hope to tax or borrow from the populace.

Walking a Tight Rope

The supervisor is in a fix. It is just too tough to explain economic theory, the workings of the marketplace, the law of supply and demand, consumption propensity, corporate finance and all of the other mumbo-jumbo to Mr. Roscoe Slopoke, who thinks that he deserves a raise.

What happens? Well, an unhappy situation develops when Mr. Slopoke, who believes that he is worth more, but who actually is worth only what he is getting, confronts his boss with a request for a raise.

Various Ploys Used—Double Talk

With many variations, the following excuses are frequently used to put off the subordinate:

1. Top management (always a good scapegoat) has limited all raises (for one reason or another).
2. Salary reviews are to be made in six months (or whenever).
3. Business is bad right now.
4. Only extreme wage disparities are being corrected at this time.
5. After January 1, some new decisions will be made.
6. A new personnel manager is starting next month.
7. Because of conditions, only the divisional vice president is authorizing raises.
8. We are going to reorganize the department in July.
9. Other people have been waiting longer for a raise.
10. New merit review forms are coming out.

The Evaluation of Ploys and Double Talk

Sometimes Mr. Slopoke will read between the lines of an excuse and realize that he is being passed over for a raise in a diplomatic fashion. He might accept the double talk as personal face saving.

Generally, such ploys are only a delaying tactic. A different ploy would have to be used the next time. However, in the long run, ploys can become counter productive. Eventually, an undeserving subordinate has to be told in a diplomatic way that he is not entitled to a raise.

"It's been a while since I had a raise and I'd like to get one soon."

"Roscoe, I've been meaning to talk to you about that."

"Okay, let's talk."

"Roscoe, your work has been satisfactory—not outstanding, just satisfactory. Frankly, I don't feel that you've been applying yourself enough to warrant a raise."

"Say, Walter got a raise. Why can't I?"

"Walter, or anyone else who got a raise, has been doing an outstanding job. I appreciate your effort, but you have not been at the level that I think that you can handle."

"That sounds bad for me!"

"No, not at all—because I know that you can do better if you really try."

"What about the future?"

"Glad that you asked. If, by the next time we sit down and talk about your salary, I'm convinced that your performance has improved, I'll give you a raise. What do you say?"

"I don't know."

"Why not give it a try."

IMPORTANT POINT

The above dialogue was not specific as to what is expected of Roscoe to merit a raise. It is best that specifics are used. Otherwise, the subordinate does not have a fixed goal to work toward.

Another reason for being specific is so that the subordinate is less likely to form a "hazy" memory of what was agreed to. A boss does not want a "he-said, she-said" argument down the road.

THE BENEFIT

The subordinate has been told that the present level of effort has not been up to snuff. More importantly, the subordinate has been encouraged to try harder by the carrot of a potential wage increase.

The boss, while denying an unjustified wage request, has at least retained the interest of the subordinate in his job. All of it has been done fairly diplomatically.

WARNING

No technique, tactic, ploy, diplomacy, double talk, and so forth is going to work unless the manager or supervisor is fair in granting wage increases. If there is any hint that a subordinate received an undeserved raise, the boss's credibility will be diminished.

A MANAGER PERK

One of the best perks that managers and supervisors have is the granting of deserved raises.

The giving of justified rewards is a big reward of itself.

Sure, the giving of more money to subordinates helps the manager or supervisor primarily to do a better job. That's why it calls for care in the granting of wage requests. However, well-deserved wage increases also make the manager or supervisor feel good—because being nice is nice.

RECOGNIZING THE EVILS OF NEPOTISM IN THE WORKPLACE

"Of all of my wife's relatives, I like myself the best."
UNKNOWN

There is the often retold story of a fellow who became a supervisor at 25, a department manager at 30, a divisional vice president at 35 and president of the company at 40. His only words about his amazing success were, "Thanks, Dad!"

The hiring of family members by higher management to work within the business need not necessarily be detrimental to the maintenance of good lines of supervisory authority.

The nephew who is hired or "recommended" for work in the shipping department by an uncle in top management, can be told at the outset that the shipping department manager is his boss.

If the uncle fails to get the situation off to a good start, then the supervisor would do well to seek an early resolution on status. After all, business is business. There has to be respect for authority and the position of the immediate superior.

Excessive favoritism could develop and the department's employee morale would suffer as well as productivity and performance.

SUGGESTED COURSES OF SUPERVISORY ACTION

1. The immediate superior should distribute the assignments on a businesslike basis. No signs of favoritism.

2. If some subordinate should cry "Foul!" the supervisor must stick to his or her guns. (Problem employees are most likely to view any supervisory action as unfair.)

3. If the relative shows an aptitude for a particular function that could lead to changes in duties or promotion, it may be best to wait until that aptitude is clearly demonstrable.

The waiting period is justified by the possible reduction of any opportunity for any grievance by others.

4. A heart-to-heart talk between the superior and the subordinate, who is a relative, may be desirable along these lines

"Wimbly, you are working out okay. However, I have a problem—I cannot even look as though I'm playing favorites in the department. I hope that you understand."
"Possibly."
"I respect your uncle, but all of the people in the section have to share the load, you as well as others. You don't have any objections to that?"
"None that I know of."
"Good, then I hope we understand each other. I have a big section to run—and I need everyone's cooperation."

5. Sometimes relatives of the brass do not make the best of subordinates. There are times when discipline, including discharge, is required. The superior might do well to apprise the uncle of the situation, using clear-cut examples of any problems that have been created by the nephew. At that point, the ball has been hit into the uncle's side of the court and it is up to him to make or suggest a move.

6. If the uncle is not of assistance in resolving the problem, the superior has to go to his or her more immediate superior or to some other higher authority for help in resolving the problem.

Basic problems

What might seem as good supervisory procedures in the daytime could appear quite contrarily different over a dinner table.

It is an uneasy situation for an immediate superior. There is a tendency to bend over backwards to make matters look better than they are.

Another problem are the attitudes of the other subordinates in the group. They can range from hostility to over-friendliness to the relative coworker. Certainly, there is going to be gossip and rumor mills hard at work. There may even be an occasional "latrine-o-gram" that the boss is going to be replaced. In any event, morale suffers—so does productivity, performance and quality.

Basic solutions

Every manager and supervisor can properly justify whatever action that he or she is taking. All decisions are usually made with a great element of fairness. That's the game and good managers and supervisors are professional in how to play it.

Remember, a relative subordinate can be used to pass on all kinds of information.

"Wimbly, our section has exceeded last year's activity by 40% without additional help."

Even bad news can be given a special and biased spin. It is worth a try.

Undercutting authority

Business is business. Few people in higher authority would like to undercut a middle manage's authority. Usually, a short conversation would have been all that is needed.

Sometimes that doesn't work. Then the manager or supervisor has to try to live with the situation (not of his or her making), seek a transfer for some other ostensible cause, or take a walk down the street.

Good people are hard to find

Once in a while, push comes to shove. Nepotism, events, pressures, the "dark forces," and so on, may require that a career move be made earlier than expected. Careful evaluation is mandatory.

An experienced cleaning person had a good credo; "Never, ever throw away dirty water *until* you have clean water."

That's a good thought in contemplating a move—stay where you are until you have another secure and comfy place to go to.

AVOID HIRING CLOSE FRIENDS OR RELATIVES OF PRESENT EMPLOYEES

"I wish my no-good nephew would get a job, so we'd finally know what kind of work he is out of."
UNKNOWN

If John is a good, hard worker, it does not necessarily follow that his brother will also be one. If Mary is a problem subordinate, it is not necessarily true that her high school friend will be a problem too. In business, as anywhere else, individuals have to be judged separately.

However, hiring judgments cannot be made in a vacuum, and there are times when it is not desirable to hire a close friend or relative of an existing employee.

FACING THE PROBLEMS OF A CLIQUE

If a number of employees are hired from the same social background, a clique can develop.

A chief problem of cliques is that they tend to become counterorganizations to the formal organization. Cliques disturb lines of authority. For instance, a leader of a clique may have greater persuasion over clique members than their immediate superiors. Nonclique members can tend to feel ostracized by their coworkers.

Cliques can be injurious to team work performance in the workforce.

Even a three-member clique in one section could be disruptive to the orderly function of that section. Limitations on the hiring of friends or relatives would have to be reviewed in consideration of the possibility of clique formation.

THE SAME HOUSEHOLD CONSIDERATIONS

In smaller communities, the wider support that the Company has with the local populace, the less antagonism there may be toward Company projects.

If employment is spread over more families rather than fewer families, the greater the extent of support for the Company. One sage put in this way:

> "It is better to have two second cousins working for you than two brothers."

ACCEPT ALL JOB RECOMMENDATIONS

It is difficult to refuse to see someone who is recommended for a job, especially when the Company approves of employee recruiting. The recommending employee can be reminded of the job qualifications of the vacancy regarding experience, and so on. If he or she still believes that the friend or relative may qualify, ask that the potential candidate come in and fill out a job application.

> *Recommendation and employment are two different matters.*

The acceptance of a recommendation does not **automatically** mean that the friend or relative will be hired on the spot. Nor does filling out an application form guarantee a job. However, it does take the employee off the hook (if there was one), since the recommending employee at least got the candidate an interview. The rest is up to the job candidate.

Taking an application requires little effort and the interview but little time. Besides, it is always possible that the applicant will be highly desirable as an employee.

GOING THROUGH THE MOTIONS

While the interview can be a chore, it is a favor to the recommending employee. In the event that the applicant cannot pass muster at the interview, the applicant can be tactfully told why:

"Pete, I thought that you had more background in our type of operation. I really appreciate you coming in to see us."

"Your salary range is justifiable. However, we are paying much less right now to people who have a number of years of good experience with our equipment. Thank you for taking the time to drop by."

"I know that you could probably do the job after a while. However, we need people who are more familiar with our product (or services). Thanks for coming by to see us."

SUGGESTION: Always appreciate an applicant's effort.

Because the interview was granted, even though the person was not hired, the goodwill of the recommending employee has been largely retained. (Everything that could have been done has been done.) Few people could expect that an **unqualified** person should be hired because of a simple recommendation.

THE WALK-IN APPLICANT

Somebody walks in off the street stating that he or she is a friend or relative of an existing employee. Fine! Give that person an application and a friendly interview.

Remember, it is more than likely that there is going to be a feedback to the present employee. It is important that the feedback imply that every consideration was given to the employee's friend or relative **because** of the friend or relative.

CASE HISTORY OF HANDLING A RELATIVE

Sid Bowlby was the production manager at a electrical appliance operation that employed 1,100 people. He was second in command after the plant manager. There was a vacancy in the Production Control Department. The PC manager reported to Sid Bowlby.

Sid's younger brother, Myron, applied for and got the job.

Shortly after the hiring, Sid Bowlby called a little meeting after work attended by himself, Myron, and the PC manager. The older brother stated that his relationship with Myron was not to interfere in the superior-subordinate relationship between

Myron and his boss. There was to be no favoritism and that Myron would have to perform like anyone else.

Myron went through the on-the-job training on the new computerized control system. However, his personality rubbed people the wrong way. That attribute was a major drawback on that job.

After a six month period, the PC manager had to let Myron go as he was not working out as planned. The PC manager explained the situation to his boss, Sid. There were no hard feelings.

RELATIONSHIP AND RESPONSIBILITY

Blood may be thicker than water, but one has to limit the extent that personal relationships interfere with getting the work out. Remember, it has been said, "Christmas is over and business is business."

If a subordinate has a special relationship, then that subordinate has to do an outstanding job. He should provide 110% effort. Why? Because any failure on his part reflects very directly on the employee with whom the subordinate has a personal relationship.

> *Sales, productivity, performance, administration,*
> *cost effectiveness, and quality control suffer if personal*
> *relationships become more important than getting*
> *the work out.*

HANDLING THE HANDICAPPED WORKER

"One of the greatest diseases is to be nobody
to anybody."
AGNES BOJAXHIU (MOTHER TERESA)

Those "do-gooders" who vent their rage at "corporate greed" usually omit one area of concern—the increasing improvements in the workplace to accommodate the physically challenged. Many businesses and industries are doing more and more so that productive work is a greater possibility to a larger segment of the population.

They do so not only because of any legal requirements, which many have gone beyond, but because of two factors: (1) it is the right thing to do, and (2) the pool of available talent is increased.

A larger available talent pool results in a higher-skilled workforce.

THE LEGAL TREND

No politician who wants to be re-elected will significantly or publicly oppose legislation that favors improved accommodations for the handicapped in the workplace. That is almost an article of faith.

There is no known special interest group (lobbyist) who generally publicly oppose benefiting the handicapped.

Not only are juries likely to hang any modern-day Mr. Scrooge, but governmental agencies will fall over each other with inspections, hearings, recommendations, delinquency reports, and taking testimony if they should get any complaint.

Probably there are some lawyers who would rather defend a corporate client against a charge of covering up a very hazardous toxic and highly radioactive waste site than defend a client against a disgruntled handicapped ex-worker.

WHAT IS THE PUBLIC POLICY?

The public views that if someone is willing to work and that there is a suitable job available, that the employer fill the vacancy. Further, if in order to fill that vacancy, the employer has to modify worker access and/or the work station, then, so be it.

WHO IS HANDICAPPED?

There is a large gray area in the definition of handicapped. Even government agencies and panels cannot agree just who is protected by governments laws and regulations.

Try this out for size! If someone weighs 400 pounds, they may be obviously handicapped. What about 300 pounds? Okay! Now, how about 280 pounds? 267 pounds? Who knows!

Can someone legitimately be refused a promotion to Sales Manager because they weigh 300 pounds and would appear displeasing to customers? A court or hearing would probably mandate the promotion.

Each borderline case is going to stand on its own. However, in the meantime, employers will have to at least pay legal costs for their own defense.

REPORTED BENEFITS

Companies that have been hiring the physically challenged have noticed some distinct qualities of these people as workers. Those reported qualities, as compared to the general workforce, include the following:

1. More appreciative of being given the chance at a job.
2. Eager to learn new possible skills that increase their personal scope and job security.
3. Somewhat more conscientious.
4. Depending on transportation conditions, more willing to work overtime.
5. Fewer complaints about dull or boring aspects of a job.
6. Higher than average commitment to quality and error-free work.

7. Other than their disabilities, few present problems to their supervision.

Boost to Overall Morale Benefit

By hiring, training and integrating the handicapped into the workforce, there is an appreciable increase in overall employee morale. It might be that the other personnel, of all ranks, think that their company is doing something worthwhile.

Recommendation: Modify Now

Building alterations cost money. However, handicapped workers need access to the workplace. Work stations and desk areas need modification to handle the special needs of handicapped people. In most situations, it is a one-time cost

It is best to make such changes as soon as possible to avoid the rush when inspections or complaints make it *mandatory quickly*. That would make it cheaper to do it now.

Some Quick Steps to Take

1. Existing contracts for building or alterations should be reviewed and amended for handicapped people considerations.
2. Have an experienced architect make recommendations for improving the access facilities for the handicapped.
3. Have office layout people redesign the office areas.
4. Require the industrial engineers to consider changes in the work areas and construction or purchase of work stations that are more adaptable to handicapped persons.

A Long Road to Go

There may be *millions of people* who would be considered as handicapped—depending on the definition of the handicapped. The ultimate apparent public policy goal is to bring as many of these millions as possible into useful and *productive* lives.

By modifying the workplace and hiring and training as many handicapped people as possible, there will be more people participating in our system.

WHEN TO ADMIT A MISTAKE TO A SUBORDINATE

"It's over, and cannot be helped, and that's one consolation, as they always say in Turkey, when they cut the wrong man's head off."
CHARLES DICKENS

It should be needless to say that managers and supervisors make mistakes as well as anyone else. However, some subordinates will needle their boss about the mistakes as if a boss is not expected to make any mistakes. A few will even go as far as to question the boss's reliability in the future.

There is an old factory saying that has been politely reworded as follows: "There are two kinds of people that don't make mistakes, those who don't make anything and those who are liars."

A boss is respected because it is assumed that by virtue of training and experience the boss will make a minimum of errors. However, more important than whether errors are made is a boss's ability to handle the situation created by his or her own error. A good measure of the ability to control the situation is the extent of control on subordinate reaction.

REDUCE THE INTERPLAY

"So what?"

That question to Joe Needle, a perennial nitpicker, puts the ball in Needle's court and reduces the issue of an inconsequential mistake. What can Joe legitimately answer—if ever he had the right to bring the matter up in the first place. The two-worded question does not admit the mistake or deny it, and more important, it reduces conversation about it to the minimum.

There is little, if any, reason to admit, confess, recant or apologize for every little goof. If the boss does not want to pursue the matter any further, then:

"So what?"

WATCHING IMPORTANT ISSUES

Since the lowest supervisor or someone in the highest levels of top management can make a mistake, they have to admit to a goof now and then.

One of the reasons that European radio broadcasts of the British Broadcasting Corporation (BBC)—a government institution—were believable to the Germany enemy during World War II was their ready admission of British defeats, such as Norway, Crete, and other disasters. Such remarkable admissions created an image of reliability.

No one is going to believe that any boss is perfect, an occasional admission is desirable—in part, because more important matters will have greater credibility.

Making someone else the guilty party works only a few times. After that, the boss creates a credibility gap. (Few will believe anything down the road.) Another drawback is that the errant boss incurs poor relationships with other supervisors, managers and top brass.

PICK THE SITUATION

As one can agree, not every mistake is worthy of confession. The supervisor would do well to select the mistake that he or she wishes to admit to:

> "Nancy, I should not have told you to use the punch
> press instead of the drill press to run that job. It was
> my mistake—and it ran up production time."

The subordinate was not at fault for the time overrun—nor was anyone else. It was a natural error in judgment, and the boss took the fall.

TIMING IS IMPORTANT

The boss should not wait until being forced into admitting a mistake. If there is any waiting or hesitation, the delay might indicate a deliberate attempt to sneak the error by.

Remember, conversations about an error may tend to increase the magnitude of the error. Quick admissions cut down the yakking and will permit the boss and the section to get on with other matters—including making up time for the goof.

INDUCE GROUP (TEAM) SUPPORT

If the subordinates are treated as a unified group, they may be likely to work harder after the goof. After all, if the quarterback calls the wrong play, cannot the team be expected to try very hard to make up for lost yardage?

"Hey, fellows and gals, let's make up for my snafu!"

PRESERVING THE LEADERSHIP QUALITY

An important consideration in leadership is not to lose one's head over a mistake. It was made, caught, and corrected. That is just the time to rally the leadership dynamics.

To sit and moan after even a major snafu could indicate weak leadership ability. The point is to go on and to keep things moving.

Some people go all to pieces when they make a mistake. They bang desks, use inappropriate language, shout, and display other tantrums. To any observer of such a scene, such carrying on indicates poor leadership because of a lack of self-control.

WATCH THE BRASS

The top people in the executive wing or floor make big mistakes every day. Why? Because the opportunity for bigger mistakes is in their area. They can overestimate sales for the next quarter, fire the wrong managers, cause overages on nonmoving inventory, buy poor equipment, lose a government contract, initiate a cash crunch, and so forth.

These bigger mistakes are taken in their stride. They are evaluated and counter reactions taken. Therefore, it behooves people in middle and lower levels of management to learn how to handle their goofs, take remedial action and go on from there.

FIRING A SUBORDINATE WHO WAS HIRED BY THE BOSS

*"He was fired with enthusiasm because he wasn't
fired with enthusiasm."*
ANONYMOUS

If normal hiring practices were not followed in any particular instance, it is best to find out why. The very minimum of good management dictates that a job applicant be interviewed and approved for hiring by the person to whom the applicant is expected to report.

In any case where the immediate superior was by-passed in the hiring decision process, there should be some attempt to gain insight into the reasoning through discussions with the subordinate and the person making the hiring decision.

POOR MANAGEMENT

The problem of a higher superior making the hiring decision over the head of the immediate supervisor is that the supervisor's hands may be tied in any firing decision.

It has been said in jest (but is often all too true) that an employee is like a missile into space; if you cannot fire him, then you cannot make him work.

IMPORTANT MANAGERIAL CONCEPT

The largest disciplinary threat or the ultimate big stick is the immediate boss's right to cause the discharge of a subordinate. Any limitation of that threat capability provides satisfactory work limitations to merely supervisor persuasion or relies excessively on subordinate motivation.

Most people in higher management levels are business minded. If they have made a mistake either in by-passing normal hiring methods or in selecting an unsuitable job applicant, both of which are demonstrably adverse to productivity, they usually will be the first to try to amend the situation.

UNIQUE JUSTIFICATION

The key word above is "demonstrably." A supervisor who wants to discipline a subordinate who has been hired by a higher level of management must clearly demonstrate that there is significant cause for the discipline. Mere pique or a tantrum about the bypassing of authority is insufficient.

Of course, every action for discipline must be well justified. Otherwise, the Company would gain a bad reputation. In a case where someone in higher authority has done the hiring, it will also be necessary to prove a solid case for severe discipline.

> *NOTE: A solid case does not mean greater reason for any dismissal, but only greater documentation or proof.*

If a lack of productivity is the cause, then actual comparative figures must be shown.

FIRST TEST THE WATERS

> "Mr. Blockhead, I have a problem with Charley."
>
> "Oh, that's the fellow I hired for you."
>
> "Yes, he may not be working out as planned. Can I discuss the matter with you?"

NEXT, SEEK SOME CLUES

Let's face it, few people would like to admit that they made a mistake in a hiring decision, and even less if good hiring procedures were bypassed. (That would be a *compounded* error of judgment.) However, an early discussion with the errant boss might reveal whether he also has concluded that a mistake has been made.

If the errant boss approaches such a discussion with an open mind, he may indicate what is required in the way of justifying a firing decision.

Obtain Approval

The supervisor can present the best possible case for the desired action.

> *WARNING: Avoid any criticism of the original **hiring** decision. Diplomacy comes first.*

Facts and figures are desirable. Specifics of major snafus are helpful. (Stay away from petty stuff—it is usually insufficient cause for canning, anyway.)

There is one side issue that can be helpful—the bearing of the existing situation on the morale of other subordinates and the ability to be even handed in matters of discipline.

What if Mr. Blockhead says, "insufficient cause?" Then, the supervisor should try for the minimum concession—a future meeting to review the situation again.

In the interim, Mr. Blockhead might advise the particular subordinate of the situation. Then there may be an attempt on the subordinate's part to perform more satisfactorily.

The Probable Verdict

In most situations, there would be approval of the supervisor's discipline recommendation. If the responsibilities of running the sections or departments are given to the supervisors and managers, so too is the authority given to them.

Authority in the workplace is ineffectual unless all superiors have the use of the greatest measure of discipline, the right to fire subordinates.

The Logic of the Chain of Command

The shipping department manager is the top brass's man or woman in the shipping department. Either they have confidence in the shipping department manager or they do not.

Giving the manager or supervisor the responsibility of getting the work out in a department or section also means giving that person the tools (the authority) to do the job.

Higher levels of management, who bypass the chain of command (that they set up) are undercutting their very appointees and preventing them from fully getting the work out.

WHEN TO AVOID PUTTING INSTRUCTIONS IN WRITING

"I have only made this letter long because I have not had time to make it shorter."

BLAISE PASCAL

There are many circumstances in which communications have to be in writing. Equally, there are many times when it is inadvisable to put matters into writing or any other form of more permanent record.

Oral communication has several distinct advantages. For one thing, oral discussion permits a give-and-take exchange of views and can result in immediate feedback.

USING CROSS COMMUNICATION

A memo which explains a part of a previous memo which in turn evokes a prior memo may be a silly exaggeration. However, this illustration does describe the sort of situation that can be avoided by quick discussion of the subject matter.

A valuable attribute of oral communication is the ability to get the receiving party's opinions and questions about the topic at hand. Discussion permits faster assessment of other views more readily than the written word.

USING TELEPHONES

Memos and letters cost more than telephone calls in time and effort. Internal and external calling costs money also. While there is some effort and expense to using the telephone, it permits more possible cross communication. Even the expense of conference calling is offset by the benefits of the quick exchange of ideas. Where speed of communication is a material factor, few methods are comparable to the telephone.

ELECTRONIC MAIL

The use of computers, terminals, word processors with modems, fax machines, and so on, have a drawback over oral communications. The same interchange is slower and not as much give and take as oral communication.

TELEPHONES VERSUS MEETINGS

In most situations, a face-to-face meeting can afford more communication than a phone. For one thing, there is body language and other signs of response and depth that is not available on the telephone. The drawback of face-to-face meetings is the time consumption which telephones tend to reduce.

PERSONAL POINT FOR MANAGERS

A singular advantage for the "rising star" manager or supervisor is what the face-to-face meeting has over all other forms of communication. In addition to the message, a middle manager person on the upward move can display higher leadership qualities.

Personal dynamics, energy, enthusiasm, potential, drive, zeal, chutzpa, or whatever, can easily be conveyed to other parties via face-to-face meetings. Little of those qualities can be conveyed by electronics or paper.

BACK TO THE MESSAGE

A communication is put into writing within a certain set of understood circumstances or against a particular background. When those conditions no longer exist, will the comments in a written communication still be valid? If the answer is "no" or is in doubt, it would be better not to set the comments down in writing.

A written communication cannot possibly cover *all* of the background and circumstances surrounding a situation, and therefore its content may be viewed as out of context to whatever prompted it. A logical conclusion is that to avoid any possible future misunderstandings, certain instructions and comments need not be put into writing.

Minimizing criticism

It is far easier to criticize the written word than the spoken word.

The spoken word is a "he said, she said" battle in which memories are tested to determine exactly what was said. However, the written word is in black and white and therefore regrettably provable and much easier as a vehicle of criticism.

Applying emphasis

The spoken instruction or comment can be made to include various tones of emphasis; even salty language may be more readily included. Therefore, oral orders or requests are more commanding because the tone or voice inflection can make them so.

"Roscoe, I need the information NOW."

"Winslow, get the . . . . . order out tomorrow."

Words, words, words

Whether the media are memos, letters, speech, telephones, telexes, Faxes, PCs and modems, or whatever, the communicator has to be a wordsmith. There is no quick pill to take to improve the art of using words carefully. For the middle manager who wants to be understood and get things done, there is only practice.

Middle managers use words to get people to do something that they may not want to do.

One little trick is to use every communication as a sales letter. The communication could be selling an idea or even just the good qualities of the communicator. Therefore, the communicator should review every communication and ask himself or herself one question; "Was *I* sold on the concept?" If not, start over.

Here's some more advice on memos

An experienced executive, who received many memos each day from middle and lower managers, would review the memos not only for content but for the following as well:

1. Did the memo convey sufficient analysis? Was there a good grasp of the subject of the memo?
2. Was there an understandable flow of information through the memo to its conclusion?
3. Was any recommendation made justified by the content?
4. Were a surplus of words used?

"The most essential gift for a good writer is a built-in shock-proof s### detector."
ERNEST HEMINGWAY

USING THE PERSONNEL DEPARTMENT FOR SOME PEOPLE PROBLEMS

"The closest to perfection a person ever comes is when he fills out a job application form."
STANLEY J. RANDALL

We don't always comprehend and support all of the Personnel Department policies. That is true from one company to the next.

The policies and procedures are mandated by the powers that be—the highest levels of management. Most of the personnel policies and procedures are an attempt to be uniform in the handling of employee matters. However, people situations do differ.

THE FOREVER CONFLICT

Which comes first, productivity or procedures.

For every line manager or supervisor, getting the work out is the primary goal. Why? Because that is what he or she is told to do. By whom? By the very people who also mandate standardized personnel policies and procedures.

The line supervisory people, who have to cope with day-to-day realities of maintaining productivity, performance, quality, cost effectiveness, and so on, at times require some flexibility of employee policies.

MINIMIZING CONSISTENCY PROBLEMS

Mr. Fred Sparkplug is a very capable manager. He encourages enthusiasm among his subordinates. Some respond better than others, show more initiative, or require less supervision. Should all the people in his section be treated alike? The subordinate who knocks out 1,000 perfect widgets (invoices, purchase orders, or whatever) a day is required to get the same treatment from the Company as the slowest member of Sparkplug's team! And, error-prone Charley has equal status with Mr. Perfect.

The answer is not standardized treatment.

Company policies must be flexible and allow for exceptions in order to accomplish the overall corporate goals.

INDUSTRIAL RELATIONS VIEWPOINT

Personnel policies are definitions of limitations which include the maximum costs to which the Company is willing to go.

There has to be controls on labor cost. The personnel procedures enforce cost control. They prevent erratic or inconsistent expenditures which can set adverse precedents or can be extremely costly.

Significant breaching of the procedures might prevent attainment of other objectives of the management.

GETTING THE BEST OF BOTH WORLDS

Line managers and supervisors should try to work up a rapport with the personnel department staff. After all, everybody is in the same organization.

Using an established rapport, line people can present a particular employee-problem case to the Personnel people. (Both functional areas should apply their expertise to the problem.) From the reaction, the line manager or supervisor may encounter a hint or how to accomplish a mutual satisfactory solution.

An advantage to the rapport is that the Personnel staff can gain an insight into operational people problems.

The Personnel Department is a *service* organization. They cannot be of service unless they know how. They can only know how if their "customers" (the line people) tell them how.

CASE HISTORY OF WORKING TOGETHER

After several mergers, a reorganized department had employee problems that were created by wage levels versus the actual job functions. That is, some employees were making less money than others who were doing the same job, and even less than some performing a less demanding function. Job titles were also whacky.

Here was a successful technique. The operating manager requested the Personnel Department to a assign a personnel staff assistant to the department on a temporary basis to help with the problem.

After a few weeks of working right at the scene within the department, and by obtaining input of the department manager's objectives, the staff assistant came with desirable changes.

The operating department was able to reslot job functions and titles, make salary adjustments, provide for further near term salary reviews and to, in general, reduce employee problems of a previously inequitable structure.

WHY COOPERATION WORKED

Half of the success of the project was attributable to the fact that a personnel staff assistant geographically worked within the operating department while developing the recommended changes. The daily contacts provided some insight into the problems. The other half of the reasons for solving the department's problems was the willingness to override some personnel policies and procedures.

WHY COOPERATION SOMETIMES FAILS

"Stay off my turf."

Turfs, empires, and territories can be counterproductive toward overall organizational goals. Sometimes the management is aware of these divisions, other times not. There are many instances where the internal policies encourages acrimonious relationships.

Example. A department says, "We will enforce our policies and procedures to the letter." In such a circumstance, that declaration can mean that increased sales or deliveries (or any other corporate goal) is not a major consideration.

Top brass has to state and act emphatically that the overall corporate goals are the primary consideration in management decisions.

THE BETTER WAY—DEPARTMENTAL COOPERATION

The inability of a service department to cooperate with a line department is not the failure of any departmental manager. It is the failure of the top management to weld a cooperative team. By statement and deed, the higher levels of management (the real makers and shakers) can incur more departmental cooperation.

CHOOSING WHICH EMPLOYEES TO LAY OFF DURING A PARTIAL LAYOFF

"Personnel selection is decisive. People are our most valuable capital."

JOSEPH STALIN

In a foundering lifeboat, the skipper has to make quick decisions as to which people in the lifeboat are to get out of the boat in order to save the others. For the same reason, a manager has to select who is to be retained in a partial layoff.

The personnel retention decisions are affected by an evaluation of who can contribute most to keeping up the necessary production or performance levels and then be able to help plan and make a successful transition to full production in the future.

UNION CONTRACT LIMITATIONS—SENIORITY

Where the union contract limits the decision making, the manager may have little discretion. However, a manager may be able to review the performance fitness of employees, who are bumped into various categories based on seniority, by indicating whether they are qualified to perform certain job classifications.

Frequently, no leeway may exist where a senior machinist bumps a junior machinist. The manager may have some control in more remote shifting around, such as when a machinist wants to be an inventory clerk.

Qualifications can be a deciding factor in certain bumping.

WATCH THE NONSENIORITY FACTORS

Length of service can be a retention factor if it is also indicative of experience gained and versatility. The factors that can influence the retention decision could include the following:

1. Various useful skills of the employees. Note: retention can lean toward subordinates who can do a greater variety of job functions.
2. The difficulty of replacing certain skilled subordinates during a return to higher production levels.
3. The difficulties in training programs for certain skills.
4. Beneficial supplier relationships.
5. Good customer relationships.
6. Levels of productivity or performance.
7. Extent of error-free work. Ability at self-checking.
8. The ability to learn newly required skills and the handling of new equipment or computer routines.
9. Availability for overtime and weekend work, if required.
10. Attendance and on-time records.
11. Salary levels.
12. Capability of being integrated into a new team.
13. Attitude toward changes, particularly in the workflow.
14. Extent of unsupervised working capability.
15. Self-starting initiative.

KEY PERSON RECRUITING DIFFICULTIES

"If we let Wilbur go now, he is going to get a job quickly. When we rehire, we will have a difficult time finding an experienced skilled toolmaker (or programmer) like him. Apprentices will not be helpful. Wilbur can make beautiful tools from a rough drawing. His salary during the slack period is our investment in the future, when we really will need him."

"You know the lead time for getting our customer reports. Without Nancy's willingness to work overtime in a pinch, we wouldn't have been paid on a couple of jobs. People who are willing to work a lot of overtime on short notice, are not readily available."

"Sure, George is high salary—but he can do anything that we throw at him. We need him now and in the future because he can pinchhit almost anywhere. George knows our business; a new outsider would not."

NEW ASSET—SKELETON TEAM VALUE

The reduction in staff or workforce should reduce the remaining team to those who can obtain maximum productivity and performance while working together under perhaps difficult circumstances.

In addition to employee cutbacks, there may be other cost reduction programs that will make even minimum achievements more difficult. While a reduced team may not be expected to be as effective as a full team—there will be managerial expectations of performance—particularly with regard to cost containment.

In the selection of the minimum team, those subordinates, who could contribute most to the effort of keeping the lifeboat afloat the longest, would have greater priority for retention.

Tight retention requirements will provide more current job security for the survivors of a layoff and greater potential for a worthwhile turnaround in circumstances.

WHEN IT HITS THE FAN

For one reason or another, one reduction in force may not be enough. And, management mandates a second go-around. Sometimes, even a third.

One additional retention factor at such a (miserable) time is that managers have more insight into which of their present subordinates were best able to hold up after the prior layoff.

MANAGER HAZARD—SLEEPLESS NIGHTS

Layoffs are an experience that few managers like to go through. (Especially, multiple and large reductions in force.) In some industries, unfortunately, it goes with the territory. Even in those industries racked by ups and downs where there are such recurring expectations, there is personal trauma about layoff decision.

"Just because it is necessary, doesn't mean you like it."

MANAGER CAREER NOTE

When push comes to shove, managers can be laid off just like any nonmanagement worker. The marketplace can dictate the wholesale furloughing of managers.

Managers have to think about how they are going to earn a place in the lifeboat at a time of layoffs.

A multiskilled manager can have a more likely chance of surviving a layoff—at least more of a chance than a single skilled manager. In addition, the multiskilled manager can more readily walk across the street, across town or across the country to another possibly better job.

Needed managerial skills can provide two benefits as follows: (1) existing job security and (2) job mobility. The obvious recommendation for any manager, particularly in industries plagued by layoffs, is to learn, learn, and learn.

HOW TO MAKE MORE PRODUCTIVE USE OF SLACK TIME

"Everything comes to him who hustles while he waits."
THOMAS A. EDISON

The very nature of business is uneven. The ups and downs in customer or client demand create relative vibrations in operating requirements in most industries.

During the up (increasing volume) periods, management resorts to overtime and other techniques to meet the current requirements.

In the down periods, layoffs result up to a point as a skeleton force is frequently maintained in the event of a turnaround and to meet improvement in demand for products and services.

During slack profitability periods, it is desirable to use existing staff more effectively than usual.

SHUN MAKE-WORK CHORES

The least recommended option is the use of make-work chores which simply keep idle hands busy. Such assignments provide minimal contribution to profits, no reduction of costs, and, possibly worst, are adverse to good levels of employee morale.

Digging a hole and then filling it is a pointless chore except for exercise.

REDUCE COSTS PLOYS

RECOMMENDATION: Produce previously purchased parts in house.

Those types of parts that do not require significant further equipment outlay or large inventory changes may be the most ideal for consideration for in-house production.

An initial view is that in-house production will cost more. Not so. Get the cost cruncher people to have another look. The labor is there to be used anyway—otherwise it is idle. Then, when full production resumes, these previously purchased parts and materials will be available at little more than the material cost. The labor and overhead costs mount up anyway whether purchased parts are produced in-house or not.

In the administrative areas, consideration can be given to the development of in-house capability for performing services previously purchased from the outside.

New skills are developed in-house which can be useful in the event that future supplier bottlenecks or shortages develop when there is full production.

TEST NEW TECHNIQUES

A slack period is the better time to try out new methods and materials which can save effort or expense than when there is full production.

Revised layouts of machines and personnel can be tried, as well as revisions in the workflow. The development of alternate production methods also has the side benefit of providing versatility during full capacity in the event that there is down time on the equipment or a shortage of certain types of skilled labor.

New methods of reporting and computer systems design can be researched and tested during slack periods as well.

TOOL, MACHINE, AND COMPUTER IMPROVEMENT

Small tools can be redesigned and tested to perform particular functions better or faster. Larger pieces of equipment could be made more versatile or faster by adaption or improvement for more error-free production

In addition, new types of machines could be brought in on a trial basis for examination in an actual production environment.

Computer equipment can be updated and modified according to possible changing needs. New programs can be tested—all with a minimum of interference in normal operations.

INVENTORY CONTROL

During periods of minimum turnover, physical inventories can be taken and compared to inventory records. Differences can be researched as to causes and remedial action in reporting methods taken. More accurate inventory reporting will aid in production control efforts.

Such effort will minimize imbalances and particularly out-of-stock situations when full activity resumes.

Another ideal inventory task during slow periods is to so rearrange the inventory so that the new arrangement reduces handling effort or movement in the future. Faster-moving items would be more readily available for production needs.

DON'T SELL SCRAP

During the peak periods, parts, sub-assemblies, and assemblies that do not meet quality control standards should be retained.

In the slow periods, all of these materials can be reclassified as to their potential for being reworked into salable or useable products.

In addition, new rework techniques could also be developed which can save more of the items for future rework and use. Once again, the labor is on hand anyway.

NEW OUTLOOK

The multiskilled worker is a more valuable asset to the Company.

RECOMMENDATION: Cross train more people.

Even if standby or idle time is spotty from section to section, that is a good time to do some cross training of personnel and the lower level supervisory people.

"Waldo can handle the industrial products also."

In times of high volume or labor shortages, cross-trained people can be more quickly moved around to workflow requirements.

In union shops, they may be some hollering. However, it can be pointed out that cross training improves job security.

MANAGER AND SUPERVISOR TRAINING

If rank and filers who have more skills are of benefit to the organization and themselves, then consider how much greater the benefit there can be if front line managers and supervisors had more managerial skills.

Managers and supervisors who have working knowledge of more than their own areas are geometrically of more value because they can then more effectively appreciate the bigger organizational and operating picture.

GETTING A SUBORDINATE TO CHANGE VACATION PLANS

> *"The only one who got everything done by Friday was Robinson Crusoe."*
> JOHN PEERS, Logical Machine Corporation

Everyone looks forward to their vacation. It is a chance to be with family, see new places, and have new and exciting experiences. Personal plans are comparatively complex, involving travel and accommodation reservations, scheduling of other family members who work or go to school, arrangements at home, and so forth.

Therefore, when a manager or supervisor wants to reschedule a subordinate's vacation, it has to be done with a certain amount of regard for the personal arrangements the subordinate may have made.

ANTICIPATING PROBLEMS

> *If there is even a remote chance that the vacation schedules are tentative, the subordinates should be so apprised.*

In industries or situations where there are dramatic swings in personnel requirements, a safety step should be considered. That is, corporate policy might dictate, with exceptions, that no more than one week of vacation can be taken in any one month. Exceptions are regulated by the vacation problems of the subordinate and the needs of the operation.

The Company's written procedures with regard to vacations can indicate that employee preferences will be honored **where possible**. However, there are limitations. The obligations to plant operations take priority and that vacation scheduling is conditional to the workload and backlog situations as well as to the subordinate's superior's requirements.

AVOIDANCE OF PROBLEMS

Every attempt to avoid reshifting of any vacations should be made.

While there may be some operating inconveniences, very few people are indispensable to the operation. If they are, the workflow should be altered because although vacations can be scheduled satisfactorily, illness or other cause of absence cannot be.

RESCHEDULE VACATIONS LAST

Good management dictates that a vacation timing commitment be kept. (Even where it is tentative.)

Other remedial measures that can be considered before any rescheduling of vacations could include the following:

1. Use of overtime.
2. Saturday work.
3. Increased night shifts.
4. Use of temporary personnel or part-timers.
5. Job classification changes.
6. Reassignment of work to others.
7. Delaying certain tasks
8. Bringing in retired personnel.

The last and least favorable option is to require a subordinate to change any vacation scheduling. Every other possibility should be considered first.

EFFECT ON EMPLOYEE MORALE

Reshifting of vacation schedules is an indication of poor management capability.

Sure there are ups and downs, swings in demand, feast and famine, and season and nonseason volume considerations. They happen in the best of regulated situations. However, the ability to anticipate and handle fluctuations is one of the differences between good and poor management.

If management permits the constant practice of shifting vacation schedules, it will be a damper on employee morale. Not just because of their own plans being shook up, but as a reflection that management just may be incompetent.

HERE IS A SWEETENER—MORE PAYCHECKS

A subordinate may welcome the opportunity to get his or her vacation pay in lieu of taking the time off. In other words, the subordinate would get double pay for working during his or her vacation—54 weeks of pay for 52 weeks of work. Many people can use the extra money.

What about the extra cost? This option may be cheaper and less effort than hiring temporaries, using overtime, or any other option. Face it, if other labor options are used, the Company is paying for 54 weeks anyway and for two of those weeks, no work is being performed.

If agreeable to the subordinate, this option removes problems associated with rescheduling the workload·and can maintain productivity.

> *"It's so hard to find a good vacation spot since they closed down Devil's Island."*
> LILY MUNSTER, "The Munsters" TV Show

OVERCOMING SUBORDINATE OBJECTIONS

Whether it is a matter of getting paid double or not, the subordinate is being asked to change vacation plans. It may be desirable to find out first what plans have been made in order to assist the subordinate in making any required changes.

If nonrefundable deposits have been made for travel or other accommodations, the Company could consider standing the loss of any deposits of behalf of the subordinate.

For rescheduling, the superior can inquire if other members of the employee's family can make adjustments to their schedules. The suggested new vacation dates may work in with plans of other family members.

Giving advance notice, cooperating in making changes, and being willing to reimburse the subordinate for any lost deposits, and so on, are techniques that provide an atmosphere of acceptance of the requested change.

THE "INDISPENSABLE" SUBORDINATE

There are times when a manager or supervisor has to permit (or even encourage) the subordinate to take a vacation as planned—no matter what is breaking loose at the moment.

The crunch is on, the backlog is staggering, some people are out sick, others are already on vacation, reports are late, the sales manager wants orders expedited, the computer terminals went down, the boss is frothing at the mouth, no one "volunteers" for overtime, and good old Charley has to be told, "Have a good time in Hawaii."

Why? Because Charley may come to think that he is indispensable.

Crunches come and go. A problem with an "indispensable" subordinate may last much longer. A good front line manager or supervisor will find shortcuts, overcome shortages of almost anything—people, supplies, information, or whatever—and work around the clock to avoid favors which a boss may not be able to pay back.

HOW TO GET A SUBORDINATE TO RESIGN

"Tell me, Dobkins: how long have you been with us—
not counting today."
DAVID FROST, BBC TV

It is always more desirable that an employee and the employer part company on as friendly a basis as possible. This is not always feasible, but is still desirable. A resignation may create less animosity than an outright dismissal.

For one thing, it is a face saving ploy for the employee. Many would rather be asked to resign than be actually fired. The trauma of a dismissal can create ill feeling, perhaps undeserved, which is adverse to the image of the employee as well as the employer. The ex-employee could become disgruntled and cause mischief in many ways after leaving. A mutual understanding and a tearless parting can prevent problems which might otherwise arise.

COMPANY ERROR IN JUDGMENT

Recruiting capable people is a very difficult chore, and occasionally, an unavoidable mistake is made as to an applicant's capabilities.

In addition, every so often, a mistake is made in that an existing subordinate cannot handle changed or additional duties and/or responsibilities.

In either case, continued retention is a compounding of the original error.

Basically, it is not the employee's mistake that management erred in judgment as to whether a person could fill the bill; it is largely management's fault. Therefore, why is it necessary to penalize the employee throughout his or her working life by putting a dismissal on record? It is not necessary. If an employee is fired, he or she will find it more difficult to get another job than if he or she is permitted to resign.

LAST ONE OUT, TURN OUT THE LIGHTS

Excessive turnover is detrimental to employee morale. In addition, turnover feeds on itself.

When any job insecurity is created (for any reason), there are other employees who begin looking for other jobs—or, at least, will listen to recruiters or follow up on help wanted ads. As turnover increases—no matter what the cause—job insecurity increases.

People come, people go, so what? Look at it this way: who is the first to leave? The best and most capable people. Why? They can get a replacement job quicker!

Good people leaving is not the only downside! Who is left? Well, the *least* capable people are going to hang around—because they have more difficulty in getting another job.

A business in trouble is not like a sinking ship. On a sinking ship, the rats leave first. At a business, where there have been many firings and related job insecurity, the slow pokes, error prone, red tape artists, clock watchers, socializers, bottlenecks, goldbricks, and so on, are going to be the last to want to leave.

PARTIAL SOLUTION

In order to counter any job insecurity created by turnover, it is desirable that those who do leave seem to leave of their OWN accord. Resignations do not contribute as much trepidation regarding job security as dismissals can.

DEMONSTRATE INADEQUACIES

Early in the decision-making process of asking a subordinate to resign, the subordinate's work efforts can be shown as counterproductive. Here's how:

"Charley, this order was for 1,000 widgets. You put it through for 100."

Let Charley alibi or admit his own mistakes. Avoid harping on the same situation. However, continue to demonstrate the problems:

"Charley, you ordered 800 part B's. Do you know that you have over 5,000 in stock in your area?"

VOLUNTEERING

Charley may become aware that the axe is being sharpened for him. If nothing else, Charley may assume that his career chances at his present location are limited. Then, if Charley anticipates all of this, he may be considering resigning. He may even start looking around for a new job. Maybe, at first, he will be testing the labor market. At any rate, there is a good chance that Charley is likely to quit without a fuss.

Remember, in most instances the subordinate would rather resign then possibly louse up a quick move elsewhere.

SHOWDOWN TIME

If Charley has not read the handwriting on the wall, or he is reluctant even after several demonstrations of his mistakes and snafus, a confrontation is in order. The discussion is best held after quitting time when few other subordinates are around. In addition, a private meeting will mean that the subordinate will lose a minimum of face and possible rumors will be reduced.

"Charley, you know how your work has been lately. It may be our fault for putting you in so deep. Whatever the reason, we have to part company. Your career is important to you and we do not want a firing to affect your chances of getting another job quickly. So, in appreciation of the fact that you have tried to succeed, you are going to be allowed to resign."

The timing of the resignation, severance pay, and other exit conditions are strong factors to reinforce a decision to resign and can be presented as such.

THE LAW OF THE LAND

Courts view different resignations differently.

If there is a disgruntled ex-employee suit for any cause whatsoever, a resignation secured under duress is frequently considered the same as a discharge. What constitutes duress? A threat that the employee would be fired anyway.

Nevertheless, even if an ex-employee suit is possible or even anticipated for some reason, a resignation is better evidence in behalf of the employer than a discharge. And, as a practical matter, the resignation may discourage a suit.

> *Warning: If a suit is threatened or is considered possible by an employee as an ex-employee, contact the corporate counsel promptly.*

THE MANAGER'S CONSCIENCE

Firings and resignations are a part of any good manager's or supervisor's duty. Things have to be done that are not personally pleasant. To counter the unpleasant, the valid management concept is that it is better to terminate than to keep some deadwood on the payroll for 30 years or so.

Failure to let a subordinate go is not necessarily fair to the other subordinates who may be knocking themselves out to do more of their share of the load. However, letting the errant subordinate resign—even by duress—makes the superior's job a lot easier emotionally. And that is a big side benefit.

HOW AND WHY TO ENCOURAGE A SUBORDINATE TO TRANSFER OUT

"Every organization has a Siberia."
WARREN G. BENNIS

At times, a supervisor may wish that a particular employee would transfer out of the department to somewhere else in the organization. Reasons may include the inability of the subordinate to work with others, personality conflicts with the supervisor, or the belief that subordinate's efforts would be of greater value elsewhere.

Mandatory transfers are less well received than a voluntary transfer and can create an undesirable situation. However, if the employee does it voluntarily—even with some coaxing—the results can be better.

"I don't want the people who YOU don't want."

WHY NOT DISCHARGE?

Not every employee performs actions or has work attributes which require dismissal. Besides, even discipline for good cause has various gradients of penalties.

THE RESISTANCE

Let's face it, few employees like to be transferred. Even moves that have to be made for work volume considerations. A transfer requires a change in work environment, forming new friendships, developing relationships with new superiors, and so on.

There is also the unwelcome feeling of being just a clock number, or a hand tool to be passed around. Even if there were conflicts that troubled the subordinate in the present work situation, there is a natural inclination against a transfer. The grass doesn't always look greener in another department.

PRELIMINARY TESTING OF SUBORDINATE ATTITUDE

The extent of any emotional resistance to the change should be determined quickly. A manager or supervisor can gauge reaction to:

> "Waldo, I have a request for your services by another department."

> "Maxey, have you ever thought of working in the main frame section?"

> "Winston, your special (don't over do it) abilities can be very useful in Mr. Jones' department."

THE FOLLOW-UP—THE CON GAME

Frequently, a more accurate indicator of the subordinate's reaction is possible after he or she knows what the boss thinks of the transfer:

> "I may not like to lose you, but it could work out for the best for you and the Wire Department."

> "We sure hate to watch you transfer out, but it's best for the Company."

> "The whole team will miss you but wish you the best of luck where you are going."

> "Look old buddy, you are limited in advancement here, but this transfer gives you new possible opportunities."

THE VOLUNTARY SUGGESTION—THE STING

After gauging the subordinate's reaction to the "suggested" change, the manager or supervisor can take a position on making the transfer voluntary:

> "Your transfer could be made mandatory, but that will not look good in your personnel file—nor would Mr. Jones feel that you were gung-ho on his team."

> "If you request a transfer, I could add a memo in your file that you were very cooperative in making this switch and that it was your idea."

"If you were to request a transfer, the acceptance of the request could be timed to be advantageous for everybody."

FOR THE HARD CORE IMMOVABLE PROBLEM

"Charley, I've been nice up to now. You either take a voluntary transfer or I turn you over to personnel."

Chances are that Charley will take the walk down the hall voluntarily.

WHY PLAY AROUND?

Well, for one thing, a boss has to be kind to the egos of some subordinates. Further, a mandatory transfer might not look good to the rest of the subordinates in the department or section.

WHAT CAN HAPPEN

It is surprising how many people work out very satisfactorily with a new boss, new coworkers, new responsibilities, new challenges, and so on. A whole new world can open up. The move is ultimately good for both the subordinate and the Company.

Many people find that a lateral transfer was the best thing that ever happened to them. At first, they might have missed their old situation. However, then they grow into their new environment and fully blossom. They take roots and then they resist being moved again. It's the old repeated story.

"However,, I really like the Shipping Department (or Siberia)."

THE BEST TIME OF THE DAY TO FIRE A SUBORDINATE

"This is going to hurt me more than it hurts you."
Sign in a dentist's office

One of the more unappealing aspects of being a boss is having to fire a subordinate. Nobody likes to do it, but at times it has to be done. It is an aggravating experience at best.

Of course, the employee does not like it either.

Physical threats, crying sessions, accusations, lawsuit intimidation, and bitter words may be a part of the firing scenario. Subsequently, the subordinate as a disgruntled ex-employee could be disruptive in various ways.

REACTION OF DISCHARGED EMPLOYEES

The realization of the loss of immediate earnings is a problem but not as big as the dented ego problem.

WARNING: One cannot fully anticipate how a discharged employee will act that is in an unexpected fashion.

Whatever the cause for the dismissal and even if recognized by the subordinate, the discharged employee may act irrationally or antagonistically toward the boss or the management.

There is no predictive device to determine how a fired subordinate will take the dismissal. Some will take it with a shrug. Others may believe that there has been some kind of injustice—real or imaginary—and evince a poor reaction.

Look out for the ploys. The dismissed subordinate may be verbally abusive, attempt to see someone in top management, be a telephone nut, discourage productive efforts by other employees, act adversely toward customers or suppliers, and be a general nuisance.

"I'm very bad at firing people, Mr. Grant. I once had
to move rather than fire a housekeeper."
MARY RICHARDS, "The Mary Tyler Moore Show"

THE SUNRISE EXECUTION

Early morning drama is okay but not for firing. If the firing
takes place in the morning, the boss has all day to contend
with his or her own emotions about having to fire someone. A
superior has feelings too—that could affect performance and a
perspective in handling other people situations during the rest
of the day. Why start a day with unpleasantness?

THE AFTERNOON HANGING

Firing a subordinate in the afternoon will leave a potentially
abusive or disrespectful employee plenty of time to react during
the rest of the day. Even if the ex-employee is off the premises
immediately after the firing, there can be unpleasant telephone
calls to higher management, other subordinates, customers, suppliers, and so on. In addition, the ex-employee can visit some
of these same people.

While a dismissed subordinate is not likely to seek revenge,
there can be expressions of resentment.

There is somewhat of a restraining influence. The ex-employee
may realize that any recommendation from his old employer in
the future may be colored by adverse action at termination.

THE MANAGER/SUPERVISOR PREROGATIVE

The immediate boss has the privilege of calling the shot. If the
boss feels that a morning or afternoon firing session is desirable
because of a variety of reasons, that's the boss's prerogative.

PROVIDE MINIMAL BACKLASH PROBLEMS

"Charley, I'd like to see you in my office just before
five o'clock."

The immediate superior can set up the appointment for a termination about half an hour before quitting time so that it is likely that the session will end after leaving time.

SUGGESTION: Keep the time gap to a minimum between setting of the meeting and the meeting.

Charley might suspect the actual purpose of the meeting, so minimal adverse "thinking" time should be reduced.

If Charley is fired after quitting time, he might be saved some face as he does not likely want to have to meet his coworkers immediately.

Remove any opportunities for employee embarrassment. A possible cause for embarrassment is the meeting of coworkers immediately after being fired. This is less likely to happen after hours.

In a quitting-time firing, most opportunities for an irrational behavior are removed. Further, the fired employee will have an overnight chance to think over adverse consequences of any contemplated overreaction to being fired. (Charley might have a chance to cool off.)

THE DEMON—THE EGO

There is no question that an experience of being fired is a large blow to one's self-esteem. Even, when the party **knows** that the dismissal was for good cause.

When someone has to be laid off or discharged, then it has to be done. It is unpleasant, emotionally and otherwise for **both** parties. No well-meaning person likes to fire anybody.

RETAIN A CALM ATTITUDE

The banging of desks, shouting, coarse language and slurs are not the ideal way for anyone in management to behave—no matter what the provocation might be. Such behavior is indicative of diminished self-control

The ability to control personal emotions is a requirement for promotion material.

Even with an unpleasant situation as having to fire a subordinate, a manager or supervisor would do well to at least act like a "nice guy." The circumstances are bad enough, so why make them worse?

Firing someone is one thing—it was necessary. However, the way that it is done has to show *class* savoire faire. As one old management saying goes, "Be nice to people on your way up, because you are going to meet these people on your way down."

DENYING TIME OFF TO AN EMPLOYEE

"I often feel I'll just opt out of this rat race and buy another chunk of Utah."
ROBERT REDFORD

If subordinates were given time off every time that they wanted it, production and performance would suffer beyond belief. It is up to the immediate superior to control very tightly the granting of any time off. While at times, the granting of time off is unavoidable, there are instances when it need not be granted.

Frequently, the subordinate, who is conscientious about other aspects of the job, will endeavor to arrange his or her personal affairs so as to minimize any interference with the job.

THE WRITTEN POLICY AS A MANAGEMENT TOOL

Company policy can be written to be very specific as to when personnel leave could be granted. Very specific does **not** mean:

"To attend the funeral of a family member."

Rather specific policy can be:

"Full day on the day of the funeral of any member of the household or mother, father, brother, sister, child, grandparent, grandchild, father-in-law, or mother-in-law."

"Two days before and one day after . . ."

"Four hours on the day of the funeral of any . . ."

CHARGE THE TIME

Unusual (not in the employee manual) requests for time off for personnel leave should be charged to current accrued vacation time. **Not because of the money**, but rather as an effort to discourage less-justified requests for leave.

If accrued vacation is not available, then straight docking has to be resorted to. Excepting for approved (in the employee manual) time off, there is no reason that the Company has to foot the bill.

OTHER WAYS TO HANDLE PERSONAL LEAVE

In some industries, personal leave is permitted up to certain limits. Some companies allow two paid personal days a year. If they are not used, the employee receives two extra days of pay once a year. Any personal leave above the two days is cause for being docked.

One company states its policy as follows:

"The Company is closed for business on 7 holidays during the year. However, each employee is granted 10 days for holidays; that is, 7 for days when the Company is closed and 3 days for whatever other holidays the employees care to take, religious, personal or other."

After the 10 days, the employee is docked.

DEVELOP A COLD SHOULDER

The average supervisor has heard just about all the stories for requests for time off ever told.

"I have to go and obtain . . . "

It is strange that only certain employees need more personal time off than the rest. First of all, there is no such thing as "making it up tomorrow (or whenever)." Someone who is out of the workflow is out of the workflow. And, that is disruptive.

When a supervisor is approached for personal time off, several questions can be sprung on the subordinate including the following:

1. Can someone else do this chore for you?
2. Can the chore be postponed? (Continuing postponement may lead to the matter being resolved some other way.)
3. Can the situation be handled on Saturday or Sunday?
4. Can our Personnel Department resolve the matter?
5. Why is not a letter written instead?

6. Can you leave it for vacation time?

7. Why don't you resolve this by phone?

8. Can the supervisor resolve this by phone?

9. Can the matter be handled after quitting time?

10. Is someone else at home?

11. Would an extended lunch hour be sufficient?

12. Can the legal department take care of it?

13. Can the nurse or doctor on the premises handle it?

14. Is it okay to pay someone else to take care of it?

15. Can the Company messenger deliver a package or message for you instead?

16. What happens if nothing is done?

17. Can a neighbor accept delivery?

CREATE ALTERNATIVES

By merely suggesting possible alternatives, other than having the day off, the supervisor may witness the withdrawal of the request by the subordinate. In addition, by an offer of Company help in the matter, the justification for any time off has to be that much greater.

THE UNAVOIDABLE

At times, the supervisor has to be understanding. It is not a matter of being a pushover or a wimp but recognizing that some people cannot regulate their lives so that other matters do not interfere with work.

Outside circumstances, even for the most conscientious subordinate, cannot always be controlled. The supervisor who can be understanding in a subordinate's personal crises, is not only a better supervisor, but a better person.

HOW SOCIAL SHOULD YOU GET WITH A SUBORDINATE

> *"Never let your inferiors do you a favor—it will be*
> *extremely costly."*
> H.L. MENCKEN

"Boss, join us for a draft beer at the bar at the Blue Bird Tavern."

Well, you know that the Blue Bird has the best draft beer this side of Calumet City and that the bar has the best after work ambiance this side of the Top of the Mark in Frisco. However, you also know that being too social with subordinates is not always a good manager ploy.

"Maybe some other time."

You probably played it right. No feelings should be hurt as would be the case with an outright "no." A few polite similar rebuttals in the future should indicate where you stand.

THE HAPPY HOUR SYNDROME

No one is advocating that a manager or a supervisor should be anti-social. The more important issue is where do you draw the line as to whom you should be social with.

The Happy Hour was invented so that the working class like front-line management people could relax after a long or tough day. More important, its purpose for management people is to exchange gossip and comments about work—a source of good information for someone who wants to know what is going on in other departments or areas.

Chances are that subordinates are largely going to provide information only on matters that you already know. However, if you choose to relax with other management people, you have a better opportunity to get more wider input.

FAMILIARITY VERSUS DISCIPLINE

The British say, "No man can be a hero to his valet." Does it mean that if someone gets to know you too well, then that person could see through your image or facade? Very likely! And, that's a distinct danger in supervision.

Front-line management people are clothed in authority. It is derived from higher levels of authority.

A subordinate with whom you occasionally have a beer is not necessarily going to counter any of your instructions at work the next day. However, it may become difficult on your part to issue a more obtuse instruction to him. You might be likely to hand such a person the easier assignments.

DEPARTMENT PROBLEM

Favoritism is deleterious to department employee morale.

You have been a drinking buddy with one of your subordinates. Even if you are not partial in any way, can other subordinates in the department believe that no favoritism is being practiced? You might have to bend over backwards to prove that you are always fair.

It is very difficult to be fair in just normal situations. There is always some appearance of partiality. (Aren't there some workers that you like better than others?) Think how difficult it can become in abnormal conditions or where only an accusation is remotely possible.

The rumor mill sends out latrine-o-grams based on allegations.

It is an unfair world. Being sociable with any subordinates can start tongues wagging. People who create other problems for their superior are often too quick to jump on his or her possible indications of favoritism.

Avoid providing detractors with ammunition.

RECOMMENDATION FOR NEW MANAGERS

You have just been promoted. Congratulations! Maybe you have a new office or new surroundings. Certainly, there are new and different responsibilities. What about your old rand and file friends? They can still be old friends, but with one big difference.

Unhappy as the decision has been, you may have decided not to socialize with them any more. The real friends should be happy for you and will understand. The rest may not matter.

EXCEPTION CIRCUMSTANCES

There will be times that you will want to socialize with a subordinate. For instance, if you have been invited to a wedding of a child of a subordinate, it might be a good idea to show up, be introduced around, have a drink (not too many), have your picture taken with others, and so on. Chances are that you wouldn't stay too late.

That is the kind of social obligation which makes you more personable. Good to do and fine feelings are engendered.

Those types of circumstances are few and it is wise to make an exception for the socially correct thing. There is not likely to be much backlash on the more formal social obligations.

OTHER INSTANCES

Being a front-line manager or supervisor is not the job of a snob. When there is a company outing, picnic, bowling night, Saturday softball game, and so on, it is a good idea to be friendly with subordinates and others at these occasions.

SUBORDINATES OF THE OPPOSITE SEX

Today, more than ever before, one has to be very careful about socializing with subordinates of the opposite sex. Both parties can have a lot to lose in their reputations.

While no one is publicly against romance, privately all too many people, who should know better, view such relationships in the worst possible light. Gossip, rumors, snide remarks, slurs, and jests become the coin of circulation.

ON-PREMISES FRIENDLINESS

There is nothing wrong with saying, "good morning," or being polite to subordinates (plus others) in the work environment. Having an outgoing personality is desirable for an image of a good manager or supervisor and certainly for one who is more career-oriented.

"He's okay, he gets along with people."

The top management slots are full of people who are good at *people-handling*. Part of that knack was developed in the lower levels of management. It is a good training ground to smooth over the rough edges of one's personality. Being sociable and friendly is a good starting plus for job survival, mobility and career advancement.

CARE AND FEEDING OF YOUR REPLACEMENT

"...duty is what one expects from others, it is not what one does oneself."
OSCAR WILDE, 1893

You are leaving, transferring elsewhere or maybe moving upstairs. Your departure from the department is with good grace, because you have been given two weeks to break in a new replacement.

Ah, but that catches you between the horns of two threatening contrarian whammies.

The first threatening whammy is that you do not want the replacement to do a better job at your old job than you did!

Why? If the replacement turns out that good, then the front office makers and shakers were wrong about your management potential! And that affects your future prospects.

The second threatening whammy is that you do not want to be perceived as undercutting the chances of success of the replacement. That ploy would be perceived as sabotage of a decision by the boss and/or the front office makers and shakers. And that also can affect your future prospects.

WHAT IF I AM LEAVING?

Well, good luck. The catch is that reputations, all too frequently, have a way of catching up. Maybe not on the immediate next job, but possibly on the one after that when someone checks back with an old employer.

"Oh, yeah, Chester, we're **glad** he is gone."

Very often, the way that you handle your departure sticks in peoples' mind at your old place. All the many years of faithful and devoted service could be forgotten.

Doing anything in bad taste prior to leaving can haunt a management career for many years.

As everyone in management can know, good reputations and excellent images can go down the tubes in 5 minutes.

RESIGNING WITH NOTICE

Maybe the reason that you are leaving your old job has something to do with how they have been treating you. Then, maybe, you do not have a very positive attitude toward your old organization.

Curb your feelings.

> **"There's no money in revenge."**
> Old gangster saying

A perceived negative attitude toward your updating or helping your replacement is going to become known to your boss and/or the front office makers and shakers—no matter how thinly disguised. And that attitude can affect your career down the road.

"I had always thought that Chester was okay until he was leaving."

BENDING OVER BACKWARDS

The theorists say that you should do the right, kind, decent and professional thing and bring the replacement up to your level of competence in the job. That's baloney!

Sure, you are not indispensable, but the replacement cannot be as good as you were anyway. Why? Well, for one thing, he does not have your experience in the job! What's more, no matter how talented he is, there is no way that years of experience are going to be crammed into two weeks.

In management, there is no such thing as a "ten-day wonder."

The other side of the coin is that if the replacement can do as good or better a job then you did after only two weeks, what was the justification for keeping you all those years?

There is low personal reason to make your replacement look too good.

Solution: Take the Middle Road

You don't want to appear to be sabotaging the next guy **and** you don't want him to look too good. Be cooperative, but not *fully* cooperative. That's a tough ploy, but it can be done.

One-on-One Initial Meeting

Very early in the relationship with the replacement, sit down with the replacement and find out a few things for yourself.

Ask what objectives in the department the replacement would like to accomplish. Because the replacement is too new to the department's operations, this stunt might reveal what the brass have in mind for the replacement and the department's operations.

This provides insight to you as to a direction that you might want to take in orienting the replacement and in keeping the boss and/or the front office makers and shakers reasonably happy with your exit performance.

The "Grand Plan" Solution

"In this area, our overall objective is . . ."

In orienting a replacement, think in terms of what work is to be accomplished. Avoid, if you can, "how to." The "how to" can be, more or less, "presumed."

Answer all questions. If you are avoiding the details and the replacement has a question about a detail, answer it completely. Otherwise, there can be an allegation that you are not being fully cooperative.

Should you be truthful? Yes! There could be a backfire and the creation of an image of deceit on your part. In such event, you could be asked to leave sooner than planned.

What About Incomplete Projects?

The best way to stay on both sides of your fence is to prepare a written status report on each incomplete project. A copy to your boss should be mandatory.

The important part of each status report is "remaining work" to be done. Once again, you can resort to "Grand Plan" wording with slight downplay on "how to." Provide enough detail to seem cooperative.

THE LOOKING-GOOD PARTING SHOT

> "Listen, if I can be of any help down the road, here's my new telephone number at work. Please call."

Tell that to your replacement and to your boss. With one swoop, you have shown how cooperative you can be. Of course, you may or may not get such a call. If you do, you will be well able to handle it.

ETHICS REVISITED

Your conscience may bother you about not being completely above board. Well, consider a couple of things first.

They are going to talk about you when you are gone anyway. No matter how righteous you were. Not every snafu that pops up is going to have your name on it. However, you will not be there to prevent any unfavorable talk.

Next, your education included attending that tough school named after Mr. Hard Knocks. That on-the-job training did not come easy. However, when you think about it, let's face it, that experience did you wonders. Similarly, it could do a great deal for your replacement. Giving your replacement a chance to learn the same way may be doing him a favor.

> *"Practice is the best of all instructors."*
> PUBLILUS SYRUS, c. 42 B.C.

PART 6

HOW TO PROTECT MANAGEMENT RIGHTS IN UNION SHOPS

WHAT MANAGEMENT RIGHTS ARE AND HOW TO USE THEM

"Christmas is over, and Business is Business"
FRANKLIN PRICE ADAMS

This will come as a shock to many people, but even in operations where there are the toughest anti-management union contracts, the management has rights. Many rights—both in and out of the union contract.

That is the good news. The bad news is that many managements (including in well-managed companies) fail to use (partially or fully) these rights. And, many of these rights are lost because of the disuse.

SIMPLE EXAMPLE

The Balsa-Wood Manufacturing Company has its ups and downs in the demand for gear shafts or whatever. As a result, there are occasional layoffs and then rehirings. During the layoffs, those workers with greater seniority have retained employment in company jobs but not in their primary occupation.

A worker can get bumped into a job which is quite different from his or her normal function when the plant is operating at full capacity. Fine, that's in the contract and that's the way the company has been handling such matters for years.

Fred Sparkplug, a department manager, reads the fine print in the contract and finds that the contract permits testing of bumpers if they can handle the new jobs. Which, he starts doing. He determines that certain people with less seniority are more capable of doing the work in his department and Fred demands that those more qualified be bumped into his department.

Sorry, Fred. The company may have lost its rights to use that clause in the contract. (One can't pick and choose when to exercise one's rights.)

Here's why. By precedent, the Company had decided (by non-action) that the testing was not a material factor in bumping—only seniority.

Actual case on precedents

A union member had received a written warning about drinking beer on the premises. (Under the contract, consumption of alcohol on the premises was cause for discharge.) Subsequently, the employee was discharged. However, the employer's supervisors had known for years of his drinking on premises.

A labor arbitrator caused the worker to be reinstated because of management's tolerance in the past of the worker's acts. (Independent Meat Packers Assn versus Teamsters Local 626).

The shoe on the other foot

Some good news. The reverse is also true. The union can lose some of its rights (even those in the written contract) by any failure to continually protect (by usage) its rights.

At the Rinky Dink Company, workers were constantly being temporarily transferred on short notice to accommodate changes in the workload or flow requirements. It was a common practice. The temporary received his or her regular pay regardless of the pay rate of the type of work performed.

One day, a worker, dissatisfied with a temporary transfer, read the contract fine print and discovered that management was required to provide *adequate* notices. His grievance met a stone wall. Why? The union had failed to require the exercise of this procedure in the past.

No other worker had ever complained about the practice.

Evaluation

Rights by either party to a union contract can be gained or lost by inactivity.

> *Precedent can outweigh all contract printing, bold, fine or somewhere in between.*

> *RECOMMENDATION: On any significant matter, legal advice should be sought on rights.*

Light years ago

Our present labor and management concepts of rights and other matters had their origin in old English law of master and servant (now, employer and employee.) A master could hire a servant for work as directed by the master and at conditions of hours and wages as agreed by both.

It was an informal and usually unwritten contract but enforceable in the courts and by law.

To this day, *every* employment is by contract, both written and unwritten. Even where there is a written contract and certain matters may be omitted from the written contract, the rights of the parties are protected by law derived from centuries ago.

Example

At Cardboard Luggage Company, the union contract did not have any disciplinary provision for the poor attitude of union members.

It was proven that one of the workers consistently harassed his supervisor, was personally disrespectful to him and was a general malcontent. The supervisor maintained a record of the incidents and of a number of warnings were given to the worker. The worker was dismissed satisfactorily.

Evaluation

Where the union contract is silent about matters, management may have certain rights by virtue of long standing law and court decision. Even where the contract has "fuzzy" wording, there may be rights accruable to either party.

How to know management rights

There is more noninformation and misinformation about rights spread through most operations than anyone can care to admit.

The first step is that every manager and supervisor should have a copy of the collective bargaining contract and should read it thoroughly. There is no substitute for being informed of the *minimum* information on how to handle the union rank and file.

The second step is to be aware of the outcome of grievances that have been made. Once again, precedent is important. It governs all new decisions on the same circumstances.

The third step is to discuss with the industrial relations people and upper levels of management any matters which may seem vague. Remember, ignorance of any rights tends to lose those rights.

HOW YOU CAN PREPARE FOR A STRIKE ACTION

"Mother, let me correct you, Rodney works every day—
on a picket line."
UNKNOWN

A strike is not a pleasant experience for anybody. It is a union weapon that is used when management refuses to make further concessions to demands. Few can be winners in a long strike. Production and sales efforts are lost, as well as employee wages.

Sometimes, these items are recovered in future periods, but not always. Just as labor leaders discuss their strike strategy, it is only proper that management considers the various possible procedures in the event of a strike.

THE BASIC DECISION

Management can review the pros and cons of trying to continue operations at a stricken plant. Certain industries, such as utilities, must continue operations.

The continuance of operations, even at a reduced level, *even if costly*, is an emotional weapon against a strike. Why? It is indicative that the striking union does not have the complete upper hand.

A closing of a struck plant is, at least, a partial victory for striking unions.

PREPARATION STEPS FOR REDUCED OPERATIONS DURING A STRIKE

1. *Develop a Strike Manual for Use by the Managerial Personnel*. The manual will outline the legal requirements, security procedures, community relations techniques, production and operating priorities, and so on.

2. ***Prepare a Strike Organization Chart***. As supervisory
   and management personnel will be taking over the more
   routine functions, they should know what their assignments
   will be. In this way, there can be some preparation and
   training in the functional routines in order to keep operations
   at a more nearly normal level

3. ***Assemble a Strike Telephone List***. A listing of supervisory
   and management personnel should be updated to include
   home and other emergency telephone numbers. Police and
   other emergency numbers can be included.

   In the event that there is a sudden or wildcat union action,
   nonstriking personnel can be alerted so that they are not
   surprised when they arrive at work.

4. ***Pay for Overtime***. Nonstriking personnel who work excessive
   hours should know that the Company will pay for their
   unusual efforts. By deciding pay procedures in advance, nonstrikers are apt to be more cooperative. Oral promises are
   not recommended.

   In addition, any overtime pay should be paid as promptly
   as possible. Meal reimbursement and other allowances should
   also be worked out in advance.

   The paying of any premiums (including overtime) to
   nonstrikers is a significant discouragement to strikers.

   "Those guys (scabs) are making more money because
   we're out."

5. ***Provide Alternative Reporting Methods***. If a multilocation
   operation is struck, arrangements as to which location the
   more skilled supervisors are to report to is necessary. The
   inventory of functional skilled supervisors should be spread
   out as far as possible.

Nonstriker Orientation

Well in advance of the strike and during the strike, management
should organize meetings of managers, supervisors and nonstriking
personnel. The topics of the meetings can include the following:

1. Explanations of the contract-negotiating difficulties.

2. Review and amendment of the Company's strike policies and procedures.

3. Instructions and possible changes as to where and under what circumstances the nonstriking personnel are to report.

4. Methods of continuing job training during the strike.

5. Suggestions for control of violence, sabotage and other illegal acts.

6. Various production or performance priorities, suggestion on nonessential cutbacks, handling of backlogs, sub-contractor considerations, freight problems, and other matters which affect operations.

7. Overtime and other payment procedures.

8. Special commuting problems and possible solutions.

9. Suggestions for improving operations.

THE TRACK RECORD

Those companies that are more prepared for a strike action, or for any unpleasant or adverse circumstance, are more likely to be better economic survivors. And, face it, that is what a strike is all about—which party is more likely to remain an economic survivor.

There are noneconomic issues involved in many disputes, but *a strike is an economic weapon.*

Skeptical? Try this on for size: the immediate ploy of a strike is not to turn out less widgets, but to cut off the cash flow to the Company. The longer the strike, the less bucks are coming in and the more willing management may become to accept the striker's demands.

On the other side, the longer a strike, the more willing the strikers become to accepting less than their original demands. After all, they have expenses to meet also.

The side that can withstand the economic pressure longest has the most to gain.

One way of fighting an economic war is to try to have as much cash as possible coming in during the strike. Labor unions establish strike benefit funds and individual union members supplement it by having a rainy day fund.

Likewise, employers build up their money coffers in anticipation of a strike, and well-managed organizations plan as to how to keep money-generating operations on line during a strike.

"THERE ARE NO WINNERS"

It has been said that a strike is costly, frequently in excess to both sides. Strikers try to minimize their loss.

It falls on the shoulders of management to keep the Company's loss during a strike to a minimum. Sales, services and deliveries are not going to be what any financial executive would like. However, by planning, a strike need not be the economic threat that it could be.

The reason some people say that there are no winners in a strike situation is that they believe there has to be a better way than economic warfare between two parties who should be cooperating to help each other.

AVOIDING MOST DIFFICULTIES AFTER A STRIKE

> *"The chickens have come home to roast."*
> JANE ACE

The chief function of the management personnel, at all levels, after a strike is to jack up the operations back to normal. Unfortunately, there has been the arousing of many emotions, which frequently have not run their complete course.

First, there is the animosity of the strikers against the nonstrikers. Then, both groups against the management personnel (who sometimes, feel like they are caught in the middle).

"Scab, why didn't you join us on the picket line?"

The end of a strike does not necessarily bring peace.

THE HANDLING OF RETURNING SUBORDINATES

There is an opportunity for a quick return to normalcy when deciding how to handle the striking subordinates when they return to work.

The extension of an attitude that "bygones are bygones" can overcome a certain amount of feelings of antagonism. It is a condition where positive thinking could beget positive thinking.

This ploy does not mean that the past is forgotten by anybody. It can mean that management and labor can try to forget their past differences in the interest of meeting common goals.

The "welcome back" ploy does not always work with the hard core anti-management employee.

AVOID USELESS DISCUSSIONS

Front line managers and supervisors would do well to avoid being brought into any discussions of the strike issues. Nothing is going to be settled other than what has already been settled.

After all, there was no point in the strikers' returning to work unless they felt that they had settled for the best that they could get.

WATCH OUT FOR THE DANGER SIGNALS

The manager or supervisor can be alert for certain signs that are indicative of continued strife including the following:

1. Refusals of strikers to work (in whole or in part) with nonstrikers.
2. Offending remarks to the superior or others.
3. Unnecessary congregating in various areas.
4. Shoving matches (even assault) among employees.
5. A higher than usual error rate. Even minor sabotage.
6. "Legal" countering of supervisory instructions.
7. Lower volume of productivity and performance.
8. Greater reluctance to work overtime.

In some operations overtime work at this point is critical in order to play catch up on deliveries or service.

CONFRONTATION

Either the strike is over or it is not!

The disgruntled employees who perform adverse acts can be singled out for discipline, or specific examples can be made. It may be best to have another supervisor present when any confrontation is made. Allowing the continuance of adverse acts will embolden others and the situation can get completely out of hand.

The management attitude can be, "We welcome you back—but we do not welcome trouble of any kind."

PROTECTING NON-STRIKERS

The nonstriker may have crossed the picket line for a number of reasons including the following:

1. Loyalty to the Company.

2. Loyalty to the immediate superior.

3. Insufficient personal financial resources during a prolonged strike.

4. Lack of sympathy toward the union's viewpoint on the strike issues.

5. Disputes with the local's officers.

6. Divided loyalty within the union.

7. Some combination of the above.

Whatever the reasons, the right of employees not to strike has to be protected along with the rights of others to strike. At the end of the strike, the nonstriker should be treated on an even-handed basis along with returning employees. Any "teacher's pet" partiality will be viewed dimly by the other subordinates.

Never-the-less, somehow, the nonstriker's service has to be appreciated.

STRIKER DISENCHANTMENT

Some strikers become "locked in" on the original union demands. When a settlement is reached, they are disenchanted with the process and the results.

"We got sold out."

It could be, but chances are that many strike diehards do not comprehend that strikes are no longer the weapon that they once were. Prolonged strikes encourage the management in self-defense to look for other areas or countries for their operations in order to minimize or eliminate the threat of a strike.

If relocation is not viable, then more automation and computerization becomes desirable.

Both alternatives, relocation and increased automation are a threat to union membership.

Managers and supervisors are keenly aware that the disenchanted striker does not always consider the long run.

HANDLING THE DISENCHANTED

Charley, the subordinate, who is disenchanted with the strike results, is a problem employee—even in a *passive* way. Why? Because his dynamics and attitude are not geared for fuller productivity or performance.

The front-line manager or supervisor has to bring Charley along with the rest of the team. While the strike is over, a little sympathy won't hurt. Remember, he thinks that he lost.

> "Well, Charley, you can't win them all. You tried. So, let's get on with the business."

THE LONG RANGE DOWNSIDE

Charley isn't a bad guy. He just wants the most money for his effort, fringe benefits, a decent pension and job security. Isn't that exactly what everyone in *management* wants for themselves?

The problem is that Charley thinks that he can get it by striking. Well, the biggest money benefit that Charley can hope to obtain is *job security*.

CHALLENGING COLLECTIVE BARGAINING TECHNIQUES

"Shop Steward: From now on all wages are doubled, holidays are increased to twelve weeks and we shall only work Fridays.
Voice from the Back: Not EVERY bloody Friday?"
GUARDIAN NEWSPAPER (Britain)

The front-line managers and supervisors have many gripes about union contracts. But the fact remains that every attempt has to be made to live with what can often be termed a "disagreeable agreement"—the union contract.

THE MANAGER/SUPERVISOR VIEWPOINT

Few things irritate the front-line management more than the realization that the union contract helps prevent the most efficient flow of the workload. Restrictions, upon what used to be known as "supervisory authority," exist for the following circumstances:

1. Limited ability to fire a subordinate for a lack of productivity or performance.

2. Inability to transfer subordinates according to their skills and for productivity requirements on an economic basis.

3. The low ability to promote a more qualified subordinate ahead of someone with greater seniority.

4. Low opportunities to modify the work rules according to production changes and other requirements.

5. Difficulty of applying discipline for minor infractions.

6. Procedural problems in granting or requiring overtime or weekend work.

7. Cumbersome or work delaying grievance procedures.

MANAGEMENT SELLOUT

Just as some union members believe that, at times, the union or union local management has not been representative of the worker's wishes, some managers and supervisors harbor a similar feeling about the Company management. In many operations, a certain percentage of management personnel believe that the front office makers and shakers have "sold out" certain supervisory prerogatives.

They believe that at the bargaining sessions, the following happens:

1. That management lawyers and industrial relations specialists make unwarranted concessions.

2. That management representatives are not familiar with operating conditions.

3. That concessions are made that have adverse ramifications on supervisory authority, productivity, performance and cost effectiveness.

JUSTIFICATION

What may seem like an innocent request on the part of the union representatives may actually limit or cripple improvements in productivity. And, the management negotiating team may be unaware of the new limitations until it is too late.

Another defect in communications is that the rank and file supervisory people are not fully aware of the negotiating process. They may have little comprehension as to what concessions have to be made in order to obtain other, perhaps more important, changes in the collective bargaining contract.

RECOMMENDATIONS TO THE IVORY TOWER

1. The top management should become aware of the problems that the front-line managers and supervisors have with the old contract.

2. The management negotiating team can survey department managers on the suggested solutions to their supervisory problems.

3. Install negotiating feedback. As negotiations are in process, there should be feedback reporting to the front-line people. Modifications to the existing work rules should be presented in detail.

4. Management negotiators should seek alternative suggestions to union proposals from operating supervisors.

5. Create a committee of manager and supervisors to advise the management negotiators. This will permit quick decisions to be made.

6. Create a management board of consultant-observers from among representative managers and supervisors to sit in on negotiating sessions.

7. Circulate drafts of significant changes to the contract to certain lower level management personnel.

WHY SHOULD THE IVORY TOWER BOTHER?

The top brass ought to improve communications between the management negotiators and the front-line management for the same reason that the unions do! Shop stewards and other union local officials go to contract discussion meetings and provide their input.

Who has to live with most of the restrictions and provisions in a contract? The front-line managers and supervisors!

Take work rules. What can negotiators know (even very knowledgeable ones) about the day-to-day contention with unwieldly work rules? Not nearly as much as the lower levels of management—the front-line supervisors and managers.

RECOMMENDATION TO MANAGERS: GRIPE

In the analogies of what comes first, there is added: "what comes first, the union contract or getting the work out?"

If it is agreed that the first duty of a front-line manager or supervisor is to get the work out, then it is also agreed that any impediments to getting the work out has to be reduced or eliminated. Therefore, contract provisions which severely limit the front-line management from performing their first duty deserves griping.

Supervisory personnel should write memos to higher levels of authority seeking future modifications to the existing contract.

This puts the brass on notice, and changes may come about.

To gripe privately about the union contract is one thing, but to do something about it is quite another. Frankly, the front office makers and shakers would like to know what is going on. Who is best to tell them than the management person who lives with the contract every working day.

If one has to bypass normal channels to gripe, so be it. But, do it with lots of grace and diplomacy. The same result can be achieved, but with less sand in the gears.

HOW OTHERS DISCOURAGE UNION ORGANIZING

> *"I'm going to my cake-decorating class. I don't really*
> *want to, but we're electing a new secretary and it's*
> *like everything else; if the rank and file don't go, the*
> *militants take over."*
> ALAN BENNETT

While the unions have enjoyed protective legislation and there is a certain amount of estrangement between the worker and the boss, there is a continuing long-term decline in the percentage of the work force that are members of unions.

The unions are quite aware of the threat of reduced memberships (and reduced dues income) and are constantly striving to reverse the trend. In some areas, it is a matter of slowing the trend.

A part of the reasons for decline in union membership is that managements are not "laying down" as readily when an organizer first appears at the plant gate.

THE LAW OF THE LAND

Legislation prevents discrimination against an employee
because of organizing activity.

Any attempt to discipline an employee for what that employee does away from the job can create more problems for the Company than the advent of a union local. National and local agencies come quickly to the defense of the disciplined employee who may have been engaged in union organizing activities.

HOW UNIONS HAVE BEEN SUCCESSFUL

Here is a common management weakness: employers fail to provide a feeling that the employee is a part of the Company. Unions, where successful, have been able to fully exploit the employee's need to feel that they **belong** in the working environment.

How does the union fill the gap? Easy. The union provides off-the-job social functions such as athletic events, outings, dances, and so on, where relatives and friends can meet co-workers. Frequently, even going down to the meeting hall is a social event.

Where employees feel that they cannot communicate with management, or that the job situation cannot relate to a social need, unions can readily step in to fill that need.

WHERE UNIONS FAILED TO ORGANIZE

Knowing what one is up against is just what unions sought to find out. A national union performed a survey—just like a market study performed by any business. The purpose of the study was to determine the reasons for the failure to organize certain businesses.

Here are the findings of the study as to why certain operations could not be organized:

1. Superior working conditions existed and few complaints could be justified.
2. More than adequate fringe benefits.
3. Considerable management efforts on communications with all ranks of employees.
4. Managers and supervisors were trained to contain any rank and file dissatisfaction.
5. Quick correction of any cause for discontent.

Notice that wages, of themselves, were not a factor.

IMPLICATIONS FOR MANAGEMENT

*Unions have not won **every** attempt to win the majority of the hearts and minds of employees in an organizing drive.*

If management provides **group thinking** and group action rather than individual performance standards, the employees are more likely to feel that they belong and are a part of the team.

Where possible, management can permit groups to work together, helping each other to meet group standards.

Companies can tolerate the discussion of management-employee issues. There are mutual problems to be solved. The front-line management may avoid dogmatic answers in the defense of management policies or actions.

If new production levels are required (up or down), there can be discussions of various possibilities to accomplish the change. (Some good ideas may develop.)

LOYALTY AND BELONGING

Many old line managers scoff at trying to win the hearts and minds of the rank and file. However, their ways have not worked either. Winning the hearts has worked.

If management's policies are recognized as providing fair treatment, and if the employee feels that he or she has some amount of input into the policies by some direct communication channel with policy makers, most employees would opt for the employer.

Under such circumstances, the employer is not an antagonist to the employee.

The proof is that in operations that are not organized, there is a higher degree of *employee identification with the Company*. The front-line managers and supervisors can consistently solidify that identification.

RECOMMENDED SUPERVISORY ACTIONS

1. Realign work flow so that employees work as a team.
2. Try to minimize individual effort.
3. Reward the group; avoid individual incentives.
4. Approve requested transfers more readily, even if there is some inconvenience to production or performance.
5. Encourage training and self-improvement. Provide training aids and effort.
6. Try to make employees more dependent on one another for technical assistance. "Waldo, show Willis how to handle that job."

7. Encourage the creation of bowling teams, softball leagues, and other off-premises activities. The Company should pay for rentals and the purchase of sports equipment.

8. Management and other personnel can join in supporting community events and activities.

9. Top management should get away from their desks regularly and appear on the operating scenes and talking and LISTEN to the rank and file.

    "I talked to the V.P., and he isn't such a bad guy after all. We talked about our kids."

WHY DOES GROUP WORK WORK?

A team member tries hard not to let the team down. The managerial concept has to be to weld the rank and file into teams in order to prevent outsiders (union organizers) from doing the same thing.

USE GRIEVANCE PROCEDURE—GET WORK OUT DURING A GRIEVANCE

"Our grievance conference table is 20 feet long and 6 feet wide, and sleeps 10."
JEAN WALLACE

While the grievance procedures are a core area of most union contracts, certain other provisions give important rights to the front-line managers and supervisors. It is important for managerial people to comprehend the interrelationships of these provisions as it affects day-to-day operations.

Most union contracts state that grievance differences must be settled "immediately." However, while there may be a definition within the contract of "immediately," there is some reliance on court and arbitrator determination of that term.

"The impossible we do right away, the unconstitutional takes a little longer." Attributed to Henry Kissinger.

FIRST—WORK

The plant or operating floor is not a scene that can be set for a debating society.

If Charley objects to a supervisory order, he can be reminded that he can only file his grievance after he does the work so ordered. However, there are three important exceptions to the "first—work" rule as follows:

1. If compliance to the order would be an *obvious* threat to anyone's health or safety.

2. If the work is not to be performed in the relatively near future.

3. If the order had a substantial element of confusion.

Experienced supervisory people do not usually issue orders that can jeopardize anyone's well-being and usually issue orders

449

when the work is needed to be done. And, they tend to minimize any confusion with fairly complete instructions.

Therefore, in most cases, Charley has to do the work assigned and then resort to the grievance procedures *later*.

Charley's downside is that he may be subject to discipline for insubordination (for not working first). Further, by not working first and arguing later, Charley may have created a cause for dismissal of *his* grievance.

EMPLOYEE REPRESENTATION CAN BE A BENEFIT

The grieving employee is entitled to representation to protect his or her interest from the very outset of the dispute. It is of utmost importance for the superior to apprise the employee of this right as soon as possible. That avoids an unfavorable decision (down the road) if the employee's rights to counsel or representation have been violated.

Charley may find that his representative does not believe that he has a valid grievance. Either the type of complaint has been settled before, or there are insufficient grounds, verifiable proof, or whatever. For any number of possibilities, his representative (usually the shop steward who has more experience in these matters than the employee) may suggest, or more readily be willing to accept, a quick solution to the dispute.

CONCILIATION AND COOLING OFF

The grievance procedures spell out the requirements of employee representation, and the management would do well to observe strict compliance with those requirements. While it is an employee right, it can work out well for management. For one thing, the machinery of representation reduces the emotional heat with which an issue is sometimes charged.

The employee's representative, in preparing to present his client's argument or point of view, will at least ask the employee for the "facts." With knowledge of some of the facts, union provisions and precedents in similar matters, the representative may be more conciliatory than the employee.

LEARN THE RESTRICTIONS ON UNION MEMBERS

A rank and file union member or a steward can complain every day in every way. If such actions are in good faith, they are protected by law and contract. However, at times some become too zealous.

Management should not turn its back on its managerial duty.

No matter how valid the apparent motivation, most union contracts prohibit the following:

1. Encouraging insubordination.
2. Calling a wildcat strike.
3. Certain other "informal" union member actions.
4. Destructing property.
5. Violating safety rules.
6. Refusing work assignments.
7. Assaulting any persons.
8. Threatening bodily harm to others.
9. Countermanding orders.
10. Performing any illegal activity on premises.

If a contract does not have the foregoing, it should after subsequent re-negotiation.

AN ACTUAL CASE

Here is an important point. During the period of a grievance, the union or its representative has no authority to interfere with a superior's orders.

In the case of the International Paper Company versus UPP Local #1210, the landmark ruling was that the union had no authority to countermand an order—even where the work assignment was **believed to be improper**.

Until there is a ruling on the grievance, the immediate superior can require that the work ordered be performed, with the knowledge that disciplinary measures are available.

IMPORTANT EXCESSIVE GRIEVANCE REMEDY

If an operation is suffering from significant interference in productivity related to grievance procedures (or their misuse), the Company's labor counsel should advise management of the remedies that are available in contract or otherwise.

Repeated grievances over the same issue, grievances filed while similar ones are as yet undecided, petty grievances, delaying tactics, and so on, may be a cause for some sort of legal action.

There have been plants that have been shut down because of excessive grievances and their effect on productivity and cost effectiveness.

HEADING THEM OFF AT THE PASS

In many situations, the people that can prevent most worker complaints are the front-line managers and supervisors. Through "salesmanship" and other ploys, they can head off many a grievance. Sometimes, they have to give a little to get the work out. If the front office makers and shakers were to be more supportive of these give-and-take types of effort, it would be helpful in the day-to-day running of a shop.

MINIMIZING TROUBLE WITH UNIONS

"Under capitalism we have a state in the proper sense of the word; that is, a special machine for the suppression of one class by another."
LENIN

Lenin, the would-be defender of the working class, who never worked a day in a factory, didn't tell us who was the suppressor or who was the suppressed. In some plants and operations, it is hard to tell.

In the union shop, the management is not the complete master of employee activity. Workers cannot be just ordered around. Considerations of seniority, job assignments, incentives, overtime, work rules, discipline, and so on are shared responsibilities between workers and management.

While front-line managers and supervisors are charged with getting the work out, there are limitations on their actions with respect to their unionized subordinates. The capable operating management recognizes these limitations and still does the job.

THE UNION CONTRACT

Read and know the contract.

Contract clauses that may seem remote to immediate areas of responsibility may, once in a while, be good to be able to resort to for unusual circumstances. Provisions of particular significance most of the time include, seniority and bumping, discipline procedures, grievance ramifications, incentives and rates, job definitions, time off, and a few other provisions.

Questions of terminology or application (including precedents) can be directed to a superior or to the industrial relations staff for further elaboration. Management meetings are ideal times to discuss the ramifications of certain contract clauses. Other supervisory personnel may have had the experience that could benefit the group.

To be effective, the operating management has to fully understand the contract limitations to authority. This is more important in actual practice and in how operations are affected.

For example, there may be a clause in the contract which the union has not sought to enforce. By cross-discussion with other managers and supervisors, higher management and the industrial relations staff, the concerned manager or supervisor can know how to proceed regarding consequences of that clause.

THREE TYPES OF AUTHORITY IN A UNION SHOP

1. *Complete*. These are areas where the immediate supervisor can direct the work as the supervisor sees fit. There is no further authority required.

2. *Partial*. The immediate supervisor must apprise others of certain actions that he or she intends to take. The "others" include the shop stewards or higher levels of management. Well-oriented supervisors know when advisory steps have to be taken.

3. *Extremely Limited*. Little discretion for action is permitted to the supervisor. Abuse of authority in these areas can lead to adverse union reaction.

REDEFINITION OF COMPANY PREROGATIVES

With the classifications above in mind, the immediate supervisor can reread the union contract and analyze the extent of the authority granted to the employer. By analyzing each type of Company right as to who in the Company can exercise that right, a supervisor can determine just where his or her own authority starts and ends.

Any gray areas should be immediately cleared up. For instance, if the Company has the right to transfer employees within a department, does the department manager have that right to so move subordinates, with or without notice to anyone?

PLAYING THE PEOPLE GAME

Some stewards are as productivity minded as any large stockholder would be. Others are plain sticks-in-the-mud. They would not go along with any good idea, period.

However, there are people in all walks of life that are like that. What else is new?

Sure, the contract says things in black and white. But that was written in the wee hours of the morning in a smoke-filled room by people on **both** sides who didn't know a drill press from a punch press. Conditions change.

"Rangle, as shop steward, can you see your way clear to allowing the work flow to . . ."

Only liars win them all. Some effort at getting union help is going to be wasted. On the other hand, there are times when good ideas will see the light of day despite the union contract.

Cooperation is the key to improved productivity and job security. Both are worthwhile goals. It does take a little people-to-people conditioning.

SHARED RESPONSIBILITY

Does the union want problems? Not really. Nobody likes hassles and crises. It is stressful and isn't any good for the blood pressure anyway.

Because a shop is unionized, even supposedly by a tough union, does not mean that there has to be a cold war between the two parties.

"PROTECTOR OF THE WORKING CLASS"

Of course, Nikolai Lenin thought that he had a better way for shared responsibility in the workplace. After usurping power, this "champion" of the workers forbid all strikes and nationalized the unions. (That's why his system never worked.)

THE BETTER WAY

Our system is a better way—one that is constantly being improved. It is based on shared responsibility and cooperation. To minimize trouble with unions, management has to start at the grass roots. By listening to, and supporting, front-line managers and supervisors in their attempts at give-and-take with rank and file people in order to get out the work, real cooperation is possible.

HOW JAPANESE MANAGEMENT TECHNIQUES COUNTER UNIONS

"Fewer things are harder to put up with than the annoyance of a good example."
MARK TWAIN

The Japanese industry resurgence has been fueled by the fact that in general the Japanese are hard workers. However, that is only a part of the reason for their success.

The Japanese have been exporting products to most of the rest of the world and beating out some big players in the process. However, products are not the only thing that is being exported by the Japanese. They are exporting management techniques as well. Techniques that make, not only better products, but better workers.

The Japanese have been setting up plants and operations all of the world—not with Japanese workers. If it is not the Japanese hard worker that has made these plants and operations so successful, what has? Their management policies.

WHO IS COPYING WHOM

Excepting for some traditional and home-grown peculiarities, the Japanese management techniques are copies of management techniques preached in the United States, Great Britain and Germany as well as some other countries.

Preached? Yes, but not widely adopted. For instance, greater cooperation between management and labor had a tough time seeing the light of day in many non-Japanese industries.

As a matter of fact, the Japanese did not have to steal a single management technique—they were given them. In visits to the United States and other countries' plants and operations as *guests*, they learned and noted varied management techniques. They picked the best of the management ideas for incorporation into their own management systems.

Thus, *without the costs* of trial and possible error, they adapted some of the world's best methods for production and other operations.

ATTENTION TO DETAIL

In Japanese management, the details are never ignored. In the handling of people, machines and money, the details are studied very carefully. They know that experience, their own and others, indicates that what trips up a project quickest are the details.

Part of the regard for details includes how every company person is considered in the scheme of things. A Japanese executive was heard to remark, "Now let's get the opinion of everybody from the janitor on up."

PARTICIPATION WORKERS

If one is going to go for the comments of everyone from the janitor on up, then worker participation ensues.

True worker participation offends unions. The key word is "true." Not lip service and advisory committees. Japanese management techniques provide channels of communication from the lowest levels to the highest.

Each worker is considered a part of the total company team. (In some operations, company uniforms are provided.)

NOTE: It is difficult to "strike" against your own team.

THE CONCEPT OF WA

Wa, a Japanese word, is not from an Eastern mythology. The concept has been around in Western civilization for quite a while. Briefly, wa is *self-sacrifice* for the common good.

The industrial aspect of the concept requires that you do not consider your immediate goals but those of the Company first. The idea is that if the Company benefits, so do you.

In more practical aspects, wa means that one is willing to work overtime and weekends in order for the Company to prosper, grow and provide job security.

It is difficult to visualize that you are being exploited by an employer, if you are volunteering for a lot of extra work.

THE CONCEPT OF KAIZEN

In Japanese, *Kaizen* means constant push. That's been around also. Whatever you did last month, you have to do better this month. Not necessarily in total, but once again recognizing the importance of details.

Small upticks in productivity, performance, quality and cost effectiveness are constantly being sought. Nothing great necessarily, but small improvements everywhere.

Kaizen is the constant drip, drip of improvements. Once again it is getting back to not ignoring details.

> *It's hard for unions to organize people that are*
> *constantly trying to improve company profitability.*

THE OVERALL THRUST

There is true participation, attention to detail, wa and even kaizen. What else can there be?

John Donne, an English poet of several centuries back wrote, "No man is an island." The Japanese believe that no worker is an island, that **each is a part of the Company**. To back up their belief, Japanese companies, with exceptions, offer lifetime careers to their employees.

Note the "with exceptions." In general though, Japanese employers are prone to retain people at all levels for decades and decades. This attribute has two anti-union benefits as follows:

1. Worker loyalty and lower regard for unions.

2. Job security and less of a need for unions.

There is a side benefit to the Company **and** the workers and that is that the workers have a greater commitment to the success of their Company.

> *It is difficult to recruit union members among workers*
> *who have a commitment to the Company.*

By the way, lifetime careers was a feature of many American and European companies many years ago.

WHAT IS TO BE DONE

The copying of management techniques is not an offense. Not copying worthwhile nonpatentable ideas may be a corporate illness. The fast in-between recommendation is taking some good techniques and installing them. Or, modifying existing "comfortable" methods and techniques as quickly as possible.

ABSENTEEISM AND CROSS TRAINING IN A UNION SHOP

> *"You can't imagine the extra work I had*
> *when I was a god."*
> HIROHITO, former Japanese Emperor who was deprived
> of divinity in 1945

An important clause in most union contracts is the limitations of the use of an employee in one job classification for work that falls under another job classification (job switching). In other words, a drill press operator may not be readily asked to operate a punch press.

The union logic is that job switching reduces jobs.

Sometimes, a union contract requires a job switcher to receive a drill press operator's pay plus a punch press operator's pay (double pay). Other times, just the *higher* of the two rates is the regular pay.

Also, because of the learning curve, the job switcher may be entitled to a bonus incentive pay rate while performing the second job.

SOME SITUATIONS

Therefore, if the punch press operator is on sick leave, the employer must pay the absentee for that day. If the drill press operator is switched over to the punch press, the employer may be required to pay a full day's drill press pay plus a day's punch press pay. That is a total of at least three days' pay (excluding any production incentive penalty) that must be paid to accomplish one day of productive work.

THE UNLIKELY RECOMMENDATION

In most cases, pay the three days' pay. Use the drill press operator to maintain the flow of work through the punch press department.

THE REASONING—THE REAL COST

If the drill press operator is not used in the punch press department (to cover for the ill employee), it will still cost the Company *two* days' pay for one day of productive work. That work may be for drill press parts that are not needed until possibly next month.

However, by switching the drill press operator to the punch press department, perhaps a higher priority flow of work will be maintained in the punch press department. Yes, it will cost an extra day's pay—unavoidable, for instance, if the punch press department is behind schedule.

NUMBER CRUNCHER NIGHTMARE

Cost accountants get gray early. That may be part of the penalty for maintaining desirable work flow.

Management flexibility is maintained by meeting labor needs to avoid production bottlenecks as a result of absenteeism. The additional cost may be offset by reductions of overtime and weekend work in problem departments. Remember, the extra pay is at the straight time rate.

RED FLAG: Job switching should only be used occasionally to mitigate absenteeism.

PRODUCTION PLANNING MALADY

Switching as a steady diet is not recommended. The method is too great an expense for a problem which need not be caused by absenteeism but could be the result of poor production planning.

INCREASING PRODUCTIVITY AND PERFORMANCE

When the same people are used in job switching, they can become more proficient in their temporary assignments. After an initial period, they could be as productive as the regulars. However, this requires some monitoring of performance, errors, rework, scrap, and so on. In addition, it is desirable, in switching, to select those employees who have a greater learning capability.

WATCH OUT FOR LIMITATION

Some labor contracts permit job switching based on seniority only. This restriction is serious. It limits the management selection of those who may have greater learning ability (or even better experience).

HANDLING SENIORITY

Frequently, management representatives who negotiate the collective bargaining contract are not aware of the effects of contract clauses that protect seniority. Little time is spent on these clauss as they do not effect wages, holidays, vacations, pensions, medical insurance, or other immediate money issues.

> *There are executives that do not realize that seniority adds to product or service costs very directly.*

For one thing, seniority limits the extent of which cross-training programs can be applied. Second, people, who may not be as competent, are temporarily switched. Productivity and performance suffers at increased costs.

OVERCOMING SENIORITY LIMITATIONS

Testing for even a temporary move can mitigate the more undesirable application of seniority. Fair testing provisions in a contract will permit the use of more qualified people to be shifted around.

OLD UNION POSITION

Many unions and the local reps view cross-training as a reduction of jobs and membership. (If a company is short in a particular skill, their orientation is that more people with that skill be hired.)

All of that is understandable. However, it ignores the reality of operating circumstances. First, last-minute things happen such as people calling in sick. Second, a company can not have too fat a work force and compete in the market place. Third, bringing people in during a feast means laying them off in a famine.

NEWER ATTITUDE

Cross-trained people have greater job security and job mobility.

Some individual unions are beginning to recognize that if their members are multiskilled, then they have greater job security. When a place closes down these people have greater job mobility and can get another job easier.

Someone who can operate two machines instead of just one is worth more, will have less of a chance of being laid off and can market the multiskills more readily elsewhere.

RECOMMENDED NEXT STEP

Upon contract renegotiation, some provisions have to be advanced and proposed that rank and file personnel will receive cross training (at Company expense). Even if the accepted provision is not all encompassing, a start can be made. Who knows? The rank and file might like the idea.

OVERCOMING SENIORITY IN A UNION SHOP

> *"Some employees would rather lose their job*
> *than lose their rights."*
> A labor mediator

Management representatives at contract talks frequently do not hassle over seniority clauses of union contracts. Their interests are largely concerned with wage increases, escalator clauses, pensions, health insurance and other seemingly more immediate money considerations.

Seniority is somehow usually left alone in renegotiation sessions.

Yet in many operations, the management prerogative of selecting the more capable employees to perform new duties or of switching employees to perform new duties or of switching employees to meet production requirements is severely limited by seniority clauses in the contract.

Bumping, the practice of moving people around from one job function to another, usually is for the benefit of the rank and file with the longest service. Merit, experience, learning ability, and so on, are not necessarily criteria for a move.

RECOMMENDED FIRST STEP

Seek any exceptions in the contract to the seniority requirements practice that is actually taking place. There may be little used provisos that front-line managers and supervisors can use to advantage.

OBLIGATION: RECOMMEND CONTRACT CHANGES

Front-line management people frequently ask about contract seniority clauses. At management meetings there is grumbling about those clauses—but few recommendations.

At one management meeting, there was plenty of talking about various definite examples of the problems of seniority but no one advanced an idea on what to do.

HERE IS A SHOT TO TRY

The suggestion can be made, and might even eventually find union acceptance, that 20% (or whatever) of the people moves can be made without resorting to seniority. Where there has been an influx of newcomers into the local, this change may even be *welcomed*.

HERE IS ANOTHER FLAG TO RUN UP THE POLE

In addition to any testing of qualifications (if any) 20% (or whatever) of the score could be reserved for a managerial appreciation of the bumper's aptitude for the new slot.

MINORITY VERSUS SENIORITY

Generally, seniority clauses prevent promotions of persons who are in minority groups or who are women or who are disabled. Reason: they are relatively newcomers into the work force.

While union contracts are not explicitly discriminatory, the effect of seniority clauses might amount to the same thing. Thus, an argument can be made that the seniority clauses prevent affirmative action. If the company is committed to affirmative action programs by virtue of a court order or other mandate, the seniority clauses are on weak legal ground.

The Company legal counsel should be advised of such a problem.

SOME EXCEPTION TECHNIQUES

1. Rewrite the job descriptions. This puts everybody in new job descriptions and might provide some flexibility.
2. If possible, put more senior employees in the management category. At one plant, a senior assembler, after being made foreman of an assembly section, developed a change of character. He began to wear a tie and jacket to work, became

a hard taskmaster, and was vocally anti-union. (A tiger can change his stripes.)

3. Advise the younger employees of the seniority clause possible restriction to their promotion. Frequently, the younger employees do not take an interest in union business and have low attendance at local meetings. However, there have been instances where younger members have changed the direction of the locals by increased union participation.

4. "Let's make a deal." Offer an upgrade of job classification to a more senior employee in exchange for permitting a more junior employee the right to bypass to another position.

THE ABUSES OF SENIORITY

Front line managers and supervisors that have been around know that there are typists who cannot type, inventory clerks that cannot add, toolmakers that cannot comprehend a print, mechanics that cannot understand a maintenance manual, assemblers who have low manual dexterity (all thumbs), tool crib attendants who don't know a jig from a die, electricians who produce shorts, painters who think sandy beige is a rock star, and so on.

No one company has all of these types. However, most operations have their fair share.

IMPORTANT. The saddest aspect may be that a marginally incompetent could be around for twenty years (or whatever) and have some priority for promotion by virtue of seniority.

WHAT ABOUT THE GOOD WORKERS

Consider the prospects of a hot shot, high-drive self-starter hard worker who has minimum seniority. He or she can get bypassed for many opportunities. That person can become demoralized because an important reward for hard work is denied.

Therefore, seniority is not of great benefit to the more recently hired good worker or to his or her boss who has to get the work out.

"Why should I knock myself out?"

What is to be Done

Actually, the abuses of seniority affect the operating management people first and the most. They are the ones who have to contend with a system that is not efficient in productivity, performance, quality control, and cost effectiveness.

Front-line supervisors and managers cannot readily change the system. Certainly, not as quickly as is desirable. However, in each operation, because of their more immediate experience, they can work toward recommending *modifications* to seniority. Each operation is different as to how it can contend with seniority.

It is easy to gripe about seniority and its consequence in each section and department. However, it is a far *better way* for a manager or supervisor (who usually have good ideas) to make some recommendation for change. That suggestion, almost whatever it is, would be a first step in a long march.

HOW TO GET AROUND SENIORITY OBSTRUCTIONS

"In the Far East the master is considered a living Buddha, but in Minneapolis they wonder why he doesn't have a job."

ROBERT M. BIERCE

The real nitty-gritty problems created by seniority are right down on the floor. In the operating end of the business. To tackle them is worthwhile.

Seniority represents a group of rights given to the employees by the union contract. Primarily, rank and file people with greater length of service have a first-come basis with regard to transfer, the filling of varied positions, last to be laid off, first to be recalled, and so on.

The most common right is that of bumping, where a more senior employee can displace any employee with less seniority when there is a cutback.

RESULTS ON THE FLOOR

For managerial people, seniority rights and the practice of bumping represent an interference in the selection of the best employee to do the job. In effect, on the floor, foreperson and supervisors have limited say in the selection of some personnel who work in their sections.

After a layoff and, at least, a partial recall, many new faces can be assigned to any section.

When a new vacancy is created in a section, the foreperson may have to accept, from another part of the plant, an employee who happens to have worked for the Company longer than others whom the immediate boss would have considered more suitable for the job.

Use Contract Wording to Advantage

The union agreement may stipulate the senior bumper must be "qualified" for the job. Some contracts state that the would-be bumper must be able to *immediately* perform the duties of the job. NOTE: that proviso rules out the possibility that an employee be allowed to demonstrate that he or she can *learn* the job.

"Qualified" has not been interpreted as meaning that the employee has MORE qualifications than anyone else who may be available without regard to seniority. It can mean *sufficient* qualifications to do the job. Once again, contract negotiators have to be careful.

The Job Definition Advantage

On newly created jobs, the work description can be very confining. By playing around with words, a floor boss can insert a restriction intended to upgrade qualifications sufficiently to preclude those who are likely to bump into a particular position.

In other words, a floor boss can over-qualify a new job description. For instance, a typing speed requirement may rule out some people who could bump into the position.

The Usual Testing Requirements

The use of tests to determine qualifications is well accepted. However, unless the contract specifically states that the passing of the test is the sole criterion, its use may be dulled. If the contract does not so state, then the test is weighed equally with all of the other considerations or qualifications for the job.

Tests can be either written or performance tests. They can be administered by an outside party.

Tests must be fair and fairly administered.

NOTE. Labor arbitrators have sided with grieving parties where tests have been deemed unfair and the testing procedure was not equitable.

Using trial periods

Some contracts require that a senior employee be allowed to bump into a position and retain the position if the bumper can demonstrate an ability to produce after a trial period.

WARNING: Determine the extent of assistance.

Once again contract wording is important. Assistance may have limitations. The bumping clauses can specify "only general instructions for job performance" or "training by supervisory or other personnel." And, that is a BIG difference.

Once again—precedents rule

If the contract has a seniority restriction provision which the management has not customarily taken advantage of, the management may not suddenly start adhering to such provision.

For instance, if written testing is a requirement that is written into the contract for certain job classifications and the Company has not been giving written tests, then the Company may have waived its right to require a test subsequently.

Check with the industrial relations staff as to management rights that are seldom used.

Other restrictions to bumping

The test is fair, job related, and administered and evaluated fairly. Is that the end of the story? Not necessarily! Other factors can affect bumping.

In the matter of Beckley Mfg. Co. versus IBEW Local 2011, a senior employee scored highest on a test for promotion but, a *junior* employee got the job. How come? The labor arbitrator ruled with the management that it had the right to consider other factors such as valid experience—which the junior had.

"Other factors" are a two-way street.

It is possible that a senior employee having a LOWER test score could get the job *if it* can be displayed that other factors, such as experience, are in the senior's favor.

Once again, contract wording has to provide for the consideration of other factors.

All things being equal, "other factors" clauses are a good means for improving job qualification levels.

WIN SOME, LOSE SOME

Floor management has a tough row to hoe, no matter what. They are caught between the higher management requirements of getting the work out and the abuses and evils of bumping. In this highly competitive world, they need the best people to help them. Yet, they have to go along with a system that does not necessarily provide the sharpest people-tools to do the job.

However, the system has to change. The marketplace is not going to permit low-efficiency operations to stay in business too long. Light bulbs that are made in Taiwan, telephones that are produced in Singapore, computer terminals that are assembled in South Korea, and so on, are indications which way the trend is going.

Seniority in those far off places is considered a "Western foolishness."

USING MONEY INCENTIVES WISELY FOR PRODUCTIVITY

*"I never been in no situation where havin' money
made it any worse."*

CLINTON JONES

The entrants into the labor market today are finding a world quite different from that of their grandparents. By virtue of legislation and union strength in some industries, brand new workers expect and receive a high salary that is largely unrelated to their work performance or contribution to society. By producing a rather basic quantity and quality of work, they are **guaranteed** a wage that will provide all of the essentials and a certain amount of luxuries.

Today, workers have less cause for saving than their grandparents. For one thing, most current workers are financially protected against major calamities, such as large medical expenses. Another factor is that workers today need not concern themselves with putting money away for retirement since that concern is to a major extent covered by social security benefits and other pension payments.

All of these benefits did not exist when many industries developed and installed money incentive techniques to increase productivity.

WHY MONEY ISN'T EVERYTHING

*For a minimum productive effort, workers can be
protected from severe financial discomfit to their very
graves.*

Making money, or extra money (incentives), is not as attractive now as when it was first developed as a technique to boost productivity. Oh, it is still very important, but to what extent and how much of a sacrifice an average employee is willing to make for it is an issue.

With less of a need to meet financial crises or to save for retirement, there is limited expectation that money incentives can automatically improve the quality of work performance.

RECOGNIZE THE RATEBUSTER

Wilbur drives himself unmercifully from whistle to whistle, producing more and more units (ratebuster). He may be doing it more for recognition that he is obtaining than for the incentive bucks alone. However, ratebusters are not popular with other employees for a variety of reasons. The more union conscious employees view ratebusting as a reduction of jobs and eventually union membership. The logic is that if there were fewer workers performing above the standard rate, there would be more union members working with fewer temporary layoffs.

UNION VIEWPOINT

If more of the employees worked above the standard or the minimum rate, there would be fewer workers required to get out the same volume of production. However, if all of the employees produced the bare minimum, there would be more workers in the plant and therefore more union members. The major source of income to the unions is through memberships, and any discouragement of increase in membership potential is viewed with alarm.

ENCOURAGING INDIVIDUAL INCENTIVE

Wilbur, who wants to make the extra money, is faced with hostility from coworkers. Sometimes, the resentment rubs off onto the immediate supervisor. As a result, the supervisor harbors a passive antagonism toward the "problem" employee who does not get along with the other workers. Wilbur may dislike the management as much as any other employee, but he wants to take advantage of incentive pay possibilities. The other workers regard Wilbur as a "scab" and his boss regards him as a "problem" employee.

Wilbur has rights also. Very personal rights that need protection. If the Company is offering incentive pay, why shouldn't he earn it? It's his right.

MANAGEMENT OBLIGATION

The purpose of producing units in excess of the norm or quota is so that overhead and other expenses are spread out over more units. Thus, reducing the per unit cost. Such reduction permits the Company to meet or beat the competition.

> *Rule 1: The more cost competitive companies stay in business longer.*
>
> *Rule 2: Staying in business longer means more **job security** for everybody.*

If the front-line supervisor is aware that Wilbur or others want to earn incentive pay, his boss should provide coaching as to how Wilbur can improve his output. This assistance need not look like "teachers pet" activity, but can be presented in a matter-of-fact and straightforward manner.

> "Wilbur, if you hold the clip with your left thumb, it will free your other hand to complete the assembly quicker."

RECOMMENDATION: REVERSE THE INCENTIVE

Here is a ploy to consider. If 500 units a day is the minimum, give the first hundred above the norm a higher rate than the second hundred units above the norm. In other words, the first 20% above the daily minimum has a higher incentive rate per unit than the second 20%. Sure, the more that is produced, the less the worker could make per unit. That's a drawback. But what is the payoff? The ploy will provide the faster worker with much more incentive to produce **above** the minimum.

CONTROLLING HARASSMENT

Morris and many other employees erroneously believe that they owe their jobs, overtime and second shift staffing to the concerted worker ploy of not producing incentive units. Naturally, they have unkind words for those who produce above the norm. Front line managers and supervisors should control such behavior as much as they can.

Morris and others are shortsighted. In the short run, they are right. In the longer run they are doing *themselves* out of a job—possibly, out of any job in their industry.

"NO FRILLS INDUSTRIAL RELATIONS"

Many foreign competitors do not pay for extra units produced. (Either one produces the extra units OR no work.)

The "no frills industrial relations" competitors will take jobs away from those people who are not making a significant contribution to cost effectiveness right where they are. It is up to the front-line managers and supervisors to make their rank and file people much more aware of just where their long term interests lie.

CONTENDING WITH RIGHT TO WORK RIGHTS

"The chief cause of problems is solutions."

PAUL DICKSON

We know that employees have rights against the interest of their employers. That is a common everyday matter. However, a worker may also have certain rights against a union's interest.

Let's get definitions straight first. What has been called the "right to work" may be more readily defined as the "right NOT to join a union."

THE STATE LAWS

Some states have enacted legislation which in effect says that a worker does not have to join a union as a condition of employment or continuing employment. A worker cannot be coerced in any way to join a union.

This legislation provides a wide gap in "union security" features of a collective bargaining contract. Union security contract clauses relate to the protection of the union as the sole bargaining agent for the workers. Those clauses should not be construed as protection of "job security" which relates to the rank and file having job protection.

THE TYPICAL SITUATION

Particularly in nonright-to-work states, the union usually seeks employer control of collection of initiation fees and check-off dues in behalf of the union. New employees are frequently required to join the union. If a would-be employee objects to joining the union, or wishes to resign from the union in most states, he is foreclosed from working in certain unionized shops.

UNION VIEWPOINT

The unions contend that their effort has achieved gains for all of the workers in the union shop. Therefore, a worker who enjoys those gains should be willing to support the union very directly. In addition, future gains require present support.

PERSONAL RIGHT VIEWPOINT

There is a presumed personal right of free association which is a basic and cultivated right in western civilization. This fundamental right provides protection to individuals to join or NOT to join any organization. While millions and millions do join the American Legion, the Red Cross, church organizations, or whatever, they are not under a compulsion to so associate.

COMMUNITY VERSUS INDIVIDUAL

In western civilization there is the obligation of the individual to the community. (In this case, the community being the union.) The individual draws benefit from the community (union) and therefore has an obligation to support it.

FUNDAMENTAL CLASH

Certain rights have priority over other rights and obligations. It can be contended that a personal right such as that of free association takes priority over a community (union) obligation. And, that coercion to join any organization is a violation of the right of free association.

THE LAW OF THE LAND

Federal legislation and courts have upheld the right of states to have right to work laws. The only limitation is that such laws are enforceable intra-state and not inter-state.

STATE LAW REVISITED

The state laws do not provide sufficient teeth for the enforcement of their right to work laws. It behooves a worker, who has been denied work because of nonunion membership to sue the employer for a job. (There are organizations that will provide lawyers to assist in these suits.)

THE PRACTICAL SIDE

Suits are drawn-out processes. Unless employers are willing to accept the spirit of the law, few individuals can be expected to fight for their right not to join a union.

INTIMIDATION

There have been cases of harassment of workers who refuse to join a union or who resign from a union. The harassment is more or less sporadic and is NOT advocated by any of the unions themselves.

THE PROBLEM FOR MANAGERS

While some employees are not willing to pay dues and join a union, there are some who are willing to pay dues (for services received) and not join a union.

Of course, it is difficult for management to intervene in what may be called a worker-union dispute. Nonetheless front-line managers and supervisors should prevent any harassment of any employee on the premises.

Workers are entitled to feel secure on the premises of their employer.

In addition, the work flow should not be disrupted by any dispute between any union and nonunion employees. Anyone causing problems of this kind can be subject to discipline and after sufficient warning, discharge. Such a reaction has nothing to do with rights and obligations.

Once again, it is the front-line management's duty to keep the work moving.

LEGAL RAMIFICATIONS RECOMMENDATION

When an employee or an applicant wishes to stand by any rights not to join a union, the advice of the corporate counsel should be sought *promptly*.

PART 7

JOB SECURITY AND PROMOTION FOR MANAGERS

HOW A MANAGER CAN IMPROVE PERSONAL PROMOTION POSSIBILITIES

"It takes 20 years to make an overnight success."
EDDIE CANTOR, COMEDIAN

In good times and bad, there is always a shortage of top management personnel. Why does this happen in bad times? This is when an organization *really* needs good managers.

Not that there is a shortage of those who want to be on top, but rather because there are relatively few people who are outstandingly qualified. Every lieutenant in the army would prefer to be a general; most only make it part of the way.

Moving up the ladder requires a certain amount of planning and self-discipline.

Rule 1: Develop a career plan.

Sure, you may have to adjust your plan once in a while. There are new circumstances, outside considerations, bad luck, etc. that encourage adjustment to the basic plan.

Having no set goals means that one is allowing circumstances to dictate the career course. Typical goals: high middle management in 10 years, vice president in 20 years, and so on.

Rule 2: Stick to your plan.

That's where self-discipline rears its head. Knowing what you ought to be doing is one thing, sticking to it is another. Yes, you are going to alter your plan once in a while. However, you have to be committed to the basic plan.

Believe it or not, most people are not ready for a stroke of good luck. They cannot take it. To succeed, one must be ready for some unlikely event that comes into reach. And, grab it.

"Don't worry, boss, I can run that department for you."

481

Back to basics

How does one improve his chances?

One of the answers is to start developing a positive plan or program and to stick to it. We have said that change is okay. Be sure that *you* believe in your program. This adds confidence if a "wild card" opportunity should arise.

Another answer to the basic question is in the form of a question, "What am I now?" Part of being able to go some place successfully is to know where your starting point is so that you have some idea of direction. Many people spin their wheels moving sideways because they do not evaluate themselves properly. Therefore, "up" can seem to be in almost any direction.

By having a plan, knowing where you are now and in what direction you would like to go, you are more than likely to avoid getting to a dead end job (one with limited promotion possibilities).

Train an understudy

> "We cannot move Fred Sparkplug up! There is no one
> to take his place in the good job that he is doing
> now."

Do not put off training someone who may turn out to be your replacement. If you wish, limit his external contacts if there is a fear that HE can take your job away. The balancing act is that your chance for promotion is improved if there is a viable replacement versus doing yourself out of a job.

It is not up to a middle manager to name his understudy as "successor." That's up to the brass eventually. However, the middle manager can usually designate him currently as "Assistant" learning the job. During vacations and at other times, the understudy can substitute to some extent.

Still worried about an understudy?

Some successful people groom more than one assistant. This technique increases flexibility, promotes competitiveness and reduces the potential for a backfire.

Too much thought may be given to creating a competitor for one's own job. If Fred Sparkplug is qualified, he is a better alternative than his assistant to continue to run the department. If the higher levels of management do not think so, then some others in a company down the street will.

Don't worry. For many really good people, the old adage that says, "Another streetcar will be along in five minutes" is all too frequently true for jobs as well. Especially, if you are a "Fred Sparkplug."

LEARN, BABY, LEARN

Exactly what is the next step up the ladder for a manager? What is there to be learned about doing that particular job? The successful middle manager finds time to determine the requirements of the next level of management. Then he finds even more time to learn those requirements. Mr. Fred Sparkplug has to master the job requirements of the divisional manager's job if he ever hopes to be in that office.

USING AWAY-FROM-WORK STUDY

The office is not the ideal place to do all of the learning that has to be accomplished. Each industry has magazines and other reading matter that indicate trends and industry topics of discussion. These matters are always of interest to top management people, and they appreciate the effort of the lower levels of management who keep up to date and are knowledgeable about industry problems and solutions.

"Last week, I read an evaluation of the new vinyl converter in the Chemical Monthly."

BE POLITICAL

For those managers who want to move ahead; "Every management job is 90% political and the other 10% is technical."

Fred Sparkplug knocks out the work, has outstanding leadership ability, knowledgeable about the next job up the ladder, high integrity, and is darn good promotion material in general. So what if no one who is a corporate maker and shaker in a higher echelon actually knows about Fred's good qualities.

INCREASE PERSONAL VISIBILITY

Here are some ways of increasing one's visibility:

- Participate in social functions that include the upper levels of management.
- Become involved in community affairs that include the brass.
- Be available to work on the pet work projects of the higher levels of management. "I am available for the budget committee."
- In the absence of intermediate levels of management, bring certain ideas and matters to the attention of superiors. "We can improve customer service if we . . . "

THE WORST EXCUSE: "I don't have the time."

Why is that the worst excuse? The answer is a question. How can anybody be good promotion material if he or she cannot be an able administrator of his or her own time?

IMPROVE YOUR "PEOPLE-HANDLING FACTOR"

Is the political capability as a requirement for success over-emphasized? No way. Consider that the higher levels of management require more ***administrative know-how*** than the lower levels. So, higher level jobs require better administrators. Now, it has been said that a good administrator is one "Who gets ***others*** to do the work of still others."

Remember, those others who are going to do the work not only includes subordinates but a whole crock of other types of people including coworkers, colleagues, outsiders, and other busy bodies, and, at times, superiors.

> *The bigger an administrator that you are, the more you need to obtain the cooperation of others.*

WARNING: DON'T BUCK THE TREND

Operations are becoming even more complex. It takes a greater variety of skilled people to manage and run an operation. And, that trend will continue. Accordingly, the "people factor" is becoming more and more important.

PROPER ALLOCATION OF A MANAGER'S TIME

> *"I'm going to stop putting off things,*
> *starting tomorrow."*
> SAM LEVINSON, Comedian

The job itself often dictates where and how a manager will spend most of his or her time. An old hand will say, "getting out the work is what a manager's job is all about." However, isn't something as important as training a new subordinate a real part of "getting out the work"?

A review of the activities expected of most front-line managers and supervisors would include the following:

- Maintaining productivity or performance levels.
- Personnel problems and administration.
- Use of the equipment and machines.
- Quality control and error correction.
- Providing supplies and hand tools.
- Obtaining proper space utilization.
- Seeking improvements in work flow.
- Attending management meetings.
- Coordinating with other managers and supervisors.
- Handling outsiders and other busy bodies.

All of these activities (and for some people there are many more) vie with the number one activity, getting the work out.

Yet, time that elusive commodity, has to be found for all of those other managerial requirements.

REDUCE TIME DEMANDS ON MANAGERS

> *"Ordinary people think merely how they will spend*
> *their time; a man of intellect tries to use it,"*
> SCHOPENHAUER, 1845

If the number one function is to get the work out, why does the brass continually load up the managers and supervisors with more and more other chores? These middle and lower level managers have demonstrated the unique ability to fit additional duties into their schedules. However, the fact that Fred Sparkplug, the hotshot manager, can handle the additional duties is not a valid reason to continue to load him up.

Eventually, the function of getting out the work has to suffer.

By demanding more and more of Mr. Sparkplug, sooner or later his department's performance or productivity will ease. Usually, quality control and error correction are the first to dissipate.

MIDDLE MANAGERS AS COORDINATORS

Any experienced hand will acknowledge that there are at least five distinct groups with whom middle managers have a day-to-day working relationship. They include the following:

1. Subordinates—both as individuals and in groups.
2. Union—shop stewards, business agents, and so on.
3. Staff specialists—engineers, accountants, personnel, and so on.
4. Other middle managers—for coordination to maintain productivity, performance and service.
5. Superiors—higher levels of management to whom the middle manager reports.

In some industries and operations there are outside relationships as well. These include: customers, suppliers, auditors, consultants, transportation people, government inspectors, outside contractors and service organizations, community groups or representatives, and so on.

It is no wonder that Fred Sparkplug, over the years, is devoting a smaller and smaller percentage of his time to actually getting the work out.

GETTING RID OF ADDITIONAL CHORES

When someone seeks to put new duties on the back of a front-line manager, the critical question which should be asked is:

"Does the new chore directly help in getting out the work?"

If the answer is "No," or "Could be," or "Maybe," then the new chore should be assigned elsewhere. It is true that others may not be as suited to accomplishing the new chore. Then again, others are not as suited to getting the work out with a minimum of errors or problems as the middle manager might be.

TOP MANAGEMENT RESPONSIBILITY

Therefore, in order to use Fred Sparkplug's skill to the greatest advantage, his efforts should be directed toward productivity, performance, and quality control. The challenge to the brass is as follows:

> *To arrange the administrative functions so that there is a minimum of interference with the primary duties of the front-line managers and supervisors.*

PROGRAM FOR INSTANT RELIEF

1. Determine what the front-line management is doing now.
2. Reassign duties that can be handled by other administrative functions. (Limit considerations of capability.)
3. Prevent the introduction of new administrative duties to the front-line managers and supervisors.

WHAT IS IMPORTANT?

Sure, there are administrative chores that Mr. Sparkplug has to perform that are "important." However, the more "important" chores that he is required to perform, the less widgets, or whatever, get to be moved to the shipping dock and delivered.

WHO HAS PRIORITY?

Hands down, the customer comes first. In the marketplace, the customer is king. He hires, fires, and from time to time, he curtails or closes down a plant or operation. Chances are very good that *he will shut the doors of any operation* that has too much administrative effort and costs. He wants to pay only for the direct product and service costs—nothing, more.

Now, picture this: there is the customer standing in the showroom, or on the supermarket floor, or listening to a salesperson, or thumbing through a catalog, or whatever. Perform a survey on him. Ask that customer if he wants to pay for weekly status reports, "make-work" procedures, budget reviews, memos that get filed, management meetings, forms in triplicate, or tons of computer printout, or whatever.

We know that in a competitive world, the customer is going to angle to try to get *the most for his buck*. He does not want to pay for "foolishness." And, if the customer is so inclined, shouldn't a company's management be the same way?

MAINTENANCE OF THE MANAGERIAL CHAIN OF COMMAND

"You've got a goal, I've got a goal. Now all we need is a football team."
GROUCHO MARX

The theorists generally condemn organization and the chain of command concepts. Their thinking is that such corporate paraphernalia stifles creativity or at least independent thinking.

Well, maybe in their work they need creativity or more importantly, practical creativity.

No business (and most other enterprises) can hope to succeed without a chain of command. Imagine if everybody went their way, each doing his own thing. Some good ideas may emerge. But who would put those ideas into fruition without an adequate chain of command?

HISTORY AND PURPOSE

At first, there was a boss-owner and the workers. Businesses grew and then there was a need for sub-bosses. (After all, you couldn't have scores and scores of people reporting to just one person.) Industry evolved into becoming more complex and specialist-bosses had to be trained and brought in.

There was the development of two types of management: the specialist managers (marketing, production, finance, and so on.) and the generalists (being significantly multiskilled).

RESPONSIBILITY DOWNWARD

"This is your areas, take charge of it."

Instead of having people wander wherever they care to, a boss divides up his or her responsibility among subordinates—even subordinate bosses.

"Here, this is your piece of my (the boss's) action (turf)."

With the delegation of responsibility goes authority related to that responsibility. ("You do what is necessary to accomplish your responsibility.")

RESPONSIBILITY UPWARD

With any responsibility goes targets of productivity, performance, quality and cost limits.

Compliance with instructions is an upward responsibility. A part of compliance is that the instructions were followed within certain other restrictions of, for instance, cost limitations or a time element.

"We got the order to the customer," also means that it was shipped on time, within budget, and to a certain quality standard.

THE REWARD SYSTEM

Rewards of pay raises, bonuses, promotions, and so on, cannot faithfully exist without a chain of command. Does everybody do their own merit review? That would be a great place to work!

HIRING METHODS

Taken to extreme, having a limited chain of command would permit anyone walking off the street to take any job. The purpose of having a competent boss handle his or her own staffing is to assure that other competents are brought on board.

Should the vice president for marketing interview a sales trainee or should it be done by a sales manager for whom the interviewee is going to work? The interviewer should be someone who is in the business of hiring and later evaluating the sales trainees.

PEELING OFF LAYERS

It is unfair to illustrate extremes. However, the theorists are quick to point out extremes in existing chains of command. Sure, there are companies that have too much management fat.

Anybody who knows how to spell "consultant" can go through any company and chop many heads. Interview middle managers and find one who reports to another middle level manager and say, "His work is duplicated." Repeat the process several times. Submit a consultant invoice, collect the fee, and advance to go.

These hired guns have exploited a gold mine discovered by the theorists. The never-ending lode is "peel away the fat."

BODY COUNTS ARE INVALID GAUGES

The proper objective of peeling away fat is not body counts but rather improvement in managerial communication. Now that's hard to quantify—chopped heads are of course easier to count.

"We chopped 100 managers in that division."

Fine, but can that division turn on a dime if the competition forced it to? Has the through-put time on special orders or services or whatever been improved? Is the span of control too excessive to permit prompt feedback reporting? Can new corporate policies be implemented overnight?

The best that one can expect from such questions is a "definite maybe." Even that bet can be well hedged.

BACK TO BASICS

The chain of command is here to stay. Maybe instead of ten layers of management, there will be seven. Or, instead of seven, then five. Each operation has to look carefully as to how to restructure.

By decreasing the number of layers of management, each manager will end up having more subordinates, including subordinate managers and supervisors, under his or her umbrella.

By reducing the number of layers, more managers will have more responsibilities. Firms who have had five section heads reporting to each manager could have seven such section heads for each. However, the chain of command will still be there.

SUCCESS REQUIREMENT: Learn more skills in order to manage a greater variety of people.

CAN CREATIVITY CREEP IN?

Creative people are in greater and greater demand—even among the most formerly conservative operations. Actually, the chain of command system is fertile ground for new ideas. How? It can more easily test and implement any sound concept more quickly than any other method.

BYPASSING THE CHAIN OF COMMAND

Can chain of command bypassing be allowed in a well-managed organization? The answer must be a resounding "no." Why? For one thing, it would take all the fun out of bypassing. Seriously, bypassing can only be justified for the following circumstances:

1. The jeopardy of the health or safety of others.
2. To report a commission of an illegal or unethical act.
3. When major corporate objectives are being thwarted.

Otherwise, bypassing is cancerous to the body of a healthy well-managed organization and its chain of command.

HOW TO BACK UP THE INSTRUCTIONS OF AN ASSISTANT

"If two men on the same job agree all the time, then one is useless. If they disagree all the time, then both are useless."
DARRYL F. ZANUCK, CEO, TWENTIETH CENTURY FOX

If a person is given a job to do, then that person also has to be given the tools. One of those tools is superior support for the decisions that are made.

Authority goes with responsibility.

A simple direct order or instruction within the responsibility of an assistant may only lend itself to obedience. However, some employees, for a variety of reasons, will attempt to undermine, countermand or reduce the effectiveness of the assistant.

MANAGER EVALUATION

A front-line manager or supervisor is limited in the potential to rise up the corporate ladder if there is a failure to use assistants as effectively as possible.

First of all, higher levels of management require more effective use of assistants and staff. Second, and very important, without a capable assistant, immediate promotion is doubtful as there is a question of the capability of any replacement.

GIVE THE ASSISTANT THE TOOLS

If an assistant is given the responsibility for the performance of a group of employees, give him or her the authority to give orders to those employees—even if the assignment is temporary. Of course, an assistant can be expected to make mistakes—but then, doesn't everybody?

The better way for an assistant to learn the job is to make mistakes.

The Personal Benefits of a Good Assistant

1. The boss can cover a wider area of responsibility.
2. Routine matters can be delegated to the assistant freeing the boss for more important functions.
3. A good assistant is a favorable commentary on the boss's training ability.
4. There is greater input in any decision making process.

Backfires

An assistant, who is not working out, has to be replaced promptly.

Just as a good assistant is a favorable reflection on the boss's ability, a poor assistant is a highly unfavorable commentary. Keeping a poor assistant longer than necessary only compounds the situation.

Sometimes the difference between a good and a poor assistant is the lack of confidence that the boss has in the assistant.

Explain Areas of Authority

The manager can explain just what the assistant is expected to accomplish. Then, the manager can define the types of orders and instructions that can be issued to the relevant subordinates. A good technique is to use an example as follows:

"Miss Kao, if you need to switch any people around to get the job done, just tell them where you want them."

Initial Notice

It is a good idea to notify subordinates of any change in the command structure as soon as possible. (This makes the job of the assistant easier.)

"Waldo, Miss Kao is going to be my assistant and will be running the special jobs."

PEOPLE CREATED PROBLEMS AND COMPLAINTS

There is nothing like listening to some rank and file complaints. (One can wonder if certain people are hard at work or dreaming up grievances.)

It is the boss's prerogative to wait to reply to comments and questions. By the way, complaints do not a poor assistant make. The boss should hold off any responses until the assistant has explained the situation or possible ramifications.

"Charley, I left Miss Kao in charge. You have to follow her instructions. She knows what she is doing."

RECOMMENDATION: NO WEASEL WORDS

Any hesitation, weasel phrases or other failure to fully back up the instructions of the assistant is going to undermine the authority of the assistant for a good long time. Subordinates might think that the assistant is a wimp. Bounce the ball right back into the complaining subordinate's court right away as follows:

"Randy, old boy, tell Miss Kao your problem. She gave you the assignment and the instructions."

WATCH FOR THE OLD END RUN PLAY

Naturally, some subordinates might try to get around the chain of command of an assistant. What else is new? The least of experienced managers and supervisors can recognize that gambit and block it quickly.

"Randy, once again, see Miss Kao."

ASSISTANT PERFORMANCE REVIEW

Once in a while, in a private office, the boss can review that assistant's progress with the assistant. When the discussion centers on problems caused by the assistant's instructions, the superior should listen carefully to the assistant's point of view. Only then can the boss make any warranted criticism. The purpose of the criticism is a learning exercise. At the end of such a session, the boss should reinforce the policy that the assistant's orders and instructions will be supported.

CARE AND FEEDING OF ASSISTANTS

In this cost-effective world, all managers and supervisors have more than they can handle. That's why the cultivation of good assistants is highly important. Words of encouragement are not wasted but help the assistant become more self-reliant and add a certain amount of esteem.

A good assistant doesn't just happen. It takes training and some good old coaching—not only in the technical end but on the people-to-people factor. It is worth the time, because a good assistant is an asset, not only to the Company but to the boss.

FEMALE MANAGERS VERSUS MALE SUBORDINATES

"The only question to be settled now is,
are women persons?"

Susan B. Anthony

To some men, the implications of working for a woman are difficult to face on a daily basis. The superior-subordinate relationship may imply to some men that they are somehow inferior, or, at least, less than they are supposed to be.

The fact that a manager is a manager because of ability is immaterial to some men if the manager is a woman. Even outstanding ability is of little consequence to some male chauvinists who would rather work for a male superior.

THE MALE EGO

The trouble is that some men believe that they are superior to women. Although there has been some change in this attitude, the change has not yet reached the point where the sex of a superior can be ignored.

THE SEXIST DEMON—ROLE PLAYING

As a result of early conditioning, which is improperly reinforced by the general society, many men do not view themselves in a subservient role to women. And, who is doing this reinforcing of male roles? Both men and women!

Fathers, mothers, brothers, sisters, and so on, all contribute to this sexist role playing. Guidance counselors in high schools and colleges are known to give different career advised to young people of different sexes—but not necessarily because of different abilities.

PROOF BY EXCEPTION INDUSTRIES

Can female managers handle male subordinates? Yes. The proof is that in certain industries, women managers and executives are quite common. Publishing, apparel, cosmetics, finance, retailing, the military and many others are finding that women make good managerial material. There is a long way to go, but the times are changing.

THE LAW OF THE LAND

National and local legislation and labor regulations give women certain rights with regard to promotion. The top brass would do well to make their employees aware of the law and its ramifications.

> *The fact that some male employees resist the concept of working for a woman is absolutely no defense against a charge of discrimination because of sex.*

In addition, some employers must take remedial action to put a larger percentage of women into managerial and supervisory position.

WATCH OUT FOR SILLY PLOYS

A frequent hallmark of unsatisfactory superior-subordinate relationship is the attempt by certain subordinates to work around the female superior by bypassing and other techniques.

Additional evidence is the disregard for instructions, "legal" countering of orders, and the deliberate misinterpretations of instructions by the male subordinates. The adverse attitude is expressed in courses of action that border on outright disloyalty.

THE PENALTY OF MALE CHAUVINISM

Duke Macho is an unhappy male subordinate. He doesn't like to work for a woman. What can he do about it? Nothing. Mr. Macho can be expected to use silly ploys that are intended to cause his female superior to fail as a boss. Those ploys can be easily countered.

Will Duke resign because of the situation? Not likely. Why? Because he may have a certain amount of difficulty in getting another job too quickly when the real reason for leaving is discerned. Besides, he can imagine what kind of a work reference his female boss, whom he tried to undercut, will submit.

Generally, Mr. Macho is trapped. The self-induced penalty for Duke is that he has to swallow his pride and male ego in one gulp.

STICK TO THE BOOK (NORMAL PROCEDURES)

The woman superior can follow the simple rules of supervision (meant for all), applying discipline when necessary, in order to have an easier time of supervising. No attempt at coddling or toleration of abuses of discretion or otherwise need be made.

While sticking closely to the rules of good supervision will not change any attitudes (conditioned by decades of role playing), it will maintain productivity and performance. For, getting the work out is still the best measure of a manager, male of female.

THE RECOMMENDED "KNOCK-EM-DEAD" EXAMPLE

Here is a technique to consider.

One experienced manager assigns the more onerous jobs to troublemakers until they show some change in attitude. The justification: "someone has to do the dog work."

"Charley, on Friday, bring in some old clothes, you have some area housekeeping to do."

As the troublesome subordinate mellows, the disliked chores are more carefully and/or evenly divided among the others.

MANAGING YOUR BOSS—MR. HARDHED

"No one can help liking the guy; if you do not,
he fires you."
UNKNOWN

Whether you inherited your boss (by virtue of a reorganization, or whatever) or he hired you, there is no reason to believe that you have to automatically get along with him.

He or she has faults, you have faults, but as an up-and-coming manager, you need your boss to help you.

Yesterday, he chewed you out in front of your subordinates. So what? You cannot quit. Why? Because you shouldn't resign unless and until it is in *your* interest.

You can brush up your resume. Nothing wrong with that. However, because your timing may be off, you have to make the most of a disagreeable situation.

GOING WITH THE FLOW

"Hey, I can't work with the guy."

Sure you can. Bite your lip, eat crow (or whatever), have a couple of draft beers at the Blue Bird Tavern during the happy hour, and stick it out—until *you* are ready to move on.

Many people damage their careers because of an unreasonable boss. They can make a careless quick move based on emotion. One that goes from the frying pan into the fire. Are you going to be one of those whose career got sidetracked because of someone else—even a boss?

Inopportune resigning is letting the boss win. Not you.

NONRECOMMENDATION: BEING A MARTYR

You really do not like the guy and therefore you are going to resign so that everyone in the Company will know how bad a fellow he really is. You are going to be a martyr. Forget it!

Six weeks after you leave, no one is even going to remember your name—much less what your sudden resignation was all about.

You are not indispensable. The Company existed before you got there and will continue on its merry way long after you are gone. Your old boss will still be up to his old tricks. Nothing will have changed, except you won't be there any more.

THE BETTER WAY

Being headstrong may make you feel good—at least for a while. However, there is a better way to feel good about yourself and your career track: Finesse the boss.

"Mr. Hardhed is too tough for that."

The tougher they are, the more hardboiled they are, the easier it may be to eventually *outfox him*. In order to advance in the management world, you have to develop a keen ability to apply your people-handling games techniques. Why not use that ability on the toughest of targets—an unreasonable boss?

Your techniques for getting people to do what they do not want to do have to be used as ploys on your boss. As a matter of fact, you should have been using your "people-smarts" all along on Mr. Hardhed.

HARDHED'S EGO IS BIGGER THAN YOUR EGO

A higher-up almost always has a larger ego. If nothing else, by virtue of the position. Because of other possible failings, Mr. Hardhed is very conscious of his position.

Think about this; a larger ego requires more stroking.

Clinical symptoms of a boss's enlarged ego include the following:

1. Unreasonable demands of subordinates.
2. Quick to place blame on (guess who?) subordinates.
3. Seldom admits his own mistake.
4. Requires prerogatives above his station.
5. Believes that colleagues and others are inferior.

6. Occasional loss of self control.

If a subordinate is going to stroke Mr. Hardhed's ego, he has got to play up to his peculiarities, abnormal requests, and unusual behavior.

"You want this report out 'yesterday'—sure thing, boss."

You may not get the report out until next week, but that is another matter for which Mr. Hardhed has to be handled then. However, at the moment, his ego has been stroked.

BASIS FOR MANAGING A BOSS

Look at it this way. You have learned how to manage subordinates—and some of them are tough cookies, right? Well, a new *challenge* appears—managing a superior. Some of the same people ploys have to be used on people higher up on the corporate ladder.

Is there a difference? No. People upstairs are just like people downstairs. Maybe their grooming and clothes are different, but underneath, where it *counts*, they are all the same. Particularly emotionally.

And, whatever people techniques that you use to get subordinates, colleagues, coworkers, customers, suppliers, accountants, inspectors, and others to work with you, you now have to use on Mr. Hardhed plus a few more "nice guy" methods.

Managers who do not use "people-smart" methods on superiors are less of promotion material.

True, it is easier to use people games on people with whom you have some sort of leverage. No question. For bosses like Mr. Hardhed, you have to remember the street-smart rules that you picked up on your journey in the business world.

THE BUSINESS ENVIRONMENT IS A STAGE

Mr. Hardhed has his script. You can even guess his dialogue in any forthcoming scene. Your dialogue and actions have to fit the scene and be part of the greater scenario.

Yes, it's play acting. If you are going to remain in the business world, you have to play a part. You will speak words that are not "your" words and move about the stage and react to other players as required.

Your survival and success in the play is highly dependent on your being a professional actor rather than an amateur. A professional will train and be more convincing in his part.

TRY FOR AN ACADEMY AWARD—AN OSCAR

"Mr. Hardhed could see through an act."

Most likely. So what? He is acting his part as a stick-in-the-mud boss. Believe or not, chances are that he quakes and shakes about his own inadequacies. Not publicly, but inside.

Your ploy is to take advantage of that phenomenon.

BEING A MANAGER MEANS BEING POLITICAL

"When dealing with people, let us remember we are not dealing with creatures of logic. We are dealing with creatures of emotions, creatures brisling with prejudices and motivated by pride and vanity."

DALE CARNEGIE

"Politics is a dirty word. Ability and hard work are what counts toward success."

It's okay to have ability and hard work as criteria for success. However, the able and hard working manager is not always necessarily a successful person—even by his own standards.

A mule has the ability to do its job and also works darn hard, and we all know what the mule gets as a reward—the opportunity to keep working harder. When the mule stops working hard, it gets sold for glue and/or dog food.

Managers are not mules Most managers want career advancement—a taste, if nothing more, of a better life.

THE SUCCESS TRACK

Let's say you want to be a senior manager in 5 years, a division manager 10 years after that, and a corporate officer 10 years later. This is not a bad plan.

What are you doing about fulfilling your plan? Well, you are working hard as well as learning and picking up new technical skills. Good! However, is something missing? Maybe. There is a chance that you may not be sharpening your people-to-people skills.

YOUR MANAGEMENT EXPERIENCE

You have been around the track and you have witnessed that people (subordinates, colleagues, bosses, and so on) do not always do what they are supposed to be doing. Even when they are being paid to do it. And, even when it is in their job descriptions.

People have to coaxed, cajoled, spoken to harshly *or* softly, scolded, stroked, pleased, bargained, harassed, argued, bribed, pleaded, and begged, in order for them to do something that they should have been done anyway.

As a manager or supervisor, you may have done many of those things yourself in order to get your department or section's work out. Chances are that you are still using those ploys to meet productivity and performance requirements. And, why not? They work.

Those are simple "people-to-people" skills that you have been using.

Here's how you may have been using those skills; you make an assessment as to the possible emotional reaction of the other party. Then, you undermine or counter it with an emotional response intended for you to get your way.

You have been running your group, section or department at a certain required level of your people-to-people skills. Now, consider if you were one further step up the management ladder. You have become a boss of about five or eight subordinates who are just like you are right now.

They are "people-smart" also. All of them have been using and will continue to use the same ploys that you have been using previously. You, as their boss, have to try more sophisticated ploys.

You are no longer fishing in a small pond. There are bigger fish who need a different kind of bait. Platitudes, kind words, and soft soap have to be added to your repertoire.

Your new colleagues at the new managerial level are playing for different and bigger stakes. They do not want a newcomer to their level outgunning them. They want to show him up, do him in and make him (at least, partially) fail at his new job.

You do not think so? Well, examine carefully the remarks made at the first few management meetings at your new level. Pay special attention and discern the motivation of the remarks. Are each of them trying to make themselves look good? Chances are they are will continue to do so—even at the expense of others.

MANAGEMENT PROMOTION MATERIAL

*There is no way that someone without good
interpersonality skills is going to continue to be promoted.*

If you signed up for a career in management, you have agreed to use and improve your ability to handle people. Management is not tightening up nuts on a widget assembly line or going door to door peddling a product or service. Management is largely the ***purposeful handling of people***.

The higher rungs on the corporate ladder require people with the ability to handle a more diverse type of still other people. There are people to be handled of varying disciplines, as well as different functions and responsibilities—marketing, production, distribution, administration, finance, and so forth. Even within the same function, there are people of varying specialities. All of whom have to be handled.

STOP! Put a bookmark or ruler on this page and quickly flip to Appendix V; Action Checklist for Wheeling and Dealing with Others in Management.

THE POLITICAL ANIMAL JUNGLE

There are two-legged sharks, jackals, coyotes, and what have you out in the business world. They are quick to turn and snap at anyone (especially a chicken) that gets in their way. Their game is survival and moving up.

Is there doubt? Well, consider what happens when someone, who wants to look good has his achievements pop up looking bad, Is he going to' come out and say, "I blew it"?

It is more likely that blame for snafus may be placed elsewhere. Maybe quietly and surreptitiously on the unsuspecting.

WARNING FROM AN OLD CARD PLAYER

If you are in a hot and heavy poker game with sharp gamblers and high stakes and you do not know who the patsy is, then chances are it is ***you***.

THE POLITICAL CARD GAME

You are not going to eliminate company politics. Whether you want to play or not, you are in the game. There are only two real options in the Company political poker game. Either you are a patsy or you are one of the more serious professional players in a game of high stakes. Your bet.

SHOULD A MANGER LIE, STEAL OR CHEAT FOR THE COMPANY?

"Everybody has a little bit of Watergate in him."
BILLY GRAHAM, 1974

There are many theorists out there who are busy developing corporate ethical codes of conduct. Actually, their work was done for them by the publication of the Ten Commandments and the Sermon on the Mount.

Their real problem though is that they were never in a position of being a front-line manager. What could these theorists know of real life career pressures, the risk-to-reward ratios and expediency?

DEFINITION OF ETHICS

Corporate life is a part of Western civilization which is based on a system of values which mandates that each individual is required to treat every other individual as he himself wishes to be treated. We do not want *other people* to lie, steal, or cheat from us and therefore, we should refrain from doing the same to them.

However, corporate life presents some very undue pressures that were not visualized by the old sages, religious leaders or ancient philosophers. In those days there were no 30-year mortgages that had to be paid or careers on the line.

THE LAW OF THE LAND

There are laws which protect society from corporate lying, stealing and cheating and provide stiff punishments for the culprits. Who writes these laws? Politicians; all too many of whom have been caught (you guessed it) lying, stealing, and cheating.

PROTECTING NUMBER ONE

Looking out for number one is a part of being street smart in the corporate jungle. Sure, there is the "team" concept. However, do not fool yourself as to who may be thrown to the legal sharks (who wear badges) first.

Front-line managers are the ones who actually get something done. That's their job. They are more usually in a position to give instructions or provide information that can backfire. In any showdown, they are going to hit that proverbial fan first.

11th COMMANDMENT: Thou shalt not get caught.

EASY RECOMMENDATION

To comply with the 11th Commandment, the easy way is not to do anything that is unethical. As difficult as that may be to many people in corporate life, for the long haul, it may be the best approach. There are many good managers walking the streets, looking for some kind of a decent job, who got caught in a squeeze between the short-term corporate expediency and their own personal long-term interests.

THE DRAWBACK OF CORPORATE CRIME

The problem of the corporate criminal is that too many others in the organization would likely know about the criminal act. Any one of those other people, for their own reasons (like protecting themselves), could spill the beans. ***Whistle blowers and "do-gooders" are all around us***. A work-alone bank heist artist does not have that problem.

ACTS SUBJECT TO BACKFIRE

For the middle manager, corporate crime could include misleading customers (consumer fraud), misleading creditors, contaminating products, providing incomplete data to auditors, governmental agencies, inspectors or other busybodies, padded insurance claims, false tax info, non-compliance with labor laws, deceiving employees on rights, failure to provide due credits, incorrect invoicing, phony shipping claims, and much more.

NOTE: Most of the above acts can be known to others (the accomplices) in the Company.

THE NUREMBERG DEFENSE

Absolutely, positively, and without question, using a defense that your boss told you to do it is *not* valid in any court of law, investigation, audit, hearing, arena or anywhere else.

"My boss ordered me to do it" is a nondefense, period. It is an excuse that carries no weight whatsoever—either in law or morality. It is not even a mitigating circumstance. The fact that your job or career was at stake is immaterial.

FORGET THE OTHERS-DO-IT DEFENSE

Others in the corporate would may have committed the same acts and have gotten away with it. Few can contend that justice also means overall fairness. The issue of fairness relates only to the accused in a particular matter—not to others.

REVISITING ETHICS

Personal ethics in business is important. It allows us to sleep nights. However, the larger reason to maintain an ethical standard may be the *risk of consequences*. Look at the risks which can include loss of a career, a prison sentence, heavy fines, and crippling legal costs. True, not everybody gets caught. However, the risks are still there and some do have to pay the full price. Is it worth the risk?

> *"First, there is the law. It must be obeyed. But the law is the minimum. You must act ethically."*
> IBM BUSINESS GUIDELINES FOR EMPLOYEES

THE CHALLENGE TO ETHICS

If you do not lie, cheat or steal for your Company, your superiors might get someone else to take your place and do it. That can be a real threat. And you have the 30-year mortgage to pay, and so on. The cheaper way is to take a walk if you're forced to. Remember, it's tougher to pay off a home mortgage while earning 30 cents an hour sewing mail bags at the government hotel in Barsville. You can figure it out.

It is not necessarily ethics that keeps you on the straight and narrow. You would rather work in a fast food outlet kitchen that in a prison kitchen. If that's the case, it's consequences, not ethics, that wouldn't allow you to lie, steal, or cheat for your Company.

THE BETTER BUSINESS WORLD

As strange as it seems to noisy media-crazed critical outsiders, corporate greed is *not* universal. The overwhelming majority of companies do not want their managers to lie, steal, or cheat for them. The corporate critics wouldn't believe that there are many, many companies that bend over backwards just to be sure that they do not even appear to be unethical—much less unlawful—in any way whatsoever.

The comparatively few companies that have given in to corporate greed have learned the hard lesson that it is cheaper and a lot easier not to lie, steal, or cheat.

THAT LAST REVIEW

For some of us, there is an expectation that there is going to be a final management evaluation or performance review somewhere up there in the great sky. It would be nice to enter that assessment process with a clear record.

IMPROVING YOUR CHANCES FOR MANAGEMENT CAREER SUCCESS

"The trick is to make sure you do not die waiting for prosperity to come."
LEE IACOCCA, CHRYSLER CORPORATION

We all are guilty of procrastination and putting things off for another day. Even the chance for success. Almost everyone who has made it advises not to wait, but to start working on personal management success now—today.

WHY WAIT?

A reason that most people go from year to year at the same job, although they have potential for a higher management level, is that they think that someone or something is going to come down the pike and they are going to be handed success. While that does happen, the probability is extremely low. It may be worse odds than trying to win the lottery.

THE THREE SUCCESS STEPS

1. Have goals.
2. Make plans.
3. Follow plans.

There it is in only three very short steps. There are two big catches to this concept. The first catch is that *you have to start*. The second catch is that *you have to stick to it*.

GETTING STARTED

In order to get on board the train for success, one has to be in the right depot. That means knowing just where you want to go. By the way, where do you want to go? Not sideways, and certainly not down. It is a matter of working out what your goals should be.

Having no goals is a plan for failure.

Giving some thought to your goals is important. Why? Because you do not want to work very hard for a great number of years to attain those goals and then you are dissatisfied.

You have arrived at your very own "dream" castle in Spain and look, there's no plumbing, sweetheart!

How to set goals

First, do not worry about being unrealistic. There are many people who made it to the top slots with less going for them than you might have. Let's face it, if you do not make it to your top goal, but made it to the step below, at least you have given it your best shot.

Second, do not consider your present abilities, talents, skills, personality traits, technical expertise, and opportunities. All of those factors and circumstances are *going to improve* as you work toward your goals. There are going to be intermediate goals that you are going to have to get to before you can reach your final goal.

The intermediate goals are way stations on your trip. Hopefully, these local stops will be of short duration. Here are some generalized abbreviated goals for a manager to consider:

- Department manager in five years.
- Division manager in ten years.
- General manager if fifteen years.
- Corporate officer in twenty years.

Those are generalized and abbreviated goals. Your individual goals have to be more *specific*. You have to include the function that you want to be in and the type of operation that you want to manage at each stage.

The easy trick for making plans

Find out what other successful people around you in your field have done and adopt their plan as yours. Their scenario worked for them. It could work for you with the same, or even better, results.

If a winning formula or plan did career wonders for someone else, who may not have been nearly as capable as you are, it sure can work again—this time for you.

Copy from a few plans so that you get the best of all worlds. Try to find out the following:

1. What were the various steps on the way up?
2. What kind of skills and technical expertise had to be acquired? At which points or steps?
3. What personality traits helped these others achieve success?
4. What kind of opportunities had to be grabbed?
5. What other plan features do I have to adopt?

Accumulate all of the information that you can. Analyze all of it. Now, do your own personal planning. Draft it in writing—about two pages. Date it, because you may modify it down the road to some extent if circumstances change severely. Put it away in a drawer.

Review it in about two weeks. Make some changes if your thinking has changed, The final version is your personal plan for success in the field of management.

NOW, THE DIFFICULT PART—ACTION

You have goals and a plan of action. You have spent some time taking personal assessments, evaluating a plan, and patting yourself on the back for what you have accomplished to this point. Up to now, it is all just wishful thinking.

Now the real work starts. Acquiring additional skills, improving your interpersonal abilities, learning new management techniques, promoting your own possibilities, picking up new ideas, and so on, are areas of your new concern. It is going to be a long road. However, others, many of whom had less on the ball, have done it and so can you.

An overnight success takes many years. If you are hesitant because the journey will take so long, think about this; if you do not start now, will the trip to success be any shorter later on?

AN ANALOGY

Many army lieutenants would like to make it to general. Most do not. However, *every* lieutenant that became a general wanted to become a general. It was a long journey with many stops. There was a lot of competition at each stop. Nevertheless, some always make it to the top.

This is true in business and industry as well. Those who *want* to move up have a better chance. Those who work harder at a plan have a still better chance. It is only a matter of you improving the odds in your favor. Start today!

CAREER ENTHUSIASM—THE BREAKFAST OF CHAMPIONS

*"Success is not the result of spontaneous combustion.
You must set yourself on fire."*
REGGIE LEACH

Look around you. There are men and women all about in job slots who are going to be in those *same* slots until someone gives them a gold watch and pushes them out the door.

You know them. They are the deadwood or almost deadwood. Some of their attributes are as follows:

1. They stopped learning anything new about the business about umpteen years ago.

2. They have not changed the way that they handle their responsibilities in about the same amount of time.

3. Most of them think that computers are a passing fad that wouldn't work. (New communications equipment are toys.)

4. Any ideas that are newer than sliced bread won't work either.

5. They do not try to walk on anyone else's turf.

6. Most of them are strictly nine to five. No weekends.

7. Each one of them survived 5 bosses, 8 management consultant head choppers, and 14 personnel directors.

8. The number of management seminars that they *all* attended in total can be counted on one hand and you would still be able to pick up a martini with that hand.

Exaggeration? Maybe, but not completely. The extent of exaggeration is not the point. What is more to the point for you is that the competition for moving up the corporate ladder is not all that fired up.

THE LOW OCTANE COMPETITION

All of the competition wants to sit in the back seat.

All of the deadwood and the others who have not installed a new idea since who knows when want a *free ride* in the back seat. For them, driving is to chancy and subject to hassle.

Consider the virtues of the back seat: low criticism, few people taking potshots at them, being comfy with the herd, no rocking the boat, a smoother ride, and less worry about survival. There is also the opportunity of taking potshots at the driver.

ALONG COMES MR. SPARKPLUG

You can readily understand that Mr. Fred Sparkplug, the hot shot department manager, is a dangerous threat to all of the "backseaters." Why? Someone in the ivory tower just might expect all of the slower moving backseaters to perform as Mr. Sparkplug does. His work habits include the following:

1. He arrives at work a half hour before start time in order for his department to get a leg up on the daily load.

2. Fred spends a number of evenings (and Saturdays—sometimes on Sunday too) at work getting squared away.

3. The hotshot manager coordinated with the computer people to install a new overall reporting system. He has a PC on his desk to monitor projects.

4. In addition to computer classes, he attended industry seminars to be abreast of competitor and other trends.

5. His subordinates have been cross-trained and are multiskilled. Absenteeism does not affect the work flow.

6. Fred's boss hands him all of the special and rush jobs and projects. (For good reason.)

7. In addition to productivity and performance gains, he has become a bear on quality and cost effectiveness.

8. Fred is always welcoming new assignments and additional responsibilities.

Now, you have to admit two things about Fred. One is that he is a definite threat to his competition. Second, he is on the make to move up.

If he knocks out the competition for any upward movement, then top management has to move him up.

FOLLOW FRED

You can do exactly what Fred does—maybe even better, because what he does is not mind boggling or impossible for someone else to copy and to do right away.

Be fired up about work, getting more work, learning more skills, trying new things, improving existing skills, copying successful techniques, and so on.

Move, move, move—keep plugging away—bang, bang, bang—knock out the work—exude and gush enthusiasm. In short, do not wait for someone to give you a push in the direction of success—*light a fire under yourself.*

"But all those other people are better than me."

Even if *all* of those other people had more skills, better education, more technical know-how, longer experience, and so on—most of them lack one tremendously big thing—they are not generally enthusiastic about their work.

Let's face it. There are all too many managers who are slow pokes, bottlenecks, nervous nellies, error prone, social lions, red tape artists, goldbricks, clock watchers and plain old deadwood. (Every organization has its fair share of them.) On the other hand, there are very few who are like Fred Sparkplug.

From now on, add enthusiasm to the start of your day. Be eager to go to work and knock the competition dead.

*Make like work is a **challenge**, not a chore.*

Here is what you have going for you. Sure, there is a great deal of competition. For now, ignore the quantity and look at the *quality* of the competition. Most of them cannot hack more work, won't learn new skills, and are against any new ideas. They are lack-luster performers.

WHEN WILL RECOGNITION COME?

As soon as you leave the herd, the others in the herd are going to take potshots at you. They cannot stand anyone who is really trying to get ahead.

Everyone from the janitor on up is going to know that someone is becoming more success-oriented. Rumor peddlers and gossip mongers are going to send out dozens of latrine-o-grams about the new hotshot on the premises.

"He came in at *what* time? Left *when*?"

A manager who becomes all fired up about the work situation is immediately going to be so known by his boss, coworkers, subordinates and maybe the people on the executive floor—the corporate makers and shakers.

THE SWEET SMELL OF SUCCESS

"He is going to be a general manager in time."

If you look and act as if you are going to succeed in your career goals, some people (including the corporate makers and shakers) will give you a wider berth and due recognition. They have sniffed out the smell of success. The ingredients for that smell include hard work, proven learning ability, and *enthusiasm*.

Going to work with a lackluster attitude is out. Come on, almost everybody does that. Showing up *fired up* with enthusiasm is going to mark you for success. Got a match?

YOU NEVER GET A SECOND CHANCE TO MAKE A GOOD FIRST IMPRESSION

"The reason for having diplomatic relations is not to confer a compliment, but to secure a convenience."
WINSTON S. CHURCHILL

It is an unfair world. People who may be instrumental in your success at work can develop an unfavorable impression of you within 20 seconds of meeting you.

It takes a great deal of back-bending effort and time to counter an unfavorable first impression. Assuming that you know that the impression is unfavorable. First impressions never go away completely.

The worst part about first impressions that we make them usually within 20 seconds. In that short period of time, a false assessment is very possible.

HOW DO I COME ACROSS?

Your boss walks into your office with a stranger.

"Winslow, I'd like you to meet the new Vice President for Engineering, Mr. Erhardt."

They have an exchange of platitudes and they leave. You do not know if you came across as a yo-yo or a hot shot. Worse, you may **never** know.

Unless you have been working hard at improving your first impression capability, you may not have come across as well as you would like to.

Portraying good first impressions is a matter of practice.

THE IMPORTANCE OF FIRST IMPRESSIONS

It is a lazy way of doing things. We categorize people and apply labels because our mind does not want to be bothered at the moment with a deeper assessment of what the eyes and ears tell it. It is stereotyping at worst.

We rely on labels and stereotype thinking to form judgments. Not necessarily based on the true facts. It is a handy way of going about the world doing things. We haven't the time to analyze everything to death.

The problem is that we seldom admit that our judgments—even those made in haste—are wrong, or even possibly wrong.

As this phenomenon relates to the work place, we must bear in mind that appraisals made upon a first impression could directly affect our work and career situation. Maybe, for a long time.

"Winslow, my first impression of you was wrong."

It is highly unlikely that anyone is going to say that to you. Proof: how many times have *you* said such a thing?

JUDGEMENTS BASED ON RESPONSE

Think for a moment how you develop an assessment of someone that you meet for the first time. Consider carefully what you are watching for. How about the following attributes for starters:

1. The tone and pitch of the other party's voice.

2. His possible choice of topics.

3. The use of certain words and phrases which instill interest.

4. His grooming and his clothes.

5. Facial expressions and body language.

6. The apparent impression that he is trying to make.

7. Overall attitude and possible motivations.

8. Flattery and platitudes.

If you are using those qualities as a guide, then others are using them and possibly much more.

Improve your own capability to judge others on a first meeting.

What to Avoid at First Meetings

Here are a couple of points to consider *not* doing when first meeting someone new:

1. Avoid any indication of hostility.
2. Do not use foul or intemperate language.
3. Keep any anger about anything to yourself.
4. Show no signs of fear.
5. Do not show any signs of disinterest.

Suggested Things to Do at First Meetings

1. If possible, prepare yourself in advance.
2. Try topics of common interest. If disinterest is displayed, change the subject.
3. Stand tall and provide a firm handshake.
4. Appear confident and act friendly. Smile to put the other party more at ease.
5. When speaking, keep an even level quality, pitch, tone, pace, and volume.
6. Reinforce good points with minor body language.

You have to develop your own style of how you come across when meeting new people. That style should add other good points to the above.

How to Practice

Naturally, you could go home and practice the first impression routines using a full-length mirror and a small tape recorder. It is a good idea in that it works out some of your more rougher edges which can become readily obvious to you.

The best practice might be in the on-the-job training. You meet new people almost everyday. Watch how you handle those situations—even minor meetings. Observe yourself and the other party.

WHY RUN LIKE HECK UP THE DOWN ESCALATOR

"Depend on the rabbit's foot if you will, but remember it didn't work for the rabbit!"
R.E. SHAY

Fifteen million people in this country have indicated that their occupation is management according to the U.S. Census. That is a lot of people not only statistically, but as possible personal competition for you.

Look at this way: there are millions of people who would like to have *your* job. There are millions of people who would like to land on the next rung up the ladder from your job. But that's statistics. Quantity does not presume quality.

> *The practical side is that there are only a comparative few that can handle your job and still less that can handle the next job up the corporate ladder.*

Even if it is one person that would like to displace you and even if there is only one other person to compete for your next job up the ladder, there is still competition.

RABBIT'S FOOT ORIENTATION

Too many people rely on luck for their career. You can see it all around you.

"Gee, I hope that I luck out and get that promotion."

Maybe chance will help you. However, the better bet, even if you believe in sheer luck, is to give yourself a better break.

CAUTION FLAG—OVER RELIANCE ON LUCK

Maybe you have had some good breaks in the past and you think that your good luck will continue. This kind of thinking is chancy. What happens if your luck does not hold out?

Well, you could be working in a management capacity which is well below your actual abilities. That would be a career failure and cause for discontent with your life's work.

BOTTOM LINE: You can be getting less pay than you are worth.

> **"If it weren't for bad luck, I wouldn't have no luck at all!"**
> DICK GREGORY

TRY THE BETTER WAY

Don't count on luck!!!

An experienced executive said, "It took 25 years of hard work to be lucky enough to be a vice president." Another management sage said, "The harder I work, the more luck I have."

Sure, there are other things that are important. Personality, technical ability, creativity, learning capability, and image go a long way toward job security and upward mobility. A part of that image thing is being recognized as a hard worker. Maybe there isn't much you can do about your personality and other personal qualities. However, almost anyone can work harder.

> **"The sleeping wolf doesn't taste mutton."**
> FRENCH PROVERB

HARD-WORKING MANAGER

To improve your image of being a hard worker consider the following attributes:

1. Works frequent evenings. (Sometimes, late at night.)
2. Puts in a couple of Saturdays each month. (During peak periods, an occasional Sunday.)
3. Provides extra effort on rush, panic and special assignments. ("No job is too tough.")
4. Takes work home.
5. Is an "early starter" at work.

6. Does not take excessive time for lunch.

7. Seeks shortcuts in all work assignments.

8. Very serious about meeting deadlines.

9. Not a "time waster" on the job.

10. Personal leave or time-off is minimal.

HOME LIFE SCHEDULE FOR A WORKAHOLIC

Being a "workaholic" and having a home life are not incompatible. Sure, there are personal chores to accomplish. However, those routines and tasks have to be scheduled to fit into a master time schedule that has regard for your career objectives.

It is not a matter of which comes first. It is more of a matter of overall scheduling. There are priorities—at work and at home.

WORKAHOLIC "DON'TS"

Most people who are very hard workers consider certain personal activities a waste of time. They have learned to cut down on the nonrewarding activities—whether at work or at home. They also apply their at-work efficiency techniques to other areas of their life.

All activities are subject to priority considerations.

WHY KNOCK YOURSELF OUT?

Even if the good competition is few in number, they are hard at work. As one manager in a very competitive career environment said, "You've got to run very hard just to stand still."

Even "standing still" (keeping your present position) can require some hard work. Look at all of the people that would love to have your present job.

There are many very good managers and capable supervisors on the street who would grab your job and for less pay and other goodies. They are victims of mergers, acquisitions, reorganizations, layoffs, slimming down, restructuring, down-sizing, budget cutting, and so on.

That's just people on the street. What about others in your own place or at work across town or across the country?

Maybe it cannot happen to you. Remember, it has happened to others who thought that they had a "lifetime" job.

WHY DOESN'T EVERYONE WORK HARD?

First, some people are not career oriented. They are content with where they are. Second, for job preservation, many do not believe that they will be laid off. If that thought does occur to them, they have the back-up belief (sometimes, unfounded) that they could get a meaningful replacement job readily. Third, many people believe that promotions will come in time to those who wait. Sure, that does happen. However, it is too infrequent and too drawn out. (You do not want to die waiting for prosperity.)

JOB SECURITY PLUS CAREER PATH

If you do not have a "laid back" attitude and/or are not content to rely on luck, then you have to run like heck up the down escalator. Because that escalator is only going to take you downstairs or where you do not want to go—career-wise.

IMPROVING PERSONALITY FOR LEADERSHIP

"You do not play well with others."
KINDERGARTEN TEACHERS EVERYWHERE

You are not going to hit that subordinate or other manager down the hall on the head with a block. Adults have different ways of expressing tantrums. Some of them are as deleterious to our careers as using a block.

We all have little tantrums. However, most of us learn to control our inner drives to dent somebody's head with a block. It is not necessarily a major personality defect and there is little need to go see the shrink about it.

Over the years, we develop the ability to cope with our rough edges of our personality. In this day and age and in some operations, the pressures are tremendous. The workday can be long with one panic after another. Yet, somehow, we almost always manage to keep an even temperament.

"I think that maybe in every company today there is always at least one person who is going crazy slowly."
JOSEPH HELLER

CHECKLIST OF WORK RELATED SEVERE TANTRUMS

1. Banging or pounding on the desk.
2. Shouting or using a very loud voice.
3. Use of abuse language with the intent of being abusive.
4. Foul language (not "shop" talk) and barnyard noises.
5. Racial, ethnic or sexual slurs.
6. Throwing or slamming things.
7. Wild gestures.
8. Stated deep resentment against certain top management people.

9. Never admits a mistake.
10. "Everyone" is always watching.
11. Has low respect for formalities—seldom polite.

Anyone that does **all** of those things, of course, is close to a nervous breakdown or the "funny farm."

LESS SEVERE PERSONALITY PROBLEM CHECKLIST

1. Refuses to hear answers on question that are asked.
2. Seldom is cheerful. Never advances a "hello."
3. Extremely authoritarian in orders.
4. Overcriticizes quickly without all of the facts.
5. Seldom appreciates assistance.
6. Hardly ever compliments subordinates or others.
7. Slow to admit a mistake.
8. Has low regard for the problems of others.
9. Is cooperative with colleagues only when necessary.
10. Is frequently disparaging of some in higher levels.
11. Maintains overimportance of personal privileges.
12. Sometimes, failed projects are cause for placing blame elsewhere.
13. Generally, shuns gestures of friendliness.

MORE COMMON PERSONALITY PROBLEM CHECKLIST

1. Doesn't always listen carefully to others.
2. Not always willing to accept good technical advice.
3. Exhibits an apparent forced politeness.
4. Often stereotypes people and things.
5. Makes small effort for a first good impression.
6. A few people are almost always in the "dog house."
7. Slight depression when matters are not going well.

8. Attitude toward colleagues and associates fluctuates.

9. Uneven self-confidence.

10. At times, slightly anti-authority.

EMOTIONAL PROBLEMS—SO WHAT?

Everyone has emotional problems, from the cradle to the grave and from the mailroom messenger to the chairman of the board. The only distinction between all of us is how we each handle our own emotional problems. Those comparatively few who cannot tackle their peculiar problems require professional help.

The rest of us have learned to cope. We hide our frustrations, hang-ups, immaturity, and so on, under a facade. Some of us are better at doing that than others.

PERSONALITY IN THE WORKPLACE

At work our behavior patterns are under more scrutiny than in other areas of our life. Therefore, we become more skillful in how we portray ourselves in that environment. In our jobs we each become three different personalities as follows:

1. What we show of ourselves to others.

2. What we think we really are like.

3. What we really are.

For purposes of job success, we try to improve ourselves and how we behave when others can be observant of our behavior. For example we are polite when we do not want to be.

CHECKLIST OF PLUS PERSONALITY TRAITS

Some of the more desirable personality traits that a front-line manager or supervisor could have would include the following:

1. Outgoing. Quick to be friendly—even with strangers.

2. At ease. Makes people feel emotionally comfortable.

3. Politeness. Provides proper formalities—even in adverse circumstances.

4. Understanding. Shows awareness of the problems of other people.

5. Small talk. Shows interest in nonwork situations.

6. Listens. Wants to receive as much information as possible.

7. Fairness. Avoids being too critical.

8. Language. Declines to use certain words and phrases that are "triggers" for emotional resentment.

9. Integrity. Tries to keep promises. Assumes any blame for personal mistakes.

10. Ethical. Avoids questionable activities.

11. Character. The sum total of all of the good personality qualities that one has.

Not everybody is going to score 100% on the above checklist. However, the basic idea is to have (or display) as many of them as possible.

One thing is for sure. If you do not have many of those good qualities and in a certain amount of depth and with consistency, you may have less of a chance to move up the promotion ladder.

"WHY CHANGE ME?"

As Mr. Elwood P. Dowd, the main nonrabbit character in the play and movie Harvey, said, "In this world you have got to be oh so smart or oh so nice. I tried smart: I recommend nice."

In the business world, if you do not have all of the other abilities in full measure that are needed for success, you can make up for those omissions by having a desirable personality. It is easier to change the way we outwardly behave than, for instance, to become smart.

KEEPING THE MOTIVATOR RUNNING

"It doesn't matter how small you are if you have faith and a plan of action."

FIDEL CASTRO

Despite the theorists and behavioral scientists, we will NEVER know what motivates people. One person is turned on and another one is not. The "why" is hard to know.

We do know one thing: without motivation there is no success. Talk to anyone who has achieved some measure of success. You will note that they have a high drive and are aggressive when the chips are down.

Motivation can beat out ability, talent, creativity, and even brute force.

The theorists think that money, perks, prestige, power, being your own boss, and so on., is the motivation to knock yourself out on your job. Not so. Think of all the multimillionaires and even billionaires, who have all of those things and much more, but who keep working a 60-hour week.

Money and those other things are goals or payment for services rendered. Ignore that these rewards are uneven, unstable and/or often delayed. At best, they are incentives.

THE REAL MOTIVATOR

You might climb a mountain because it is there. If a bigger one shows up on the horizon, you might try to climb that one also. At home, you might pick up the daily cross word puzzle and spend three or more hours trying to get at least half of it completed. Climbing the mountain or struggling with the puzzle doesn't provide economic or material gain.

531

Laid back attitude

Frankly, in our system, you can eat pretty regularly by just doing a job. No knocking yourself out with long hours, additional education or training, thinking of better ways of making widgets, or whatever.

Charley could make more money and perks by working a couple of evenings plus every other Saturday, and taking up computer systems or programming. He knows that. And, he has seen others who follow that path to try to get ahead. We say that Charley lacks motivation. Actually, Charley would like to have more of the trappings of success, but he does not accept the challenge.

Some people want to go from A to B while sitting down.

Old Charley and others would like more in their paycheck, some stock options, big bonuses, a limo, a title like vice president, sitting in on board meetings, a 20 by 20 office, two secretaries, and an administrative assistant. Those are all what theorists call motivational items.

Everybody knows that those items are there, yet they do not try for them. Why? Because most people do not accept the challenge to try to get them.

Mountain climbing and job success

Lindberg soloed the Atlantic because it was there. Hillary climbed Mount Everest because it was there. Astronauts have gone to the moon because it was there.

If the TV evening news reported that an explorer found a mountain twice as tall as Everest, then, tonight, there would be some people packing their snow shoes and oxygen tanks and heading for it. Similarly, at work, there are some people who have accepted the challenge of trying to get to the top—maybe, step by step (promotion after promotion).

No special ability is required

People who accept the challenge of climbing mountains in the work place do not necessarily have any special ability.

Those fellows and gals who are moving toward the top of the corporate ladder put on their snow shoes just as you do—one shoe at a time. They seldom are more creative or have any more talent than the rest of the management people around them.

As a matter of fact, a good number of people made it to the very top of the business world on their own with less than average talent. ("On their own" means excluding the "thanks, Dad" stories.)

How about hard work?

Hard work counts but that's not a motivator. It is the result of being motivated. You might work hard an/or do a score of other things to help you overcome the challenge.

And politics?

Politics is a good tool to use to meet the challenge of others. Unless you want to move up, politics is just a nice office game.

Aren't skills important?

Skills are important, and what you need you pick up along the way. Most people are not willing to learn any new skills unless they are challenged.

How to keep the motivator turned on

Fred Sparkplug has seen the light and accepted the challenge of success. He has witnessed how others have arrived at, or near, the top. People who have no more on the ball than he does!

"If that lummox can do it, so can I."

Mr. Sparkplug is moving, moving, moving. His motivator is running full blast all of the time. He is hot to trot.

Fred is not waiting for lady luck or someone to get around to recognizing him. He is picking up tricks of the trade, finding shortcuts, cutting red tape, soft-soaping people for cooperation, learning new skills, increasing productivity, improving quality, volunteering for more responsibilities, seeking expanded authority, meeting targets, finding new customers, cutting costs, inspiring subordinates, pleasing superiors, and finding out how to finesse up to the next job up the ladder.

If the makers and shakers on the executive floor are alert, they will eventually help Fred Sparkplug move up the corporate promotion steps. If they are not alert and savvy, Sparkplug will move to the competition—who could always use another hot shot.

KEEP YOUR MOTIVATOR RUNNING

Look around your place. You can assess that good higher level management material is hard to find. That's no secret. Now, look around at your colleagues. Most of them are content to be where they are. (That's the competition!) If you are not content, then develop a plan for success and take up the challenge. It is just a matter of starting your own personal motivator today and keeping it going, going, going.

TECHNIQUES FOR JOB SURVIVAL

"No river is deep to one who can swim."
UNKNOWN

In the business world, some say that this is the computer age or the age of high speed management. The reality to too many people is that this the age of mergers, acquisitions, restructuring, slimming down, downsizing, reductions in force, budget cutting, layoffs, and pink slipping.

Many of those people are concerned with resumes, references, job openings, employment agencies, unemployment checks, want ads, interviews and rainy day runds that are going downhill.

Not only is there the financial drain of being out of work but the emotional trauma of being out on the street.

When you sign up to work for someone else, you accept the hazard of being laid off.

In many industries that have been hit hard, there are all too many very capable managers and supervisors looking for work. They were good at their jobs but they didn't survive retrenchment.

CAN THIS HAPPEN TO ANYONE?

Unless you are the beneficiary of a "Thanks, Dad" scenario, it can happen to you. Good management people who thought that they had some kind of "guarantee" are out looking for work.

Maybe, not today nor tomorrow, but down the road anyone that works for someone else has to take their chances on job longevity.

From among the Fortune 500 companies, market secure companies, powerful banks, public utilities, government agencies, as well as lesser enterprises, cutbacks have discarded management people like so many old shoes.

Cut personnel and reduce debt.

One company gobbles up another and seeks the economic benefit by cutting staff. That ploy is called cost effectiveness by volume—higher sales and cash flow with less people. The additional cash flow is needed to pay for the acquisition.

Dog eat dog world

"What about Joe Doakes in the next office?"

Well, it's either him or you. The makers and shakers in the front office (the head choppers) have to make that decision. You know that and he knows that.

The good news

A cutback does not have too be bad news for you. Because you can do a certain amount about the competitive situation.

Law 1: Only the fit shall survive.

Law 2: You can make yourself more fit to survive.

The front office cost cutters and head choppers are usually going to select the people that are needed most in a slimmed down organization for retention. If you are needed more than Joe Doakes then you are going to get to stay in the game.

The bad news

Chances are that Joe Doakes wants to stay in the game also. That means you have to start applying yourself even more to making yourself the most needed manager around. That effort cannot wait until the last minute. One has to start on the survival track "yesterday."

Becoming "indispensable."

No one is indispensable. However, the trick is to become as nearly as indispensable as one can get. You have to so position yourself that a front office head chopper will think twice before canning you.

The cost-cutting head chopper has to think that your capabilities are vital—or, at least, of more importance—than others under the gun.

CONSIDER THESE PROTECTIVE SURVIVAL STEPS

1. Take on more responsibilities. (Look for more work.)
2. Broaden your experience. (Put your nose in other types of work.)
3. Increase your skills. (Learn all that you can. Everyday, teach yourself something new and exciting.)
4. Improve your people-to-people ability.
5. Enhance your managerial image. (Act and look like you are important to the organization.)
6. Display career enthusiasm—the breakfast of champions. (People appearing to be on the move upward are more likely candidates to stay in the game.)
7. Make special efforts for success on high visibility assignments. "Oh, you are the person who did that."
8. Develop more friends among higher staff levels. Keep the communication lines open.
9. Steal the ideas and techniques of others that can make you look good. (It's either them or you!) Anyway, credit should go to the successful promoter of a good idea.
10. Use more initiative on panic jobs or projects that have high customer interest.
11. Anticipate and consider how to take personal advantage of managerial changes.
12. Stay away from "losers." Do not get painted with the same brush as people who may be out of favor or have a lot of duds to their unfortunate credit.
13. Keep evaluating yourself as compared to the competition. (Work on your survival weaknesses.)
14. Sell yourself to your boss that you are doing at least a 100% job. ("What you want boss, is what you get.")
15. Do not "advertise" any failures. (If necessary, admit mistakes, but do not overdo. Avoid giving ammo to the competition.)

16. Have outward confidence in your abilities and staying power. (Inwardly, keep plugging away at improvement in your chances.)

PERSONAL SIDE BENEFIT

After acting on the above checklist, if push comes to shove and you are out on the street, then you may have an improved chance to move more quickly to another job. Why? With increased abilities, you can be more of an asset to another company.

KEEP UP CAREER MOMENTUM

Today, self-improvement for all management personnel is a "must." Not only for job security and/or mobility, but for moving up the corporate promotion ladder. To become a front office maker and shaker yourself requires multiskills and varied experience. Why not start on that success track right now? You have nothing to lose but job insecurity.

WHEN ALL ELSE FAILS—TRY COMMITMENT FOR SUCCESS

> *"As we say in the sewer, if you're not prepared to go all the way, do not put your boots on in the first place."*
> ED NORTON, *The Honeymooners* TV Show

The average person in management is average. It's simple and straightforward and rather commonly known.

However, let's dissect that statement as it relates to your chances for success. There are millions of people in management with average managerial abilities. Their chances of going up the organization promotion ladder in a desirable time frame are rather low.

THE RATIONALE

All of those people (your competition) have average leadership ability, technical know-how, integrity, political savvy, and so on. In other words, all of their qualities that are needed to move to further succeed in the management world are—that's right—average.

What keeps them average despite the potential rewards built into our system? Well, some of them are happy with their present lot. (They are in the millions.) Some just haven't got the innate ability to improve their management qualities. (They are in the millions, also.) Others are locked into a security blanket, the herd instinct, and may be fearful of rocking the boat.

HOW TO BREAK OUT OF A PATTERN

Maybe you have upgraded and improved your managerial ability but you are still in square one. You are learning something new almost every day, increasing your skills, and sharpening your "people smarts." Yet, personal advancement progress has been too darn slow. When all else fails, here is one word that you have to put into your mind-set: commitment.

ANOTHER LOOK AT THE COMPETITION

"Benson is a hard worker."

What are people (including the front office makers and shakers) thinking when they hear that statement about Benson? First, he is not one of the herd. Second, there is the implication to some that Benson is "on the make." That is trying to succeed and to be so recognized.

There are people in management who, when it is five o'clock, it is best not to stand between them and the elevator or the parking lot or the commuter lines. There are coworkers of Benson who never put in any overtime, nor come in early nor show up on weekends at the office or plant.

Some people want to go from A to B sitting down.

WHY COMMITMENT IS IMPORTANT

Commitment can be a displayed favorable attitude to superiors of involvement in the job and to the accomplishment of the organization's objectives.

HOW TO IMPROVE YOUR COMMITMENT IMAGE

While each type of operation varies as to just how to increase one's commitment image, here are a few hints:

1. Put in a more than an adequate amount of overtime.
2. Be ready to accept as many responsibilities and new duties as you can. Don't shirk work.
3. Accept and install changes for improvement readily.
4. Try to learn "why" as well as "how" about all matters in your immediate area.
5. Understand the problems of your boss, higher levels of management and the organization.
6. Include "cost-effectiveness" into everything that you do. (Act like a big stockholder.)

7. Do not overlook details. Remember, the small matters can kill a grand plan.
8. In sales and service situations, maintain the customer as the king of the marketplace.

THE "INDISPENSABLE" ISSUE

We know that no one is indispensable. The Company existed before you got there and will continue to make and sell widgets, or whatever, after you are gone. However, try to approach some level of being an important cog in your area. That means that if you were not there, then there would be a great deal of scrambling around to fill the gap.

Commitment will not make anyone 100% indispensable. What sufficient commitment can do is to make someone very important to a smooth flowing operation.

"Harry knows how to handle that."

ONE EXEC'S VIEWPOINT

A very successful executive told a friend, "Tell me what a fellow does evenings and I will tell you if he will succeed in a management career."

He was using his own yardstick for measuring commitment. It is one measure of evaluating management candidates. To a major degree, it has validity. Why? There is a distinction between the commitment to the more leisure pursuits and the commitment to a career.

WHAT WE KNOW

People with rock-solid commitment to their job and organization have a greater chance to move up the promotion ladder than those who do not have such commitment. Abilities, education, experience, talent, creativity, or whatever, frequently not withstanding.

Look around your shop or office. If your place is like many others, then there are people who are in relatively high position that may have less on the ball than you. Probably, they may have some higher level of commitment. Not a lot, but just enough to make the scales tilt in their direction.

Let's tell it like it is. If you were the top mogul in your place, wouldn't you want people with commitment around you? If someone has little or no commitment, all of his or her other good points might be wasted!

THE BOTTOM LINE FOR YOU

If you have tried everything else to improve your job situation, then it is time to consider tying to develop greater job and organizational commitment. Yes, you may have to realign personal priorities. (You set other priorities all day long; so that's easy.) Nor, does it have to be done all at once. You can let commitment creep into your scheme of things.

> *"Chiefly, the mold of a man's fortune*
> *is in his own hands."*
> FRANCIS BACON, 1625

HOW MUCH ARE YOU WORTH?

"You know what makes this country great? You do not have to be witty or clever, as long as you can hire someone who is."
TED BAXTER, "The Mary Tyler Moore Show"

One of the first things that one learns when entering the field of management is that not every management person receives the same amount of bucks in the paycheck. Even for the same job!

Of course no two jobs are exactly the same. Nor do any two people have the same capabilities.

Jones gets X thousand dollars a year. Smith gets double that. Jones may take a week to get a task completed, while big-bucks Smith accomplishes the same task with one phone call.

Hold it right there! We are assuming that Jones and Smith are playing (being managers) on a level playing field which only happens in theory, and therefore never happens.

The front office makers and shakers let many, many factors influence the salary package of each manager. The biggest influence should be accomplishment. Sometimes it is and at other times other combined factors are more decisive.

For instance, if you have been doing a real bang-up job lately, you may not even be able to ask for a raise because, of all reasons, you just got one a few months ago. (Reward doesn't always follow on the heels of accomplishment.)

However, someone could be transferred in at greater salary to do a similar job. Worse yet, you could be replaced by somebody from the outside for more money.

You may knock out tasks with simple 10-minute phone calls but you do not get along 100% with the VP for Manufacturing. Therefore, your salary raise request may sit on the back burner for some time.

RULE 1: You may earn more than you make.

RULE 2: You may make more than you earn.

Here is a slice of management life: most of us feel that we are in the category of Rule 1 (we are worth more than we are making). We think that many others around us are in the category of Rule 2 (they are worth less than they are making).

WHAT'S WRONG WITH SALARY RANGES?

Fred Sparkplug does a bang-up job. Fred knocks out the work, is constantly improving productivity or performance, is quality conscious and is very cost effective. The people in the fuzzy sports jackets put this hotshot manager in the same salary range as all of the same-level managers including those who are the slow pokes, gold brickers, clock watchers, error prone, misfits, and plain old deadwood.

In his "spare" time, Fred is increasing his education or picking up new skills and staying on top of new trends. The others in his management level may be watching reruns of reruns on the boob tube. Yet, all of them are in the same management salary category.

"We have exception procedures for people like Fred."

Many operations do have salary raise exception policies and procedures. No question. However, many of them are just paper procedures. In actual practice, they are seldom resorted to.

WARNING: Salary ranges are not fully rewarding to the gifted, talented, creative, hard-working managers in any organization.

Why have salary ranges? Frankly, it is frequently because it is easier to use than rooting around and trying to find out what a particular manager is actually worth to the organization!

There will be no change in the compensation system in any organization overnight.

What to do Now

Evaluate your own image.

To decide if you are worth more than you are making, you have to have a frank "discussion" with yourself. This is not a time to be less than truthful with yourself about something as important as your potential lifetime earnings.

Rate yourself as to your worth to the organization as:

1. Marginal. (Doing an adequate job in most areas under your control.)
2. Good. (Accomplishing most duties and assignments on time with high quality and maximum cost effectiveness.)
3. Outstanding. (Knocking all work out right away with 100% quality and lowest possible cost.)

There are some areas in which you are marginal and others in which you are outstanding. However, we are talking about the overall rating.

For those areas where you are marginal, you should concentrate your effort in those duties and assignments and bring them up to a higher level of accomplishment.

Use some public relations techniques.

There is little **monetary** point in being a hotshot manager in a corner where no one else knows of all of your good work.

Outright boasting is out of the question. It is poor form in any operation. However, there are less obvious ways to get your P/R pitch across. Each working situation has its own potential and particular circumstances for letting others know the good job that you are doing. You have been around the track long enough where you are to know how to do this.

Here is a Good Ploy

There is nothing like using a battle-tested ploy to improve and get recognition for your worth to your organization. Just add four words to your bag of trick as follows:

"I can handle that."

Use those four words in situations similar to the following:

- Upon receiving ANY new assignment.
- Installing a new system or procedure.
- Being given a tight deadline. (Rush jobs are your bag.)
- Having to squeeze another nickel out of costs.
- Upon assuming responsibility for a project gone haywire.
- During a meeting discussion of a problem.

The ploy is to say those four words and then to try your best to deliver on your words. You wouldn't always succeed on delivery but you will be known by your desirable managerial attitude and your solid try.

GOOD MANAGERS ARE HARD TO FIND

If ABC Widget Company is not going to pay you what you are worth, then XYZ Widget Company just might pay you more than you are worth. It happens.

Few people signed up to work for a lifetime in one place. The managerial labor market is just like any other part of the free enterprise system. Those consumers (employers) in the market who are willing to pay more should get the best.

We are not advocating constant job hopping. However, checking around to see if the grass is really greener on the other side of the fence doesn't hurt either.

You know that good managers are hard to find by taking a good look around your place. A management pundit said, "Some managers have retired on the job."

Every operation has its fair share of managers who are red tape artists, nit-pickers, work shirkers, gravy train riders, social lions, nine-to-fivers, malcontents, political sharks, and others who are overpaid for what they really contribute.

THE PERSONAL BOTTOM LINE FOR YOU

The easy two-sided trick is to be worth more and to let others (who matter) know that you are worth more. If you can do those two things and there isn't recognition for you, then it is time to carefully check around for another place that can and will provide what you are worth.

THE QUICK ACTION CHECKLISTS AND FAST WAYS TO EASE MANAGER WORKLOAD

WHAT THE MANAGER SHOULD EXPECT OF THE INDIVIDUAL SUBORDINATE

1. The subordinate is directly responsible for accomplishing the specific objectives of his or her position.

2. Can interpret orders and instructions reasonably well. Knows how the work affects other areas.

3. Can suggest changes in methods and objectives and can implement desirable improvements.

4. Is able to change the work techniques that will improve productivity, performance, quality and cost effectiveness.

5. Has the capability of doing some work planning.

6. Is able to anticipate problems created by his work.

7. Guides and counsels others in related work situations.

8. In evaluating, inspecting or auditing the work, can distinguish causes and effects.

9. Is able to appraise the work of other persons at the same operating level.

10. Initiates and expedites material, services, and information requirements of his own areas.

11. Can communicate within the requirements of the position.

12. Recognizes special or rush job situations and knows how to seek assistance if necessary.

13. Comprehends the performance requirements of his job.

14. Respects cost controls and budgets.

15. Knows and observes the administrative requirements associated with his function.

16. Has learned self-correcting techniques and does take corrective and remedial action on his own initiative.

17. Developed working ability with computerized operations that relate to his function.

18. Uses the variety of tools, machines and equipment related to his job.

19. After training, can perform minor repairs on equipment that he uses.

20. Is aware of the maintenance requirements of his equipment and follows such procedures.

21. Has familiarity with the Company policies and procedures that affect him and his job.

22. Displays a reasonable attitude toward new instructions or job requirements.

23. Uses judgment in seeking high level advice.

24. Does not abuse sickness leave policies.

25. Telephones in early if out ill or there is a delay in arriving at work.

26. Does not encourage others to be problem employees.

27. Has significant pride in his own workmanship, in that of the department and the Company and in the products and services.

28. Takes and appreciates constructive criticism.

29. Understands some of the burdens of his immediate superior.

30. If promotion oriented; is willing to learn the skills of the next step up the ladder.

31. More often than not, is willing to work overtime and weekends upon request.

32. When possible, helps co-workers with their jobs or provides technical advice.

CHECKLIST OF EMPLOYEE DESIRABLE SKILLS

1. The employee inspires a favorable response from new people upon contact.
2. Is fairly quick to gain some rapport with persons of varied background.
3. Understands the requirements of others in the work flow.
4. Fairly readily recalls names and their association.
5. Has easy coordination of eyes and hands.
6. Has the required stamina for the job.
7. Can do a certain level of math without the aid of machines or calculators.
8. Is able to check if reported quantities appear "reasonable."
9. Has a knack to explain abstract ideas.
10. Can readily determine which parts are a part of an assembly.
11. Fairly good at expressing thoughts in speech.
12. Has the ability to explain things in writing.
13. Is not mystified by more complex equipment.
14. Able to read and easily comprehend written instructions and manuals in connection with his job.
15. Fairly well understands drawings and prints.
16. Is able to recheck his own work.
17. Inspires an attitude of confidence.
18. Develops some new methods of performance.
19. Can spot errors fairly quickly.
20. Institutes corrective action on his own.
21. Can copy information with minimum of errors.
22. Is able to do more than one task at once.
23. Knows his limitation on technical matters and will seek assistance when needed.
24. Can retrieve information from computer terminals.

25. Has an understanding of the computer system as it relates to his job.

26. Has good knowledge about the overall work flow.

27. Knows the administrative portion of his job.

28. Can complete the forms that are necessary for his job.

29. Has some measure of respect for immediate superiors and others in authority.

30. Maintains good housekeeping in his work areas.

31. Can easily grasp the benefits of many changes in the operation.

32. Tries some improvements of the tools used in his work.

33. Knows what substitutes can be used in the event of any shortages.

34. Has some interpersonal skills with coworkers and service groups.

CHECKLIST TO REDUCE GOLDBRICKING

1. Is each employee assigned a definite work station or desk?

2. Are as many work stations and desks as possible in direct view of a supervisor or manager?

3. Are those employees, who move about to perform their duties required to report back to their superior periodically?

4. Does each subordinate have substantially MORE work assigned to them than can be completed within the work day?

5. Can the work be arranged into short interval scheduling for notation of progress by a superior?

6. On the larger assignments, can milestones be designated for the purpose of noting of progress by the superior?

7. Can chores that require leaving the department such as going to the supply room, tool crib, mail room, and so on, all be assigned to just one person within each section?

8. Can the work be arranged in a flow so that a break in the work flow will be readily noticed?

9. Can overtime be denied to suspected goldbrickers who desire to work overtime? As a punishment?

10. Can overtime be required of suspected goldbrickers who do NOT desire to work overtime? As a punishment?

11. Are the conscientious workers rewarded sufficiently?

12. Are there occasional expressions of appreciation made to hard workers?

13. Is there sufficient top management support for the discipline actions against proven goldbrickers?

14. Is time reporting properly monitored?

15. Are areas subject to employee congregation under some management observation?

16. Does new employee orientation STRESS the importance of productivity and performance?

17. Is this orientation periodically reinforced?

18. Are managers and supervisors setting a good example?

19. Do all middle level managers take an observing walk around the premises once in a while?

20. Are unused areas secured against interlopers?

EMPLOYEE ORIENTATION CHECKLIST

INSTRUCTION: To be prepared by the new employee's superior and forwarded to the Personnel Department.

Employee Name: _____ Dep't: _____

_____ 1. Shown the locations of coat room, locker, bulletin board, restroom, cafeteria, etc.

_____ 2. Introduced to coworkers and others.

_____ 3. Has been explained the starting and quitting times, lunch hour, break times, etc.

_____ 4. Indicated when and how paid.

_____ 5. Discussed overtime requirements and weekend work.

_____ 6. Indicated potential shift changes.

_____ 7. Discussed the probationary period and the employee requirements.

_____ 8. Indicated whom and when to call when late or requesting sick leave.

_____ 9. Explained the sick leave policy and procedure.

_____ 10. Explained the vacation and holiday pay policies and procedures.

_____ 11. Oriented the new employee to departmental organization.

_____ 12. Explained the rules on personal telephone calls, dress requirements, tardiness, housekeeping, etc.

_____ 13. Indicated the flow of the work and how the new employee's function fits into it.

_____ 14. Showed the employee where to obtain equipment, tools, supplies, etc. that are needed for his job.

_____ 15. Explained the expected levels of productivity and performance.

____ 16. The employee was shown the end products or services of his work.

____ 17. Quality control standards were explained and stressed.

____ 18. Showed the employee how his job is to be performed.

____ 19. Showed the employee how to control waste and possible rejects.

____ 20. Explained ALL of the safety rules.

____ 21. Showed the employee where first aid and other health and safety equipment was located.

____ 22. The employee was shown the hazardous equipment and dangerous areas.

____ 23. Discussed training sessions and requirements.

____ 24. Explained the promotional possibilities and the requirements.

____ 25. Discussed the procedures for merit pay increases and the requirements.

____ 26. Provided copies of work manuals and instruction sheets in connection with his job.

____ 27. Showed the employee where additional manuals and references are available.

____ 28. Provided up-to-date Company publications.

____ 29. Provided literature on the fringe benefits.

____ 30. Informed the employee as to who to contact in the event of a fringe benefit claim.

____ 31. Explained the employees' suggestion and awards system.

____ 32. Explained how to report an accident on the job.

____ 33. Indicated the parking and other commuter facilities that are available.

____ 34. Provided any information on car pooling.

____ 35. Indicated smoking and non-smoking areas on the premises.

____ 36. Made a special orientation effort on the rules regarding drugs and alcohol on the premises.

____ 37. Discussed group and individual incentives.

___ 38. Indicated possible Company awards for certain recognition.

___ 39. Introduced the new employee to an alternate superior.

___ 40. Invited questions from the employee.

___ 41. Offered help or suggestions on problems.

___ 42. Instructed the employee on further availability in the near future for any follow-up on the orientation.

___ 43. Other areas discussed included

_____

_____

QUERY TO SUPERVISOR: Did you find the employee receptive to your orientation? _____

Date:_____ Signed: _____

TO: _____   _____
　　　　　NAME OF SUPERVISOR　　　　　　　　　　　　　　DEPARTMENT

To be prepared in duplicate. Original for absentee's supervisor.
Copy for personnel records.

ABSENCE REPORT

CLOCK OR
PAYROLL
NAME_____NUMBER_____ DEPT._____

ADDRESS_____ PHONE_____ SHIFT_____

LAST DAY WORKED_____ WILL RETURN IN APPROXIMATELY_____DAYS

PERSON REPORTING ABSENCE_____ PHONE_____

REPORTED TO:	BY PHONE	BY MESSENGER	OTHER MEANS	DATE	HOUR

REASON FOR ABSENCE
(CHECK APPROPRIATE REASON)

ACCIDENT ON DUTY		HOLIDAY		SICKNESS—SELF	
ACCIDENT OFF DUTY		JURY DUTY		VACATION	
DISCIPLINE		LEAVE OF ABSENCE		UNEXCUSED ABSENCE	
DEATH IN FAMILY		SICKNESS IN FAMILY		EXCUSED (OTHER)	

NAME OF HOSPITAL_____ NAME OF DOCTOR_____

REASON FOR ABSENCE EXPLAINED (AS REQUIRED)_____

_____

_____

_____

DATE_____   REPORT RECORDED BY_____
　　　　　　　　　　　　　　　　　　　　　　　　　PERSONNEL DEPARTMENT

558

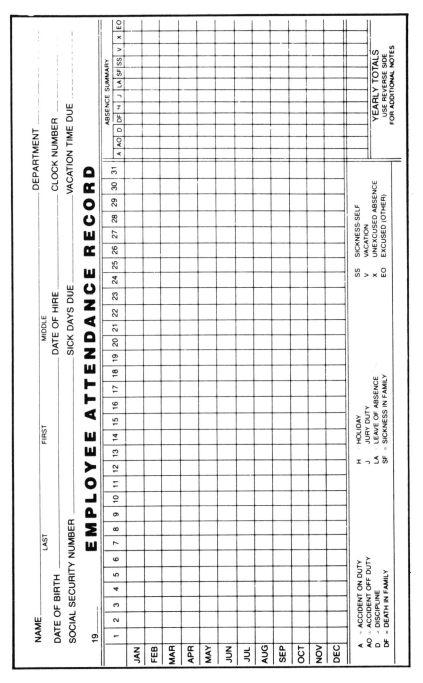

EMPLOYEE ATTENDANCE RECORD

NAME _____
LAST   FIRST   MIDDLE

DATE OF BIRTH _____   DATE OF HIRE _____
SOCIAL SECURITY NUMBER _____   SICK DAYS DUE _____

DEPARTMENT _____
CLOCK NUMBER _____
VACATION TIME DUE _____

19___

	1	2	3	4	5	6	7	8	9	10	11	12	13	14	15	16	17	18	19	20	21	22	23	24	25	26	27	28	29	30	31
JAN																															
FEB																															
MAR																															
APR																															
MAY																															
JUN																															
JUL																															
AUG																															
SEP																															
OCT																															
NOV																															
DEC																															

ABSENCE SUMMARY

A	AO	D	DF	H	J	LA	SF	SS	V	X	EO

YEARLY TOTALS
USE REVERSE SIDE
FOR ADDITIONAL NOTES

A = ACCIDENT ON DUTY
AO = ACCIDENT OFF DUTY
D = DISCIPLINE
DF = DEATH IN FAMILY

H = HOLIDAY
J = JURY DUTY
LA = LEAVE OF ABSENCE
SF = SICKNESS IN FAMILY

SS = SICKNESS-SELF
V = VACATION
X = UNEXCUSED ABSENCE
EO = EXCUSED (OTHER)

559

PROCEDURE FOR STRIKE PREPARATION

INTER-OFFICE MEMO

TO: All Department Managers   DATE: October 27
FROM: Vice President for Manufacturing
SUBJECT: Procedure for an Anticipated Strike

It may be likely that our Company will be subject to a strike action after November 15th. Our negotiating people are making every attempt to avert such an action.

The department managers are to prepare in ADVANCE for such an eventuality, using the following guidelines:

1. Develop a listing of the home telephone numbers of the management and other nonstriking personnel in the department.

2. Circulate such listing to the appropriate management members of the department.

3. As soon as possible, notify the Purchasing Department of the parts and supplies that may become critical in the event that deliveries are interrupted.

4. Have your people aware that administrative and other non-collective bargaining people may decide to respect the picket line.

5. Reschedule the workload to take effect as soon as possible and coordinate with the Production Control staff.

6. Shelf items and certain other items should have minimal priority.

7. All of the nonstriking personnel are cautioned against responding to hecklers on the picket line no matter what the provocation might be.

8. Only the main gate will be used.

9. Only parking lot C will offer adequate security personnel.

10. The local police department will assign their manpower to observe the picket line in appropriate strength.

11. In the event of any fracas in entering or leaving the premises, comply with the instructions of the police and our security personnel.

12. In the event that the picketing is too hectic, your personnel may be expected to stay home.

13. If individual duties require, the management personnel will be paid for overtime. The Department Managers will handle this matter in conjunction with the Payroll Section.

It is stressed that the Company is doing everything that it can to postpone and/or avert any strike. Because a strike is not pleasant for either party, we hope that if there is a strike, it will be of short duration.

Management personnel are obliged to prepare for the strike eventuality as if it were imminent.

BASIC DISCIPLINARY NOTICE MEMO

INTER-OFFICE MEMO

TO: Personnel Department   Date: March 23
FROM: John Hughes, Shipping Manager
SUBJECT: Warning Notice to William Walter

According to Company procedure #3-23, an employee who intends to be absent must call in or have someone notify his immediate superior by 9:30 A.M. of the day of absence.

Mr. William Walter, an employee in the Shipping Department, is aware of the procedure. He was reminded of the procedure and given a copy of the procedure when he returned to work after being absent on February 14th. On that date, no advice of absence was transmitted to the superior.

Yesterday, the 22nd, Mr. Walter was absent again without any notification to his immediate superior.

If Mr. Walter is absent another time and fails to give notice as provided in the procedure, his employment will be terminated. A copy of this memo is being given to Mr. Walter as a warning notice. Your office is hereby requested to retain this memo in the employee's file.

cc: W. Walter

Simplified Guide to Training Requirements

TRAINING TECHNIQUE	EMPLOYEE REQUIREMENTS	MANAGEMENT REQUIREMENTS
Self-instruction	The employee takes on the task of teaching himself. Usually, this is at his own speed.	Providing manuals, job aids, working models and other self-training
Tutorial instruction	The employee applies himself to a one-to-one relationship for instruction.	Providing an instructor or coach who will provide guidance and instruction, usually at the work station.
Group instruction	The employee and others participate in a classroom setting to obtain at least the fundamentals of the job.	Classroom or conference environment.
Combination of more than one method	The employee understands how the program works and what part he is to play in it.	In addition to the individual technique requirements, a method of monitoring individual progress must be installed.

CHECKLIST OF BENEFITS OF TESTING EXISTING EMPLOYEES

Not everybody is in favor of testing the existing work for (both rank and file and managerial) to determine the pool of talent that can be available. Here are some of the advantages of such testing:

1. Helps in the selection of the best qualified employees for cross training.
2. Can be used to develop standards for replacements and additions to the work force.
3. Determines fitness for existing jobs that are held.
4. Provides an inventory of available skills for matching to existing or REVISED requirements.
5. Indicates any potential for improved productivity or performance.
6. Discovers potential supervisory or management trainees.
7. Indicates benefits or drawbacks of existing training programs.
8. Develops causes for revision or updating of the present methods of on-the-job training.
9. Provides a valid comparison to testing of employees' aptitude when tested for their present position.
10. Improves mutual understanding by the superior and the subordinate of the job requirements.
11. Reduces the costs of training.
12. Minimizes turnover during training.
13. Provides easier assessment of expectations of further training for some employees.
14. Reduces favoritism by use of objective testing.
15. Reduces the potential for employee grievances.
16. Increases the confidence of better performers.
17. Isolates unfit employees.
18. Develops standards for incompetency and causes for dismissal.

19. Testing is a reinforcement mechanism for previously acquired information or skills.

20. Tests provide guidance to the immediate superiors of their subordinates' capabilities.

21. Testing can reveal desired creativity.

22. Counseling combined with testing can determine which employees are not occupationally settled.

23. Some tests can aid in determining which employees have greater drive or ambition.

24. Some tests can aid in determining which employees are good team workers. Or, are better as individual performers.

FAST ACTION CHECKLIST FOR TRAINING EMPLOYEES

You have read the "how-to" training manuals and the operating training manuals and maybe you have gone to class to learn *how* to be a better trainer.

Yet, what happens? The graduate trainee goes out into the workforce and his immediate supervisor has to begin the trainee's job education from square one.

The problem is that the "established" training methods have been developed by ***professional*** trainers who frequently have not worked with the product of the training classes. In contrast, the following nitty-gritty checklist is provided to improve your training capability.

1. Motivation. Do you devote 5 minutes of each lesson to why the trainees should be learning what you are teaching?

   (Without a motivation for learning, there is NO learning.)

2. Is the training area conducive to learning? Make the training environment as professional looking as possible.

3. How about the written materials? Even photocopied instruction sheets are better than nothing.

4. Do you require trainees to take notes? The notes are a good reinforcement of what is being said.

5. Are the trainees told just how their particular job will fit into the overall picture?

6. Is efficiency and performance stressed? Are they expected to produce 1 widget an hour or 100?

7. Does the trainee KNOW why he or she is being trained? That is important for self-esteem of being a learner.

8. What incentives can you provide for those trainees that do well? It does not have to be just money!

9. Are visits to actual situations interspersed into the training program? "Let's visit the computer department."

10. Can you round up a few guest speakers to provide some good insight into actual performance? Other than yourself!

11. Do you constantly encourage the trainees to ask as many questions as they like? Do you compliment those who have good questions?

12. Are the answers fully and completely answered?

13. Do you provide periodic testing? Remember tests are a learning reinforcement and are helpful to you to determine where the training is weak.

14. Is there any way of monitoring your own performance as an instructor?

15. Can you determine which trainees need additional exposure to what has been taught? WARNING: In any class, some will be slower learners than others. Such situations are not the instructor's fault.

16. Have you used the sparkplug students in the class to inspire the others? If possible, let them do a little "coaching" to others.

17. If some students are much faster in learning than others, can you sidetrack them to learn more advanced techniques?

18. Have you thought of having a "graduate" level class for superior trainees?

19. Are trainee washouts more suitable for other types of jobs? Do you separate them out fast enough?

20. Can you install a grading system as an additional trainee incentive?

21. Can you have a follow-up program after completion of the course? This step will also provide an insight into which training methods have been the weakest.

22. Do you encourage comments and suggestions from the training course graduates? Do you follow up on the worthwhile ideas?

23. Have you sat in on other training classes to get some good training ideas?

EMPLOYEE EVALUATION FORM

NAME: _____ DATE: _____

DEPARTMENT: _____ JOB TITLE: _____

Purposes of this Employee Evaluation:

To take a personal inventory, to pin-point weaknesses and strengths and to outline and agree upon a practical improvement program. Periodically conducted, these Evaluations will provide a history of development and progress.

Instructions:

Listed below are a number of traits, abilities and characteristics that are important for success in business. Place an "X" mark on each rating scale, over the descriptive phrase which most nearly describes the person being rated. (If this form is being used for self-evaluation, you will be describing yourself.)

Carefully evaluate each of the qualities separately.

Two common mistakes in rating are: (1) A tendency to rate nearly everyone as "average" on every trait instead of being more critical in judgment. The rater should use the ends of the scale as well as the middle, and (2) The "Halo Effect," i.e., a tendency to rate the same individual "excellent" on every trait or "poor" on every trait based on the *overall* picture one has of the person being rated. However, each person has strong points and weak points and these should be indicated on the rating scale.

ACCURACY is the correctness of work duties performed.

Makes frequent errors.	Careless; makes recurrent errors.	Usually accurate; makes only average number of mistakes.	Requires little supervision; is exact and precise most of the time.	Requires absolute minimum of supervision; is almost always accurate.

ALERTNESS is the ability to grasp instructions, to meet changing conditions and to solve novel or problem situations.

Slow to "catch on."	Requires more than average instructions and explanations.	Grasps instructions with average ability.	Usually quick to understand and learn.	Exceptionally keen and alert.

CREATIVITY is talent for having new ideas, for finding new and better ways of doing things and for being imaginative.

Rarely has a new idea; is unimaginative.	Occasionally comes up with a new idea.	Has average imagination; has reasonable number of new ideas.	Frequently suggests new ways of doing things; is very imaginative.	Continually seeks new and better ways of doing things; is extremely imaginative.

FRIENDLINESS is the sociability and warmth which an individual imparts in his attitude toward customers, other employees, his supervisor and the persons he may supervise.

Very distant and aloof.	Approachable; friendly once known by others.	Warm; friendly; sociable.	Very sociable and out-going.	Extremely sociable; excellent at establishing good will.

PERSONALITY is an individual's behavior characteristics or his personal suitability for the job.

Personality unsatisfactory for this job.	Personality questionable for this job.	Personality satisfactory for this job.	Very desirable personality for this job.	Outstanding personality for this job.

PERSONAL APPEARANCE is the personal impression an individual makes on others. (Consider cleanliness, grooming, neatness and appropriateness of dress on the job.)

Very untidy; poor taste in dress.	Sometimes untidy and careless about personal appearance.	Generally neat and clean; satisfactory personal appearance.	Careful about personal appearance; good taste in dress.	Unusually well groomed; very neat; excellent taste in dress.

PHYSICAL FITNESS is the ability to work consistently and with only moderate fatigue. (Consider physical alertness and energy.)

Tires easily; is weak and frail.	Frequently tires and is slow.	Meets physical and energy job requirements.	Energetic; seldom tires.	Excellent health; no fatigue.

ATTENDANCE is faithfulness in coming to work daily and conforming to work hours.

Often absent without good excuse and/or frequently reports for work late.	Lax in attendance and/or reporting for work on time.	Usually present and on time.	Very prompt; regular in attendance.	Always regular and prompt; volunteers for overtime when needed.

HOUSEKEEPING is the orderliness and cleanliness in which an individual keeps his work area.

Disorderly or untidy.	Some tendency to be careless and untidy.	Ordinarily keeps work area fairly neat.	Quite conscientious about neatness and cleanliness.	Unusually neat, clean and orderly.

DEPENDABILITY is the ability to do required jobs well with a minimum of supervision.

Requires close supervision; is unreliable.	Sometimes requires prompting.	Usually takes care of necessary tasks and completes with reasonable promptness.	Requires little supervision; is reliable.	Requires absolute minimum of supervision.

DRIVE is the desire to attain goals, to achieve.

Has poorly defined goals and acts without purpose; puts forth practically no effort.	Sets goals too low; puts forth little effort to achieve.	Has average goals and usually puts forth effort to reach these.	Strives hard; has high desire to achieve.	Sets high goals and strives incessantly to reach these.

JOB KNOWLEDGE is the information concerning work duties which an individual should know for a satisfactory job performance.

Poorly informed about work duties.	Lacks knowledge of some phases of work.	Moderately informed; can answer most common questions.	Understands all phases of work.	Has complete mastery of all phases of job.

QUANTITY OF WORK is the amount of work an individual does in a work day.

Does not meet minimum requirements.	Does just enough to get by.	Volume of work is satisfactory.	Very industrious; does more than is required.	Superior work production record.

STABILITY is the ability to withstand pressure and to remain calm in crisis situations.

Goes "to pieces" under pressure; is "jumpy" and nervous.	Occasionally "blows up" under pressure; is easily irritated.	Has average tolerance for crises; usually remains calm.	Tolerates most pressure; likes crises more than the average person.	Thrives under pressure; really enjoys solving crises.

COURTESY is the polite attention an individual gives other people.

Blunt; discourteous; antagonistic.	Sometimes tactless.	Agreeable and pleasant.	Always very polite and willing to help.	Inspiring to others in being courteous and very pleasant.

OVERALL EVALUATION in comparison with other employees with the same length of service on this job:

Definitely unsatisfactory.	Substandard but making progress.	Doing an average job.	Definitely above average.	Outstanding.

COMMENTS

Major weak points are—	Major strong points are—
1._____	1._____
2._____	2._____
3._____	3._____
and these can be strengthened by doing the following:	and these can be used more effectively by doing the following:

Rated by _____ _____

(Name)   *(Title)*

(If not used as a self-evaluation form, the employee should sign below)

A copy of this Report has been given to me and has been discussed with me.

_____ _____

(Employee's Signature)   *(Date)*

MANAGER SELF-HELP QUIZ

Managers and supervisors can know how to do a better job, can get their subordinates to do a better job, but what about their own future? There are little things that you should be asking yourself in order to improve your chances for personal success in the business world.

Here are some TOUGH queries that you can ask yourself. Your personal appraisal and FRANK answers may be of help in promoting your career or, at least, being more appreciated in your present situation.

1. Does your *personal* attitude toward the Company help or hinder your success? Can it be DISPLAYED in a better way for your benefit?

2. What is your assessment of what your boss REALLY thinks of you? Can you quietly determine it?

3. Can you slowly change the boss's assessment of your capabilities? Is it worth the effort?

4. If you were your boss, would you think that someone like you is one of the better members of his team? Can that situation be changed or improved?

5. Are you acquiring additional skills in order to handle some greater responsibility more readily?

6. Do you conduct the administrative portion of your job as well as can be expected? Do others recognize you as a good administrator. (Remember, higher level jobs require greater administrative ability.)

7. Are you aware of industry trends? Do you know what the company's competition is doing?

8. Have you appraised you OWN technical performance carefully? Are there areas that could stand improvement?

9. Are your relationships with other managers as harmonious as possible? (Good inter-personality skills are a major criteria for success.)

10. Without being pushy, do you try to maintain or pursue contacts with the more senior members of management?

11. Do your subordinates respect your leadership and technical skills? Could you improve on the situation?

12. Do you handle mutual problems with other departments or divisions reasonably well?

13. Have others indicated that you have above-average integrity? "Is your word, your bond?"

14. Have you resisted acceptance of new responsibilities?

15. Are your superiors slow to give you the really tough assignments, or rush and special jobs? If so, is there some adverse reason that you have to spend effort on?

16. Do panic jobs make you "sweat?" Can you improve your track record on such jobs or assignments?

17. Can everyone who works with you say that you are open-minded about suggestions for improvement?

18. Do you sometimes experiment with new techniques?

19. Are you considered objective-oriented?

20. Do you have sufficient self-control? (Do you engage the gears of your mind before engaging the gears of your mouth?)

21. Can your decision-making capability use improvement?

22. Do you act in the *most* professional manner that you can?

23. Would *anyone* else consider that your grooming and dress is LESS than appropriate?

24. Is there reason to believe that your work area indicates that you are inefficient?

25. Do you recognize management politics associated with your job to the extent that you should?

26. Off the premises, are you considered sociable?

Sure, those questions are tough. Any self-evaluation has to get to the nitty-gritty, otherwise, it could be a waste of time. (In order to go from A to B, you have to know where A is—at least, in the formula where A is your current job assignment or title.)

Today, more than ever before, managerial people have to self-appraise their own image, work habits, personality, skills, professionalism, and so on. Why? Because, without such appraisal, it is difficult to know where to apply more effort for some improvement.

Without self-appraisal and subsequent improvement, there is less of a chance for success—even if success is defined as hanging in there where you are right now.

QUICK CHECKLIST FOR RATING YOUR SUBORDINATES

NOTE: This is a quick-action simplified guide for the rating of your subordinates. Depending on job requirements, some areas of concern may have greater emphasis.

1. Technical ability and work area knowledge
   a) Understands all phases of day-to-day work.
   b) Knows how to use the equipment associated with the job.
   c) Can handle a certain amount of new technical problems.
   d) Knows how his work is used subsequently.
   e) Has the ability to catch his own errors.
   f) Can take corrective action without further problems.
   g) Is familiar with computer techniques.
   h) Can explain the technical end of his job to coworkers.

2. Dependability and integrity
   a) Desires to meet most targets and/or deadlines.
   b) Attempts to follow instructions completely.
   c) Promptly reports any stumbling blocks to goals.
   d) Frequently cross checks results.
   e) Provides realistic estimates of effort required on assignments.
   f) Co-workers have indicated reliance on his promises.

3. Interpersonality Capability
   a) Gets along with coworkers.
   b) Has been willing to help others.
   c) Other departments are willing to be cooperative with him.
   d) Confines any dissatisfactions.

e) Moves to resolve disputes as quickly as possible.

f) More than willing to listen to others.

g) Accepts constructive criticism fairly well.

h) Work problems to do not alter behavior.

i) Has fairly good composure. Reacts well in stressful situations.

4. Productivity and/or Performance

a) Maintains a good level of output.

b) Has a minimum of wasted effort.

c) Handles rush and special assignments well.

d) Realizes importance of quality control and error containment.

e) Revises methods that cause errors or poor work.

f) Does not provide additional red tape.

g) Finalizes all details of assignments.

h) Is fully aware of cost-effective requirements.

5. Attitude toward the work situation

a) Tries to overcome work difficulties.

b) Is a good team worker.

c) Respects his immediate supervisor and other superiors.

d) Is willing to train others.

e) Is seldom argumentative.

f) Does not present false issues.

g) Is supportive of rules and procedures.

h) Does not abuse employee privileges.

i) Is not anti-managerial or anti-company.

6. Housekeeping

a) Has a neat workstation or desk area.

b) His file systems are in good order.

c) Can locate work readily.

d) Observes the safety rules.

e) Properly disposes of trash and waste.

f) Stores materials and supplies carefully.

g) Keeps equipment in good order.

7. Attendance

   a) Has a minimal absentee record.

   b) Reports to work with minor ailments.

   c) Is available for weekend work.

   d) Calls in early when he is out ill.

   e) Seldom requests personal leave.

   f) Complies with vacation policy.

8. Punctuality

   a) Has started work on time consistently.

   b) Reports back to work promptly after lunch.

   c) Seldom has to leave early.

   d) When late due to outside events, he manages to get to work as quickly as possible.

9. Potentiality

   a) Enjoys training others.

   b) Studies or trains for more responsibilities.

   c) Seeks to be recognized for expertise.

   d) Has success as a group leader.

   e) Seeks to resolve work difficulties by himself.

   f) Tries to learn the context of jobs that others are doing.

   g) Wishes to be multiskilled. Wants cross-training.

   h) Requests higher level assignments.

10. Adaptability

    a) Supports changes in job methods.

    b) Quickly learns uses of new equipment.

    c) Understands problems of old methods.

    d) Shows willingness to be retrained.

    e) Wants to learn more about computer techniques.

    f) Is aware of industry trends.

PROCEDURES FOR NON-DIRECT INTERVIEW TECHNIQUE

THE DO'S AND DON'TS OF NONDIRECT INTERVIEWING

The presumption is that an employee, or a job applicant for instance, does NOT want to tell you everything about a matter or himself. However, there is a method gaining wider acceptance which relies on a unique emotional quality. (See the explanation near the end of this appendix.)

Basically, this technique relies on the interviewer avoiding asking any questions. The interviewer merely states the topic and lets the interviewee expound on it.

Here are some pointers on using the method:

1. The interview should be held in a private office.
2. The circumstances should limit the possibility of an interruption to zilch. NO POSSIBLE DISTRACTIONS.
3. The interviewer should face the interviewee very directly.
4. Both of the parties should be comfortably seated.
5. A preliminary platitude is desirable. If the interviewee is apparently up tight, try some small talk about the weather, sports results, or other impersonal topics.
6. The interviewee should not only be physically comfortable but apparently emotionally at ease as well.
7. The interviewer should make a BRIEF reference to the interview topic. "Let's talk about absenteeism."
8. "Let's talk" means let him talk.
9. Do not interrupt. Do not interject. Try to just listen.
10. Provide no response in words, expressions, body language, or deeds. (See step #15 for an exception.)
11. Permit the interviewee to ramble. Let him decide the course of the conversation.
12. When the interviewee stops talking, merely repeat his last sentence.

13. Repetition of the last sentence by the interviewer may cause the interviewee to expound on that statement further and continue his one-person dialog.

14. When the "conversation" has run its course, the interviewer can summarize what has been said. If further clarity on a particular point is required, repeat the interviewee's statement with regard to that point.

15. If a statement is made which is apparently questionable, repeat that statement with some body language cynicism. Let him expound on it and put himself in deeper or extricate himself with a correction or whatever.

16. If after 15 to 20 minutes, the interviewee is repeating himself or new ground is being covered, go on to the next topic or terminate the interview.

17. Important. Any hostility by the interviewee must be tolerated without any comment or reaction by the interviewer.

DOES THE METHOD WORK?

Many times, the nondirect interviewing technique has revealed fibs on resumes and/or applications, petty thefts, drugs on the premises, animosities against management people and others, and, even collusion in serious fraud.

WHY NONDIRECT INTERVIEWING WORKS

Most people like an audience. Some even like to entertain an audience with slight revelations, behavior departures, etc.

The underlying principle is for the interviewer to be an audience—but with NO reactions. The rationale for "no reactions" is that the interviewee is thus being encouraged to be "bolder" in trying to induce a reaction in his audience.

SELF-PROTECTION IRONCLAD RULE

GOOD IDEA: Be aware of when this technique is being used on you. It is an old Turkish proverb which says, "Your tongue can be your own worst enemy."

CHECKLIST FOR OVERCOMING EMPLOYEE INDIFFERENCE

> *"The trouble with this world is apathy."*
> GRAFFITO

> *"Who Cares?"*
> SUBSEQUENT GRAFFITO RESPONSE

1. Does the employee as fully as possible understand the job?
2. Has the employee been shown how his contribution fits into the total organization's objectives?
3. Can it be said that discipline is applied fairly and evenly?
4. Are any subordinates "favorites" or "teacher's pets?"
5. Do subordinates receive job orientation from their immediate superiors or from co-workers?
6. Were productivity and performance requirements explained to the subordinate?
7. Was quality control and cost effectiveness stressed in the orientation to the job?
8. Does the subordinate really comprehend what his immediate superior expects of him?
9. Has the subordinate been expressly told what other departments, customers, etc., expect of him?
10. Was the subordinate shown just how to catch and correct his own errors?
11. Were instruction sheets, written procedures or manuals provided to the subordinate? Were they up-dated recently?
12. How frequently and in what depth was the on-the-job training reinforced?
13. Can a good-example "coach" be assigned to a problem subordinate?
14. Is the immediate superior a good representative of management?

15. Is there an impression that the immediate superior's work habits are poor?

16. Does the superior provide sufficient monitoring of the subordinate's activity?

17. Has the merit wage salary procedure been explained to the subordinate?

18. Have the promotional opportunities been explained to the subordinate?

19. Has any special effort on the part of the subordinate been recognized and acknowledged?

20. How often has the indifference problem been discussed with the subordinate?

21. Has the subordinate given any *valid* reason for the indifference? Has something been done about the reason?

22. Are the right tools, machines, equipment, computer terminals, etc., being provided to the subordinate?

23. Have all of the changes in working methods or techniques been adequately explained to the subordinate?

24. Is the subordinate's work station or desk conducive to better performance?

25. Are available incentives *promptly* distributed?

26. Does the subordinate know the extent of cost expense of scrap and/or flawed work?

27. Is the subordinate aware of the industry competitive market place?

28. Was any request for a transfer denied?

29. Is there another type of work available for the subordinate that can provide more interest?

30. Would a team effort type of work be more ideal for the subordinate?

31. Is the subordinate aware of discipline (including discharge) which can be applied to him for displaying a poor attitude?

CHECKLIST: DEALING WITH INFORMAL GROUPS (CLIQUES)

Frequently, there are relationships between employees that develop amongst themselves which are not along the proscribed organizational lines of authority. These informal organizational relationships (cliques) can cross recognized organizational lines.

Sometimes, such cliques are anti-managerial or anti-supervision. In some situations, they are healthy and in others they are deleterious to discipline. Cliques can have a loose code of morals including the following:

1. Members of a clique avoid seeking favoritism from a superior.
2. Most clique members seldom speak unfavorably about another member of the clique.
3. At times, they become bottlenecks as higher productivity may be counter to group informal goals. "Don't do more than you have to."
4. Work assistance to clique non-members is seldom.
5. At times, clique members are known to take advantage of sick leave and other employee privileges.

There are techniques for countering or dealing with **adverse** attitude clique groups which include the following:

1. Observe employee attitudes and note relationships.
2. Encourage more discussions between the superiors and the subordinates.
3. Cross-train subordinates so that different employees can handle the same jobs.
4. Increase the number of subordinates with key skills.
5. Revise the flow of work in line with the more formal organization.
6. Increase employee trust in management by being fair.
7. Increase internal communications keeping varied interests in mind.

8. Provide for employee input into possible procedural, production or performance changes.

9. Stagger lunch hours or rest periods for members of an adverse attitude clique.

10. Stagger shifts or overtime requirements of the more hostile attitude clique members.

11. Involve group leaders as substitute supervisors or straw bosses.

12. Improve and reinforce employee orientation.

13. Delegate responsibility as widely as possible.

14. Involve rank and file employees in the development of production and performance goals.

15. Have a private meeting with a clique leader and warn him about attitude problems.

16. Keep the clique off balance by surprise changing of individual duties.

17. Assign occasional "dog work" to poor attitude problem subordinates.

WARNING

Where a superior has "teacher's pets" or practices subordinate favoritism, adverse attitude cliques have a central cause for existence and their attitudes.

THE FLIP SIDE OF THE COIN

There are instances where a clique can be useful to a superior after their poor attitudes have been modified. For instance, in work that involves team effort, a healthy attitude clique can form a good work group. Or, in operations where high cooperation is required.

Where cliques do not have adverse attitudes, clique leaders are frequently ideal coaches or minor supervisors to other employees.

CHECKLIST TO REDUCE EMPLOYEE TURNOVER

1. Evaluate and update the recruiting practices.
2. Redevelop minimal hiring standards.
3. Consider the advisability of employing "job-hoppers."
4. Analyze training and orientation procedures and content for new employees.
5. Install exit interview procedures for departing employees to determine areas of possible dissatisfaction.
6. Compile statistics on causes for departure and functional areas affected.
7. Consider using trial periods for new employees.
8. Review the grievance procedures.
9. Determine what can be done about areas of high employee dissatisfaction.
10. Increase the use of nonfinancial incentives.
11. Review causes of excessive overtime or weekend work.
12. Check to determine if promotional opportunities are well understood.
13. Have subsequent reinforcement of employee orientation.
14. Attempt to promote largely from within.
15. Open more communications channels to higher levels of management.
16. Provide copies of written policies regarding employees to the employees.
17. Consider changing the merit wage procedures.
18. Increase the frequency of early merit wage reviews.
19. Improve housekeeping methods.
20. Install an informal suggestion system.
21. Provide more orientation to lower managerial levels as to purposes of corporate policies.

22. Determine wage and benefit levels in nearby operations in the competitive labor market.

23. Improve the employee facilities such as cafeterias and wash rooms. Provide a more pleasant decor.

24. Improve the lighting and decor of all work areas.

25. Make the work stations and desk areas more functional.

26. Consider increasing the number of Company annual outings and other social opportunities.

27. Subsidize a bowling league or soft ball teams.

28. Increase management participation in community events and affairs. Adopt a local charity.

29. Install a partial or full tuition reimbursement program.

30. Start an after-work on premises school for additional skills (typing, computer orientation, print reading, etc.).

31. Increases efforts to instill pride of workmanship or service. (Have Company sales managers provide pep talks.)

32. Consider installing a deferred compensation plan with benefits accruing *early* in employment.

33. Give more meaningful awards for attendance, punctuality, and for length of service.

34. Whenever possible, attempt to re-hire former employees.

35. Higher levels of management should attempt to learn the first names of as many rank and file as possible.

36. Where possible, install work teams rather than rely on individual efforts.

37. Permit more rank and file to determine how their work is to be accomplished rather than mandating methods.

Analysis of Arbitrated Grievances

The American Arbitration Association conducted a study of 1,000 grievance cases brought before its labor arbitration panels. The analysis is as follows:

	Type of Grievance	Percent
1.	Discipline problems	25
2.	Seniority problems including promotions, transfers and layoffs	21
3.	Job evaluation and assignments	12
4.	Overtime	5
5.	Vacations	5
6.	Incentive plans	2
7.	Holidays	2
8.	All other, including fringe benefits, working conditions, safety, specific contract clauses, work clothes, etc.	28

CHECKLIST FOR EVALUATING A SUBORDINATE SUPERVISOR

It is always difficult to conduct a "standard" performance review of subordinate supervisors. Usually they each have different functions to perform and are working under varying circumstances. Nonetheless, here are some guideline areas to consider:

1. ACCURACY. Does the supervisor promote self-checking procedures among his people? How about reasonableness checking?

2. ALERTNESS. Can the supervisor quickly grasp changing conditions?

3. ATTENDANCE. Is the work flow in the supervisor's area affected by extensive rank and file absenteeism?

4. COMPLIANCE. Does the supervisor support the rules, regulations, and policies of the Company? Does he properly enforce them? Is he supportive of his superior?

5. COST EFFECTIVENESS. Does the supervisor's section control waste and duplication of effort?

6. COURTESY. Are the supervisor's people polite to others?

7. CREATIVITY. Are there a number of significant changes made on the supervisor's initiative?

8. DEPENDABILITY. Are the supervisor's people able to fulfill assignments on time?

9. DRIVE. Is the supervisor sufficiently aggressive in getting the work out?

10. FRIENDLINESS. Does the supervisor appear to have interpersonality problems which hinder the work?

11. HOUSEKEEPING. Does the supervisor's geographical areas appear neat and efficient?

12. JOB KNOWLEDGE. Does the supervisor have sufficient expertise in his various responsibilities?

13. ORGANIZATIONAL SUPPORT. Does the supervisor understand the importance of the chain of command?

14. OVERALL PERFORMANCE. Does the sum total of all of the supervisor's qualities compare favorably with other supervisors of equal responsibility?

15. PERSONAL APPEARANCE. Does the supervisor apparently appreciate outward dress and grooming? Do his people follow a good role model?

16. PERSONALITY. Do the supervisor's behavior characteristics conform to job requirements in relations with others? Does he have an even temperament?

17. PHYSICAL FITNESS. Can the supervisor handle the more physical aspects of the job? Are there complaints of fatigue?

18. QUANTITY OF WORK. Is the extent and/or volume of activity excessive for the supervisor? Can he really handle more?

19. SELF-IMPROVEMENT. Is the supervisor trying to increase his variety of skills? Is he learning more in depth about existing skills?

20. STABILITY. Does the supervisor panic in a crisis? Are there times that he loses self-control?

21. TRAINING. Is the supervisor a good trainer of his people? Do they respect his technical skills.

MANAGER, KNOW THYSELF

Of course any boss can use the above checklist to gauge his or her *own* abilities to be a boss. And, we know that the problem of any self-evaluation is FRANKNESS. But, why not be frank if that is going to lead to improvement in being a boss. Only you will know if you are too harsh on yourself or that, maybe, just maybe some personal improvement might be in order.

Self-improvement is the best survival weapon.

Your friends may be kind and not tell you of your performance or leadership weaknesses. Your enemies, well, they are not going to tell you, no way, because you just might take corrective action.

Then who else is there? Only you! So, to do a better job of being a boss, reread the above evaluation and then do what you have to do.

SELF-HELP QUIZ TO IMPROVE MANAGER PERFORMANCE

1. Are you learning some new skill for the job environment as often as you can?

2. Have you tried any new methods or techniques in your section or department lately?

3. Are you recognized by your superior as being innovative?

4. Do you know where most of your subordinate supervisors and direct subordinates are at any one time? Are you control oriented?

5. Are you performing chores that should be more properly done by someone else in the department? Are you going to delegate out those chores?

6. Do your colleagues and coworkers have reason to believe that you have a good business personality? Can your inter-personality ability use improvement?

7. Are your communicative skills among the best in your division or company? Are your memos and/or reports "sales devices" for your capabilities?

8. Have you been upgrading your computer knowledge? Have you computerized as much as you can in your department?

9. Are your political skills adequate? Do you know what is going on in other departments, divisions and company locations?

10. Have you delegated enough so that you can accept more responsibility quickly? Are you personally ready to take on more?

11. Are you tempered? Did you experience any personal loss of control lately? Are panic jobs a problem?

12. Does your boss and other superiors respect your professionalism about the job? Do you convey such respect among co-workers?

13. Do you handle yourself at meetings in a managerial manner? Are you always well prepared for meetings?

14. Do you believe that outsiders or new people get a good first impression of you? Are you outgoing?

15. Can your handling of authority be improved? Does your boss give you reason to believe otherwise? Is there some cause why your boss has not granted more authority to you?

16. Do people that you work with consider you very reliable?

17. Can your knowledge of the equipment used in your department be increased? Can you handle the computer terminals?

18. Does your department maintain good housekeeping? Can it be improved to reflect greater efficiency?

19. Is the morale in your department in good shape? How do you know? Have there been complaints? Have you been particularly unfair with any subordinates?

20. Do you put in as much overtime as you can? How about weekend work? Do you want an image of being a hard and conscientious worker?

21. Do you allow outside interests to **materially** interfere with your work? Your career goals?

22. Are your plans for promotion constantly being sidetracked? Do you have a career target for 5 years? 10 years? Is there something that you can be doing currently to accomplish your goals?

23. If you were one of the movers and shakers in the executive office, what would be **your** opinion of someone like yourself?

24. Do you believe that many people do judge a book by its cover? Accordingly then, do you dress and groom for a successful and/or higher role in management?

TODAY'S REALITY

Many managers are not further success oriented and need little in the way of self-improvement to do their jobs. Fine! They are content with the status quo—at least, for the moment. That's okay! The problem is that in this changing business world the "status quo" can change overnight. Either by the market competition, merger or acquisition, or corporate re-structuring and/or "slimming down."

In such event, and if for no other reason but for survival insurance against such event, self-improvement is a protective procedure. Many current management victims of corporate change wish that they had taken timely protective steps to insure themselves more against the actions of the front office choppers and/or those pencil-pushing cost cutters.

CHECKLIST: WHEELING AND DEALING WITH OTHERS IN MANAGEMENT

NOTE: See important justification at the end of the checklist.

1. The cooperative approach to others in management is that "you scratch my back and I'll scratch yours." Or, in the more trusting sense, "one hand washes the other and BOTH together, wash the face."

2. Cooperative approaches are maintained when *both* parties have CONTINUING leverage against each other. If one has nothing to offer to the agreement, then the agreement to cooperate may be UNenforceable.

3. Know which of the other people in management are generally supportive of your efforts. They can be designated as FRIENDS.

   A friend in need, need not be a friend any more.

4. Those management people who are LESS supportive of your efforts are your ENEMIES. For instance, they will hurl slings and arrows against your proposals.

5. Those who are neither friends or enemies are NEUTRALS.

   Keep neutrals away from enemies for fear of conversion.

6. Keep your enemies off balance by fluctuations in your attitude toward them.

7. Seldom divulge information to enemies or neutrals.

   Info and its use are assets.

8. Use your friends for public relations activity on your behalf. "Waldo, mention my proposal in your report."

9. Voice appreciation for any favors by friends. When required, support their efforts.

10. At lower levels of management and certain rank and file, observe who are the KEY people in some sections. Go out

of your way to maintain good rapport with these people. (Sometimes, they have good input routes to higher sources.)

11. NEVER display any animosity to any person. Even if there is provocation. Your claim to fame is "cool." Be friendly in the worst of circumstances.

12. Save "ammunition" (derogatory info) about an enemy until the best possible moment for use. Constantly seek to increase your supply of such ammo.

13. Be prepared to loan subordinates, equipment, parts, supplies, etc., to those parties who favorably wheel and deal with you.

14. Know all of the corporate unwritten policies very well. Be able to use such data to your advantage.

    Never let on the source of such info.

15. Use exceptions or omissions in the written procedures to your advantage in wheeling and dealing.

16. IMPORTANT. Network people throughout the operation. Know first names of remote potential helpmates. "Remote" includes other departments, divisions, subsidiaries, and geographical locations.

17. Attend all significant company social events. Try to mix with all types of attendees. (Don't stand in ONE corner.) Such events (even a bowling night) are opportunities to increase your network.

18. CRITICAL. Try to have an occasional lunch with people on a higher management level than you. At least, try to lunch with people who can help you in some way.

    Don't keep lunching with the same old crowd. (Taking lunch almost constantly with the same people provides nothing new to you.)

19. Distinguish between **born** "winners" and "losers" in the management hierarchy. Associate and emulate "hot shots," "sparkplugs," "rising stars," "management teacher's pets," and others who appear to be on the move upward.

20. Minimize your association with "status quo" career people or obvious "non-movers."

Don't get painted with the same brush.

21. Use the happy hours at the local "Blue Bird Tavern" or wherever the management gang meets for acquiring information—not for undue draft beer intake.

22. NEVER divulge your network contacts to *any one.* Have others operate through you. (If you divulge contacts, who needs you?)

23. A worthwhile network contact can ONLY be divulged while undergoing Far Eastern extreme torture applied to *all* extremities, or 10 minutes AFTER your last rites. Otherwise, you will suffer remorse.

24. In most situations, no one should EVER realize that you are a wheeler and dealer. While to some it is admirable, others take offense.

WHY WHEEL AND DEAL

No chairman or CEO of any Fortune 500 company actually works the assembly line, sweeps the floor, maintains a sales route in East Cornfield, Iowa or anything like what people call every-day work. The rationale for their LARGE paycheck, sky-high bonuses, "boo-koo" stock options, and big perks is that they can handle people *very successfully* who can handle other people to do those more technical operations.

Technical ability is important. And maybe, your CEO can handle a pneumatic wrench or a crimp press. Fine. But, he did NOT get to the top by being the best widget assembler around. Heck no! He moved up the corporate promotion ladder, rung by rung, by being the best people-handler around at the time.

Take another walk around the executive suite, offices or floor, ivory tower, or whatever it is called around your place. Don't look at the plush carpets, look at the people. Some day, they are going to retire or move on, right? And, other people wheelers and dealers are going to take their place. Right? Only the better ones will. That's the system.

RESUMES THAT PROMPTLY MAY BE THROWN AWAY

Your resume is one of the best chances that you have of using your communicative skills. While resume content is highly important in job switching, *other factors can negate* your good and valuable experience.

While certain industries have informal guidelines for resumes, here are some types of resumes that are more than likely to be thrown away and have a *low* chance of being read:

1. Resumes that do not have a cover letter. Or, the cover letter is improperly addressed. Or, is makeshift.

2. Resumes that exceed two pages. Reviewers and recruiters do not want to *bore potential decision makers* to death. (Your autobiography is needed when you are rich and famous—not before.)

3. Resumes that are in binders. They become too cumbersome for reviewers and recruiters and are not easily torn apart.

4. Poorly organized content resumes. (Remember, you are trying to show your administrative capability also.) Your education and experience should be in a logical order.

5. Colored paper resumes. White is standard and can be more easily copied *clearly* by the prospective reviewer if desired.

6. Gross or very glaring misspellings of important terms.

7. Resumes that are not neat, are poorly typed or duplicated. (Neatness counts.) A resume is a SELLING device.

8. Resumes that, upon quick glance, are not germane to existing or potential openings. NOTE: the resume content ploy is to TARGET possible openings.

THE ABSOLUTE PROOF OF THE PUDDING

You may have experience in recruiting. There are certain types of resumes that are more appealing to you. And, there are certain types that "turn you off." Use that good experience to YOUR advantage to develop your own type or style of resume. You can still be individualistic but you know the **established limits** of being creative on a resume and what kind of communicating that YOU want to do.

The real proof of any type or style of resume is the bottom line—does it get you good interviews and job offers. If it does, fine. If not, IMMEDIATELY go back to the drawing board and re-work THAT resume.

See Appendix X, "What to Exclude from Your Resume."

WHAT TO EXCLUDE FROM YOUR RESUME

There is a great deal of literature on what should be INCLUDED in a management person's resume. Not all of that good information has always worked when it should have.

Therefore, in the interests of **balanced advice** and to make job switching a lot easier, this checklist has been made available. This is a list of some of the matters and information that should be EXCLUDED from almost any management person's resume:

1. Do NOT misspell any words.

2. Do not use poor grammar—even to make a point.

3. Never, ever mention that any project, government or otherwise, that you were connected with over-ran by more than 3 months. Whether you were responsible for the over-run or not.

4. Do not use the words "bankruptcy" or "insolvency" in connection with the naming of any former employer. (Let them find out.) Such mention MIGHT mean that you had something to do with creating the situation.

5 Do not say that you lost or left any job because of politics. Such cause for leaving DIRECTLY implies that you do NOT have sufficient interpersonality ability.

6. Avoid mentioning any assignment which has become commonly known in your industry as a dud. "I designed the Edsel," is not recommended.

7. Do not mention that you lost a job as a result of a merger or reorganization. That means that you were low man on the **ability** totem pole.

8. Avoid mentioning any jobs that were held more than 20 years ago as the experience is not current or even possibly germane.

9. Do not give your age or date of birth. It is expected that you know the law with regard to discrimination on account of age.

10. Do not include references. The references can be submitted down the road. (It is assumed that you will get reference permission first.)

11. Do not use excessive technical language. Stick to general terms for accomplishments. The technical terms may indicate that your experience is too narrow where the job calls for a broader background.

12. Avoid "flowery" language or to much self-promotion. Try to let your accomplishments speak for themselves.

For additional help, read Appendix W.

LIST OF TOUGH JOB INTERVIEW QUESTIONS

You do not have to have gone around the block many times to know that obtaining applicant information is only ONE of the purposes of the interview questions. Particularly on the tough questions.

The purpose of the tough questions, in addition to gaining some insight into the technical capability of the applicant, is to ascertain capabilities of articulation, personality, and reactions to more stressful situations.

Here are some tough job interview questions which can reveal quite a bit about the applicant:

1. Can you tell me something about yourself?
2. What have you been able to accomplish at ABC Company?
3. How did you get along with the people there?
4. Why do you want to leave the ABC Company?
5. How do you see yourself in 5 years from now?
6. What are you good at doing?
7. Which part of your job didn't you like?
8. Why did you pick this area of work specialization?
9. If we make you a job offer, why would you accept?
10. What can YOU do for us at XYZ Company?
11. What are your references likely to say about you?
12. How much were you making at ABC Company?
13. What salary are you looking for now?
14. Why couldn't you make that salary at ABC?
15. How would you handle a panic job like . . .?
16. Is there anything adverse in your background that we should know now?
17. Why did you attend THAT school?
18. Would relocation be a large problem for you?
19. Is frequent travel a problem?

20. Could you accept X dollars a year to start?
21. What do you do in your off hours?
22. Why haven't you obtained additional education?
23. How much do you know about computer systems?
24. Would you be willing to start as an assistant . . .?
25. Can you start on . . .?
26. Is there anything that you would like to add?

No one is likely to hit you with all of those questions. However, you, as an interviewee, have to be ready for those questions and possibly more. With practice answering the tough questions, you are less likely to get "rattled" and to present the best possible side of yourself. Besides the content of your answers, you should try to display *a grace under pressure*.

TRY ROLE PLAYING

To increase your chances of handling an interview well, have a friend or relative play the part of the interviewer using the above questions and you play the interviewee. A few practice sessions will make you more of an old pro at the interview game.

If nothing else, practice leads to more self-confidence.

HOW TO KILL A CAREER IN MANAGEMENT

Almost all of what we read about management is devoted to what to do to improve your career chances in management. Well, there are people who have read that material and have NOT improved their own chances for success. It could be that some managers have not been exposed to what they should **not** do in everyday work or what constitutes a negative attitude.

Here is a quick action checklist of things that managers should NOT (repeat, NOT) do UNLESS they want to kill their career in management real fast:

1. Tell your boss all of the truth because the truth will set YOU free.

2. Accept blame for all of the mistakes that are not yours.

3. Tell colleagues EXACTLY what you think of them. Why shouldn't they know?

4. By-pass your boss on all important matters and occasionally on a few unimportant issues.

5. Accept NO constructive criticism whatsoever. You always know best how to do your job.

6. Seldom keep promises. Your word is NOT your bond. "Isn't business a matter of dog-eat-dog?"

7. Never recheck your department's or your work. After all, you know how to do things right the first time, EVERY time.

8. Be over-authoritarian with subordinates. You don't need them!

9. Never be on time with rush or panic assignments as others would come to expect too much of you.

10. Do not bother with personal self-control. Lose your head. Shout and bang on the desk. Rant once in a while.

11. Do not hesitate to use abusive language because it helps you to express yourself and can make a point.

12. Abuse all privileges because you are entitled to. Rules are made to be broken by people at your level.

13. Keep people off of your turf but gladly walk on theirs. (What's mine is mine and what's yours is mine.)

14. Never trust anyone's word as you would lie if you were in their shoes.

15. Fire subordinates without cause. (They have to take their chances.)

16. Ignore housekeeping and safety requirements in your area as you have more important things to do.

17. Use the Company facilities for personal needs. They are there for your personal convenience.

18. Never attend a Company social function as your time is, after all, your own time.

19. Do not let people know where you are if needed as they can wait for you to show up.

20. Your lunch hour is flexible as to length.

21. Budgets and cost controls are limitations on what YOU think the Company should spend in your area.

22. Assume that computer methods cannot help make your department's work any easier—despite proof otherwise.

23. Take your vacation days at inopportune times for the department and/or the Company. Your time is your time.

24. Never appreciate a subordinate's superior effort as it is part of his or her job anyway.

25. Form or support cliques that are anti-managerial. Of course, freedom of speech is your right.

26. Be tough on minorities, women and the disabled as your own employee policies are better than the Company's.

27. Sleep at management meetings as they are not arenas for learning what is going on.

28. Do not support company community projects as you have little to gain personally.

29. Keep your boss waiting for you on mutual appointments as you are busier than he is with more "important" things.

REALITY AND THE FINAL FRONTIER FOR MANAGERS

In reality, there isn't anyone in management that is guilty of ALL of the above. Heck, no! However, there are a few people who have done or are doing a few of those things. Or, at least, shadings of them. The safest bet is to reflect and to be darn sure that your own attitude is not your own worst opposition in the fight to stay and succeed in management.

In the end, at that final, final manager evaluation or performance review in the great sky (whenever it takes place), it would be good to know that we each tried our best to be our best.

MASTER SUBJECT FINDER

W